The
Divided
Heart

The
Divided
Heart

Scandinavian Immigrant Experience through Literary Sources
BY DOROTHY BURTON SKÅRDAL
with a Preface by Professor Oscar Handlin

UNIVERSITY OF NEBRASKA PRESS · LINCOLN

Published in Norway by
UNIVERSITETSFORLAGET

Published in the United States of America and Canada by
THE UNIVERSITY OF NEBRASKA PRESS

ISBN 82 - 00 - 08978 - 9
ISBN 0 - 8032 - 0840 - 5
Library of Congress Catalog Card Number 73 - 94120

Printed in Norway by
Edgar Høgfeldt A/S, Kristiansand S.

Contents

Preface by Oscar Handlin

Pforzheimer University Professor, Harvard University

Historians of immigration, like students of popular culture in general, have long overlooked a rich source of material with a bearing upon their subjects. The spread of literacy in the nineteenth century and the technological changes that lowered the costs of paper and of printing produced a vast outpouring of written matter directed specifically at readers with little formal education. The market for the products of the printing presses expanded far beyond the upper and middle classes who had earlier been their mainstay. Men and women from all walks of life were now among the purchasers of books and periodicals; and the columns of the newspapers and the pages of the cheap volumes filled to overflow with stories and poems written to appeal to the tastes of the masses. Like the oral literature which to some extent it displaced, the new popular literature reflected the attitudes, ideas and emotions of thousands of people who turned to it for an enhanced understanding of their own lives. Used with care and sensitivity, these writings form an important pool of evidence, indeed sometimes the only available data, on the experiences of people in societies undergoing rapid change. Certainly few sources are as rewarding in the light cast upon the human problems of migration, adjustment and acculturation.

Popular literature tends to focus upon that which is normal and usual rather than upon that which is exceptional in the human experience. Precisely because its themes must be comprehensible to a wide audience, it seeks out for description situations which are common, depicts emotions shared by many, and finds the heroic in the victories and defeats of everyday life. It thus offers information for a consideration of aspects of the immigrant experience all too readily overlooked by scholars.

The migration of Europeans to the United States was, after all, a mass movement involving millions of families, most of them drawn from the humblest levels of society. Nevertheless, with rare exceptions, historians have devoted most of their attention to the minorities of rather exceptional individuals who distinguished themselves by success in the New World. Partly that distortion was the product of conscious of unconscious efforts at self-justification; each immigrant group sought to defend itself against attack and to demonstrate its worth through a display of the contributions by famous names associated with it. But the emphasis upon the notables rather than upon the masses was also the product of a bias in the data to which historians most frequently turned. It was not the common man whose papers the libraries collected, whose orations were recorded, whose biographical materials were preserved or who figured prominently in the news columns of the press. Hence it was easy to overlook him, and the common woman also.

Immigrant literature offers the means for correcting this distortion. Precisely because it was directed at the mass of newcomers, because it reflects their ideas and emotions, it provides the alert scholar with an instrument for the analysis of the men and women who found meaning in it. This is a hitherto neglected resource for the social history of immigration.

The difficulties in the way of use of this material are imposing. They involve first the daunting problems of identifying and locating the physical survivals. Immigrant literature appeared in fugitive publications; many of the periodicals had but a brief life span and even those which endured did not achieve a broad circulation outside the communities which they specifically addressed. They did not therefore normally pass into the holdings of the great collecting libraries and archives. The scholar who wishes to employ these materials must have the persistence and patience to hunt them out in scattered repositories and must often be satisfied with only fragmentary results.

In addition, the use of immigrant literature calls for linguistic skills not commonly possessed by many Americans. The newcomers brought with them the languages of Wales, Germany, Greece, Poland and many other parts of the world. No single scholar could master all these tongues; few could master several; some, none. Yet without these essential keys, the treasures of immigrant thought and feeling lie beyond the reach of the investigator.

The linguistic problem has had the incidental effect of exaggerating the distinctiveness of each immigrant group. Historians, limited by language, generally concentrated upon a single group and tended to overstress what was peculiar to it, tended to overlook what it shared with others.

Above all, the effective utilization of popular literature requires novel techniques of assessment and evaluation. The critical methods appropriate to formal literature are inappropriate to writings composed for another purpose and for another audience. No easy alternative model of analysis lies ready at hand; and the historian who ventures to struggle with these materials must, as yet, devise his own methods for doing so.

Dorothy Skårdal's thoughtful book si an important contribution to the understanding of immigration and of popular immigrant literature. It has a good deal of value to say about the experience of the Scandinavians and about the quality of Scandinavian writing. But it also has more general implications bearing upon the experience of all immigrants to America and upon the quality of all immigrant writing. She is of course aware of the distinctive qualities of the rare writer of great talent like Rølvaag; but her attention nevertheless rests upon the larger body of literature from which his novels stemmed. As a result she has been able to tell us much about the character of immigrant literature and the character of immigration. On both accounts, she has made a valuable contribution to American social history.

Acknowledgements

Three one-year scholarships made possible the basic research on which this book is based. The first was a Fulbright grant for a year's study of Danish and Norwegian literature (and observation of Scandinavian life) at the University of Oslo in 1950-51. The second was an advanced research fellowship from the American Council of Learned Societies in 1952-53. This year I spent reading in various historical libraries of the Middle West. The third was a grant from the Norwegian Research Council for Science and the Humanities in 1964, enabling me to read still more books from emigrant archives in the three Scandinavian countries, especially autobiographies. Without this financial support my reading could not have been so extensive.

I owe warm personal thanks to Professor Oscar Handlin of Harvard University, my thesis advisor, for his interest in this work. I married a Norwegian and moved permanently to Norway in 1953 after having barely begun the writing of the doctoral thesis which was the original form of this book. My own trials as an immigrant, combined with various full-time teaching posts and the responsibilities of motherhood, forced me to lay the study aside for many years. Without Professor Handlin's patient, persistent prodding and encouragement I might well never have taken it up again. Certainly I could not have done so if Harvard had then had a time limit for completion of the doctoral degree. I began general course work on this highest level in the fall of 1948; my degree was awarded *in absentia* in March 1963. I am not the proper judge of whether or not the scholarly world has gained because I was allowed to finish, however belatedly, but I could not have resumed my calling as university teacher without this degree. Since 1965 I have taught American Studies at the University of Oslo. Advocates of strict time limits for higher degrees, please notice.

Numerous other individuals have also contributed to this study, including librarians at Luther, St. Olaf, Augustana, Grand View, and Dana Colleges; at Minnesota, Wisconsin, Illinois, and Nebraska state historical associations; at Universitetsbiblioteket in Oslo, Udvandrerarkivet in Aalborg, Denmark, Det kungliga biblioteket in Stockholm and Emigrantinstitutet in Växjö, Sweden. A dozen American scholars of Scandinavian background have kindly read the thesis manuscript and corrected several mistakes. Three first-generation immigrant writers also read the thesis manuscript and have offered their comments: Simon Johnson, Norwegian-American, Arthur Landfors, Swedish-American, and Enok Mortensen, Danish-American. The revised manuscript, text of the present book, has been read by Professor Handlin and the Norwegian Professors Sigmund Skard of the American Institute, and Ingrid Semmingsen of the Historical Institute, both at the University of Oslo. The National Archivist of Norway, Dagfinn Mannsåker, has also read the final text and suggested some corrections. My husband, Olav Skårdal, has offered criticism and comment from the viewpoint of his field, social psychology. There is no excuse for mistakes or misinterpretations which may be left, but I am sure there are many—for which I alone am responsible.

This book now appears under the joint imprint of the University of Oslo and the University of Nebraska, its printing costs in large part defrayed by The Norwegian Research Council for Science and the Humanities. I hope it may both symbolize and contribute to cooperation between Americans and Europeans in the study of our common culture and our mutual past.

Chapter One
Ends and Means

I. How This Book Came to Be

A tapestry hung on the dining-room wall of my childhood home. In sub-dued tones of grey-green, blue, and gold it showed a panoramic scene: In the foreground, small steamers were headed toward or tied up beside a streetside wharf. Horse-drawn wagons backed up to transfer piles of freight. Tiny people promenaded on broad walks, boarded a tram, sat on park benches. Across the water stately buildings rose behind banks of trees. The central one, I knew, was the King's palace; it was the largest and finest, and shone like gold when lit up by the morning sun. Woven into the border at the bottom was the magic word: Stockholm.

Outside the sun-filled windows was the dull Omaha street of my everyday life, but that tapestry was my talisman of romance. It was proof that in far-away Sweden a royal family still lived in a palace, like in fairy tales. My mother had seen this scene with her own eyes, and described the quaint cobblestone streets and clustering shops of the Old City hidden behind palace and Parliament. She told about dancing around a maypole on Midsummer Night's Eve, about carpets of wildflowers in ancient forests where nightingales sang in the white summer night. Sometimes she took out a black velvet cap with long red tassels and the bright striped apron of a peasant costume, or let me look again through the book of queer old pictures, one to each thick board page, which showed the town of Vimmerby in Småland where our cousins lived.

Shortly after the turn of the century, my mother's brothers had scraped together the money to send my grandmother and her, then in her early teens, on a summer's visit to Sweden. This was my grandmother's sole return to her native land; after emigrating alone in 1868 to join her fiancé, she saw her family again only this once, as a widow of many years. I have no record of how my grandmother felt then (or any time), but my uncles often said the trip added at least ten years to her life. I know, however, how my mother felt: that summer had been the high point of her youth. Brought up a bilingual in Stromsburg, Nebraska, she could hold her own with any Swede. She made such an impression on some of her Swedish cousins that they remembered her half a century later. A few she continued writing to until her marriage.

But she married a native American, and by the time I was old enough to dream under that golden tapestry she seemed to have lost interest in Sweden. She never spoke of it except when asked, never found time to teach me any Swedish, though I begged and begged. She was busy, of course, as high-school teacher of Latin and English; but still she managed to take active part in several local women's clubs, so long as they were purely American. When I heard of a Swedish society with its own hall in South Omaha, and wanted to go and see what it was like, she wasn't interested. Then troubles closed down around our family: the crash and the depression, suicide, sickness, lingering death. I forgot about Sweden too.

Yet I never stopped wondering about the Swedish grandmother I had never known. How had she felt when she came from ancient woods and nightingales to our dusty Nebraska plain? What had it been like to be an immigrant? The frontispiece in my school history book gave one answer, a picture of the Statue of Liberty with its famous verse beneath:

> Give me your tired, your poor,
> Your huddled masses yearning to be free . . .
> I lift my lamp beside the golden door.

But what about that golden tapestry? Its answer did not agree. Many years later I began the study of immigrant history in an attempt to find the truth. I soon discovered one thing, at least: that my mother's and my behavior had been typical. Those of the second generation who feel insecure as immigrants' children tend to reject the foreign heritage, while the third generation, securely American, often turn back to it.

One day I stood on Strömgatan in Stockholm and looked across the water at palace and Parliament, recognizing the stately old buildings from that faded tapestry. Boats still tie up in the foreground, but now the street along the waterfront is choked with cars and buses. The people on the broad walks hurry instead of promenading, but the park is still there with its benches, and the skyline of the Old City is unchanged. Vimmerby too I recognized from the queer old pictures in that long-lost book. On various research trips I've been back many times, gradually learning family history from the years between: how that branch declined while this one rose; how luck struck here and tragedy there; how distant cousins had spread all over Sweden, and some first learned of each other through me. In time I came to see them not as Swedes or Europeans but as human beings, each with his own personality and problems, just like my relatives back home. Once, a bit diffident

14

about returning to Vimmerby so often, I asked a favorite second cousin and his wife if they really wanted me to come again.

"Oh, yes," they said, "you bring a breath of the great world into our dull small-town life!"

II. What This Book Hopes to Do

What was it like to be an immigrant? My unknown grandmother may have inspired the question, but I never thought there might be an answer until I read *Giants in the Earth* in college. That novel dealt with Norwegians in Dakota, not Swedes in Nebraska, nor had my grandparents been pioneers; but it rang so true!

I found authorities who agreed with me, experts in both history and literature. For instance, Vernon Parrington praised Rølvaag's psychological realism in portraying the human cost of both immigration and pioneering:

> . . . it is because *Giants in the Earth,* for the first time in our fiction, evaluates adequately the settlement [of the frontier] in terms of emotion, because it penetrates to the secret inner life of men and women who undertook the heavy work of subduing the wilderness, that it is quite apart from all artistic values a great historical document.[1]

Terms of emotion, the secret inner life of individual men and women— *that* was always lacking from conventional history. Already as an undergraduate I began to wonder if it might be possible to use literary works as historical documents, in an attempt to preserve the depth, vividness, and complexity of individual human lives within the broad generalizations of history.

Social history, I soon discovered, was moving in that direction. I found Theodore C. Blegen's two-volume account of *Norwegian Migration to America* undertaking to describe "the whole experience of an immigrant people."

> In grappling with social history on so broad a scale I have encountered many difficult problems of research and used some unusual sources, including the findings of linguists who have probed immigrant speech and the writing of novelists who have probed immigrant souls.[2]

Professor Blegen used emigrant songs and ballads, too, but always checked these unusual sources against more conventional historical materials: newspapers and official records, immigrant guides and handbooks, letters, autobiographies, eyewitness accounts of many kinds.

Suppose I went a step further, or in another direction, and tried writing history out of literature *without* the check of such conventional source materials. Suppose I put together a composite picture of Scandinavian-American experience from imaginative literature which immigrants wrote about their own lives. Would such a picture be complete? Would it be coherent? Would it be valid? Certainly it would be an "inside story," but would it be true?

The book which follows records the results of this experiment. It traces social and psychological change in the patterns of behavior of an ethnic group during the process of turning from Europeans into Americans. Ignoring the *facts* of their history, it focuses on how they viewed those facts, on opinions, attitudes, feelings about their own lives as immigrants expressed in fiction and poetry by two generations of Scandinavian-American writers. There were an amazing number of them in the roughly seventy years during which this little-known branch of American literature developed and declined. Chapter Two describes its magnitude, variety, and extent, as well as some of its special problems of publishing markets, reading public, and language. The general reader who finds this chapter about the source material dull is advised to skip it and go on to Chapter Three, where the story of immigrant experience begins.

III. Definitions and Demarcations

I use the term *Scandinavia* to refer to only the three nations of Norway, Sweden, and Denmark, eliminating Finland and Iceland. This is in accord with current usage in the nations concerned, where the word *Nordic* includes all five of them (as in the Nordic Council), while *Scandinavian* is reserved for the first three collectively. These terms reflect a long and complex history: that Sweden, Norway, and Denmark share close-knit anthropological, political, economic, and cultural interrelationships developed continuously through many centuries, while Finland and Iceland have had relationships (mostly political) with one or another of the three countries only at certain periods. (The word *Nordic* as defined above is very recent indeed.) The languages of the five countries symbolize their relative closeness: a Swede, a Norwegian, and a Dane can communicate with one another with little difficulty when each speaks or writes his own language, but they can understand only a few words of Icelandic and nothing whatever of Finnish. A minority of the Finnish population do speak Swedish, descendants of a colonizing upper class, and some of them took part in the migration to America. Only one published any literature of note, however, and he was not an immigrant but a visitor.[3] In any event this minority was too small measured against the total emigrated population of the three larger countries to be worthy of special notice in this study.

Immigrant writers of the Scandinavian nationalities, on the other hand, not only felt themselves related, but revealed such similar cultural traits when thrown into relief against the American background as to prove beyond any shadow of doubt that they must be classified as members of a single ethnic group. There are real differences among the three nationalities, of course; Norwegian, Swedish, and Danish are separate languages, and the histories of the three countries are not identical, only similar. Immigrant life in America emphasized the similarities, however, and gradually dissipated the differences, so that *Scandinavian* denotes even greater ethnic unity in reference to immigrants in the New World than to natives in Europe.[4] One of the original purposes of this study was to demonstrate this historical fact not only by recording the immigrants' own observations of it, but also by giving parallel examples from each of the three branches of the literature in every case. Scholarly readers interested in this issue will find the full evidence in the manuscript dissertation which was the original form of this book.[5] In the interest of greater brevity I have cut many of these duplicate examples out of the present text, but I hope enough remain to convince the general reader of the homogeneity of this ethnic group.

Ethnic is thus consistently used in this book in reference to the Scandinavian immigrant group as a whole. When considering its three elements separately, I use the term *national,* or the name of the nationality itself.

I should point out that most students of this ethnic group have not reasoned along the same lines. Although the immigrants themselves founded many Scandinavian-American societies and associations, historians and historical societies in most cases have limited themselves to one of the three nationalities. No definitive study of Scandinavian immigrant history as a whole has yet been written, although one or two attempts have been made.

I had personal reasons for including all three nationalities in my study. Rølvaag was Norwegian, while my own family was Swedish; if I insisted on both of them, I could hardly omit the closely related Danes. Besides, in the beginning I was afraid there might be so little material produced by each national group that I would have to include them all to get enough.

Instead I found an embarrassment of riches. In historical collections of the Middle West I was ushered into whole rooms of Scandinavian-American published writings, including magazine and newspapers files which included countless items that could be grist to my mill. Faced with such masses of material, I felt I had to restrict my choice of literature to the central genres of fiction and poetry, or risk never getting through. Within the field of fiction, I limited my reading to stories which, so far as I could judge, portrayed immigrant life contemporaneous with

17

the author. Stories laid in the Old World or elsewhere, tales of long ago and never-never I put aside for possible later reading. They too revealed attitudes and feelings, but at a farther remove from daily life. It was the authors' views of their own *immigrant* life I was after, so I chose only stories dealing with characters who were immigrants to America. In the few cases in the following chapters where I have cited from novels written by non-immigrants, or by second-generation authors who could not have observed themselves what they were describing, I have called attention to this fact in a footnote. In such cases I have used that source because its description was the best I found, and was in full accord with other evidence.

In my original dissertation I also limited myself to fiction laid in the Middle West. I argued that the full span of Scandinavian immigrant milieus existed within this region: from lonely frontier settlements to thronging cities, from primitive logging and railroad construction camps to complex factories, including farm communities, towns, and cities of every size and stage of development. Within this region existed also all possible variations of immigrant concentration: colonies composed exclusively of Norwegians or Danes from one province or valley; those made up of one nationality but collected from all over the home country; and all conceivable shifting combinations of admixture with native Yankee and other immigrant stocks. I am still convinced that all variations of Scandinavian immigrant life were fully represented in this single region, but here I have eliminated this restriction of geographical space. By adding the few books of fiction I have found with settings in the Northeast and the Northwest, I can now claim that my study includes the picture of Scandinavian immigrant life recorded in the literature everywhere in the United States.

From the first I accepted only those limitations of time imposed by the source material itself. As described in Chapter Two, Scandinavian-American literature began in the 1870s. A full generation and more of earlier migration was thus not covered by the material, or was represented only in books based on secondary sources. These I eliminated in order to rely solely on authors writing out of their own experience. Apart from this initial hiatus, the literature covers in full the development of the Scandinavian group in America from the 1870s until the 1940s, reflecting its growth and consolidation, its cultural flowering, and its gradual dissolution through assimilation into the surrounding American society.

The history of the group itself is still not finished. Some of its members continue to define themselves to some extent as Norwegian-, Swedish-, or Danish-American, rather than plain American. A variety of social, cultural, and other organizations based upon this ethnic origin continue to exist, and a handful of newspapers in the original European languages still appear regularly for a declining number of readers.* The revival of interest in American ethnic groups since the 1960s may enable also Scandinavian group definition to survive indefinitely, although in what forms and with what meaning remains to be seen. It is difficult to judge how much genuine Norwegian culture lives on in such a typically American enterprise as the annual three-day Nordic Festival in Decorah, Iowa, begun in 1967. There is, however, no doubt that whatever the state of the distinctive sub-culture which produced it, Scandinavian-American imaginative literature itself is all but dead. What little the surviving immigrant authors still write in their own language is published in the few remaining immigrant newspapers, in the European homeland, or not at all.** English-language writers of Scandinavian descent are now practically indistinguishable from other American authors; they can hardly be said to be carrying on a distinctive tradition in another tongue. The development of Scandinavian-American literature is over. It belongs to history.

It also describes history, not objective facts but complex inner processes involving mysteries of human identity. Historians have spoken so glibly of the melting pot, of assimilation and Americanization, of immigrants made over into Americans as though by some inevitable alchemy. Even now, when they have begun to write about the lasting ethnic groups of a pluralistic society *beyond* the melting pot, too often they do not realize the complexity of the processes involved. Sociologists and

---

* About 800 newspapers and magazines were published by Norwegian-Americans in their own language in the United States. Of these, five newspapers were still appearing in 1971. *Decorah-posten* (Decorah, Iowa), a weekly newspaper with 44,000 subscribers all over the United States in its heyday, printed only 4,000 copies of each number in 1971 and ceased publication in early 1973. See Olaf Holmer Spetland, "Den norsk-amerikanske presse," *Aftenposten* (Oslo) for 24 Nov. 1971, p. 4 (morning edition).

   For figures on Swedish-American periodicals, see Sture Lindmark, *Swedish-America 1914-1932* (Uppsala, 1971), pp. 221-32, and Finis Herbert Capps, *From Isolationism to Involvement, The Swedish Immigrant Press in America, 1914-1945* (Chicago, 1966).

** Reminiscences and historical studies still occasionally appear under the auspices of one of the immigrant newspapers—for example, Karsten Roedder, *Av en utvandrer-avis' saga, Nordisk Tidende i New York gjennom 75 år* (From an Emigrant Newspaper's Saga, *The Nordic Times* in New York through 75 Years, Brooklyn, 1966); but I am aware of only one book publication of imaginative literature by a living first-generation immigrant author in recent years: Arthur Landfors, *Träd som bara grönska* (Stockholm, 1962), a volume of poems most of which originally appeared in the Swedish immigrant press. Another volume of Swedish-American verse which has just appeared was published as a memorial to its departed author: Hjalmar Björk, *Stigens rosor* (The Swedish Cultural Society in America, 1973). A number of now unpublishable manuscripts of fiction by elderly first-generation immigrants exist. I shall draw upon some that I have read in subsequent chapters.

   The reader should note that titles in a Scandinavian language which are not translated when mentioned in footnote or text will be found translated to English in the bibliography at the end of this book, except when they are self-explanatory.

psychologists, on the contrary, know how little they understand of the intricate interdependencies between individuals and social groups. They know that identity and culture belong together. In a stable cultural situation, identity is no problem to the individual; but when a person leaves the culture in which his personality was formed, and plunges into a society whose ways are strange to him but where he means to stay, the confrontation will force him into painful personal change. This cultural shock was common and central to all immigrant experience. Therefore it is the central theme throughout Scandinavian-American literature, whereas it has seldom appeared in either American or Scandinavian literature. Crisis of or quest for identity as a theme in modern national fiction is a different problem: it reflects the experience of persons growing up in a culture in such flux that they have failed to form a stable identity at all.

The immigrants' problem was having to adapt personality and behavioral patterns developed in one social situation to a different setting requiring different patterns. This was an extremely complex matter, and would be difficult enough to trace even if the initial and terminal stages of the process remained stable. The societies at both ends of the process, however, were undergoing radical transformation at the same time. Think of the profound changes in the Middle West from 1875, for instance, to 1930. The fundamental reconstruction of Scandinavian society which took place during the same period was not less drastic. The initial impression given by the source material is that of movement in different directions: in Europe, the gradual breakdown of an old, rigid order inherited from the Middle Ages; in America, the rapid emergence from unfinished, amorphous fluidity of a new order—that of the modern world. From a wider viewpoint, however, the development is seen to have been roughly parallel in both places: from rural toward urban, from agricultural toward industrial organization of society. For many reasons this revolution in human life began later in Scandinavia and developed more slowly there, so the impression of most immigrants was that their homeland stagnated in the past while America hurried into the future. Since their image of the Old Country tended to remain fixed in the stage at which they had left it, only the minority who revisited their birthplace after long absence saw the drastic transformations which had also taken place there. Because of this continual change at varying rates on both sides of the Atlantic, all generalizations comparing the two cultural systems must be qualified by a sense of time. Yet beneath the flux of these years something remained comparatively constant, patterns of behavior which may be called typically Scandinavian on one hand and typically American on the other. Both patterns emerge from the variegated source material of this study, in the constant comparisons the immigrants made between their old homes and the new. Here I will venture into that suspect field which attempts to define national character, armed with the surprisingly consistent observations of two generations of marginal men.

Variations of place as well as time of settlement by Scandinavian immigrants have also caused problems of generalization. Within the same period, those who came to settled communities found quite another social and cultural situation from those who went to the frontier—and many did both in turn. Those who stayed in settlements dominated by their own nationality met less intense problems of adjustment than those outnumbered by other groups. Those who remained in rural areas encountered a different kind of American life from city dwellers. Scandinavians were Americanized—that is, adopted patterns of behavior appropriate to American society—at a speed proportionate to the amount of their contact with native Americans; yet even the most isolated and exclusive settlements succumbed in time to the pressure of the larger society around them. Thus in both group and individual life the general movement was away from typically Scandinavian toward American patterns of identity and behavior. I have found in imaginative literature records which describe this complex process of assimilation more vividly and in greater detail than any other historical source material.

IV. Problems of Literature as Historical Source Material

Yet literature has obvious drawbacks as source material for history. The evidence of any one book is highly fragmentary, limited not only by the author's purpose but also by his experience and his talent. Even a hundred fragments fitted together may lack many parts, how many and how important only other sources can reveal. Among several hundred books, one or two alone may treat a given topic, and they may be biased. Fiction especially abounds in elements relevant to its own purpose but useless to the historian: love interest, mistaken identity, deus ex machina—all the involutions of plot and exaggerations of character by which an author may seek to hold reader interest. What is of value to the historian is often present incidentally, even unconsciously: local color, concrete detail, attitudes revealed through both expressed opinions and slanted situations. Above all, no writer is obligated to stick to the facts as he sees them. He may omit, distort, or overemphasize, express a passing mood as an eternal verity, insist upon his own view as the only valid one.

To deal with these problems I have used techniques of analysis from both history and literary criticism. My first task was to classify the authors in terms of their importance, as measured by the number of books they published, the recognition accorded them by contemporary readers and critics, and their artistic ability. I have included the general results of this classification in Chapter Two, where I distinguish between major and minor writers. My judgment of the individual authors' relative importance in their own literary tradition underlies every citation I make from their work, but here I have made no attempt to write evaluative literary history. Later I hope to make a contribution in this quite different field. At present there are many minor figures about whom I know nothing beyond the fact that a book with their name on the title page is to be found in a certain library. Anonymous works especially I can judge only by internal evidence. I may therefore have inadvertently included some books by European visitors to the American scene rather than by true immigrants, but these can be neither many nor significant. As a rule an author revealed in subtle ways whether he was looking upon immigrant life as an outsider or a participant.

I have used techniques of literary criticism to probe beneath what the authors say, to what they *mean*. I have assumed that the opinions and experiences of fictional characters are significant only insofar as they reveal the judgments of their authors. Those especially critical of American life were apt to distort both characterization and plot for purposes of satire or in moral indignation. Unskilled minor writers often wrote a novel with a single distinct purpose, such as attacking saloons; these clearly showed any bias they had, often commenting or moralizing in their own person. A few authors, however, were talented enough to create characters independent of their own personalities, who expressed divergent or even opposing views. All of these better writers produced enough material for me to undertake more detailed analysis of their basic attitudes. Usually they also partook in printed polemic about the merits and demerits of life in America, and about whether or not their fellow immigrants should fight to preserve their ethnic identity. (A general discussion of these underlying attitudes will be found in Chapter Four.) Armed with such knowledge of the viewpoints and purposes of individual authors, I have been able to judge better the reliability of their evidence in specific issues. Where I have cited a deliberately exaggerated account for a special reason, I have pointed out the bias involved. Otherwise the illustrative quotations I have chosen, although in the form of comments by or about fictional persons, actually express typical views of real people—the authors.

The sheer bulk of the literature has enabled me to distinguish between observations and comments which were typical of the authors as a group and those which were anomalous, whether meant to be or not. I have considered recurrence of similar events, reactions, and (in poetry) moods in variant settings as evidence of validity, weighing of course how often and how widely distributed they occur. I have discarded unique or aberrant examples except in a few special cases, where they are labeled as such. Otherwise I have indicated the amount of evidence supporting a generalization by such phrases as "practically all of the authors," or "some writers," or "a few."

However, I consider the most important fact which my study uncovered (verifiable by any scholar who investigates the evidence) to be that in the court of history these literary witnesses *agree*. Their description of immigrant experience is amazingly consistent, when seen in reference to place and time. This general agreement I have organized and discussed in the form of themes—for instance, homesickness, which all authors recorded, although some insisted its suffering was more than outweighed by social betterment while others maintained the opposite. Thus they agreed in general on what happened to immigrants in America, and how; where they disagreed was on their *evaluation* of what happened. They exercised comparatively little literary license in these books.

A number of factors influenced most of these immigrant fiction writers toward literal realism in recording the life around them. In the first place, most were too unskilled to be inventive. To the last man they were amateurs as literary artists, earning their living in a multitude of callings while their writing was of necessity relegated to leisure time. What would be more natural than that they should take as their subject matter what lay most immediately at hand? Many admitted or boasted in forewords or postscripts that their work was based on actual events, with only names changed.* It was precisely what lay at hand—the cultural shock of their daily lives—which seems to have motivated so many ordinary people untrained in literature to attempt self-expression in literary forms at all. Even Rølvaag was first inspired to study and write in America.

The taste of their reading public too was dominated by naive realism —well expurgated, of course. Much of one of the earliest Norwegian-American novels, *Fra begge sider af havet* by Tellef Grundysen (Chicago, 1877), was so realistic that the author's neighbors in Fillmore County, Minnesota, could identify the principal characters and recognize several episodes as based on local occurrences of the recent past. But the plot included forgery, embezzlement, and a prison sentence for the Norwegian

* "The content of this story is based partly on my own experiences and partly on accounts which I have from the tellers' own mouths. Most of the names of the participants have been changed, but otherwise everything is the unvarnished truth. Imagination has no part whatever in the story. From actual life I have tried to present some of the causes which impel and often compel people to leave their native land, and how life in America often develops for the emigrants." Eilert Storm, *Alene i urskogen* (Kristiania, 1899), p. 3.

villain—and no such horror had ever occurred in that settlement. In a preface Grundysen had claimed to be telling a true story. Fearing that he would be believed, twelve of his neighbors published a statement in a leading Norwegian-American newspaper "condemning the novel as a base fabrication and a libel on the immigrants from the author's own valley."[6]

Such reader reactions, to be sure, might exert pressure on writers to idealize their characters even more than to portray them realistically, and not a few novels and short stories showed a marked tendency to make heroes and heroines of the same national background as the author and readers, while villains were Yankees and Irishmen. On the whole, however, the fact that most prospective readers had lived through similar experiences tended to influence the authors toward literal realism in the picture of daily life which they recorded as framework and setting for their stories, however wild their flights of fancy in constructing plots. A Danish-American author in his foreword disclaimed any artistic merit in his tales of immigrant life, "but they are presented as artless, unpretentious sketches of the life and conditions of [my] countrymen in America. . . . I hope that my countrymen west of the great sea will acknowledge their truth and authenticity."[7]

When the literature included evidence of diametrically opposed opinions on various aspects of immigrant life, it reflected the reaction of unlike personality types to similar situations. Some authors, like their characters, proved able to make satisfactory adjustment to American conditions, while others remained discontented and therefore much more critical. The books expressed attitudes arising from greater or less success in adapting an old identity to a new environment. In many cases sheer chance involved in time of arrival and choice of place exercised decisive influence on the individual's adjustment. Characters who came early enough to acquire free or cheap land in the rural Middle West, or who settled in communities of their own kind and there made good, tended to approve of life in America and to be glad they had emigrated. Later comers, on the other hand, who met declining economic opportunity and disintegrating exclusiveness of Scandinavian settlements, emphasized increasingly the trials and suffering of cultural shock.

Yet in all periods and places some characters remained homesick and unhappy in America irrespective of the degree of prosperity they won. Usually the personality structure of this type of individual proved too rigid to adapt to new conditions. He or she was too old and fixed in his ways at emigration, or too bound to family, friends, and all the emotive symbols of a meaningful life left behind in the homeland, to be able to develop new emotional ties in a strange setting. The sensitive, the introvert, the tender-hearted and thin-skinned were shown invariably

24

to make the poorest immigrants. Above all those who took their own European values most seriously found adjustment to the unexpectedly different value orientation of another society most difficult. A number of characters were portrayed modifying their original patterns of judgment and behavior under the constant pressure of another social system around them, and these usually made satisfactory adjustment to American life. But those unable to change their identity remained outsiders unless they lived together in sufficient numbers to establish their own community. In this case the entire community remained "outsider," open to the accusation of being clannish, different, and un-American. However, this resolution of the problem of cultural shock for members of the first generation only postponed its solution for their children. Sooner or later the second or third generation had to move out into the larger encroaching society on its terms, completing the process of assimilation and ending the immigrant experience because their personal identity was no longer European in any significant sense but wholly American. Individual characters might still claim Scandinavian-American family background, the way I did (and do), without it affecting their identity as Americans.

All these variants of immigrant experience, also those extending beyond the first generation, appear in Scandinavian-American literature as defined in Chapter Two, and will be described in the following study. But how can one be sure that what these authors saw and experienced was representative of the life of the entire group? I have three kinds of evidence to support this claim: First, the fullness and variety of the description of Scandinavian-American life which the literature gives. The reader can judge the validity of this evidence for himself, since the sole purpose of this book is to present it. Second, the testimony of contemporaries who read the literature, such as this unsigned editorial from 1924:

> It is characteristic of this immigrant literature that it is honest, candid, and at times even painfully realistic. It is a series of plain stories of everyday life among Scandinavian settlers in America and as such it has a cultural value that cannot be overlooked. . . . The prose as well as the poetry written by Scandinavian pioneer authors grew out of life itself and therefore, often in a crude way, expresses the emotions, the drama, the hopes, and the affections *not only of their writers but of the entire nationality whom the writers represent.*[8]

Third, the independent evidence of other sources—that is, conventional history. The expert in Scandinavian immigrant history will recognize all aspects of the following reconstruction of the life of this ethnic group with the possible exception of one, which I shall discuss in an epilogue. I do not maintain that this evidence is sufficient to prove that a couple of hundred writers and critics fairly represent a group numbering some millions (including the second generation), but I have found no evidence to the contrary. Therefore I lean toward the assumption that the claim is true.

I do not need to insist upon it, however, any more than I need insist that the truth of Scandinavian immigrant life was what these authors said it was. I am content merely to record what a small, clearly defined group of persons professed to have felt and seen as they moved through a complex and painful process of adjustment—painful even for people of this ethnic background, always assumed to be closely related to the Anglo-Saxon and the Yankee. At least these writers tell clearly what it was like *for them* to be immigrants to the United States through nearly four score years. This book is thus a study in the history of ideas, recording the series of images developed by persons who had uprooted themselves from the old familiar and were striving to transplant themselves to the new and strange—images of the home they had left and the home they found, colored by nostalgia, anxiety, and hope.

Chapter Two

The Source Material:
Scandinavian Immigrant Literature

> We can call these works and poems provincial or emi-
> grant literature, but then we give the child a wrong
> name. For they are not that: they are American litera-
> ture in the Norwegian language.
>
> Ole E. Rølvaag.[1]

Who ever heard of Scandinavian-American literature? The general reading public in both the United States and Scandinavia may remember
O. E. Rølvaag's *Giants in the Earth,* but as far as they know his work
is an isolated phenomenon without forerunner or fellowship. American
scholars of Scandinavian background may have heard of a handful of
other immigrant authors: Waldemar Ager, Johannes B. Wist, Simon
Johnson among the Norwegians; Adam Dan, Carl Hansen, Kristian
Østergaard among the Danes; Vilhelm Berger, Ernest Skarstedt, Johan
Person, Anna Olsson among the Swedes. Yet few specialists in any of
the three national groups are aware of even the leading figures in the
others, and no one has attempted so much as an outline of the broad
field of Scandinavian-American creative writing. What accounts of
literary history have been published are limited to one nationality and
include little more than lists of the best known authors and their works.[2]
Even bibliographies are few and incomplete. Only the Norwegians have
undertaken an exhaustive listing of all individual titles printed by first-
generation immigrants in the United States and Canada before 1930.[3]
There are in fact many hundreds of volumes and pamphlets of short
stories and novels, poems and plays, reminiscences, autobiographies,
essays, travel sketches, and historical accounts published by Scandinavian
immigrants in their own languages, now gathering dust in the collections of Luther College at Decorah, Iowa, St. Olaf College at Northfield, Minnesota, Augustana at Rock Island and North Park at Chicago,
Illinois, Grand View College at Des Moines, Iowa; in state historical
society libraries throughout the Middle West; and in emigrant archives
in Sweden, Norway, and Denmark. Rølvaag's achievement stands not

alone but as the climax of a literary tradition that began in the 1870s and is not yet completely dead.

The definitive appraisal of this little-known branch of American literature must wait until a number of specialized analyses have clarified its content and worth; but since the following study is based upon part of the material—fiction and poetry—it seems necessary to attempt a preliminary definition of the field as a whole. The following survey will trace its boundaries in the borderline between two cultures, analyze its special problems of audience and language, and consider the intriguing questions about how and why such a large, rich, and varied literature could develop among a transplanted people, written for a public severely limited both in number and in cultural interests, and coming to full flower after its language had begun to die.

I. Publishing Markets

1. NEWSPAPERS

Undoubtedly the early development of foreign-language newspapers provided the first stimulus for immigrant authors. The two first Scandinavian-language newspapers known were both founded in 1847. *Nordlyset* (The Northern Light) was published in Norwegian in Muskego, Wisconsin, while *Skandinavia* in New York City appealed to Danes, Swedes, and Norwegians not only by printing news from all three native countries but also by using both Dano-Norwegian and Swedish languages.[4] The rapidly multiplying newspapers that were published for all three groups continued to reprint poetry and, later, tales and serialized novels by authors in the Old Country, as well as verse and prose writings by their own staffs; but before long they were also accepting contributions from readers. Letters to the editor often appeared in news columns; but what became a particular plague of the Norwegian or Swedish newspaper was the persistent stream of amateur verse sent in by subscribers. Most of this was very bad poetry indeed, and some of the most amusing accounts of immigrant journalistic life describe the moral struggle of editors torn between their outraged artistic judgment and their fear of insulting contributors if they neglected to print their efforts.

But by no means all the verse published in the Scandinavian-American press was bad. The larger and better newspapers, which could afford to pay (although very little) for contributions, usually were the first to publish even the major works of poets in the immigrant tradition. Smaller journals then reprinted them, often again and again. Introductions to collected volumes of verse usually acknowledged previous publication in newspapers much more often than in magazines. Such journalistic verse was the earliest and most regular literary expression of the transplanted writers, and even the worst of it carried many of the same themes and attitudes as the most finished poetry in their literature. The poets constantly complained of lack of reader interest—and indeed their collected works sold as poorly as those of their American colleagues —but their serious and their popular efforts did not differ so much as those in English publications. The difference between good and bad poetry written by Scandinavian immigrants was largely in form, not content.

Most of the verse printed in newspapers was written by the immigrants themselves, but the fiction usually was not. Perhaps one reason was financial: the poems, on the whole, were gratuitous contributions; even those furnished by better-known writers were bought for small fees. Moreover, the press used less verse than fiction. Only on special occasions, such as Christmas or the Seventeenth of May, did two or three poetic efforts appear in a single issue of a newspaper, and often weeks would pass when smaller papers printed no verse at all. But the press used fiction in astounding quantities. Literature interested some editors more than others, and a few of their organs—*Emigranten* (Inmansville and Madison, Wisconsin), *Decorah-posten* (Decorah, Iowa), and *Skandinaven* (Chicago)—held for certain periods a reputation of being almost literary journals. But almost every one of the immigrant papers, no matter how small or short-lived, ran not only short stories and sketches but also serialized novels, not infrequently two or even three novels at the same time. Most of the stories were reprinted, translated from American fiction or adapted from European sources. Some editors had a predilection for French murder mysteries, others for German romances; but all drew copiously on the authors of their home countries. Occasionally this policy was aimed deliberately at building stronger ties with the homeland, but, especially in the twentieth century, the reprinting of cheap popular fiction in the Scandinavian languages was simply the easiest way of getting copy. Often during the nineteenth century the source of the work was not acknowledged, a novel merely being labeled "From the French" or "Translated by X . . ."; but even after copyright regulations became stricter, most of the novels and many of the short stories in this foreign-language press were second printings. The fiction produced by the immigrant group itself was by no means large enough to satisfy the demand.

In addition, some newspapers instituted literary supplements. *Ved arnen: et tidsskrift for skjønliteratur* (By the Fireside: A Magazine of Belles-Lettres) was undoubtedly the most important of these; it was issued as part of the weekly *Decorah-posten* at Decorah, Iowa. As a medium for Norwegian-American literature, it published the work of such writers as Antonette Tovsen and Ruth Fjeldsaa, whose novels never appeared in book form, as well as that of Rølvaag and other leading authors. In numbers for two years, 1927-28, were serialized Waldemar Ager's *Gamlelandets sønner,** H. A. Foss's *Valborg,* and Rølvaag's *I de dage* and *Riget grundlægges*—first publication in America for the last two, which were later issued in English under one title, *Giants in the Earth.* The quality of fiction printed in *Ved arnen* varied sharply, however. From Dickens and Anatole France in translation and Bjørnson and Jonas Lie in the original Norwegian, the range extended to Zane Grey and Gene Stratton-Porter, and their equivalents in Europe.[5]

Newspaper presses sometimes issued novels or collections of tales as books after setting them up for serialized publication. These were sold through the newspaper's bookstore, if it had one, or offered as premiums to subscribers who paid in advance. Thus one finds under the imprint of Norwegian or Swedish publishers in the United States wild West stories, tales of European court intrigue, cheap romances, and murder mysteries from many tongues. Occasionally an immigrant novel would find its way into book form in this manner. The phenomenally popular *Husmandsgutten* by H. A. Foss ran in *Decorah-posten,* 1884-85, and then went through several editions as a book from B. Anundsen's press. This serial was said to have attracted six thousand new subscribers and saved *Decorah-posten* from bankruptcy at a time of crisis. It set the style for what became a whole school of fiction in this tradition, the Horatio Alger story translated into immigrant terms.

2. MAGAZINES

Church periodicals were the earliest magazines founded by the Scandinavian group. The first and most persistent type was the organ of a synod or other affiliation of churches, and contained news of theological appointments, social events, and mission doings, as well as discussions of doctrine. In 1851 the two earliest Norwegian religious periodicals were established: *Maanedstidende* (The Monthly Times—Racine, Wisconsin), published by the conservative Norwegian Synod; and *Kirketidende* (The Church Times—Racine), which defended lay preaching and attacked the Norwegian Synod's high-church predilection. As various new synods grew out of the bitter controversies among Scandinavian Lutherans, and as independent churches of Scandinavian Methodists, Baptists, and others grew strong enough to unite in larger groups, each founded its own organ. Some of these were among the periodicals surviving longest in the original languages.

---

* The reader is reminded that titles not translated in the text will be found with English translation in the bibliography.

Such church news letters carried no fiction, although poetry on purely religious themes, contributed by ministers or leading parishioners, appeared occasionally. The synods were not slow, however, to found their own magazines of "Christian entertainment," some designed for family consumption, others to provide moral and inspirational reading for children. Perhaps the earliest of the latter type was *Børne-blad* (Children's Paper), published monthly at La Crosse, Wisconsin, 1875-89, and weekly at Decorah, Iowa, 1890-1902. Weekly Sunday-school papers were common. Stories, serials, and verse in these publications naturally ran to a pattern. Most were translations and reprints, but original contributions also presented the "true faith," praised Christian virtues (especially obedience to parents), and glorified God. After the turn of the century the inclusion of more and more material in English marked the growing Americanization of the younger generation.

Annual almanacs and calendars were issued for varying periods by several of the synods, as well as by a few immigrant newspapers and publishing houses. The religious ones carried calendars of Lutheran holy days, sermons, poems, lists of church members who had died during the year, reports on missions, and often a short story or two on a religious theme. Sometimes there were historical sketches of early congregations, reminiscences by leading pastors, and tales of Lutheran martyrs. The secular yearbooks ran to statistics: lists of fraternal societies and church synods, of important businesses and businessmen of their nationality, of schools, periodicals, institutions such as orphans' and old people's homes, of festivals and meetings held during the preceding year, sometimes even of lecturers and artists who had come on tour from the Old Country. These almanacs thus preserved a wealth of factual detail about the organized group life of that nationality all over the United States, one year at a time, as well as printing some poems, essays, and stories about and by members of the national group.

Christmas annuals, based on Old-World models, began to appear during the nineties; several proved important as markets for leading Scandinavian immigrant authors. *Julegranen* (The Christmas Tree— Cedar Falls, Iowa, 1896-1950) published work of all the best Danish writers in the United States, and included short stories and poetry, travel sketches, articles about artists and famous American men and places, and some historical accounts. As late as 1953 a new annual called *Dansk nytaar* (Danish New Year) began publication at Blair, Nebraska, succeeding *Dansk almanak,* which had been issued there by the Lutheran Publishing House since 1922. The new periodical carried on the tradition of *Julegranen* by printing articles and stories written by Danish immigrants about their own lives, but ceased publication in 1961.

Of the several Norwegian and Swedish Christmas annuals, those of the Augsburg Publishing House in Minneapolis have been most significant. The beautifully illustrated *Jul i vesterheimen* (Christmas in the Western Home—1911-57) published only original contributions, often solicited from the best-known Norwegian-American and Danish-American authors, written both in the European tongues and in English. O. E. Rølvaag was interested in this magazine, and gave most of his short stories and a couple of poems to it. Over the years *Jul i vesterheimen* reflected well the changing interests of the immigrant group, including in its pages stories of pioneer days and incidents in lumber camps and gold mines, accounts of the city life of the second generation, of Americanized Norwegians during the depression, and of elderly folk waiting for death in old people's homes. Since 1931 the Augsburg Publishing House has printed an annual called *Christmas* entirely in English. During the last forty years a considerable number of English-language Christmas annuals have been published by various religious groups (especially Lutheran) of Scandinavian background; but they show little trace of immigrant origin.

By far the greatest number of Scandinavian-American non-English periodicals, however, have been free of church affiliation. Some meant for family consumption did emphasize the word "Christian" in their subtitles, and their short stories and serials were as consistently moralistic as those of the church-sponsored magazines. Their founders constantly proclaimed their mission of filling a long-felt need for uplifting and educational reading matter for their language group in America. Although these publications flourished in considerable numbers from the 1870s to the 1920s, most proved short-lived.[6] Probably these periodicals, as well as those freer of moralizing, were begun by individual publishers as moneymaking projects. This would account for their extremely varied contents, designed to attract every possible reader interest. The articles covered natural history and astronomy, popularized and applied science, accounts of American history, famous men and places, and travel in remote and exotic parts of the world. Much of this material was reprinted from other sources, as were many of the serialized novels and short stories. Sometimes, however, the periodicals included what they proudly labeled exclusive contributions; and the first novels of Norwegian-American life appeared in one of the oldest of the family magazines in 1874. These serialized novels, written by Nicolai Severin Hassel, were "Alf Brage, eller skolelæreren i Minnesota," and "Rædselsdagene: Et norsk billede fra indianerkrigen i Minnesota." Both ran in 1874 in *For hjemmet* (For the Home—Decorah, 1870-87).

Occasionally a literary magazine was designed to preserve Old-Country values in the New World. One such was the Swedish *Val-*

kyrian: Illustrerad månadsskrift (The Valkyrie: An Illustrated Monthly Magazine), founded in New York, January, 1897, by Charles Johanson, an editor of the newspaper Nordstjärnan (The North Star). To encourage circulation, the price was set at only one dollar a year, the main costs being borne by profits from Nordstjärnan. The editor, Edward Sundell, printed many excellent Swedish-American tales and novels, including some of his own, but the magazine survived only thirteen years.[7]

Similar in aim but with weaker financial backing were the organs of the fraternal and cultural societies. The immigrants formed lodges in which they could speak their own language, wear Old-Country costumes on festive occasions, or discuss books from the homeland and papers written by members. Many of these clubs soon lost all but their social aspect, and the periodicals became news letters; but at least two, though comparatively short-lived, preserved valuable literary and historical material. Symra was published at Decorah, 1905-14, by the Norwegian reading and discussion club of the same name, and the Kvartalskrift (Quarterly) of Det Norske Selskab i Amerika lasted from 1905 to 1918. In the latter are many discussions of prospects for a Norwegian-American literature, as well as short stories and poems which proved that it did exist. For several years Det Norske Selskab gave an annual prize for the best piece of writing submitted by a Norwegian immigrant.

Comparable to these were special publications of Swedish and Danish groups interested in literature. Prärieblomman kalender (The Prairie Flower Calendar—Rock Island, Illinois, 1900-13) provided a market for leading Swedish-American writers, as did the literary magazine Hemmets vän (Friend of the Home—Chicago, 1903-05). Smaablomster fra vor lille have (Small Flowers from Our Little Garden), published monthly during 1901 at Grand View College, Des Moines, made available assorted poems and tales by leading Danish-American authors. Each small issue was devoted to three or four poems, or a short story, by one person. Dagen (The Day—Minneapolis, 1900-04) and Norden (The North—Racine, Wisconsin, 1903-15) were other Danish magazines printing tales and poems.

The Norwegians were especially active in forming bygdelag, associations of people from one valley or province in the home country.[8] These clubs flourished in the first quarter of this century, many of them putting out yearbooks modeled on similar magazines in the Old Country and containing not only social notes but poetry and sketches, both reminiscent and fictional, about the home valley and group settlements from there. Collections of these publications at the Wisconsin and Minnesota state historical libraries and in the archives of the Nor-

33

wegian-American Historical Association provide a little-known source of shorter literary compositions, many written in dialect. Rølvaag, for example, made several contributions to his regional society's yearbook, *Nordlandslaget*. These regional associations have numbered nearly fifty in all, and some of them still exist.

A minor group of periodicals published by Norwegians and Swedes in the United States consisted of humor magazines, some copied directly from examples in the homeland, others patterned on American models. Put out mainly in a few large Midwestern cities during the nineties, these were printed on cheap newspaper stock and featured verses, funny stories, and cartoons. *Spøgefuglen* (The Joker), a Danish-American satirical periodical (Minneapolis and Perth Amboy, New Jersey), survived 1893-1931. The Norwegian *Spøg og alvor* (In Jest and in Earnest) ran a couple of serial novels, including a reprinting of *Kristine: En fortælling fra Valdres* (Kristine: A Tale from Valdres), by H. A. Foss.

Even one-man magazines appeared among the Norwegian-Americans. The most long-lived was printed monthly, beginning 1901, in St. Paul, and was entitled *Smuler* (Crumbs) by its editor, publisher, and chief contributor, O. S. Hervin. The little periodical discussed, criticized, and made sophisticated fun of everything in the Norwegian-American world; occasionally it printed short poems sent in by readers. *Dølen* (The Man from the Valley), on the other hand, issued irregularly at Joice, Iowa, and Minneapolis after 1902 by Jon Norstog, crusaded seriously for the preservation of Norwegian culture. It was a direct imitation of a magazine published in Norway by the poet Aasmund Vinje. With few exceptions, Norstog printed only his own poems and short stories. A third of these one-man periodicals was called *Buslett's* by its publisher, O. A. Buslett. In four issues of irregular dates put out in Northland, Wisconsin, in 1922-23, the author reprinted his first poetry and tales from newspaper files of forty years earlier. He had planned to issue his entire collected works in paper-bound periodical form, but evidently lacked financial support. Sometimes a *bygdelag* magazine was also largely a one-man undertaking: *Telesoga* (Fergus Falls, Minnesota, 1909-1924), put out by Torkel Oftelie, is a good example.

To such periodicals writers of Norwegian, Swedish, or Danish could look for publication in the United States from the 1860s on.[9] They provided a market with considerable variety of taste. Moral tales or innocent romances sold most easily to Christmas, family, and children's magazines; humorous sketches might appeal to the comic periodicals; but serious, realistic, critical fiction had a much more limited market. The few good literary publications were comparatively short-lived, and they flourished only from the nineties until the first World War;

magazines that did survive changed their literary standards with their editors. Therefore many authors looked to book publication for works which were either too good or too bad for the periodical press.

3. BOOKS AND PAMPHLETS

Getting books printed was not difficult, even before the establishment of immigrant publishing houses in the major cities of the Middle West. Newspaper presses did the work either at the printer's cost and profit, or subsidized by the authors. The first novel of Norwegian-American life to appear in book form was put out by the newspaper *Skandinaven* in 1877, after it had run as a serial: *Fra begge sider af havet* by Tellef Grundysen. It proved popular enough to run through at least three editions by 1896, the later ones reprinted by the John Anderson Publishing Company of Chicago.

The method an author used for publishing his own book was described by Ole Amundsen Buslett, who paid the printing costs of his first little volume of verse in 1882 and then of his novelette, *Fram!* This fictional bit was an assignment in a course in Norwegian at the University of Wisconsin for Professor Rasmus B. Anderson, whose advice the young man followed in peddling his pamphlets from farm to farm in the surrounding countryside. Many writers of all three nationalities, notably poets, paid to have little volumes of their works put out by newspapers and job-printing plants, in small villages as well as larger cities, until the depression. Such private editions were small, and a number of them may have been totally lost; but enough remain to indicate that many of these books of fiction and poetry were published at the authors' expense.[10]

A third type of publication was done by the synod presses, for example the Swedish Augustana Book Concern in Rock Island, Illinois, and the Norwegian Augsburg Publishing House in Minneapolis. Besides hymnals, volumes of sermons, and doctrinal tracts, these firms put out quantities of stories and some collections of poetry of high moral tone, aimed like their magazines at providing inspirational reading. A considerable amount of material was reprinted from Old-World sources, especially in the early years; but much was original, and by the turn of the century most of the best immigrant writers in all three languages were being published by synodal companies. These presses also commissioned the translation of suitable stories from other languages for book publication under their imprint.

Last to develop were the Scandinavian-American commercial publishing houses of the Middle West, mainly in Chicago and Minneapolis, which accepted for publication only works which they believed would sell. They were often associated with newspapers with which they shared a common economic fate, as well as the type and presses. They tended to be both smaller and more short-lived than the church-subsidized companies, and not many survived the transition to English-language publishing, which the big synodal firms took in their stride. Since the major immigrant authors usually preferred publication by church presses, the commercial companies were often left with second choice of manuscripts, but they provided an outlet for literature whose moral tone did not meet the strict standards of the religious concerns.

II. The Scope of the Literature

Privately printed or commercially published, the amazing fact about these Scandinavian-language books is their number and their range.[11] Among the novels, novelettes, collections of short stories, fictionalized reminiscences, compilations of jokes and yarns, Christmas books, religious and moral tales, juveniles and mysteries, the scope extends from deliberate obscenity and scandal, through attacks on specific institutions such as saloons, to the most serious social criticism; from shallow Cinderella stories through utopian novels to the most realistic tragedy —all within the framework of immigrant experience. The setting of the very first novel written by a Scandinavian in the United States, Hjalmar Hjort Boyesen's *Gunnar,*[12] was Norway, and later writers of all three nationalities turned out reams of romances picturing the homeland through a rosy haze. Other stories dealt with various topics, from fantasies laid in Viking days to tales about African natives. Much of this fiction, however, pictured the immigrants' daily life in many places and at all stages of its multiform development, seen optimistically or humorously or critically as the case might be but almost always on the level of simple realism.

Just as original verse was published earlier than fiction in newspapers and periodicals, so poetry appeared first in book form for all three national groups. The year 1871 saw the first volume of Norwegian-American poetry, Rasmus O. Reine's *En liden samling af psalmer og religiøse digte,* two years before the first fiction by a Norwegian appeared in America. The Danish clergyman Adam Dan had published poetry in Denmark before his emigration to the United States in 1870, and the next year he put out another volume in Copenhagen; but it was 1874 before the first book of Danish-American verse appeared in the United States—*Ved Øresund og Mississippi* by J. Waldemar Borchsenius. The Swedes' first books were also of poetry, probably the earliest being a pamphlet entitled *En svensk sång om den store branden i Chicago af Anders Nilsson, arbetskarl* (Chicago, 1872). The author was the journalist Magnus Elmblad, who wrote so fluently that his first volume of collected poems was published in Chicago in 1878.[13]

The range of subject matter and artistic competence was fully as wide in poetry as in prose for all three national groups. Much of it was abstract, dealing with generalized love of God, nature, fatherland, or family; only in certain types of lyrics and a few narrative poems did it express specifically immigrant themes. The most persistent of these was homesickness, but there were also many verses comparing the old home with the new in praise or criticism, urging preservation of the imported cultural tradition, or celebrating some achievement of the poet's group. Didactic verse included considerable social and economic criticism of American life, especially prohibition songs, and there were great quantities of humorous verse and occasional doggerel.

III. The Reading Public

The wide scope of this literary output indicates that the immigrant tradition reflected in miniature the same diversified reading public as one finds in the general American population, although not in equal proportions. Because religious controversies long absorbed most of the Scandinavian immigrants' intellectual energies and interests, almost all of their first books were doctrinal tracts and sermons. Moreover, much of their early poetry was religious; and the conservative pietism of certain elements remained a constant factor, stronger proportionately even in the present century than in corresponding native American writings. A considerable proportion of immigrant writers were, in fact, ministers. But there also developed a reading public amused by scandal-mongering and *double-entendre,* as witnessed by the phenomenal success of Lars A. Stenholt. This writer poured out cheap paperbound books during the nineties and the first decade of this century, attacking rich people (especially bankers), Jews, and above all Lutheran church and cultural leaders, in libelous fiction, with characters so thinly disguised that his Norwegian-American readers could easily identify the persons. These he accused of every possible sin, from hypocrisy to adultery. His books, published by Waldm. Kriedt in Minneapolis, were sold like magazines on trains and newsstands, and proved so popular that Stenholt was said to be the only writer of the immigrant tradition who made a living from his pen.[14]

Although all the elements of the American reading public were present in the foreign-language audience, the number of prospective book buyers in the latter group was so small that no immigrant author

37

(with the possible exception of Stenholt) could earn a living from his work. To judge from the complaints of the writers themselves, only a small fraction of the immigrants ever bought books produced by one of their own number. The literary needs of most were satisfied by a newspaper subscription and an almanac or Christmas annual; the better-educated minority who read fiction and poetry usually turned to the authors of the home country. As one leading Norwegian-American author complained, church and politics furnished the immigrants' sole cultural interest; nobody wanted or missed books. "What on earth was the good of fiction and poetry? Would it bring taxes down or land prices up? And so they smothered the brat, or nearly did. . . . Those who had something to say soon learned to address themselves to themselves. It is characteristic of our most gifted authors that they have worked under the conviction that they have no public."[15]

IV. The Authors

Lack of a reading public meant that writing had to be a spare-time activity for the Scandinavian immigrant authors. They were all amateurs. Perhaps this is the main reason that they must be judged as minor figures when compared with the major writers of any national literature. Within their own ranks, however, they showed such wide differences of ability and achievement that a critic can and must classify them as major or minor along a scale which measures, among other criteria, the number of works an author produced, the seriousness of his intent as an artist, and his reputation among his own people on both sides of the Atlantic.

1. THE FIRST GENERATION

a. *Education and background*

A great many "major" writers among all three immigrant nationalities earned their living as newspapermen, ministers, or teachers. Despite their varied backgrounds, most of them were better educated than the average immigrant. Many were distinctly untypical because they came from the cultivated upper classes of the home country. An example of this group was the journalist Magnus Elmblad, mentioned earlier as the first of the Swedish-American poets. He was also acclaimed as the best of them, although he remained in the United States only thirteen years, editing various newspapers. Son of a teacher at a Stockholm college, Elmblad took a degree at Uppsala University before emigrating in 1871. He had begun his prolific writing in Sweden, and continued to publish there even while he was in America. His epic poem, "Allan Roini," received the rare distinction of an award from the Swedish Academy. Unquestionably the outstanding minister-author among the immigrants was Adam Dan, who was trained at the University of Copenhagen and served as a missionary for two years in Nubia and Jerusalem before coming to the United States in 1870. He continued to issue his works in Denmark as well as in America until his death in 1931.[16]

Of scholar-authors trained in European universities before their emigration, one could name several outstanding examples. Hjalmar Hjorth Boyesen was author of the first novel by a Norwegian in America; he wrote it and his other works in English. Son of a Norwegian army captain, he took a degree at the University of Christiania before coming to the United States in 1869. He became professor at Cornell University and finally at Columbia University. The Swedish linguist, August Hjalmar Edgren, took his degree at Uppsala, came to America, and enlisted in the Union Army during the Civil War. He returned to Europe, became an officer in Sweden, studied further in France and Germany, and returned to the United States to take a doctorate in science at Cornell in 1871 and another degree in linguistics at Yale in 1874. A recognized authority in the science of language, he spent the rest of his life as scholar and poet alternately in Swedish and American universities, torn between his love for both lands. He died in 1903. A woman professor bearing a name famous in Norway, Agnes Mathilde Wergeland, student at Munich and Zurich, was the first Norwegian woman ever to take a doctoral degree (in Switzerland). Finding no place for her talents at home, she came to the United States on a scholarship from Bryn Mawr College in 1890. Her first years of lecturing at Illinois and Chicago universities were a time of bitter financial struggle; she was finally called to a professorship in history and French at the University of Wyoming in 1902. Beside scholarly works, she wrote two volumes of exquisite poetry in Norwegian before her death in 1914.

Contrasted with these educated leaders from the Scandinavian upper class were writers who were also editors, ministers, or teachers, but who came from the lower ranks of Old-World society and received their training in America. Many would have had no opportunity for higher education in Europe and probably would never have developed as authors there. Best among these, of course, was the fisherman's son from north Norway, Ole E. Rølvaag. After the customary early years of manual labor that most immigrants had to endure, he took his bachelor's degree at St. Olaf and spent a year studying in Norway before being appointed to a lifelong post as teacher at St. Olaf College. Other professions were also represented in this group: the chief librarian for many years of the John Crerar Library in Chicago, J. Christian Bay, and the Chicago dentist, Emanuel Nielson, were both Danish-born writers.

On the other hand, a number of the authors who can be classified as major never received much formal education. They earned their livings, often precariously, in various ways. Perhaps most of them were journalists, as was the Norwegian-American novelist Simon Johnson. Growing up in pioneer days in the Red River Valley, he received only the sketchy public and parochial schooling available there. A few were businessmen, as was the lumberman and poet Julius B. Baumann. Equally occupied in his business by day and as lecturer and leader at prohibition meetings and fraternal lodges in the evenings, he usually found the opportunity to write only in the dead of night or while traveling. Often he hardly had time to revise a poem before sending it off to a newspaper or magazine which had requested a contribution.

Some writers were homesteading farmers, eking out their meager incomes with odd jobs as mail carriers or game wardens. Some were Jacks-of-all-trades; the ambitious Ole A. Buslett, when he discovered he could not sell enough books to support his family, became farmer, storekeeper, postmaster, justice of the peace, and member of the Wisconsin legislature. Olai Aslagsson was hobo, cowboy, and sheepherder; his animal and adventure tales were published in Norway as well as in the United States and were translated into both English and Swedish. Tellef Grundysen was a drugstore clerk when he turned author; the Swedish Ernst Skarstedt became almost a professional hermit in the Pacific Northwest; the leading Danish-American poet, Anton Kvist, was a bricklayer in Chicago. Such were the immigrants whose compulsion to write Simon Johnson described in an essay:

> I know one who in stolen hours, preferably when bad weather hindered work outdoors, sat in a cold room and with numb fingers scrawled stories and poems about his people in this land. I know one who the whole day long—and it was not a mere eight-hour day either—followed his plow and harrow and composed verses which he tried to memorize until in a pause for rest he could scribble them down on a piece of wrapping paper. I know one who sat in a jolting mail wagon on the prairies of South Dakota and tried to set lines of verse on paper. The sun burned, the wind howled, storms broke loose—but this man wrote poetry. In the end he died of tuberculosis.[17]

b. *Aims and motives*

These were the dedicated souls of the tradition, motivated by their need to tell the story of themselves and their own people. Such a self-conscious artistic aim, of course, depended on membership in a group which was aware of its identity and had developed pride in its own accomplishments. During the first generation after Scandinavian immigration began in considerable numbers in the 1840s, such a situation was impossible. The physical struggle for survival in pioneer days occupied most ordinary people, and their intellectual leaders, most of them clergymen, were concerned almost exclusively with church organization and theological conflict. But by the seventies and eighties the shaping forces of national group consciousness were already strong: language, church, newspapers and magazines, fraternal organizations, cultural and political activities of many kinds within the limits of the national group. Fuller discussion of these forces and institutions will follow in Chapters Three and Six; here we wish to consider only varying attitudes of immigrant authors toward the *norskdom, svenskhet* or *danskhed* of their group.*

The three groups varied considerably in the fervor of their cultural nationalism. The Norwegians were by far the most enthusiastic, the Danes the least, for many complex reasons. And even within these groups, authors varied widely in their attitudes toward *norskdom* or *danskhed.* Some of the first generation advocated the most extreme abandonment of everything European. H. H. Boyesen dramatized this attitude in his own life, stating that after setting foot on American soil he never spoke a word in Norwegian except when absolutely necessary. As professor at Cornell and Columbia, he left completely behind him the Norwegian world, and recommended in his novels that his fellow immigrants do the same.[18]

Most of the leading Scandinavian-American authors, however, advocated maintaining the closest possible ties with the home countries and preserving their own hybrid culture within the larger environment. Some believed their transitional society could be only temporary, but thought that it could make positive contributions to American society while being melted into it. The bilingual editor and author Edwin Björkman typified this attitude; he began his career in immigrant newspapers and moved on to American papers, but he never disavowed his Swedish roots; see, for example, *The Soul of a Child* and *Gates of Life* (New York, 1922, 1923). Both Björkman's autobiographical novels and his books of essays were written in English. The best major writers, however, were the firmest believers in the value of their own culture in transplantation. Swedes pointed to the continuing existence of a strong island of *svenskhet* in Finland; Norwegians re-

---

* "Norwegianness," "Swedishness," and "Danishness" are the awkward English translations for these conceptions of national culture as expressed in language, art, religion, history, literature, folklore, and the collective personality of the people. These are European terms and concepts, applied to their own situation by the immigrants in America.

membered the survival of Norse culture through many hundreds of years in Iceland. So O. E. Rølvaag led the battle for the preservation of European language, history, and literature in America. Let the second and third generations continue to be bilingual, he argued, and lead richer lives for being able to draw on the cultural wealth of two lands.

Some authors in this tradition directed their fire against what they considered undesirable carry-overs from European life; Kristofer Janson, for example, attacked bitterly in many tales the power of the Norwegian Lutheran church in the Middle West.[19] Others assailed the evils they saw in American society: economic injustice, business immorality, overwhelming materialism. An institution that was a great menace to immigrants, especially on the frontier, was the saloon. Hundreds of poems and songs, plays, short stories, and even novels were written in the fight for prohibition. Especially among the Norwegians, there was hardly an author or journalist who did not give some part of his time to lecturing and writing against drink.

This cause, more than any other, furnished incentive to the minor writers, those of little or no ability, many of whom published only one or two books. The impulse to support worthy ends moved many otherwise inarticulate immigrants to take up the fictional pen. Some attacked specific institutions, as J. A. Harildstad did the treatment of the insane in *Bondegutten Hastad under asylbehandling i den nye verden* (Minneapolis, 1919). Other writers burned with indignation at economic and social injustices, wrongs done naive newcomers, conniving by wealthy bankers, oppression of the laboring class. One of the most vehement novels was E. L. Mengshoel's *Mené Tekél: Norsk-amerikansk arbeiderfortælling fra slutten af det 19. aarhundrede* (Minneapolis, 1919). The author portrayed laborers, struggling to organize a union, who were crushed by the superior power of evil capitalists.

Most of the minor tales, however, were written in a more optimistic vein. Their heroes usually won through to fame and fortune in the New World, and returned to their peasant homes in the Old Country only long enough to fetch their loved ones back to the land of the free.

Minor versifiers displayed the same cheeriness and banality in following set themes: glorification of church and faith, admiration of the equality and opportunity of the new land, upward-and-onward exhortation—although a shadow of melancholy fell across their work in the universal refrain of homesickness, above all at Christmastide. Many an amateur realized how unoriginal his little book was, and apologized in a brief foreword for offering yet another privately printed volume to an unresponsive public. Some confessed they hoped to earn a little extra money—not always for themselves, by any means; often it was announced that proceeds would go to a mission or to charity. Frequently the claim was that only at the "urging of friends" had the author consented to print his unworthy efforts. He hoped to further a little the good cause of religion or temperance, or to bring a little sunshine into someone's dark day. Underneath perhaps were obscure yearnings for self-expression and for the publicity and prestige of breaking into print.

The major writers were by no means immune from such motives. They were especially eager to publish in the Old Country. No doubt many realized, particularly after World War I, that they were fighting a losing battle to preserve their language. Soon if they were to be read at all it could be only across the sea, and meanwhile the homeland offered a larger potential audience. For others, artistic recognition in the land they had left would help justify their departure. Nearly every author had somebody back home to convince that he had made good, and a book published under the higher requirements of a European concern was respectable evidence. For immigrant writers of any skill recognized the lower standards of local reviewers, so eager to further the cause of an infant literature, so aware of the difficulties a man had to overcome to write at all. The best authors, exposed to the dreadful amateurishness of so many of the immigrant books, and cut off from American critics by their language, preferred to measure their achievement by European criteria.

c. *Special problems of language*

However, immigrant writers faced problems more complex than any author in the home country might meet. Their most immediate subject matter, the life around them, was American; yet they must treat it with European concepts and terminology. At first the contrast between what they found and what they had left tended to sharpen their observation but dull their comprehension; it was simpler to criticize than to understand. When they learned in time to interpret and explain, their initial conceptions had changed, and although they might be aware of the transformation, their original language was often inadequate to express it. Consider the simple Norwegian words *bonde* and *gård*. The first meant yeoman, a freeholding farmer, the second meant a farmstead, freehold, or estate; but the equivalent terms in English lacked the complex of social, legal, and historical associations involved with the Norwegian words. Immigrant writers found themselves forced to incorporate the American words "farmer" and "farm" into their Norwegian text, inflecting them after the rules of their own grammar. Then they had the problem of possible noncomprehension by readers in the Old Country. To solve this, many books by immigrant authors aimed at a European audience included footnotes or glossaries explaining American terms.

43

Authors who had not been educated in Europe faced further language problems because most Scandinavians spoke dialects which lacked written form. The same dichotomy between the speech of ordinary people and that of the educated class which existed in the Old Country was preserved in the new. When the mother tongue survived in daily speech even to the third generation, it was usually as a dialect; yet students who went to Scandinavian-American colleges studied the language and literature of church and court across the sea. Most immigrant authors chose quite naturally to write in the more formal linguistic form, but when their characters were of peasant stock the problem of dialogue arose. Should speech be transcribed in the dialects actually used, or formalized by regular spelling and vocabulary? This question faced writers in the home countries too, but in the United States it was complicated by strong admixtures of English in daily speech, creating a still more involved idiom that a few authors used deliberately for comic effect. Sometimes an author chose to write a poem or sketch in his original pure dialect, transcribed into approximate phonetic spelling, to give a special flavor or for publication in one of the *bygdelag* magazines, which printed contributions in dialect. Then, however, he ran the risk of being more or less unreadable to fellow countrymen from provinces other than his own.

The situation was further complicated for Norwegians by the New Norse (*landsmål, nynorsk*) movement at home.[20] The war between this new tongue, based on dialects and growing out of cultural and social reform, and the Dano-Norwegian, which had previously been the only written language, developed in full fury during the latter part of the nineteenth century, and raged largely among the literary classes; thus most immigrants had little contact with the battle before their departure. Neither did they develop interest in the conflict in America, being concerned with more immediate problems, such as the survival of any form of Norwegian at all. Their main cultural institution was the church, which had a vested interest in preserving the older, more conservative tongue of the Bible and the catechism. Those of their leaders who had been trained in Norway brought with them the almost unanimous rejection of New Norse by the upper classes there; those educated in America had studied only Dano-Norwegian in school.

Judge then the stone wall of indifference, not to say hostility, which faced a would-be New Norse author in America! Such a one was Jon Norstog. His mother was cousin to the *landsmål* poet Aasmund Vinje, in whose strongly traditionalistic province, Telemark, Norstog had grown up. He had studied under teachers who advocated return to the roots of peasant culture, and his first book of poems, *Yggdrasil* (Christiania, 1902), leaned heavily on Old Norse symbolism. The unfavorable reviews this book drew may have been a factor in Norstog's emigration the same year. Throughout his life he continued to write in a New Norse influenced by his own dialect, a style which his fellows in America found virtually unreadable. He printed on his own hand press thousand-page novels, huge Biblical dramas, volumes of poetry, which he bound himself; then he drove in a wagon over the Dakota prairies, trying in vain to sell his books—surely the ultimate in author publication. Of undeniable talent, he had a great deal of value to say to his fellow immigrants; but, being a poet, he could and would write only in the language of his heart, regardless of the inability of others to understand it. When he died in 1942 he was probably the least read of all the better-known immigrant authors.

Norwegian-American newspapers deplored the New Norse movement back home, foreseeing that it would increase the difficulty of cultural communication with the mother country. During the past fifty years both Dano-Norwegian and New Norse have been so changed by progressive "reforms" designed to bring them closer together, with the aim of ultimately combining the two, that elderly immigrants complain they can hardly read newspapers from Norway at all. In America, meanwhile, the language has been more static, especially in spelling. During the 1920s, when some leading immigrant authors had novels brought out on both sides of the Atlantic, their orthography had to be completely overhauled for the Norwegian editions. This has been a problem for people from Sweden and Denmark as well, because growth and change have also taken place in the official languages of these two nations. Emigrants revisiting the homeland after many years' absence often discover that their speech sounds rather quaint and bookish to friends and relatives who have never left home.

2. THE SECOND GENERATION

Similar problems faced second-generation authors. None grew up with the conviction that their parents' idiom was the only acceptable mother tongue. Those who lived in communities where Swedish or Norwegian was still widely used were rather bilingual. Except in families of upperclass or urban background, a dialectal type of the European language was transmitted from parents to children; but authors of the second generation nevertheless wrote in the literary form, learned at school or self-taught, because this was the only one they saw in print. They were inclined to seek more education than average even if their opportunities for schooling were limited; in that case they read on their own. As a result many were more culturally self-conscious than the usual farmer, laborer, or businessman, whose indifference to things of the spirit they strongly criticized. Not having memories of the Old Country to draw on, they often laid their stories in Scandinavian-American or purely American settings. Their poems celebrated the beauties of prairie and inland lake rather than glacier and salt sea. When their subjects were thus American, the language they chose for expression became a less crucial matter; for even their foreign tongue had become adapted in vocabulary and connotation to American life. The choice between English and Norwegian (or Swedish) then usually depended on the audience they were writing for, although a few were not completely at home in English.

One such writer was Anna Olsson, daughter of a leading Swedish-American minister and educator who for many years was president of Augustana College at Rock Island, Illinois. Miss Olsson, although born in Sweden, was brought to Kansas as a baby and grew up so completely the product of a hybrid background that she won her greatest literary success with short stories written in the everyday mixture of Swedish and English spoken by most immigrants. This crossbred dialect is still quite funny, although few can read it easily now. She published memories of her prairie childhood in normal Swedish in 1917, but when she translated the same book into English ten years later the stilted style revealed that she had not completely mastered the latter language.[21]

Dorthea Dahl, on the other hand, was equally competent in Norwegian and English. She was brought to the United States at the age of two and went to school in South Dakota; in 1902 she entered St. Olaf College at Northfield. She began writing her many stories of small-town and farm immigrant life exclusively in Norwegian, publishing in a variety of periodicals. Her first collection of tales, *Fra hverdagslivet* (Minneapolis, 1915), won the annual literary prize of Det Norske Selskab i Amerika. Her second collection, published five years later, contained only stories in English. Her one novel was written in Norwegian.[22]

3. ENGLISH-LANGUAGE WRITERS

Most second-generation authors of Scandinavian background wrote in English. They may well have spoken their parents' tongue, at least in childhood, and they may have maintained a lifelong interest in their foreign roots; but as writers they felt fully at home only in the American language. Several first-generation immigrants also published exclusively in English, in time losing full command of their original idiom. The Norwegian Hjalmar Hjorth Boyesen and the Swedish Edwin Björkman have been mentioned; the Danish journalist Jacob A. Riis must not be forgotten. A trio of Swedes may represent a group of minor novelists who emigrated when still young enough to absorb English well, but old enough so that their personalities had been primarily formed in Europe. Laying most of their plots in the Old World, Flora Sandström, Gösta Larsson, and Edita Morris had a number of novels published by New York firms during the 1930s and 1940s.

Scandinavians who wrote in English had little opportunity to publish in magazines put out by their own people. The synods and sects did issue some juvenile and family publications and a few Christmas annuals in English, providing a limited market for moralizing tales. A few magazines were directed at Scandinavian-Americans who read only English, but the little fiction these carried was usually translated from European literature. *Scandinavia*, a monthly, appeared in Chicago as early as November, 1883; it carried articles in English on ancient and modern phases of life in the three countries of origin, including translations of literature and criticism from the other side of the sea. It lasted three years. Another English-language *Scandinavia* with a Danish editor was founded at Grand Forks, North Dakota, in 1924.

The Northland Magazine, begun in Minneapolis in 1898, was intended to acquaint English-speaking people with Scandinavian folk; it was published "especially for those of Swedish descent who no longer know the language." An account of the Norwegian-American press in 1914 listed three nonreligious periodicals currently appearing in English for readers of Norwegian background, as well as several synodal magazines.[23] *The American Swedish Monthly,* published in New York, celebrated its fiftieth anniversary in 1957. Historical associations of the three nationalities issued publications printed in English. The author of short stories and poetry, however, tended to turn to the native American magazines. There his special background usually played no role.

Books in English by second- and third-generation writers were frequently published by regular American firms. Many had nothing to do with the special background of the author's childhood, and are of value in the study of Scandinavian immigrant literature only to demonstrate that here the process of Americanization had been carried to completion. Examples were the wild adventure yarns of Henry Oyen, written during and just after World War I. With titles like *Gaston Olaf, Twisted Trails,* and *Tarrant of Tin Spout,* these romances glorified virility and sex appeal for the rental-library trade. On a more serious level, a third-generation Swede, Nelson Algren, produced several books about the seamy side of Chicago life. Many of Algren's petty gangsters and prostitutes were of immigrant background, but they were not Swedes. The greatest of the completely assimilated authors of Scandinavian background was, of course, Carl Sandburg. Born of Swedish parents in Galesburg, Illinois, in 1878, he became a symbol of the American Middle West. Such authors help define the limits of immigrant literature because in spite

47

of their parentage they fall so indisputably outside it. By no stretch of definition can they be considered anything but wholly American.

A number of other second-generation prose writers occupied the borderland between Scandinavian-immigrant and general American literature; they were evidently influenced in choice of subject by their special background, but did not always treat their material with insight. Here the dividing line would seem to run between those who wrote from personal experience and those who were dependent on research. Among the latter were several historical novelists, some attracted to Old-Country themes, others interested in the more distant past of their group. Thus Ottilia Adelina Liljencrantz, born in Chicago of Swedish parents in 1876, during the rage for historical fiction at the turn of the century produced some thin romances of Viking days.[24] Martin Wendell Odland published *The New Canaan* (Minneapolis, 1933), a novel about the Norwegian sloopers of 1825, and Stuart David Engstrand based *They Sought for Paradise* (New York, 1939) on the Swedish religious colony founded at Bishop Hill, Illinois, in 1846. To a fictional setting laid so long before his own time no author could bring special understanding because of his ethnic background.

Other English-language novelists of Scandinavian background can be classified according to their interest in immigrant themes. Among authors of one or two volumes, some privately printed, James A. Peterson may represent those who wrote only about immigrant life as they knew it at first hand. *Hjalmar, or the Immigrant's Son* (Minneapolis, 1922) and *Solstad: The Old and the New* (Minneapolis, 1923) communicate many of the problems and attitudes of two generations of Norwegian immigrants, despite awkward construction and style. Other men devoted their single efforts to subjects unrelated to their mixed national origin, as for example Alexander Corstvet in *Elling, and Some Things That Helped to Shape His Life* (Milwaukee, 1901).[25]

More than one author of Scandinavian stock published a number of books of which only one dealt with his immigrant background. Perhaps he felt compelled to exorcise the ghost of his hyphenated past by confrontation before he could continue as a native American writer. A pair of Norwegian-Americans of considerable talent were Anthony M. Rud, whose *The Second Generation* (New York, 1923) pictured vividly the conflict between Old and New World patterns of family authority, and Norman Matson, whose *Day of Fortune* (New York, 1928) alone among his several novels presented a realistic account of a Scandinavian-American family. Neither of these writers ever returned to an immigrant theme. The prolific Martha Ostenso might be included here. Scandinavian immigrant characters appeared in minor roles in several of her novels, but only in her *O River, Remember!* (New York, 1943) did three generations of Norwegians emerge as central figures. Norwegian newspapers hailed her as a leading Norwegian-American author on the occasion of her sixtieth birthday in 1960, but on the whole she seemed to have crossed the line into general American literature. She portrayed characters of Norwegian stock no more frequently or perceptively than she described Icelanders or Yankees.

In contrast, other authors of Scandinavian-American origin were primarily concerned with their own people. Sophus Keith Winter's trilogy about a tenant farm family in Nebraska was a major contribution to the story of the Danes in America. *Take All to Nebraska, Mortgage Your Heart,* and *This Passion Never Dies* (New York, 1936, 1937, 1938) could be compared to Rølvaag's Norwegian-American trilogy in intent and scope, although not in artistry. A second-generation Norwegian-American, Borghild Dahl, wrote all her fiction on themes from Old-Country and immigrant life: *Karen* (1947), *Homecoming* (1953), *The Daughter* (1956), *A Minnetonka Summer* (1960), *Under This Roof* (1957) and *This Precious Year* (1964), and two juveniles, *Cloud Shoes* (1957) and *Stowaway to America* (1959), all published in New York.

Closely related to these works were the fictionalized and reminiscent accounts of Scandinavian-American life written by people who had been part of it. Part of a literary trend based on nostalgia for a simpler day, a dozen or more books from the last thirty years portray rural, small-town, and city life as experienced by Scandinavian immigrant children from San Francisco to Brooklyn. Best known of this group was Kathryn Forbes's *Mama's Bank Account* (New York, 1943), the story of California Norwegians which, as "I Remember Mama," won success on stage and television. *The Coffee Train* (New York, 1954, reprinted 1968) and *Call Back the Years* (Minneapolis, 1966) by Margarethe Erdahl Shank recorded lasting Norwegian influences on the lives of immigrants in North Dakota. Among several stories of immigrant families in Minnesota, *Mor's New Land,* by Lillian M. Gamble (New York, 1952), and *The World so Fair,* by Karen Peyton (Philadelphia, 1963) might be mentioned; Skulda Banér's *Latchstring Out* (Boston, 1954) showed how much color and light Swedish traditions could bring to a raw mining town in upper Michigan; *Defend My Mother,* by Agnes Roisdal (New York, 1952), traced the tragic disintegration of a once happy Norwegian family in Brooklyn. A trilogy by Lillian Budd followed the Americanization of three generations of Swedish-Americans in Chicago: *April Snow, Land of Strangers,* and *April Harvest* (New York, 1951, 1953, 1959).

Authors of Scandinavian stock have written a number of children's books, as for example, Helen Forster Anderson's *Enchanted Valley:*

49

A Story of Sweden (New York, 1941). Clara Ingram Judson's *They Came from Sweden* (Boston, 1942), and *They Sought a Country,* by Norman Eugene Nygaard (New York, 1950), are examples of juveniles which sketched Old-Country background before bringing their characters to the New World; while the little girl heroine of *Home for Good,* by Erna Oleson Xan (New York, 1952), represents several young characters in similar books who were born in Wisconsin (or Dakota or Minnesota) and so grew up in the bicultural environment of settled immigrant families. The story of Scandinavian-American life is now available in books written by people of this ethnic background for every age level: picture tales for the very young, such as *Nils,* by Ingri and Edgar Parin d'Aulaire (New York, 1948); books for the nine-to-twelve level, such as Nina Morgan's *Prairie Star* (New York, 1955); novels for teen-agers like Ellen Turngren's *Listen, My Heart, Shadow into Mist,* and *Hearts Are the Fields* (New York, 1956, 1958, 1961).

A number of second-generation poets have written in English, but only Sandburg has won wide recognition. Albert Edward Johannsson, son of a Norwegian mother and a Swedish father, showed considerable promise, winning a number of poetry awards while an undergraduate; but he died young. His one book, *In Strictest Measure: 50 Sonnets,* was published in Boston in 1944. Like Sandburg, the younger poets rarely touched Scandinavian immigrant themes and only occasionally revealed their European ties by translating poems from the Swedish or Danish. Most of them fall outside the area that has been outlined here.

V. Boundaries of the Field

It should be simple to define the main body of this literature—the multitudinous volumes of many kinds written in their original languages in the United States by people born in Scandinavia who chose the New World as their home. It is American because it was written by Americans about their lives and interests; but it occupies a special field because these were adopted Americans with divided loyalties, as they signified by writing in European tongues. Yet language alone is not a sufficient criterion of membership in this group. A number of borderline figures may be difficult to classify. The long list of visitors from Scandinavia, coming only to observe and to record for European audiences, must be eliminated; but it is not always easy to distinguish between a visitor and a short-term immigrant, one who meant to remove himself permanently to America but gave up the effort at transplantation and returned to Europe, with or without American citizenship. Often, too, as the stories record, an individual who meant to stay only a few years ended by living out the rest of his life in the New World. Clearly neither the intent (when known) of the person, nor his formal citizenship (not always ascertainable either), can serve as an infallible guide.

The present writer has attempted to distinguish authors who underwent discernible modification of character ("Americanization") during their years in the United States from those who returned to Europe untouched by the process, classifying the former as members of the hyphenated tradition, the latter not. The Norwegian Knut Hamsun would thus be eliminated, for during his two stays in America he remained a highly critical visitor; but both Magnus Elmblad, who spent thirteen years in the United States, and Kristofer Janson, who after a preliminary tour stayed twelve years, would be included, or at least their works dealing with the life of their fellow immigrants would be.

The judgment of contemporaries should also be considered. To Swedish-Americans, Elmblad was one of themselves—and indeed he survived less than four years after returning to Sweden. Kristofer Janson lived for nearly a quarter century after going back to Norway, but there continued to write much about Norwegian America. During their lifetimes both men were claimed as one of their own by immigrant critics in America. Present-day literary historians of Sweden and Norway, however, insist that Elmblad and Janson were Europeans who happened to live long periods in America. In their home countries they are considered not emigrant authors but full-fledged natives—unlike O. E. Rølvaag, for instance, who is defined by all hands as an immigrant author, and discussed as such in both Norwegian and American literary histories. Declining to quibble over such borderline cases as Elmblad and Janson, the present writer claims to find in their books sufficient evidence of the effects of Americanization, and in their biographies proof of enough years in the United States to qualify their work as first-hand evidence concerning Scandinavian immigrant experience. They will therefore be quoted on equal terms with indisputably immigrant authors.

At the English-language end of the field, it is more difficult to determine when Scandinavian-American literature becomes purely American. Books by first- and second-generation immigrants about their own experiences, as influenced by their special background, should no doubt be accounted part of Scandinavian-American literature, regardless of the language used. On the other hand, authors in English who betray no trace of their ethnic origin should probably be classified as American writers, regardless of their parentage. Nelson Algren is no more an immigrant author than James T. Farrell. Here too, however, there are borderline cases; on occasion a writer of the second or third generation produced a book or two containing immigrant characters or a Scandinavian theme—sometimes with insight arising from his special heritage, but often with no more perception than if he were not of Scandinavian origin. Also in these cases the present writer has ignored hard-and-fast boundaries, and used any book which provided pertinent evidence by any writer of Scandinavian family background, however remote.

Even within the clearly defined tradition of this immigrant literature, many problems await clarification. For instance, the distinction between first and second generation is not always clear. If first-generation immigrants are defined as those who made the removal from Europe to America in their own persons, how does an individual brought ashore as an infant in arms differ from one born the day after his mother set foot in the New World? His cultural affiliation will depend not on his place of birth but on the surroundings in which he grew up, whether an immigrant or a native American community. The present writer has considered Anna Olsson and Dorthea Dahl, both of whom came to the United States at the age of two, second-generation authors, whereas Simon Johnson, who was eight when he arrived, has been regarded as first generation. This somewhat arbitrary distinction has been made by appraising the influence of cultural background on the individual, measured partly on significant memories of the Old Country, partly on the author's attitude toward his European heritage. Had Simon Johnson not been reared in an exclusively Norwegian settlement in the Red River Valley, he too might well have been classified as second generation rather than first; but the literary historian can see in Johnson's work modes of thinking as genuinely Norwegian as those of Ole Rølvaag. It seems more meaningful to designate both as first-generation authors, although one emigrated as a boy, the other as a man grown.

Many similar problems can be clarified, if not resolved, by continued research in this neglected area of American literature; but the main value of such study would be in social, not literary history. No one in the entire Scandinavian immigrant tradition can be compared with Rølvaag. There are a few other surprisingly good authors, a host of mediocre ones, and all too many who are downright bad, judged by artistic standards. As source material for cultural history, however, the field is a veritable gold mine of inside information, not only for the role of the Scandinavian nationalities in the making of America but also for problems of cultural transmission, personality transformation, and conflicts and tension within and between contending human groups. From this source material has been constructed the picture to follow of Scandinavian immigrant experience in the United States.

Chapter Three
Emerging Themes

Although Scandinavian immigrant writers varied among themselves in background and purpose, they exhibited more uniformity than native American writers during the same four score years as they constantly reconsidered themes that were part of their common experience.

Most of these people had not thought of themselves as members of a specific culture while still in the Old World; but in the New World the unending discovery of differences in almost every aspect of life made them conscious that they were like neither native Yankees nor other immigrants. Whether the writers approved of New-World ways or not, they were forever comparing American social institutions and attitudes with those they had known before: characteristics of church, family, and school; conditions in farming, business, and the professions; interpersonal and group relationships; politics and citizenship, classes and customs, ethics and ideals. To understand these comparisons, we must look briefly at the life they left behind.

I. The Old-World Background

Because the immigrant authors took for granted that their readers shared the same Old-World background as themselves, few wasted much effort on describing it, especially not in stories whose main action developed in the United States. From this source material only a fragmentary picture of European conditions can be pieced together from opening scenes before emigration and from reminiscent remarks by characters in their new home. Other sources must help supply the missing pieces and the general framework for the following account of the two distinct types of Scandinavian rural culture from which most of the emigrants came.[1]

1. VILLAGE VERSUS RURAL DISTRICT CULTURE

Village or *landsby* culture in Denmark and the more fertile regions of southern Sweden centered in villages like those on the continent, with the important difference that landowners and renters usually lived on their separate holdings. Fields divided since feudal days into narrow strips with common woodlots and pasture had been largely collected in single farm units by the end of the eighteenth century. At the same time dwellings had been dispersed from the central cluster of manorial days to the separate farms; but since this movement had been completed only two or three generations before mass emigration to America began, the older tradition of the village as the cultural and economic center of the rural community still persisted. To village markets the peasants took their produce, and from village artisans they procured the articles of handicraft they needed. Noblemen and gentry owned much land in these areas, although the number of peasant proprietors continued to grow throughout the nineteenth century. All classes of landowner rented parcels of land to cotters in return for their labor, sometimes plus a cash initial payment and annual rent. Many landowners also hired agricultural workers by the year—the lowest class of rural society, except for paupers. Almost all immigrant characters whose background was specified as Denmark or southern Sweden came from the ranks of the cotters and laborers. Few stories in Scandinavian-American literature described typical village culture, however. Either not many people emigrated from these areas, or else the bulk of movement out took place after the identification of individuals with their village had broken down in the latter part of the nineteenth century.

Since the village culture was descended from feudalism, it flourished only in the flat and fertile parts of Denmark and Sweden. Until the Scandinavian population began to grow rapidly in the eighteenth century, the heaths of western Jutland and the poorer areas of Sweden—Värmland and the western borderlands, parts of Småland and Skåne, the northern provinces—were settled thinly if at all by separate farmsteads sometimes scattered through the wilderness but usually clustered in valleys, in the second type of rural culture typical of Norway: *bygdekultur*. Here geography (together with centuries-old economic and social factors) precluded villages until railroad and steamship made possible the late development of local factories and trade centers. Even in the narrow valleys, separate small farms lay side by side, each with its own complex of buildings. As the homesickness expressed in book after book made clear, individual identification was with the family and its native homestead, where generation after generation had lived and died. Population growth of the eighteenth and nineteenth centuries pushed settlement further and further up the mountainsides and into the forests, filling in between older cultivated areas and extending their limits wherever patches of tillable soil could be grubbed out between rocks and trees.

Judging by how often this second type of country life was described in Swedish- and Norwegian-American literature, it would seem that much more emigration came from these less hospitable regions; for not village but farm life was portrayed as the dominant background of this group. The most important feature of the inland *bygd* or dispersed rural district was its isolation. Coastal and fjord districts of course had ties by water with the rest of Europe, but in the heavily forested, mountainous areas of Sweden and Norway, each valley or district had remained a separate entity for centuries. Variations in dialect, costume, traditional foods, and customs gave evidence that medieval seclusion here survived far into modern times. In the latter part of the nineteenth century, improved transportation and beginning industrialization lessened such isolation, but the process was tardy. Within their own natural boundaries most districts in the more remote provinces remained largely self-sufficient until the end of the century.

Life on the farms of each *bygd* or district was to a large extent self-sufficient too. Each homestead not only produced much of its own food and clothing but also supplied many of its other needs. Peasant farmers took their building materials and fuel from their own woods, made their wooden furniture and implements, forged their tools from crude iron, cured their leather, distilled their hard liquor, carved their own wooden shoes. What artisans there were trudged from one homestead to another with a knapsack of tools, staying long enough to cobble leather shoes or tailor garments for the family from local materials, or to bake a half-year's supply of hard bread. Peddlers brought a few manufactured items along with their news and gossip into the rural community: glass, firearms, needles and fine thread, ribbons and silken kerchiefs, knives of tempered steel. But such self-sufficiency did not necessarily mean sufficiency. Given the short growing season of a northern latitude, poor soil, and primitive agricultural methods, endless labor often produced only poor crops. Then basic foodstuffs like dried fish and grain were imported by those peasants who could pay for them, while small farmers and crofters went hungry. Those who gave up the struggle to seek a more hospitable geography and climate in the New World had been well schooled in hardship and hunger.

2. THE SOCIAL SYSTEM

Within such *bygder* or rural districts, each farm unit maintained its social separateness. Few families lived so far from neighbors that they could not see another house or at least the smoke from a chimney; but several weary miles of woods or water might lie between. In so closed a community all knew everyone—knew their past and place and possessions—but they met regularly nowhere but at church, and held social intercourse, except when courting, only at festivals like Christmas and Midsummer or the great events of a family's history: marriage, baptism, confirmation, burial. By no means all could look forward to meeting friends and neighbors every Sunday, either. In more remote areas, where one parish might include three or four valleys, the minister came to hold services perhaps once a month; or bad weather might keep the family from the long journey to church. Then the head of the house took out the book of sermons and held a private service at home.

Because the church was the cultural center of the parish, the State-appointed Lutheran minister was the greatest man in it. He too lived on a farm, assigned to him as a large part of his salary, but he was a learned man and did not soil his hands with manual labor. He supervised the work of his tenant or hired men, however, for his living depended largely on what the place produced; and he often brought new agricultural techniques into the parish to improve the local standard of living. The minister was an important government official, keeping vital statistics for his parish, performing the ceremonies of family life, reading official proclamations after service. Well into the nineteenth century he or his parish clerk was often the school teacher, for the local church was responsible that the members of the parish knew their catechism and Commandments and could read the Bible a little when they were examined for confirmation. Later, ambulatory school was held a few weeks on one farm, a few weeks at another, the children who lived nearest gathering under a schoolmaster. Older immigrants in America recalled both these types of schooling in early stories. By the middle of the nineteenth century most districts had acquired a little schoolhouse near the church, with a resident schoolmaster. As a rule the only other government official with whom *bygdefolk* came in contact was the sheriff. He was usually one of the biggest landholders in the area, and one of the least popular, since he collected taxes and carried out forced seizures and sales. A visit from the sheriff on such an errand was sometimes the final trial which forced a hard-pressed family to emigrate.

These were then the great men of each isolated community, to be greeted with bows and uncovered heads: the minister, the sheriff, and somewhat lower in status, parish clerk and schoolmaster. In Sweden this pattern was occasionally complicated by the presence of a nobleman, or at least his estate; but nobility had been abolished in Norway by its Constitution of 1814. Gentry typical of village or *landsby* culture did not appear in descriptions of dispersed rural or *bygd* culture, nor of course the wealthier shopkeepers and artisans who flourished in larger towns. In dispersed rural areas the landed peasants ranked next below the official class. Their families had often held the same farmsteads for centuries, and their traditions and loyalties were bound to it and their native valley. Although their cultivated acreage was limited, they owned forest, mountain pastures, and fishing rights, which augmented the production of their narrow fields. The small freeholders who stood below them owned tiny plots indeed. They were forced into other economic activity during the long winter—fishing or forestry, sometimes handicrafts.

Still lower in the social scale came the *husmenn* and *torpare* (crofters, cotters), landless men who had traded their labor for the right to put up a hut and clear a few patches of somebody else's soil for cultivation. Their contract terms varied greatly from one period and area to another, until laws finally provided them with minimum protection; but in general they had to work a stipulated number of days a week for their landlord at pay far below the local standard. They cultivated their crofts the way they thought best in the little time left. Some places the contract was binding on the landlord for the life of the tenant, some places it was renewed each year; but the crofter always had the right of terminating it.

At the bottom of the rural districts as of the village society were servants and laborers who hired out by the year for a pittance in cash, a few articles of clothing, and found. Practically the only local employment available to sons and daughters of cotters and small freeholders was service on a larger farm. Should two of them decide to marry, they could establish a home only by becoming cotters; and if no croft happened to be vacant for them to take over, they had to move onto marginal land and grub out a new place. Movement was thus possible between the servant and cotter groups in each community, but seldom higher. And since each district was so limited in land and opportunity, those whose ambitions or affections impelled them to cross class lines found the easiest way to do so was to leave. A very few with exceptional talent could occasionally return as educated men and function as clergymen or teachers; more moved into towns, where they were largely limited to servant positions until the development of industry; but once word of the Promised Land across the sea had filtered into their society, most left for America.

3. MOTIVES FOR EMIGRATION

Oppression of the lower classes in such a closed social system was consistently pictured by Scandinavian-American authors as the main cause of emigration. Agents sent by steamship, land and labor companies in the United States, to lure unsuspecting natives from their homes with false promises of golden opportunities in the New World, almost never appeared in this literature.[2]

Looking back from a better life in America, many characters agreed with Danes attending an ethnic festival in Iowa. One Reverend Grunding in glowing words had urged his fellow immigrants to preserve their priceless Danish heritage in exile. A member of the audience stood up to contradict him, begging leave to observe that "America gives us food and clothing for our labor, while the Old Country let us go hungry. Mr. Grunding belongs to the upper class, which Denmark always did treat well. They got the cream, while the likes of us had to be satisfied with skim milk." After the meeting people stood around discussing the issue, and most agreed that "Denmark had starved them out because they were denied the chance to own a bit of land themselves; but America gave them land in abundance." One man maintained bitterly that his class had never known anything but evil days in Denmark. "We were looked down on and treated like dogs while we were herdsboys, and we had to sleep in damp, filthy rooms in the stable both then and later, when we were hired men." Somebody remarked that things were supposed to be better in Denmark now for the ordinary laborer.

"Maybe it is better," replied Thomas Dal, "but I haven't forgotten how it *was*. And there was never any hope of getting ahead."

Some had been a little better off and had brought happier memories from their home community; but most agreed that Sam Sorenson had spoken the truth, while Grunding stood up there and romanced about something he didn't understand at all.[3]

This literature clearly reflected a serious maladjustment between the organization of Scandinavian society in the nineteenth century and the attitude of a considerable portion of its members. Distribution of privilege, resources, and esteem was still almost exclusively on the basis of social position as determined by birth. Few of the underprivileged, to be sure, faced starvation in their old homes, except in years of drastic crop failure; but many were chronically undernourished, their homes cramped and cold, their clothing poor and limited in style by their social position. Not only were they denied hope of betterment; throughout much of the nineteenth century, the lot of many Scandinavian poor appreciably worsened. The population explosion which followed from widespread improvement in health and living standards meant not only that suddenly many more babies began to live to maturity but also that older people lived longer. Both changes caused grave problems in an agricultural economy where food and jobs were limited. A Norwegian-American novel which opened in a remote valley as late as the 1880s described how the people felt that "one thing was certain: Conditions in the province were getting worse rather than better, year by year.

The things one had to buy, like grain products, grew dearer; wages, on the contrary, stayed about the same. Under such circumstances there were many who decided in desperation to leave."[4]

A generation or two earlier, the possibility of making such a decision would not have existed. But change had been slowly permeating this stable society. The acquiescence of the underprivileged in their deprivation was coming to an end. Scandinavian-American literature showed little of the causes of this deep-rooted transformation in attitude, but it recorded plainly that the change had taken place. Ideals of liberty and equality had undermined the old religious duty to be content with the lot one was born to. Worldly ambition to get ahead infected an ever-growing number of lower-class people who no longer accepted the truism that their humble birth must always deprive them of the privileges of their betters. In this situation of growing discontent, word of another type of society, where status and standard of living could be won by an individual's own performance, spread in widening rings from the reports of those who had gone before.[5] "America fever" was regularly pictured infecting worst those who were most ambitious to improve their lot and therefore most frustrated by lack of opportunity at home.

Emigration was of course not the only alternative of action available to malcontents. Those too poor to undertake such a long trip, or too timid, could hunt for jobs as servants or factory hands in the growing towns; sometimes a young man sought to satisfy his wanderlust but keep his ties of nationality by going to sea. Naturally the immigrant literature written in America was not much concerned with such as these, although occasionally stories picked up a seaman or worker who had stopped some years in such employment as a halfway station, and carried him on to settle in America. By the 1890s the children of such displaced peasants were shown joining the emigrant flood in ever-increasing numbers, and for the same reason: the desire to advance further and faster than they believed they could in a homeland rapidly changing but still offering the best of limited opportunities to the well-born. A typical exponent of the privileged official class fulminated against a low-class assistant in a Danish-American novel: "It's a confounded misfortune for a young person to be born with these notions of getting ahead!"[6]

Desire for individual betterment: all authors who considered motivation for emigration agreed that this was its basic cause. But ambition for a higher standard of living could not be separated from aspiration for a better social standing. "For Knut it was not so much a matter of growing rich but of getting ahead; but of course both these things went together, and all was for her who was waiting for him."[7] Another novel defined motivation in terms of self-respect.

In every healthy human being Our Lord has placed something called self-respect, he said. When from time to time in the history of nations people with self-respect feel themselves slighted, looked down on, and treated unjustly, they seek ways of self-assertion . . . more innocent self-assertion than peopling and cultivating the fertile plains which have lain untouched since the morning of creation, cannot be conceived. Each of us should thank God both for the opportunity and the strength to make use of it![8]

Ambition and self-respect were only two of several personality traits attributed to the majority of emigrants in this literature. Most were also accredited with initiative, resoluteness, and determination. Above all, they were portrayed as feeling deprived in the Old Country of opportunity to realize their potential, of freedom to behave in a host of ways as they saw fit. Persecution of sectarians for their deviant faith was mentioned only occasionally as a contributory factor for motivation in tales laid before the Civil War, for by that time all three Scandinavian countries tolerated religious dissent. The desire for freedom and equality repeated in endless stories and poems was thus largely economic and social, arising from what was felt as repression of natural rights. The wish to escape from environmental deprivation of one kind or another was indeed the most general motive of all emigration, although definition of what constituted deprivation varied greatly from one time and place to another. "The emigrant was and is still today a person who deliberately and of his own free will has separated himself from one or another condition into which he was born, and which in his innermost, truest being he has found repressive and base."[9]

The type of ambitious, resolute emigrant escaping from degrading restriction at home to opportunity in America did not persist unchanged. He was common in stories and poems about agricultural settlements in the Middle West, up to the closing of the frontier. Usually he was a family man, either making the trip with wife and children, going ahead to prepare the way for them, or establishing a family soon after arrival. Because the trip cost much and the risks were great, his determination had to be strong. But as the voyage to America grew cheaper and easier with the development of steamer service, and mobility away from one's birthplace became common in the late-developing industrialization of Scandinavia, an individual needed much less strength of character and ambition to pull up his roots and make off toward the west. By the end of the nineteenth century, in fact, this had become the easiest way out of a temporary embarrassment. "Disappointed people came, people who had fallen out with their existence and lacked courage to fight it out home in Norway."[10]

Later tales showed young men emigrating because they had made a girl pregnant or were passed over in a job promotion, to escape military service, or just to satisfy wanderlust. A girl emigrated because she had been disappointed in love, or heard that servants in America dressed like ladies. The motivation was still discontent with the situation at home, but the deprivation was often minor. Then it was not seldom the weakling who left, thinking it easier to start over where his past was unknown. Upper-class characters in literature were shown coming to America almost exclusively because their mistakes or misfortunes had deprived them of their privileged position: a businessman who had gone bankrupt, or a spoiled son who had forged his father's name, the scion of a leading family who had married a shoemaker's daughter. Almost the only exceptions were ministers and an occasional journalist or teacher, trained in the Old World, who responded to definite offers of a job in the New. Even in these cases, however, a number were pictured crossing the ocean because posts were scarce at home, or the pay offered and chances of advancement were greater where there were few competitors with the prestige of a degree from a European university.

All these types of emigrant made their own decision to leave. A few also appeared in this literature who were taken or sent to America more or less against their will: a reluctant wife, a child old enough to understand the difference, aged parents, the black sheep of a family shipped off to get rid of him, even a rare prisoner who had served his term and was provided with a one-way ticket at government expense. Sometimes one of these expressed lifelong sadness or bitterness over the decision made by others, as an old Norwegian woman told after many years in America: "I was still a girl when I left home with Father and Mother. When our home disappeared from view, I felt such great sorrow and longing that I cried and cried—and those tears have come back so often."[11] The literature recorded, however, that most involuntary emigrants made the move in agreement with whoever decided it. Usually the whole family had taken part in long discussions about America. A Swedish-American novel summed up most of the attractive forces of the great land in the West:

Around that country fantasy had twined its many-colored threads, aided by accounts from over there. Now people talked of Indians, buffalo, and frightful wars; now they talked about the rich natural resources of the country in the form of endless fertile plains. . . .

To these accounts was added much talk about freedom, equality and independence. There, no nobility was to be found, no bigoted clergy, no onerous military conscription. There freedom reigned unrestrained.[12]

II. The Journey

Although many authors discussed the expulsive forces of the home society or the personal frustrations which motivated their characters to emigrate, few described the long-drawn-out difficulties of preparations to leave or the trip itself. Most Scandinavian-American writers opened their action at a late stage of the initial journey, showing their characters landing at some eastern port or approaching the final destination by wagon, river steamer, or train.

Almost all those who became authors had themselves made the trip by ocean steamer and railroad. The earliest writers, who began publication in the 1870s and 1880s, were mostly journalists, ministers, a few scholars—professional men who would hardly have traveled by the cheaper sailing vessels still in use. A little later even those who came by steerage found the trip so easy and dull as to be hardly worth mentioning to readers who had had much the same experience.

1. THE OCEAN VOYAGE

Only an occasional tale recalled the trials of a personally experienced crossing by sail, as a Norwegian-American novel of 1918 told briefly of a sixteen weeks' voyage to Quebec a half century before.[13] Not until this late did those who set their story a generation or more ahead of their own time realize that the more difficult transportation of an earlier day might be of interest, and include some description of it in their accounts: how friends and relatives banded together, packed elaborate supplies of salted and dried foods, hired carts to transport their heavy baggage to the nearest port, collected there with others to wait for a vessel bound for America, and bargained with the captain for passage. Even in such novels, however, details were few; descriptive passages were usually limited to storms, seasickness, and dramatic rescues.

Apart from such secondary evidence, Scandinavian-American literature contributed to the story of the sea voyage by sail only a few popular ballads from the middle of the last century.[14] These tended to exaggerate the perils involved, with graphic descriptions of sickness and death. A humorous ballad by Magnus Elmblad, evidently inspired by the excesses of his anonymous predecessors, pictured the trip under sail as such a purgatory that the hero sold his travel chest as soon as he went ashore in New York to pay for his immediate return by the same transport to Sweden![15]

Most accounts of the crossing by sailing ship showed emigrants traveling in groups which remained units from the time they left their home community until the arrival at their destination far inland in America; and the ship in which they embarked from their own shore carried them all the way to their port of entry. Descriptions of the voyage in the 1870s and 1880s, however, recorded two important changes in this pattern. As the trip became progressively shorter, cheaper, and easier, single families and lone individuals, even young girls, undertook it without hesitation; and the journey was broken into segments. The most usual route led across the North Sea to England, although many Danes headed south to Hamburg. From such major ports a British or German steamship line with fast and frequent service carried the emigrants across the Atlantic. An occasional tale pictured the overlapping of both types of ocean voyage during the transition from one to the other, as when a Norwegian in a novel published in 1884 earned enough in a year to pay for his passage by sailing ship but not by steam. He had to delay his departure until the following spring, for the slower vessels set out only at that time of year.[16]

Through all the changes recorded or assumed in the first stage of immigrant experience, certain problems remained comparatively constant. The question of how to pay for the long journey was most difficult in the early days, when costs were highest relative to the resources of the poorer classes, which furnished most emigrants. Therefore as a rule only people with something of value to sell were able to undertake the trip in the days of sail; and the first break with home and birthplace occurred at an auction of livestock, goods, and sometimes land. Such scenes remained common in novels opening in the Old Country at any period, whenever a whole family emigrated at once.

But often the capital thus acquired proved insufficient. Then the balance had to be borrowed: the wealthier in a party loaned to the poorer; stay-at-homes advanced cash on security furnished by relatives remaining behind, or chipped in to get rid of a family on poor relief; a returned American paid for the tickets of those who promised reimbursement (usually with a sizable interest) from their first earnings over there. Even after the trip became cheaper by steam, the expense still kept many who wished to emigrate from going. If everybody tried to sell his land and goods at once, a Swedish-American novelist remarked, there could be no buyers. Some had to stay home, especially unmarried women. "It took a girl nearly a whole lifetime to save up as much money as the trip cost, and nobody who had any cash seemed to trust them enough to help them with a loan."[17]

The steady decline in the cost of steamboat fares, however, together with the rise in cash wages during the last years of the century, was reflected in many a story which solved the problem of trip expenses by sending the man of the family or of an engaged pair ahead alone.

A Norwegian-American novel opened at the fjord pier with a young man taking leave of his fiancée:

Both of them had worked hard the past year; she had hired out as a dairymaid on a big estate, and he had chopped wood by the cord in winter and hired out by the day through the summer. With the help of a small advance by her employer on her next year's wage, they had finally scraped together enough for the cheapest third class ticket on the cheapest steamboat line there was to be had to America.[18]

By then everyone knew how much faster the price of the Atlantic crossing could be earned for the rest of the family in the New World; and many a plot showed the faithful father slaving away alone a year or two or three to bring over his loved ones. Some tales recorded, however, that the man who had gone ahead was heard from once or twice, perhaps, and then never again. Sometimes he took a new wife and founded a second family; sometimes he was killed in an accident or drank himself to death; sometimes no one ever learned his fate. Rarely in such cases did the deserted fiancée or family later get to America on their own.

Later, travel on tickets prepaid from America became probably the most common method of financing the emigrant journey, pictured in story after story between the 1880s and the first World War. Often a relative who had been some years in America defrayed the cost, whether he initiated the offer to bring over a sister and her family, or responded to an appeal for a ticket from a niece or a cousin's son. By the turn of the century the trip had become so cheap and easy that it presented only a minor problem, and many a young hero and heroine set off for the New World without mention of how they paid their way. From first to last, however, financial difficulties remained a constant theme: how to move to America and get started there with a minimum of capital. Few immigrants were described as possessing more than this.

Another persistent theme was introduced in every account of departure from the home and homeland. During the rush and struggle to get off, few characters offered a thought to the pain of parting—and those few were invariably women. At the auction, seeing their familiar household goods and livestock carried off, many felt their first misgivings; but at the hour of saying farewell to family, friends, and home, all were pictured overwhelmed by sorrow.

When one leaves his dear ones and the place one loves most in the world, it's as though something breaks—something of the carefree and buoyant, of whatever it is that makes the strings of the heart vibrate in joyous song.

Thus felt the girl from Sundelv, when her mother embraced her for the last time and prayed for God's blessing over her future life, and when the boat glided away from the pier and her father took the oars to row her to the steamship, but laid them quietly down, bowed his grey head against his daughter's shoulder, and wept; then she felt as though she could never be happy again.[19]

The intensity of such universal sorrow at parting, felt even by those who left as black sheep, measured how closely bound to family and place of origin Scandinavian-American authors conceived their countrymen to be.

After the development of steamer traffic, it would seem that the break should not have been felt as irrevocable. "People travel over the Atlantic nowadays as easily as one can run into Jönköping," claimed a character living not far from that Swedish city on the eve of his emigration.[20] In the later literature many a young adventurer left sorrowing parents with the promise to return soon; he would stay only three years to study this, or until he had earned enough for that, and then come back for always. As many stories and poems recorded, however, the promise was seldom kept. Occasionally the emigrant did come back for a visit, but almost always he was drawn across the sea once more.

The excitement of travelling from home to port of embarkation temporarily deadened the pangs of leavetaking for many characters. Most had traveled very little if at all before this greatest trip of their lives, and the initial stage of the journey within their homeland overwhelmed them with new impressions. Several characters were amazed at their first ride on a coastal steamer or their first glimpse of a railroad train. Many had never seen a city before, and marveled at urban noise and confusion. This initial phase of the emigrant journey within the homeland introduced a most important theme: the strain of constant encounter with the unfamiliar which comprised so much of immigrant experience.

Another theme to be found thus early was the adventure of encountering strangers. Many peasants who had lived in isolated areas heard other dialects of their native tongue and met people from other provinces for the first time now. Finding nevertheless that they could talk with these strangers about common interests, many emigrants unconsciously took the first step toward realization that they were natives not only of a given locality but also of a nation. A Swedish ballad described this experience when the singer, arriving footsore and weary in Gothenburg, found a flock of other travelers collected there.

> Friendship was soon established, we shook each other's hand,
> We were all sons and daughters of the same fatherland.[21]

Fuller consciousness of nationality was described awakening in one story and poem after another as emigrants watched their native shore fade behind them. Believing that they had already suffered everything involved in leaving home, few had anticipated the pain of this second farewell; but many found it even worse than the first one.

> Long he stands at the rail looking back. He sees the last glimpse of Copenhagen disappear; the green-clad banks of the coast glide past and are lost to view; as

65

Kronborg passes he is seized by a strange melancholy, an oppressive sadness, which he cannot explain.

He knows that this is the last he will see of Denmark for many years, perhaps forever.

All the best and most glorious memories of his life sweep past him now—yes, even more—it is his very youth that calls to him and bids him farewell.

He clutches the rail and feel his eyes grow dim, and his heart swells with a hot and violent wave of longing—a first feeling of homesickness—the need to clasp it all in his embrace.[22]

In this universal experience, described in nearly every account of embarkation, was introduced the theme of what it cost to lose homeland as well as home when one became an emigrant.

The route to America mentioned most often led across the North Sea to Hull in England, and from there by train to Liverpool. For a number of characters this was the first rail trip of their lives. Neither were they prepared by brief contact with a small Scandinavian port city for the speed and confusion of English urban traffic, the size of buildings, the noisy crowds babbling in a strange language—all a foretaste of what awaited them in New York.

The restless commercial city [Liverpool] gave Adam an unpleasant impression. Everything seemed strange and abnormal. The horses were as big as elephants and pulled loads like small houses. The men looked hungry and the women artificial.[23]

Slums the emigrants had never seen either, and the majority of rural background were shocked by the glimpses they caught of industrial poverty. A Norwegian poet in a versified novelette expressed horror at finding, close by the splendid royal palace in London, such destitution as he had never dreamed existed.[24] In England many travelers also met the first attempt to cheat them. A Swedish folk ballad related the sad experience of a group who bought an exchange order for their gold from an English bank to be paid in New York; but when they tried to collect on it, the money had already been taken out.[25]

Most stories including description of the transfer from North Sea to Atlantic liners in England mentioned efforts by the steamship companies to protect their passengers from such risks. In a typical Norwegian-American novel, a representative of the English steamship line met the boat from Norway at the dock and led the passengers on foot to the railroad station. They walked holding on to each other so they could gape at the marvelous sights. After the train trip they were herded to the proper dock in Liverpool.[26] Other accounts complained about the service considered good enough for mere emigrants, as Swedes grumbled over the lack of toilets on the train to Liverpool, and the shabbiness of the hotel where the travelers were sorted out for the different liners to America.[27]

66

Reports on boat accommodation across the Atlantic varied considerably. Norwegian peasants leaving Liverpool in the 1880s were favorably impressed with their liner, which seemed as fine as a palace. They stood in line with their plates to receive each meal doled out and thought the food very good, though scanty in some items; they were used to more than one potato apiece for dinner. The boat was far bigger and faster than any of them had ever seen before, carrying both engine and sails. When mechanical power failed for a couple of days, the sails were unfurled and the voyage continued to the playing of fiddle and concertina for merrymaking on deck.[28] In a Danish-American account published in 1892, passengers fetched loaves of white bread, slabs of butter, and cans of water to pass out at mealtime in the large bunkrooms for unmarried men and women. In the married people's quarters, "An unpleasant chorus of the crying of children, scolding and laughter of women, drunken uproar from a couple of tipsy Holstein men who were playing cards, harmonica music, and the groans of seasick people rolled at him through the nauseous air of the room. He looked around at the bunks of raw, rough pine, where bedclothes and wearing apparel lay in utmost confusion among chests, footgear, food and drink, and where here and there an untidy woman's head stuck out. Children lay and crawled on the floor or in the bunks, tumbled over with the tilting of the ship, and screamed."[29] Charges of "indescribable and meaningless filth"[30] in the steerage quarters were common. The sudden appearance of lice was the only event which broke the monotony of a dull trip for some Swedes, although the young folks amused themselves for the two or three weeks at sea with games and dances.[31]

The most detailed contemporary account of the ocean voyage appeared in a Danish novel published in 1890. On the German liner out of Hamburg, rich tourists and business people traveled in first class, returned Americans and other solid, respectable folk in second, and emigrants in third. The food provided for the last was reported in detail: for breakfast, coffee made with condensed milk, bread and butter; dinner of fresh soup with boiled meat the first day, thereafter ordinary sailor fare of salt meat and fish or dried peas or beans; supper of tea, bread, butter, and cheese, sausage or herring. After-dinner coffee was not served, but boiling water was given out from the galley to those who wanted to make it themselves. Fortunately most had not taken literally the promise of the company to furnish them with everything, but had supplied themselves in Hamburg with such luxuries as coffee beans. The passengers had to furnish their own plates, cups, and other tableware. They were served by stewards carrying around buckets and large trays, and sat either at small tables in the crowded dining rooms or wherever they could find space—on a bench, a staircase, the edge of a bed. Anyone who wished to wash his plate after use was free to dip up water from the ship's side. Washing of any kind was a big problem, for the ship provided fresh water only to drink, passed out by the cupful at certain hours. Nor was any place provided for passengers to wash. In the big sleeping rooms below deck, where families, unmarried women, and single men were assigned to different quarters, the doubled-decked iron bunks were so crowded that it was hardly possible to squeeze between them; and there was room for nothing else, not even a wash basin. Not until the last day at sea, when all danger of delay was past, was fresh water given out in any quantity to whoever asked for it. In good weather the emigrants stayed on deck all day; in bad, they crowded into the dining rooms, where the air was a little better than in the sleeping quarters. No one was allowed on deck in rough weather, for the company wanted no accidents. Dancing on deck in the evenings furnished the only occasions when emigrants of different nationalities mixed freely. Otherwise each group—Danes, Germans, Poles, Russians —kept to itself. But after a day or two at sea the Danes were friendlier and talked more freely with each other than an acquaintanceship of months would have permitted back home.[32]

Reactions to meeting other nationalities for the first time were described in several accounts of the Atlantic voyage. When enough Scandinavians of any kind were present to form a group, they automatically kept to themselves, shocked at Irish drunkenness or Jewish filth. Only occasionally did a young individual making the trip alone seek acquaintanceship with members of other nationalities. A Norwegian hero, fair-haired and handsome, proved quite the cock of the ship's walk in spite of language difficulties on a British steamer; dark Irish colleens found him especially attractive.[33] Rarely indeed did characters feel any human fellowship in their shared status with emigrants from other lands. Reacting against the differentness of others, they rather held aloof in mingled contempt and fear. A Danish-American novel offered an apparent exception, in which the young hero sailing over the North Sea to England met an older Dane who had already been some years in the United States. He pointed out to the inexperienced youth how Swedes and Danes were all mixed up together on the crowded boat, so they could hardly be told apart; and after being stirred together just as thoroughly with Irish and Scottish emigrants on the next lap of the voyage, they could all be poured out of the pot in New York as good Americans already. As they looked over the crowd of passengers disheveled from seasickness and filth "who lay and crept about helter-skelter like a swarm of wet flies," however, neither Dane seemed to feel as though he shared their fate.[34] Such concern with one's own family and group, at most including only those of the same national background,

68

remained typical of Scandinavian immigrant authors throughout the literature.

2. THE ARRIVAL IN AMERICA

Various Atlantic-coast cities were ports of arrival for fictional Scandinavian immigrants until the turn of the century. Sailing ships often docked at Quebec, from where the travelers proceeded by steamer up the St. Lawrence and through the Great Lakes to Milwaukee or Chicago. A little later, steamboats disembarked their passengers at Philadelphia and Boston. New York was named more often than any of the other ports at all periods, however, and from the turn of the century became practically the only one. Details of changing requirements and procedure for admission to the United States therefore appeared in accounts of the New York harbor at different periods.

Most stories mentioned either Castle Garden or Ellis Island as the reception center for immigrants. The exceptions either were laid before the day of Castle Garden, and pictured their characters going directly ashore into swarms of runners and confidence men, or omitted mention of landing formalities altogether. In a typical account, a party of Norwegians were herded ashore into the huge rotunda of Castle Garden. They found courage to proceed into the pandemonium only when their guide assured them that all who looked like good workers would get through. Customs inspectors rummaged a little in their painted chests before directing the immigrants through a narrow gateway where they were carefully looked over; and all were allowed to pass.[35] Other stories mentioned families overnighting in the huge hall, napping on bundles and baggage; or exchanging currency and buying railroad tickets, with various complications from language difficulties. No contemporary fictional account complained of discourtesy or cheating by the officials. On the contrary, a number of peasant characters remarked on the novelty of being treated with respect by government functionaries, or at least no worse than anyone else. This was their introduction to American democracy, and they highly approved of it.

Stories laid in the 1890s and after regularly mentioned Ellis Island as the immigrant reception center. A few more detailed narratives also recorded changes in admission regulations from time to time. A Danish immigrant in a novel of 1890, for instance, was a bit nervous when his boat steamed into New York harbor; he had heard that immigrants were not admitted so easily any more. A returned American with him concurred that the law had recently been made much stricter, but claimed that it was applied with indulgence. People who had served prison terms or seemed likely to become paupers were rightly kept out; but the requirement that every immigrant must possess a certain amount of cash was overlooked when a person was young and healthy. The only passenger on this steamer refused admission was a young girl who said she was to meet her fiancé. He did not appear, and the address he had given her turned out to be fictitious. First and second class passengers were not subject to immigrant entry procedure, but those in steerage were given a superficial medical examination before being taken by ferry to Ellis Island. Here were a restaurant and waiting rooms, telegraph and money exchange offices, provision for every need of the immigrants. Runners and agents were denied entry, and government employees were not permitted to recommend any hotel or business enterprise even when asked.[36]

A quarter century later, admission requirements were stricter still. When a Danish liner entered the harbor, it was met by a customs boat bringing doctors and inspectors. First and second class passengers were subjected to a hurried medical examination before being allowed ashore, while all in third class were taken by ferry with their baggage to Ellis Island. There they went through turnstiles while doctors looked them over and inspected their eyes. Those held back were sent to another hall for a more thorough examination, while the others were lined up for interrogation. Women traveling alone were cross-examined with special care. Any man who admitted that he was under contract for work in the United States was immediately sent back at the expense of the steamship company, in accordance with a law forbidding importation of foreign labor. Those who declared they were coming to look for a job, however, were admitted when they fulfilled the other requirements concerning health, moral character, and possession of at least $25 in addition to a ticket to their final destination. The majority who passed this examination were herded into the great "Railroad Hall" where they could exchange their money and buy rail tickets. Each immigrant then received a colored card indicating his railroad line and went to the main hall below where he could buy food and send telegrams. There he waited for the boat which would transport him to the proper railroad terminal for the continuation of his trip. Those who were to stop or be met in New York City were sent to Battery Place, where they had to wait behind bars while their friends or relatives proved their identity.[37] Other stories recorded the difficulties of older people in gaining entry from immigration officials afraid they might become public charges. This regulation gave a decisive twist to the plot of a Rølvaag novel, when an old father who had come to look for his lost son in America was refused admission because he had too little money and no guarantee. However, the Norwegian immigration commission then in operation tried to find the son before the old man was sent back.[38]

Common to all accounts of both Castle Garden and Ellis Island were descriptions of immigrants' fear and dismay at the confusion and uproar of the reception halls. Not only were the newcomers afraid of the uniformed officials who possessed such power over their future, but also they often felt completely lost in the milling throngs. On board the big liners they had been able to build circles of acquaintanceship and within these exchange information on their backgrounds and prospects; but now, reduced to ciphers in endless lines, over and over they complained that they felt like sheep, or drops of water, or buzzing flies. This unpleasant experience proved their introduction to yet another theme in Scandinavian-American literature: the sense of helplessness and loss of identity in a strange and hostile environment.

It was with a decided feeling of disgust that Meinhardt, together with hundreds of others of different nationalities, was driven to a New York railroad station. It seemed to him that he had been reduced to an unutterably small fraction of an aimless, swarming mass.[39]

Many immigrants discovered that the strange environment was dangerous as soon as they had passed the entry gates. Outside swarmed the runners and confidence men pictured in every account of landing in America. Most claimed to be agents of cheap hotels and labor bureaus, some reputable and some not; and a new arrival certainly could not tell the difference. The literature showed the characters usually forewarned against this danger: "He did not dare ask anyone for advice, since like most Norwegians he believed that the main occupation of Americans consisted of cheating all more unsuspecting and unsophisticated people in the world."[40] Yet those traveling alone were so confused when plunged into the turmoil of New York that all too often they greeted as a friend anyone who could speak a few words of their language. Short stories from a decade or two before and after the turn of the century recorded hapless newcomers being cheated, robbed, even murdered by dockside crooks. Earlier than this, group migration with guides had protected large numbers from such exploitation, and stricter government regulations and guidance by immigrant aid societies reduced the danger later.

Rarely was a wronged immigrant able to avenge his loss. Exceptional was the Danish sailor who, after he had been sent to a nonexistent job by a bogus labor bureau, returned to hunt for the man who had deceived him. He knew better than to bother the police with such a trifle, and besides, the confidence man had "pull." By a lucky chance he found the fellow again, busily conning some German newcomers. Threatening to expose his racket and beat him up, the Dane got his money back with interest and went his way; the fate of the Germans was not his concern.[41] "Look out for thieves!" a Danish-American poet saw posted everywhere in public places, and concluded that no one could trust anyone in this ruthless land.[42] Every man for himself, preached story after story, was one of the first principles that immigrants had to learn.

Feeling themselves automatically defined as fools because they were strangers disturbed a number of immigrant characters too. A landowner from Norway, arriving with $1500 in gold, was dismayed at the discovery that the runners who swarmed around him at the docks were laughing at him as a greenhorn. When he took a walk along the crowded streets in a spirit of interested curiosity, people he might have considered his equals also seemed to reject him. "His Norwegian attire, which he had used since childhood, and whose suitableness it had never occurred to him to doubt, suddenly seemed ridiculous and queer; and the half curious, half contemptuous glances which the men and women gave him, made him think how foreign and strange he must look in their eyes."[43] Such uneasy awareness of being unlike others became an important theme in this literature, driving most of the immigrants to try to conform to American expectations.

The very climate increased the initial discomfiture of these Northmen. Most characters were pictured arriving in the late spring or early summer. Those who intended to become farmers always hoped to get a crop into the ground the first year, and those who planned to look for work knew from America letters and guidebooks that jobs were difficult if not impossible to find in the winter. Although many had been warned that summers were hot in the New World, no one expected such suffocating heat so early in the season, and these northern people were wearing their usual woolen clothes. Suffering from the heat became a recurrent theme in the literature, even after the immigrants had adopted lighter clothing.

Difficulties with language, on the other hand, all had foreseen, and a number had tried to prepare for them in advance. One of the main advantages of traveling in groups with a guide and interpreter was avoidance of the language problem. As group migration gave way to that of single families and individuals, however, language difficulties grew in number and complexity. Few tales pictured problems of communication at the official reception centers, where usually interpreters were at hand; but as soon as they set foot outside those protected shelters most newcomers felt the utter helplessness of persons suddenly struck deaf and dumb. Even those later and better educated immigrants who had studied some English at home found the rapid pronunciation of American speech impossible to understand at first. The numerous practical problems arising from inability to communicate with other people, as well as the frustration and emotional atrophy which resulted, became a dominant theme in the immigrant literature.

New York City itself made a consistently bad impression on Scandinavian immigrants. Even those who had come from the largest cities of their homeland found this one overwhelming. The reaction of an educated poet from Copenhagen, first published in 1874, was typical. He criticized the endless streets ankle-deep in filth, the screeching turmoil of Broadway; he found the huge buildings monotonous and displeasing, half bazaar and half castle, without a trace of history: "In form how big, in character how small!" The crowds struck him as cold and unfriendly—fashionable gentlemen looking down their noses, ladies painted with make-up, boys impudent and rude. Like many who followed him, this Dane felt only relief at escaping from the metropolis.[44] A Norwegian poet recording his impressions a quarter century later found the city no less repulsive. The Statue of Liberty appeared to his hero's eyes symbolically covered with rust and mold, the hurrying mobs in the streets like packs of two-footed predatory animals.[45] Most other accounts of New York in stories of immigrant arrival were briefer than these, often only a sentence or two; but practically all agreed that their characters' first impression of the New World was unpleasant.

3. THE JOURNEY WESTWARD

Almost all immigrant characters proceeded westward from their port of arrival at once, preferably on the same day. Until the 1890s the majority were peasants in search of land, and realized that to find cheap and good farms they would have to go west. Family groups in particular were apt to have a specific destination in the Middle West. The moves of Scandinavians still further west into Colorado, Montana, and the Pacific states seem to have been secondary removals of dissatisfied settlers or their children from the Middle Border more than primary settlements by immigrants fresh from Europe. Very little of this literature followed characters to the western sea. Instead, later arrived factory workers and skilled technicians were usually shown settling in eastern towns and cities.[46] A story laid in the 1890s recorded the changeover in mid-course: A pair of better-class Swedish youths on an Atlantic steamer discovered that they were the only steerage passengers who did not have a specific goal in America, such as the home of friends or relatives. The country people were without exception going further west, while the smaller group of servants and handworkers planned to stay in eastern cities.[47] The hero of the story was himself a chemical engineer, who after wandering from one job to another in both East and Middle West finally settled on the east coast. Occasionally a story showed single individuals of undecided destination being convinced by others on the boat that it would be stupid not to go west. "Out there were the rich opportunities for making money, they said; a man was foolish to stay in the East, which was already full of people."[48]

Scandinavian immigrants could go further west because practically all arrived with some money. This was no doubt the reason they so often fell victim to confidence men, who correctly assumed that most had something to steal. There were exceptions: a young Dane, for instance, set out hiking from New York because he lacked train fare; but he soon earned enough working on an upstate farm to buy his ticket further.[49] In another novel a destitute Norwegian family landed in Quebec expecting to find a money order promised by an aunt who had emigrated earlier. When this did not appear, the Norwegian consul got funds for their trip west from an immigrant commission in Chicago, which also took care of them on arrival there. With this help they finally reached the aunt's home in Wisconsin.[50] Poor immigrants traveling with a returned American were usually best off, for when they ran out of funds they had only to borrow more from the same benefactor. Thus the guide of a Norwegian party warned them in New York to buy food for three days before boarding the train west. One peasant father thought a dollar ought to feed a family of seven for so long, and was horrified to learn that five could hardly do it. But the guide willingly advanced the five dollars, and the family had enough to eat on the long train ride.[51] Other stories sometimes pictured characters who had fasted a day or two when they arrived out west with empty pockets, but every immigrant in the literature ultimately succeeded in getting where he wanted to go.

Not many authors described in detail the continued westward journey. Most only outlined the route their characters followed west, and began their action at its terminal point. Stories laid before the Civil War often mentioned transport by Hudson River steamer to Albany and then via canal boat to Lake Erie, where lake steamers carried the immigrants to Detroit, Chicago, or Milwaukee. "Conditions on these boats were terrible; the greatest filthiness reigned and there was little or no opportunity to cook or prepare food."[52] Since most books in this literature concerned immigration after the Civil War, however, the usual mode of transportation was by rail. Many characters remarked on how much cleaner and more comfortable American coaches were than English, but they were far from safe. In a Norwegian-American novel laid in the 1880s a train was hit from behind by a freight. The last passenger car, full of Swedish immigrants, was demolished; several people were killed, many seriously injured. The leader of the Norwegian group in another coach could only assure the terrified newcomers that the railroad company would pay handsome damages for casualties.[53] Even in later stories, when rail traffic had become comparatively safe, the long trip

74

in day coaches was described as an ordeal for many characters. One neat little Danish seamstress could hardly stand the discomfort of forty hours on the immigrant train to Chicago without a chance to eat, sleep, or wash properly.[54]

Impressions of the new land seen through train windows were recorded in a few tales. One Norwegian group was surprised at how early twilight came even in midsummer, although it brought no relief from the heat. Their guide explained that daylight was more reasonable in the New World; instead of light all summer and dark all winter it was more nearly the same all year round. The larger size of almost everything west of the Atlantic continued to impress the same group after leaving New York. These peasants from cramped valleys marveled at average American farms all bigger than the wealthiest estates back home, at large herds of cows and horses, at fields, pastures, and forests stretching to the far horizon. A cotter's wife thought American cows must be as large as elephants. "Just look where the cows are wading in clover up over their knees! It's almost a shame! Think how many poor folks would be glad of the chance to scrape together what those cows trample down. It hurts just to look at it!"[55] The guide warned them that farms were not so fine nor buildings so large on the frontier where they were headed; but the land was as spacious there, and the opportunities unlimited. Time after time the initial impression of immigrant pioneers on the frontier was recorded as wonder at the vastness of the fertile acres waiting for the plow. Here was land to feed all the millions of the earth! Even after the frontier had closed, a sense of the much greater scale of everything American persisted as a first reaction of all newcomers. A Danish boy arriving in 1908 thought the farms of the Midwest like royal domains; Nebraska farmhouses and grain elevators were so big that they obviously must all belong to very rich men.[56]

Confidence men also infested railroad terminals in midwestern cities, and many immigrants who had escaped them in New York fell victim to them later. A Swedish-American tale related the reception of one Erik Svensson by a Chicago crook. Speaking broken Swedish, he promised to help the new arrival find a cheap hotel and a good job. But Erik had been forewarned, and demanded to see the regular railroad agent. The runner displayed a brass plate engraved in Swedish: "Agent for Swedes, Norwegians, Danes, and Finns. Follow him! Watch out for imposters!" So Erik went along to a shabby hotel where he was knocked out, stripped of money, watch, and clothes, and left for dead in an alley. The Irish policeman who found him laughed heartily: "Another greenhorn from Sweden!"[57] Even more often it was compatriots who fleeced newcomers near the end of their journey. Fearing and avoiding

Americans, many a character appealed for help to countrymen, like another young Swede who addressed two shabby men he overheard speaking Swedish on a Chicago street. "They understood at once that a greenhorn had fallen into their clutches straight from the clouds, and without doubt they would soon be several dollars richer."[58] Pretending to befriend him, they picked his pocket of all his forty dollars and melted away into the crowd.

Once the travelers had left American cities, however, and passed through rural or frontier areas on the last stretch of their journey, they met such generosity from strangers as amazed them. A party of Norwegians were given a feast by a Yankee farmer in Wisconsin, who understood only that they were new arrivals hunting for a relative. He refused any payment, and pointed them on their way with hearty good wishes. "It was worthy of its fame, this golden America, where strangers were invited in to a banquet when they asked to buy food, where folks were so hospitable and helpful."[59] In book after book travelers on foot or by wagon were given food and shelter without thought of payment as they pushed westward; and when they finally arrived at their destination, they were welcomed by friend and stranger alike with gifts of food and offers of help. Neither in the stable society of the homeland nor in the tumultuous American cities had newcomers experienced the openhearted generosity toward outsiders characteristic of the rural West. Such extremes of treatment bewildered Scandinavian newcomers, who never knew what to expect.

On the last lap of their journey, many characters also collided with another difference in American life: disparity in the value of money. Stories of the unbelievably high wages paid for even unskilled labor had of course drawn many of them across the sea, and they soon found it true that here they could earn in a month or two what had been a year's wage in the Old Country. But prices demanded for what they bought were equally fantastic. Their little capital, which represented years of toil and sacrifice in the Old World, disappeared with shocking speed. The price of food and lodging in the cities seemed incredible, and many a family chose to camp out in discomfort rather than waste so much of their precious cash. Locally grown food declined in price as the new arrivals traveled west, but processed and manufactured goods grew more expensive. Hotels in small towns on the Middle Border, dirty, crowded, and vermin-ridden as they were, demanded such high rates that a Danish settler in Dakota was forced to buy lumber at unheard-of prices to put up a temporary shelter for his wife and child. The finished hut and rough shed of a stable cost him $150.[60]

Where public transportation ended and the immigrants had to hire their own conveyance, again they were dismayed at the expense. Many walked long distances, but they could not carry their heavy chests; and sometimes the last miles cost half the price of the whole trip. A young Danish settler in Nebraska worried through his hurried wedding because he knew he could not afford a horse and wagon to drive his newly arrived bride the last miles to his claim. She thought he should be able to pay that; it was their honeymoon trip! But he was already deeply in debt. When they reached the nearest prairie village by train, the young man was overjoyed to find a neighbor shopping in town who would give them a ride home.[61]

A large percentage of pioneers made the journey to the frontier in two stages, stopping some months or years in an older settlement to earn capital. They were then able to buy wagons and teams for the last lap of their trip. Again prices were high, but by then the immigrants had also received American-scale wages. The exorbitant cost in new communities of everything processed or manufactured was of course a result of frontier conditions, and reached better adjustment with the rest of the economy when the primitive period was over. But from first to last this literature pictured Scandinavians as having to learn to think of money as being more plentiful and having less value than back home.

4. THE FINAL DESTINATION

Throughout the various stages of their long journey, the immigrants were most impressed by the differences in everything they saw from what they had known before. It was as though the trip itself served the purpose of uprooting them from the familiar and habitual to prepare them for meeting the alien and new. Under the impact of so many new experiences, even the short time of a mechanized journey seemed long. "It's not a full month since I left home, but it feels like an eternity," began Rølvaag's first novel. "It's as though I've had three lives to live here on earth. The first two are already finished—one in Smeviken, which lasted nearly 21 years. The second was the trip from Smeviken to Clarkfield, S. Dak. And now I'm about to begin the third. It's funny to think that the second life lasted only a little over three weeks, but it feels longer than the first one."[62]

At the end of their exodus, however, those who came to Wisconsin, Minnesota, and parts of Iowa found many similarities between the homes they had left and the places they intended to settle. Despite the greater violence of American weather and the plague of swarming insects, nature in midwestern forests was much like what they had left behind. Newly arrived Norwegians on a river steamer in Wisconsin recognized and greeted as old friends crows on the wing, pike in the river, and many trees along the shore: willow, alder, ash, maple, oak, pine, and the lovely white birch, which often stood in clumps of three just like back home. "Indeed they recognized the familiar smell of the woods, though not so strong and intoxicating as in eastern Norway; but it brought them a greeting which made them feel that they were still on God's earth and would be able to come to terms with the new land in the end."[63]

Scandinavian colonies in landscapes similar to the homeland also impressed newcomers with their familiar style of building and Old-World ways. An early Norwegian-American novel described a Norwegian settlement in Minnesota as the hero approached it. A red-painted little house with white gables reminded him forcibly of Norway; he heard a Norse cattle-call, and saw a flaxen-haired girl leading a herd of cows. In the bottom of the valley glittered a long lake, lined with forests and meadows. "How could this beautiful bit of Norway have been transplanted into the heart of this mammoth-boned, huge-veined continent?"[64] Danes too found areas which reminded them strongly of home. In that rich land of northern Iowa where prairie and woods met and mingled, a Danish-American novel traced the growth of a little town so thoroughly Danish that, apart from the lack of thatched and tiled roofs, a visitor might have believed he had come to a village in the Old Country.[65]

Far more of these immigrants, however, found their surroundings at their destination fully as strange as anything they had seen during the journey there. Iowa was no flatter than Denmark, but how the Danes missed the sea! And many who came from forested mountains to Dakota or Kansas were haunted by the immense, brooding emptiness of the great plains.

Even these comparatively homogeneous immigrants from Norway, Sweden, and Denmark had left widely different landscapes back home. Some came from plains, others from mountain areas; some from dense forest, a few from treeless tundra; a number from the shores of quiet lakes, others from beside rivers or waterfalls, many from the sound of the restless sea. Within the wide expanse of the Middle West they found almost as many different types of countryside, depending on what was open to settlement at the time they came. Often a single shipload of immigrants spread out over a wide area, as in the case of a party which arrived shortly before the Civil War:

The big group from Norway had dwindled on the long trip from Milwaukee. Some had stayed in that city, others went on to Muskego in order to continue from there to the fertile Koshkonong, which had been discussed so much on board ship. Others had taken the boat from Milwaukee to Chicago, where there was said to be plenty of work but an unhealthful climate. Still others had taken the boat from La Crosse down to Prairie du Chien, to cross from there into Iowa—a fairyland which lay and waited for those who wanted to take it. But these were mostly farmer folk, who had money and knowledge of farming. Those who were left were now on the way to the woods to find the type of work which they thought suited them best.[66]

How much at home or how alien an immigrant felt in the physical environment to which he came depended thus on the combination of two variables: his memory of what he had left behind compared with what he found around himself in America. Later comers fared worst in this respect. Stories laid on the treeless plains of the last frontier emphasized how difficult it was for people conditioned to woods and water to adjust to a landscape with neither.

Pictured in this literature was also the full variety of social environments which the immigrants found on arrival: lonely pioneer settlements, more advanced rural areas and country towns in every stage of growth, large cities like Chicago and Milwaukee at various periods. Seldom did the stories portray their characters plunging at once into American life. Hampered by language difficulties, they rather sought out their own countrymen to live at least the first weeks or years as close as possible to them. But every newcomer's initial experience of adjustment was subtly different, depending on the age of the immigrant community he came to, its size and compactness, its isolation from the surrounding American society, and how much community life had been established in Old-Country patterns. In some areas practically every farm was owned by Norwegians, elsewhere perhaps one or two Danish families sat alone among many other nationalities. Here was a whole town where only Swedish was spoken, there half a dozen Norwegian families lived together near the station, elsewhere an old bachelor was the only Dane in town. In cities considerable areas were often so exclusively Swedish or Norwegian that they drew almost all new arrivals of the same nationality. In a Danish-American novel the main character wanted above all to room near Humbolt Park in Chicago, the center of the Danish quarter.

Half of the store signs on North Avenue displayed Danish names. There were more than a dozen Danish bakers; there were banks which changed crowns; there were restaurants which served open-faced sandwiches; there were food stores which sold liverwurst and pork sausage and Danish cheese. And there were saloons where one could curse in his mother tongue and drink himself to a thumping good hangover in Aalborg Aquavit.

In the neighborhood were located all the Danes' meeting places. Seven of the ten Danish churches in town were there. . . . In this area lay also all the club rooms, several secret societies, the lodge "Denmark," the Scandinavian Social Democrats' Sick Insurance Society of 1895, the Youth Club, the Gymnastic Club, and the choral societies, in all a good fifty organizations of widely different types.[67]

Whatever their setting, Scandinavian-American books were above all concerned with change. Stories of immigrant life always showed people being transformed by new experiences. The changes were regular; they reappeared as themes from one story and poem to another. Despite varying environments of settlement, the range of personality types, the diversity of experiences, the incompatible opinions of authors, there was a general pattern to the way these characters changed from Scandinavians into Americans. The process began with the journey itself, when the shock of contrast between old and new was most vivid and painful; but it was carried out in the myriad small repetitive experiences of daily life which this literature showed so well. Each author's portrayal of the process, however, was controlled by his conception of and attitude toward it; so before turning to the detailed evidence of the books themselves, it will be necessary to consider more abstract concepts of the process of cultural adjustment evinced or argued by the writers in this tradition.

Chapter Four
Theories of Cultural Adjustment

Practically every discussion of motives for Scandinavian emigration emphasized that those who left sought to change their social and cultural environment, not their native geography. Character after character expressed himself willing to put up with the long winters and stony soil of his homeland if only its social structure had permitted him to get ahead, or at least provide a decent living and future for his family. Since economic opportunity at home was largely determined by birth, however, it seemed necessary to seek a different kind of social organization, which most emigrants believed they would find in America. Few realized in advance that such desirable differences in American society were inseparably interwoven with other characteristics of New-World life which they would heartily dislike. Whether or not these undesirable aspects could be avoided or minimized by preservation of Old-World ways was widely debated throughout the literature.

I. Pioneer Days

Stories of frontier life showed that this question did not concern immigrants who became pioneers. Their problems of adjustment were distinctive in many ways. Where the overwhelming problem was physical survival in the wilderness, the sole aim of all was to adjust to prevailing conditions as rapidly, flexibly, and completely as possible. The only test of the worth of a tool or technique was pragmatic; no one cared whether its origin was European or American.

The earlier comers who pioneered in the wooded areas from the Great Lakes to Minnesota were singularly well prepared for frontier life. (These were largely Swedes and Norwegians; Danes hardly appeared in this literature as woodland pioneers.) Moving from a settled civilization into wilderness, pre-Civil War immigrants naturally carried most baggage with them: big wooden chests and heavy bags of food, clothing, and tools. Even more important, they brought along knowledge of the skills essential to subsistence farming in timber country. One Swedish immi-

81

grant in northern Iowa in the 1870s was described as "a Robinson Crusoe of the inland, for he contrived to make his farm almost as independent of the outside world's manufactures and production as though it were isolated."

For a long time the cradle-scythe was good enough to take care of his small fields of wheat and oats, so he bought only the steel blade and made the rest out of wood. . . . He kept bees and had his own honey. He made his own out-buildings of hewed logs nogged with mud. For the granary and toolshed he manufactured heavy oaken locks with oaken keys. He made iron tools at his crude forge. He used rail fences instead of wire or boards. With typical Old-Country dexterity he cobbled shoes for the family, and Mollie spun yarn for clothing. . . . He made his own candles out of beeswax or tallow. He killed his own cattle and hogs, and cured their meat. His wife made butter and cheese.[1]

Most important of all, Scandinavian immigrants from dispersed rural districts were accustomed to life on separate homesteads where each man made and carried out his own decisions on how to run his farm and his family.

Even when the frontier moved out onto the Great Plains, practical knowledge brought by woodsmen and fisherfolk from the North proved useful. In *Giants in the Earth,* Per Hansa knew the trick of steering a straight course without a compass by dragging a long rope—the sailor's trick of throwing out a line astern. He could weave nets, too, for catching trout and wild duck to salt down against the Dakota winter, and carve wooden clogs to protect feet against the cold dirt floor.[2]

Conditions in this landscape were so different, however, that much Old-World skill proved useless there. Nor did the later comers bring along such chestloads of tools. By the 1880s immigrants usually carried as little baggage as possible, and got their pioneering outfits together on the American side after some time in a settled community. A few characters who followed the advice of earlier guidebooks on what to take discovered their mistake after arriving in a changed America. A Swedish shoemaker in a novel published in 1899 did put to good use all the tools of his trade he had brought; but his wife never needed her wool carders, preferring to buy inexpensive American ready-made yarn and cloth.[3]

Scandinavian pioneers on every midwestern frontier at first found life much more difficult than at its worst back home; but conditions were most primitive of all on the treeless prairie. Beret in *Giants in the Earth* was appalled at having to live like an animal in a hole in the ground; she expressed the feelings of many a housewife who could hardly endure housekeeping in a sod hut.[4] A Danish newcomer to Dakota was disconcerted at discovering in this land of Progress hay used for fuel and oxen for draft animals. "Like in our grandfathers' time back home!"[5] In another story a mother reminisced about her pioneer days, when large families lived in a single room with a dirt floor, one door, one window. "Many had been badly off in Norway, too, so they didn't know much about anything better. . . . But none even among the cotters' families had ever lived so wretchedly as the first pioneers on the prairie."[6]

Intolerable conditions did not drive them away, however. As book after book pointed out, most of the immigrants were too poor to leave. Instead bitter necessity impelled them to work harder than ever before.

Methods of farming which the immigrants brought along proved useful under pioneer conditions in those areas which most resembled the homeland. When all a man had to cultivate were the small fields he had cleared of timber or plowed from sod, his ability to make the most of every square foot with primitive tools was all in his favor.

In the late summer Jens cut his flax with a scythe and Mary raked it with a wooden rake, for this was the way they had done in the old country. Reapers were already on the market but they were expensive and there were bills to be paid.[7]

Usually characters were shown planting the crops they already knew how to cultivate; sometimes years passed before a conservative settler ventured to try Indian corn. The main difference in farming for most pioneers at first was not in type of crop or work technique but in yield; the virgin soil and the warmer climate repaid many times over what the same methods had produced in the Old Country.

As the earth lost fertility, however, as transportation improved and the farms of the neighborhood began raising money crops, farming techniques had to change too. A little book about Norwegians in the Red River Valley outlined the stages of transition. First the harvest was all cut and raked by hand and thrashed by oxen. Then the settlement hired two Americans to come with their reaping and thrashing machinery. Later the farmers pooled resources to buy one machine of each type for all to use in turn; and finally each was able to buy his own.[8]

Only a few characters resisted the adoption of American farming methods and equipment, and they were always won over in the end. Slow-witted Per "Trot" in a Norwegian-American novel would use nothing but a hoe to prepare his fields in a pioneer Dakota settlement, though he had more money than the other settlers. He did not trust American hoes, either, but hiked ten miles to a blacksmith to get one made like those in the Old Country. But one day he had to have a new hoe in a rush, tried an American one in desperation, and found it couldn't be beat. It took him a couple of years more to get around to buying oxen, but he finally did—when his neighbors were selling theirs to buy horses.[9] The majority of immigrants, however, were eager to listen to advice on what type of plow, seed, fertilizer best suited the new environment. Especially when the recommendation fitted the framework of what they were used to, or concerned conditions so new they had no experience to go on, they welcomed any idea or tool that *worked.*

When Isak took the American ax into his hand, it seemed to fit perfectly at once—the long, strong, elastic handle which bent a little, and the weight that was just right. This was something else than the heavy broadaxes in the Old Country. With such an ax he could chop all day long without getting tired.[10]

What they learned, the Scandinavians passed on to all comers, as it had been given them. Germans heading still further west stopped to see Per Hansa's big sod hut with house and stable under the same roof. "They themselves were just beginning, and needed ideas."[11] Whatever worked best in the practical problems of frontier life was adopted without further ado, whether brought from Europe, found in America, or invented on the spot. The frontier created its own pragmatic culture, which cut across all national lines.

Pioneer conditions also molded social relations. So long as men were few, and their main concern was to keep alive in the face of natural dangers, the differences among them did not matter. Beret longed for other people on the empty plains, in *Giants in the Earth*; only after there were people aplenty did she begin to differentiate between Norwegians and Irish. These peasants had brought along strict rules of hospitality from the Old Country, for in their closed society there had been only two ways to treat an outsider—as a stranger or a guest. On the frontier the surrounding wilderness merged the two categories; and story after story recorded the mutual helpfulness, the generous sharing of everything—except their wives! one author qualified[12]—while all were poor pioneers. Differences in language were then more of a nuisance than a cultural barrier. Where the rest of the environment was foreign, however, immigrants naturally welcomed company of their own kind more than other people. Germans and Irish who passed their outpost in Dakota the Norwegians tried to talk into settling nearby, in *Giants in the Earth*; but when Norskies came—God's own Norskies!—the firstcomers practically stood on their heads to get them to stay.[13]

Conflicts in cultural adjustment thus hardly appeared in the literature dealing with pioneer life, because Americanization in the adoption of tools and techniques meant survival, because frontier conditions were similar in many respects to those at home, and because all human aid was needed in the wilderness. Only after civilization had caught up in the form of a developing community did problems of cultural conflict take form.

No more than a small part of this literature dealt with pioneer life, however. The majority of writers wrote out of their own experience, which fell after the Civil War; and by then frontier conditions lasted hardly more than twenty years at most in any given settlement. A Danish-American author summed up the typical speed of development in a novel about an Iowa town:

The same generation which had plowed the first furrows in the earth here had also built the first railroads in the valley. . . . Roads and railroads, congregations and clubs, churches and schools in older societies are inherited from one's forefathers, taken over often without a thought of thanks. In Elkdalen the first generation had built everything, as far as they had yet come. The model had been brought from other parts of the country or from Europe; but it had to be adjusted to the conditions and necessities of life at that particular spot.[14]

Conflict between models from other parts of America and from Europe, and adaptation of both to the local scene, made up a basic theme of this Scandinavian immigrant literature.

II. Pressures of Economic Life

In certain areas of immigrant life there was no conflict between European and American ways at any time. In matters economic the dictum was absolute: do it as the Americans do or not at all. Especially in farming, after the subsistence economy of the frontier had passed, newcomers often found that the knowledge they had brought along was obsolete. A youth coming directly from Norway to an older farm in Wisconsin was bewildered by the contrast in techniques of cultivation:

He had come from a land where men plowed and harvested three, five, ten acres—or in the case of the largest farm near Skien, thirty acres. There the life fortunes of an individual cabbage, or a single stalk of tobacco growing under the hot-house glass, was subject for discussion. . . . Here, where Einar brought him to the endless rows, stretching like box hedges into the horizon, he was wordless.[15]

Newcomers who stopped in an older immigrant settlement or worked for an American farmer not only earned necessary capital but also learned American agricultural techniques. One Yankee farmer's place was literally a school of American work methods and the English language for an endless series of greenhorns from Norway.[16] A Norwegian recounted how he had stopped some years in Wisconsin before pushing on to take up a claim in Minnesota.

Even the farm work was new to me—something quite different from the work at home on the croft. Here were enormous plains that seemed much too huge to harvest. And then those labor-saving machines. Good heavens, such machines!—I had to learn everything over again, greenhorn that I was.

All the same, I thought it had been easier home on the croft, even if I had to be both horse and machine there myself. . . . It all seemed so big and oppressive here.[17]

85

In later years, when agricultural techniques had been modernized in the Old World too, previous knowledge of farming again proved of use in the new environment. A Danish farmer in Nebraska in the 1890s soon learned the new technique involved in raising corn. "The small grain farming he understood from the Old Country."[18]

The farmer had no supervisor to insist on his doing things in American ways, but in other types of employment the boss took supremely for granted that every immigrant wanted to work as much like an American as possible—only harder, to make up for being a foreigner. Among themselves European workers might compare the old and the new, but they made little attempt to continue in accustomed work patterns. Previous experience in the same line was naturally an advantage, and newcomers who had received training at home usually gravitated toward the same type of work on the other side of the ocean. But skill was not enough. If previous training could not be adapted to American tools, techniques, and tempo, the man lost his job—or his life. A Norwegian-American recalled his adjustment to the difficult work in a sawmill:

Near the singing and dancing sawblades for seven long months I had carried out work which required my undivided concentration and all my body's strength every minute of a twelve-hour working day. The steam power which drove the machines was set to the utmost of a young man's strength and quick thinking. If either failed, the worker was injured or killed. But the summer season was over and all had gone well. My Norwegian heritage had passed its test.[19]

Attitudes toward work, however, were often transplanted intact to the new environment. In many stories Scandinavian pride of workmanship was highly valued by American employers, although it sometimes had drawbacks too. A Danish contractor in Chicago hired preferably Scandinavians or Germans as carpenters, for "as a rule they were people who had learned their trade thoroughly; but occasionally they disappointed him, their traditional training hampered some of them instead of helping; they did not dare depart by so much as a hair's breadth from the regulations they had once learned."[20]

Offered the choice between changing their work-patterns or starving, most immigrants naturally took the former. But throughout their years in America all faced a protracted series of choices in almost every other aspect of their lives. Their immediate surroundings or the force of habit exerted pressure toward selection of one option rather than another, so much so that they often were not aware of making a decision at all; but the choice in every case lay between a more European or a more American model of thought or behavior. The span of alternatives stretched from the minutiae of daily life to single decisions which affected their entire future. Each selection resulted from the interplay of two basic variables: the personality of the individual, and the pressures of his environment. For one whose character had already been largely formed before he left Europe, the most crucial question was whether he wished to retain as much as he could of his Old-World culture, his pre-emigration self, or whether he wanted to become as American as possible. Did then the people and institutions which surrounded him support his decision? If not, did he have the strength to oppose them? Most of the authors gave some kind of answer to these questions. The best of them were deeply concerned with the issue of cultural adjustment which underlay the whole. But they disagreed as vehemently as their characters over whether or not aspects of European culture could or should be preserved.

III. Preservation versus Abandonment of European Culture

All the writers belonged to one of two groups: those who sought to preserve as much as possible of their European heritage, and those who wished to abandon it. Those who appeared not to care lined up with the second group in every practical case. Indifference to this question meant moving in the direction toward which one was impelled by the pressure of Americanization. All immigrant authors recognized this fact; those who nevertheless argued for preservation of European culture were aware that they were attempting to stand against the tide, and that they were a minority not only as Danes or Norwegians in America but also within their own ethnic group. The evidence of this literature indicates that the majority of Scandinavian immigrants accepted abandonment of their European roots as rapidly as possible. The majority of Scandinavian-language authors, on the contrary, advocated preservation of Old-World culture; but they were unable to agree among themselves on a definition of either the culture to be preserved or the means of maintaining it.

Even the most conservative of the preservationists admitted that no one could escape certain aspects of American life. All immigrants must do their work in the U.S.A., be paid in dollars, buy their necessities made in America; they must learn English for economic as well as political reasons, for they should become citizens and vote to protect their own interests. But beyond such practical and materialistic concerns, argued the preservationists, in the cultural life of social groups and the emotional life of individuals, forms and models brought from Europe were distinctly to be preferred. Some hoped to keep their "cultural heritage" uncontaminated by American influence, presumably for their own benefit alone. Others argued that they must remain European in order to aid American development, transmitting the spiritual treasures of their native to their adopted land. All preservationists agreed, however, that they must somehow remain a separate and definite group if they were to preserve anything of their own.

IV. Definition of the Immigrant Group

Few bothered to define the qualifications for group membership; it was enough that they had been born to parents of a certain national origin.[21] But the assumed boundaries of the group shifted from one discussion to another, sometimes including all who had been born citizens of the homeland, at other times fellow immigrants and their descendants; and the homeland was invariably Norway, Sweden, or Denmark, not Scandinavia as a whole. Immigrants of the three nationalities felt special kinship and sympathy with each other, but not a sense of cultural union. They shared parallel fates, but each group stood or fell alone.[22]

1. THE BOND OF LANGUAGE

The most distinctive characteristic of each group was its language. For many conservatives, language was indeed the crux of the matter. So long as that could be preserved, they argued, its speakers would remain a separate group, and no longer. For them the phrase "mother tongue" took on special connotations, colored with sacred memories of childhood home and loving parents. First-generation ministers frequently invoked the sanction of the Almighty for continuing to use the European language in America.

> Was it not the Lord who gave us our tongue
> with all its spiritual riches, which gold cannot outweigh?
> And when we lost that language which He spoke
> to us the time we were baptized with His holy love,
> the language in which our childish hearts sought comfort,
> the language which gave wings to our youthful hopes,
> then we sin against Him, our great Master,
> then He can no longer use us as His clay. . . .
> O, what a people's sin to reject its language!
> In doing so, a people kills itself.[23]

On this topic, the didactic tone was habitual in both prose and poetry. Readers were enjoined to preserve their mother tongue so insistently that one is forced to deduce they were not doing so. However, this literature showed both how and why their language was such a cohesive force, especially for the first generation.

The most common single difficulty portrayed in Scandinavian immigrant literature was that of communication with Americans. The first and most recurrent problems these people met arose from the fact that they could understand little or nothing of what was said to them, and could not make themselves intelligible in return. One story and poem after another recorded immigrants' irritation and frustration at being reduced to the helplessness of a small child. In a Chicago restaurant a Dane flushed with embarrassment at not being able to read the menu a waitress brought. "He felt as sheepish as a dog. It was devilish stupid for a grown person to stammer like a two-year-old."[24] Such experience proved a powerful force to turn these immigrants toward those who spoke the same language, for the ability to communicate restored them instantly to their adult selves.

Yet the feeling of solidarity with speakers of the same tongue involved more than escape from practical difficulties. The process of immigrant-group formation on an emotional level was illustrated in a Danish-American short story about three Danes who sat in the same train compartment all the way from Vamdrup to Hamburg. They did not exchange a word so long as Danish was spoken around them, but as soon as they had crossed the border and heard only German—though they understood it well enough—they began speaking together in their own language, and booked on the same boat to America.[25] A Swedish-American tale also showed how the possession of a common tongue in a different-language environment proved an immediate bond. During a stop in a prairie village, a young Swede got off the train to wander about the platform. He overheard two men speaking Swedish and immediately addressed them in the same language. The friendship arising from this chance meeting held through the winter, for the three men shared a room in a Chicago slum and divided what little money they could scrape up through the jobless season.[26]

Even after many years in America, characters in these stories often found themselves in a special relationship to strangers who spoke the same foreign tongue. In a late (1930) Danish-American story, the author was riding the Chicago elevated train on a sweltering day, as usual paying no attention to his fellow passengers. When his handkerchief became too wet to mop his face any longer, he tore off pieces of his newspaper to do the job. The man sitting beside him smiled at this and said in English that was a good idea—he'd do the same. This casual contact between strangers was, of course, typically American; in Denmark no such exchange would have taken place. But the author noticed that the other man spoke with an accent. He had blond hair—could he be Scandinavian? The newspaper he took out was *Berlingske Tidende*. The author spoke to him in Danish. "He was happily surprised to discover that his seat-companion was a fellow countryman, and we shook hands and introduced ourselves cordially."[27]

The ability to understand each other's language was also a force for sympathy across the national boundaries which divide Scandinavia. Several stories related the desperation of an individual or party of one nationality unable to communicate with English-speaking people until rescued by a Scandinavian of a different stripe, who served as guide or interpreter. In a typical incident a Norwegian mother and three children arrived in Chicago outfitted only with the address of the father, who had emigrated a couple of years before. When he did not meet their train, they set out on foot to try to find the address, showing it to passers-by and trudging off in the direction they pointed—if they pointed at all, instead of just shaking their heads and hurrying away.

While we stood there utterly dispirited, a man pushed by us and bumped into Totty so that she fell on the dirty pavement. The man stopped, and Totty, who had no doubt been fighting back her tears this long time, burst out in her own Norwegian, "Jutht look what you did to my dreth!" She took her skirt and held it up to show him. "Yes, that's too bad!" he said, and at that we knew he was Swedish and could understand every word we said. He knew just where West Erie Street was and said he'd be glad to go along with us and carry Totty. . . . There was no end to what he could pile on himself, and he went with us to the door of the house, bade us welcome to America, wished us good fortune, and hoped he might see us again.[28]

Emotional attachment to one's mother tongue based on such experiences belonged of course to the first generation alone. Rarely could those who emigrated as adults attain such mastery over English that they spoke it without an accent; even those who learned it quite well thought of it as the language of their business, not their hearts; and many of the ordinary immigrants shown in this literature spoke English so poorly that they embarrassed both themselves and their children. Thus most of the first generation retained their attachment to their mother tongue as the only language in which they felt completely at home. For their children, however, the situation was altogether different. Those who grew up in exclusively Scandinavian settlements were usually bilingual, but even those who spoke their parents' language or dialect exclusively until they began public school could not share the feelings of their parents toward the European tongue, subject as the children were to powerful pressures towards use of English from the surrounding environment. All cultural leaders within the immigrant group recognized this fact, but the literature showed them divided in opinions on how to cope with it.

Many of the preservationists believed that the Scandinavian languages could and should be maintained indefinitely, not in the dialectal form which most of the first generation spoke so much as in the formal book language used in religious instruction, church services, and classes at Scandinavian schools and colleges. It was assumed that teachers outside

90

the family would give most of the instruction; yet all agreed that only the influence of the individual home, especially the mother, could counteract American pressures sufficiently to implant in the children knowledge of and affection for the parents' native tongue. Thus many writers urged parents to keep up their own language even in dialectal form and to insist their children use it at home, in the effort to preserve the linguistic bond of their cultural group. We Danes can only dimly glimpse what role God intends for us in America, wrote a leading minister, but we know that we cannot fight the good fight if we throw away all we brought from the treasure chambers of our European culture.

> . . . our generation will preserve faithfully
> what the Spirit gave us, our language, our ideals,
> and not merely preserve it, but pass it on
> to our children, as their birthright from their forefathers,
> so that our Danish people may be kept alive
> to carry out the will of our Lord.[29]

Keeping the Danish or Norwegian people alive in America, mixed with other nationalities as they must live, might at first glance seem a hopeless task; but the preservationists were aware of considerable forces already working in that direction. They hoped that conscious encouragement of these forces could so support group solidarity that it would be able to withstand the dispersive influences of American society.

2. THE BOND OF KINSHIP

In the literature recording Scandinavian immigrant experience can be found recurring evidence of concentric rings of loyalty moving out from the family center, which had been the main basis of solidarity in the homogeneous society of the homeland. The solidarity of kinship naturally continued in the New World. Where all else was different, at least family ties remained the same. Therefore if an immigrant possessed any relative however distant in America, provided he had the vaguest notion of where he might be found, the newcomer invariably headed straight for his relative as soon as he got off the boat. Ties of kinship required that the older resident do all in his power to help the new arrival, who was entitled to free room and board, introductions to friends, a helping hand toward a job. Often, indeed, the host had paid his kinsman's trip over.

Such extensive obligations toward kinfolk were by no means so binding in America as in the Old Country, however; some characters in this literature accepted them unconditionally, others not. Usually members of one's immediate family were brought over and helped without thought of return; but now and again a benefactor took a hefty interest on the

91

loan he made, or used an obligation of gratitude to hold a young relative to hard work at far less than current wages—or no pay at all.

3. THE BOND OF ACQUAINTANCESHIP

Beyond the ties of family relationship, the next ring of loyalty was that of acquaintanceship. If two men had known each other ever so slightly in the Old Country, regardless of what their relationship there had been, that older shared experience made common cause between them when both had become strangers in their new environment.

Nevertheless, oddly enough, he rather liked being together with Lomviig. It's hard to explain: an old acquaintance is an old acquaintance, and meeting again so far from the fatherland gives a special feeling of togetherness, even if they have been political opponents and at bottom despise each other.[30]

Most established immigrants also felt obligated to give extended aid to any stranger who turned up with a letter of introduction or even just a verbal greeting from a mutual friend. Usually this was enough to call forth hospitality unlimited in extent though not in time.

4. THE BOND OF PROVINCE

The next wider ring of loyalty included all those from the same province in their home country. These had shared a common dialect, a distinctive folk costume, similar variants of social customs, the same landscape and local history. Later comers from the same valley served earlier immigrants as a welcome renewal of the bond tying them to their own past. Therefore time and again, especially in pioneer days, newcomers were received with open arms by settlers who had come from the same region; and the older people came from miles around to hear the latest news of friends and family they had left so many years before. One recently arrived Norwegian had to answer endless questions from his countrymen about friends and relatives back home: "For him these conversations kept open the wound of parting, but for the listeners they breathed the beauty of memory . . . he could not avoid sharing with them this life of the home province, the great unifying force of all who live in exile."[31]

This form of group solidarity, based on common origin in space, survived long after the group members had been dispersed to the four winds. The most successful imposters and bums learned all possible dialects so that they could claim to be from the same district as their intended victim. This, of course, they could tell as soon as the person addressed opened his mouth. For in America, where all other external signs of district of origin soon vanished, classification of a given person as from one district or another was based on his dialect. Naturally only compatriots were familiar enough with the different dialects to recognize them at first hearing; a Dane would hear a Norwegian as a Norwegian, and not distinguish between a man from Telemark and one from Nordland. Occasionally a character complained over difficulty in understanding unfamiliar dialects spoken by his own fellow countrymen. A novel describing the formation of the Fifteenth Wisconsin, all-Norwegian regiment in the Civil War, mentioned the language difficulties of eight hundred men from all parts of Norway thrown together in training camp. Sometimes they had to communicate in bad English because they could not understand one another's dialects.

"God knows what kind of folks we've got in with," said Hans, "they claim they're Norwegian, and they cuss in Norwegian, but I can't make head nor tail of what they say."[32]

This classification of compatriots by province of origin was clearly a survival of Old-World modes of thought; it was most prominent among newly arrived immigrants and continued beyond the first generation only in large group settlements. Rarely did a second-generation author mention the matter, as a Swedish-American opened a short story: "There were hardly anything but Värmlendings around where the Höglunns lived. What few Smålendings and Skånings were roundabout mostly kept together by themselves."[33] But of first-generation authors, Rølvaag like many others always identified his Norwegian characters by their region of birth: in *Giants in the Earth* the settlement of Trønders near the Sioux River, the Hallings Per Hansa gave food to, the Sognings and Vossings who came twenty families strong to join the Dakota settlers; and the fact that the main characters were from Helgeland was constantly emphasized by the strongly dialectal flavor of their speech. Sometimes characteristics traditionally associated with the inhabitants of a given province in the Old Country were mentioned as surviving transplantation: merry Värmland humor, Trønder toughness and persistence, Småland slyness and tenacity and willingness to work hard.

This way of classifying fellow countrymen did not seem to serve any significant function in the new environment. Many authors—also of the first generation—never mentioned it, describing characters merely as from Norway (or Sweden), with at most bare mention of the valley or province of birth. Rølvaag implied the reason for the declining importance of this classification, in a scene where a Trønder and a Helgelænding chopped holes in river ice and sat peaceably fishing side by side. No comment on the significance of this incident was necessary in the Norwegian edition of the book; but the English-language edition carried a footnote to explain that during the winter seasons at Lofoten, fishermen from the two regions from time immemorial had fought bitter battles on the fishing banks.[34] In time, these immigrants found common nationality and language stronger bonds than district of origin. A Norwegian character remarked of his neighbors from many provinces that "they had a common childhood, for the small communities they were born in had melted together out here to one big one, Norway."[35]

5. THE BOND OF NATIONAL ORIGIN (NATIONALITY)

The most powerful ring of loyalty bound together those of the same country of birth. The mutual expectation of preferential behavior between members of this group was portrayed so consistently—indeed, was taken so for granted—that it must be seen as a significant factor in immigrant experience. Examples were legion: never did a newcomer arrive anywhere but he first tried to find a compatriot. If he was a relative or a previous acquaintance, well and good; but even a stranger was expected to give all possible assistance to a fellow countryman.

Tales of pioneer days especially emphasized this hospitality, which was of course not limited by lines of nationality but intensified within them. For instance, Norwegian characters had been at the site of their pioneer settlement on the prairie only three days when another wagon train hove into sight, the men shouting at their oxen in Norwegian.

To think that they should meet people clear out here—Norwegians, too!—what an event! Unbelievably good luck—and when did you folks come over, and where are you from in Norway? The men shook each other's hands silently and vigorously, glanced away when they had examined each other's faces, and some of the women cried.

The first arrivals dropped everything to help the newcomers, even accompanying them to town to file on neighboring land. So began the marvelous summer, when the joy of strength accomplished what seemed impossible and mutual helpfulness solved all problems. The children ran and jumped in the sunlight, ungovernably happy in their health and freedom.

There were other jumps too—jumps their minds made, though no one noticed. But here people had come from different districts in Norway and in a few weeks became like a single family in common needs and shared goals in the face of the untried and the unknown. Open hearts and open doors—there wasn't a locked door in the whole community.[36]

Story after story by authors of all three national groups underscored the sense of unity which developed in isolated frontier communities and persisted long after the country had filled up. Sometimes people of other nationalities were included and shared in the neighborliness; but as a rule, provided there were enough Swedes or Danes around to make a

94

group, the basic solidarity remained within limits defined by national origin, at least for the first generation.

Deliberate efforts were often made to strengthen the original group by drawing in other settlers of the same nationality. In one story a Danish doctor caused the main growth of a South Dakota town, because he wrote articles in several Danish-American newspapers praising the locality after a railroad had come through. The Danes who responded soon took up all nearby homesteads, and land values rose. Some years later, after church squabbles had split the community into several camps, the damage inflicted by a major storm drew the people together again; and when they appealed for help through Danish-American newspapers, Danish colonies farther south sent three carloads of wheat and corn.[37]

6. THE IMMIGRANT CHURCH

The immigrant church proved the most important single institution in support of this group solidarity. A Norwegian minister who traveled by oxcart from one prairie settlement to another mused over how the members of his scattered flocks had come from very different regions in Norway and were quite unlike each other, yet all were united by their childhood faith. "They have their religious instruction along with them. And church and divine service, baptism and communion are holy things in their minds. If only there is someone to remind them of their inheritance frequently!"[38] Although there were exceptions, the native piety of the vast majority of these peasants appeared as such a consistent theme that it was clearly conceived to be a dominant characteristic of the group. Many of the authors, to be sure, had a professional interest in the matter, being themselves ministers; but the laymen did not lag far behind. The countless religious poems, numerous scenes of praying, holding services, founding congregations, going to church, discussing doctrine, were abundant external evidence; but there was internal evidence too in the attitudes of both authors and their characters, based on deep-rooted faith in the will of God.

The Lutheran churches which the immigrants founded became the cultural centers of the new communities as they had been of the old. A Danish settler explained to a visitor what the local church meant to its members, long after the frontier had passed away:

You see, all these people have only one single—what shall I call it?—entertainment, to go to church; here everybody meets regularly every Sunday. If there's something one wants to tell his friends or acquaintances, he doesn't have to *hope* he'll meet them at church on Sunday, he *knows* they'll be there. The need of companionship which we all have is satisfied there. And besides—though you probably won't understand this—besides, we prairie folk need the church, perhaps more than other people. Out here we are all engaged in a struggle for existence harder and rougher and more violent than you can imagine.

As just one example, he told about a tornado six years before, which had destroyed the home of the Danes on the next farm and killed the father and a child; the mother and the other children made it to the cyclone cellar in time.

"That's the kind of experience one lives through out here. And not many such pass over our heads before we have use for the church.—The buildings up there," he turned around on the seat and looked back at the church and parsonage, "nobody made us build them, they weren't put up with tax money or tithes, but when we sat out here on the prairie, we scraped the money together for them, not from our surplus but out of our poverty, because we needed them."[39]

Later, when local churches had joined into synods, religious solidarity widened. Individuals who moved from one area of settlement to another could usually find their own kind of Lutheran church wherever they went. By the 1870s, however, a counter-movement of fragmentation had begun which split congregations and even synods over questions of dogma, especially among the Norwegians. For nearly a quarter century doctrinal disputes disturbed the solidarity of all three Scandinavian groups. This topic will be discussed more fully in Chapter Seven.

7. THE ATTITUDES OF OUTSIDERS

Attitudes of Americans and of other immigrants also supported group solidarity based on national origin. Typically American contempt for "dumb Swedes" and "dirty foreigners" appeared in all three branches of the literature: immigrant children tormented at school and on the streets, greenhorns cheated at every opportunity, the whole group held to menial labor. Invariably Scandinavian girls hired out as household servants when they first arrived, while young men took jobs as farm hands and lumberjacks, railroad or unskilled construction workers. Every immigrant had to suffer through his "dog years," declared story after story; until he learned English he remained at the mercy of a system which kicked him to the bottom of the scale. The only exceptions were those who could set up immediately in farming for themselves and a few who enjoyed special patronage.

An American novel traced local American attitudes toward the swarming Swedish migration to Minnesota: first contempt and amusement at these dirty, ignorant foreigners; then mounting fear of their growing numbers and envy of their ability to get ahead. Political rivalry followed, when the Swedes grew conscious of the power of their numbers, took out citizenship papers, and began to vote in blocks. In the end they were at last accepted as worthwhile citizens. But throughout the process the Swedes remain defined and treated as a separate group.[40] A Norwegian-American novel on lumbering in northern Wisconsin showed Norwegians undergoing the same experience.

Canadians, Anglo-Americans, and Irishmen had the advantage that the language of the country was their mother tongue. Although they often differed among themselves, they made common cause against newcomers who did not know the country's language or who spoke it poorly. And they were in complete agreement about treating the Norwegians superciliously. This forced these to hold together. As long as they did the heaviest work and kept out of the way of those who spoke English, they were left alone and were even shown a sort of good-natured benevolence. But an instinct told the Norwegians that they had to stand their ground also when off the job to avoid being molested and tramped down.[41]

Now and then an author showed opposite attitudes toward Scandinavian immigrants existing side by side. In one story an Irish foreman hated Swedes, but had to hire them because the boss of the factory was convinced they were such good workers;[42] in another story, an American farmer contradicted his wife when she criticized a party of Norwegian immigrants who stopped to buy food.

I'd give half my farm for those powerful muscles and such a strong body. We need just such people as these to clear the wilderness. Such a family has everything needed to find happiness in this country, because they can stand work and know how to live economically. You may well some day find that man prosperous, his children Americanized and well informed, and one of his sons in Congress.[43]

Many Americans were quoted as favoring immigration from Scandinavia because these Protestant northmen became Americanized faster than other nationalities.[44] Immigrant authors were thus aware of both approval and disapproval of their group, but both kinds of judgment by outsiders had the same effect of establishing and maintaining group identity among those judged.

8. THE SELF-IMAGE OF THE SCANDINAVIAN GROUP

Reinforced by such outside opinions, the immigrant writers were quite sure of their own identity. In numerous articles, poems, and stories they listed and analyzed characteristics of the Swedish and Norwegian people.[45] The Danes drew up fewer lists, but in editorials, poems, and tales their authors too praised certain virtues and showed their characters making value judgments which revealed a consistent group self-image.[46] Its boundaries were blurred, for although each writer felt sure enough about what belonged to his own culture, his evaluation rarely coincided in all respects with that of his fellow countrymen, not to mention that of other Scandinavians. But there was a core of agreement which could

97

be designated as typically Scandinavian, as well as overlapping areas defined more specifically as Norwegian, Danish, or Swedish.[47]

a. *Cultural heritage*

It is comparatively easy to trace the survival or discard of "cultural heritage" on the obvious level of artifacts brought from the Old World, which could become keepsakes and heirlooms in the New, and on the relatively concrete level of customs and traditions such as in preparation of food and celebration of holidays. Mention of such things or of their absence was commonplace in this literature. The matter of language too was clear, though more complex because it was subject to infinite degrees of admixture of English. The language an individual spoke could thus serve as an objective, although not infallible, yardstick of his adjustment to the English-speaking environment at any given time and place. One must distinguish between the vocabulary of authors and their characters, however, for while dialogue was often consciously "mixed," descriptive style meant to be in the formal book language often included Americanisms both deliberate and unconscious.

Such cultural elements as folk songs and beliefs on one level, and references to the literature and history of the homeland on another, were also recorded in these books. The reader can trace where interest in such survived, where it died out, where it never existed, and where it was deliberately resurrected by cultural leaders. The form of social institutions as brought from Europe in the minds of immigrants was shown clearly in plots of conflict with American models, especially in the case of family relations, church structure, and school organization. But these aspects of cultural heritage the authors did not consider the crux of the matter.

b. *Personality traits*

In defining what was most characteristic and significant in Scandinavian culture, the authors emphasized personality traits and moral attitudes. Usually they assumed that character traits were as inheritable as physical traits in whatever they defined as typically Scandinavian. "Edith Mortenson was a real Swedish-American, born in this country of Swedish parents. Her golden hair and blue eyes with their candid, open look were inherited from the land of song and saga in the North."[48] Rølvaag alone was careful to explain what he meant by "Norwegian heritage": that Norwegian-Americans had received as their birthright certain aptitudes and inclinations in larger measure than the children of other groups in the United States.[49]

The trait most often emphasized was that of personal honesty. It was called by many names—conscience, love of truth and right, a sense of honor, obedience to law—and shown in a variety of forms and situations, from a boy whose bad conscience over not returning a lost knife made him sick,[50] to a greenhorn bartender who simply could not follow the order of his boss to steal from the customers, and became a farmer instead.[51] In a Norwegian-American novel, a group of Norwegians had made the trip and got started on farms on capital borrowed from a returned American at ten percent interest. They were shocked when a crabbed and disagreeable old man of their number announced he would not pay back his debt. He had discovered that American debtor laws were different from Norwegian ones, and the moneylender could not force him to pay. "This was a doctrine which none of those present could approve of, therefore the room got so quiet. Unconditional honesty was an essential characteristic of the Norwegian immigrants."[52]

This sense of personal honor was related to other traits claimed by these authors as their own, such as reliability and thoroughness. It could also be traced in a certain naiveté or simplicity which many writers held to be a Scandinavian characteristic, taking the form of thrift and frugality in their daily lives, but in interpersonal relationships leaving them open to exploitation by unscrupulous strangers. "The Norwegians are easily swayed, uncalculating, easy to fool. Except for the coastal population, they have been out in the world so little. In this country the funny papers and vaudeville have created a Norwegian or Scandinavian type. We are characterized as strong and true-hearted but dreadfully dumb. Something must lie beneath this. . . . To the type also belong blue eyes, upturned noses, yellow hair, and big hands, people of boundless loyalty and unlimited naive trust."[53]

Family ties were universally agreed to be much stronger in the immigrant group than among Americans; some authors emphasized the greater respect of children toward their parents, some the higher authority of the father as family head, others the sacred nature of the marriage bond. Divorces were few indeed among the characters of this literature, and regarded with unqualified moral disapproval when they did occur. The Scandinavian was also a homebody, agreed these authors. The desire to own his own hearth was widely accounted as his strongest motive for emigration. The hospitality for which he was famous was always extended in his home, where he celebrated the most important events of his life and festivals of the year.[54]

Love of nature was often attributed to people coming from these beautiful northern lands, and innate interest in science and technology —an urge to find out how things work and why—that was recognized as akin to Yankee practical ingenuity. Adaptability was attributed to the group as a characteristic which helped explain their rapid Americanization.

A strong love of freedom was also counted among Scandinavian traits, stemming from the glorious tradition of the Vikings.[55] This was associated with a democratic egalitarianism which appeared in many a story, when characters preparing to emigrate expressed deep resentment at being looked down on as inferior beings in their homeland; they hated having to take off their hats to persons of authority. The absence of such traditional distinctions of class behavior was one of the things they most admired in America.[56]

No one who attempted to describe the characteristics of these Scandinavian immigrants failed to include their piety. For many authors, the Lutheran faith expressed in their own language was the most important part of their heritage:

> The God of our fathers,
> the teachings of the Bible
> the baptism of the soul and holy communion,
> the pure ore of our mother tongue,
> the annals of our church, Lutheran psalms. . . .[57]

This trait was undoubtedly closely related to the sense of honor and conscience mentioned above, for as Rølvaag pointed out, the relationship to God of the Norwegians (and other Scandinavians) was strongly personal.[58] It was always a matter of deity and the single individual; one was saved or damned alone, not in communities, and responsibility for the outcome rested only on oneself.

From this belief Rølvaag traced the seriousness, even moroseness of the Scandinavian character. This he personified in the wife, Beret, in *Giants in the Earth,* though he did not neglect to contrast it with the humor and bounce of her husband. Evidence of this sense of gloom turned up in the work of other authors as well. Waldemar Ager believed the disproportionately high percentage of insanity cases among Norwegian immigrants stemmed from this cause, for the trait was intensified in America. "Those who have traveled . . . among our people on the prairie have noticed that they are generally marked by melancholy. . . . There is little social life, and neither strong desire nor opportunity for amusement. . . . In this respect we stand almost alone among immigrant groups. The Irish brought their irrepressible humor with them . . . and the Germans and Danes their geniality and sociability. . . . We Norwegians (and perhaps the Swedes) often become introspective and despondent. It is possible that the prairie is partly to blame. We are basically a mountain people."[59]

Such a propensity toward introversion might well be related to reserve, and restraint of emotion. This trait appeared in many incidents of novels and short stories, often in contrast to the less phlegmatic behavior of the Irish and other groups. Men of a lumbering town in

Wisconsin, who had to leave their families for the winter's work in the forest, showed this characteristic. A wife was lucky to hear from her husband at all during the long winter, for there was no mail service, and the roads were often impassable. Usually news came only in case a lumberjack was brought home injured, seriously sick, or dead. When the hour of parting came, husband and wife only said goodbye, well yes, goodbye, God be with you and goodbye again.

Thus they could go on and on. The children were perhaps not mentioned, and man and wife did not so much as take one another by the hand; but there was deep pathos in the way they could never break off to part, and the way the one braced himself up so as not to weaken the courage of the other.
It was like going to war.[60]

An iron-bound, rock-grounded conservatism was another Scandinavian trait on which authors of all three nationalities agreed. On one hand, the immigrants had usually proved themselves the least conservative members of their communities by packing up and leaving; but on the other hand, perhaps because they had abandoned so much, they tended to cling the more to what little they had left, such as attitudes toward and feelings about morals, economics, and politics. An early Norwegian-American novel emphasized the traditional peasant suspicion toward change which Norse immigrants had brought to America.

Norse conservatism is as rigid, unelastic, and unyielding as the primeval granite which was the nation's cradle; therefore progress in Norway is rarely the result of individual growth, but rather the inevitable widening of the gulf which separates each new generation from the old. People with national traditions like these were already by nature molded in sympathy with the Puritanic spirit of the New World, and in a land where radicalism of all shades flourishes and liberty is apt to run riot, the Norse immigration furnishes the sort of ballast which we are especially in need of.[61]

Clannishness was a last general trait sometimes attributed to Scandinavian immigrants. As an aspect of group loyalty preservationists usually commended it, while assimilationists attacked it. In one novel a Norwegian leader started an English-language newspaper for his countrymen to help "break up the clannishness which they had inherited along with their blond hair, their blue eyes, and their stubborn self-dependence."[62]

The immigrant authors made almost no attempt to distinguish which of these traits were general European, which stemmed from agrarian social structure, and which may have arisen from given geographical, historical, and other conditions in the home country. These characteristics were considered transportable and transmissible entities which could be preserved or lost according to the will of the people eligible by inheritance to have them.

As for distinctions among the three related nationalities, the Swedes

101

professed that they were by far the most aristocratic-minded, the most impressed by titles; that they suffered from extreme jealousy of any of their number who managed to get his head above the others; and that they tended to covet strongly anything foreign and exotic to their own culture, to the extent of disdaining their own. The second trait was accredited with weakening their group loyalty, and the last with hastening their Americanization.[63]

Norwegians in a similarly self-critical mood were apt to point to their own belligerency and love of argument and contention which caused such bitter splits within their own Lutheran church. Some traced this trait back to the strong Norwegian sense of truth and individual freedom, so strong that no one who was sure he was right could compromise.[64] For reasons rooted in their own contemporary history, Norwegians were also the most nationalistic. They maintained enthusiastic celebration of their national day, the Seventeenth of May, wherever they came. Danes were only occasionally shown celebrating their comparable holiday, the Fifth of June, Swedes never—probably because they did not have a "Constitution Day" in the same sense. There were frequent references to political strife between Sweden and Norway under their common king in the Norwegian immigrant literature of the 1880s and 1890s. Independence won in 1905 was celebrated fully as warmly by Norwegians in America as at home—and the Swedes were fully as peeved.[65] Swedes, in fact, were apt to look upon their brother-folk as stiff-necked with the pride of poor relations, while the Norwegians considered Swedes haughty and arrogant. Marriage between representatives of the two groups in America was often commented on with surprise. In one story a pretty Norwegian girl flared up in anger when an Irishman called her a "nice svenska flicka. Nothing made her madder than to be called Swedish."[66]

Danes in America were the least nationalistic of the three groups. They were fewest both numerically and in proportion to the homeland population, and tended to settle in urban areas, where pressures toward Americanization were always strongest. Their national trait of modesty and unobtrusiveness, mentioned in many a story, probably influenced their stand. "We Danes are in our heart of hearts very sentimental, but we hide it bashfully in one way or another . . . at bottom we are a soft-hearted people, too shy to promote our independence as a national group over here."[67] In a Christmas annual one article claimed that "Possibly the Danes are of all nations the most cosmopolitan, the most sympathetic, and their sense of humor, their whimsy—which sees the comic even in tragedy—is a blessing in our modern world";[68] while another article in the same issue remarked that the inquisitive elf who in his own magnifying mirror saw the greatest man in the world was a better symbol of

102

Denmark than the hefty Valkyrie figure of Mother Denmark with banner and sheaf of grain. "The mixture of curiosity and unjustified self-importance which characterizes . . . the little elf is as typically Danish as the friendly, likable elf is himself arch-Danish."[69]

Most of the authors who attempted to analyze Scandinavian characteristics acknowledged that these included elements both good and bad, although they naturally emphasized the former. Sometimes less desirable traits were simply omitted from the definition, so that the national group sounded like a paragon of virtue; but as a rule such over-praise was viewed with a sardonic eye. A short story in a Swedish-American periodical portrayed a picnic at which the speaker "flattered us in the good old style, so we sat there and felt proud and lordly in our hearts that *we Swedes*—the best and honorablest and educatedest and intelligentest people on earth—carried the fate of America on our strong shoulders."[70]

Some Scandinavian vices flourished in the new environment, others withered; the trouble was that virtues often suffered the same fate. Preservationists were often concerned with the problem of how to discourage less desirable inherited traits while encouraging beneficial ones. It was the best of their heritage they always talked about saving, not necessarily the whole of it. The solution commonly given was expressed by the hero of a Danish-American novel who decided to found a private high school:

It cannot be denied that our old culture is in many ways pale and weak. It does not fit conditions here. It is too opposed to the fresh, strong American culture, which is, however, still rough at many points, not to say raw. It needs filing down, a thorough purification. . . .

But we people who have come here to stay, we must be so equipped that we are able to pick and choose. To fight the windmills of illusion, to try to cut ourselves off from everything American, is as stupid as it is impossible. And to throw away everything from home and give ourselves completely over to the alien and strange is out of the question too. There is a middle way. When we keep the best of our old Danish culture and at the same time understand how to assimilate the best of what is to be found here, then we will be able to carry out our role and exercise influence. Then we will have something to live on and to live for.[71]

Since the act of emigration had made members of this group into a minority cut off from their wonted institutions and methods of exercising influence, their leaders emphasized that group ends could be achieved only by individual actions; therefore they viewed personality traits as the most important aspect of their heritage.

c. *Group achievements*

Well before the Civil War, Scandinavians in America had created a considerable number of their own distinct local communities. The setting

103

of many tales showed that geographically delimited ethnic spheres did exist at given times in certain places, communities where practically all the inhabitants were immigrants from the same country (or the same province), where within the limits set by American law the first settlers could build their social life on European models. In one Danish colony, for instance, a young couple fell in love with the surroundings—the quiet woods, the lake with an island, all the people speaking Danish. The wife asked if they were really in Denmark or America, and an older settler told her just to wait until winter. When she saw people losing their frozen noses and ears right and left, she would be convinced this was genuine American cold![72] In other words, the weather was the only difference between this community and one in Denmark. The plot of this novel was based on conflict between two types of Danish Lutheranism, and could almost as well have taken place in Europe.

However, such spheres of a Scandinavian culture existed island-wise in pioneer times, and in rural communities only. The passing of the frontier invariably meant that the countryside filled up with other nationalities, and every improvement of communication with the rest of the nation weakened the Scandinavian aspects of local community life.

But as the ethnic exclusiveness of local settlements declined, nation-wide self-consciousness of the Scandinavian group was growing. By the 1880s these immigrants had a record to be proud of. During the Civil War separate Scandinavian regiments had fought bravely in Union armies, and were lauded to the skies in every Fourth of July address by one of their own nationality until the end of the century. They had done no small part of the pioneer drudgery of settling the Middle West; their speechmakers were fond of calculating how many thousand acres of virgin land they had broken, and how many cords of primeval forest they had cut down. They had founded innumerable churches and other religious organizations, denominational schools and colleges. They were printing scores of newspapers and magazines in their own languages, some with nationwide circulation. It was indeed a record of accomplishment to which politicians would point with respect when appealing to them as a voting group. Swedish and Norwegian Days at the Chicago Columbian Exposition of 1893 dramatized this self-approbation.

Events in the home countries, which most immigrants followed in their newspapers, caused immediate repercussions in the New World. Reports of crop failure and threatened famine at home brought sizable relief donations from countrymen in better circumstances in America. The long, bitter dispute between Norway and Sweden under their common monarchy affected these two immigrant groups in the United States, expressed not only in street brawls, angry speeches, and editorials, but in poetry and fiction. Norway's independence in 1905 caused an upsurge

104

of pride among immigrants from that nation, helping to produce a flowering of Norwegian-American culture between 1900 and the first World War. Many statues of famous Norwegians to be found in American cities date from this period.

Beginning in the seventies, tours made throughout the Scandinavian settlements by lecturers, musicians, and choirs from the home countries brought cultural interests and enthusiasms from Europe. Later, official visits of scions of the royal houses periodically fanned patriotic fervor. Organizations formed in the Old Countries to maintain ties of culture and friendship with emigrated brethren founded branches in America, and sent over publications and representatives.

The immigrant group itself founded early and continued to develop every possible type of organization based on ethnic origin: insurance and mutual aid societies, social and athletic clubs, dramatic, music, debating, and reading groups, hospitals, orphan asylums, old people's homes; historical associations and the American-Scandinavian Foundation; societies for the preservation of European culture, such as *Dania* and *Det Norske Selskab i Amerika*. Many of these appeared in the literature. If group identity can be measured by individual activities, this ethnic group could be quite satisfied with its image by the time of the first World War.

V. Immigrant Group Goals

The authors defined the ends of their group as first, to maintain its identity, and second, to contribute certain of its elements to American culture.

This literature provided overwhelming evidence that the Scandinavian group in the United States did succeed in establishing a way of life which was uniquely theirs, neither European nor American but composed of elements from both. Many first-generation immigrants, after years of trying in vain to become Americans, returned home only to discover they no longer belonged in the Old Country either. Second-generation characters who grew up in Scandinavian-American communities often found their only home in that hyphenated culture—or nowhere. One Swedish-American heroine, born and educated in the United States, was always looked on by her American neighbors as an immigrant and foreigner. In the course of the plot she married a Swede and went to live in Sweden, but discovered that there she was considered not a Swede and incapable of ever becoming one. She who was so fluent in the language found herself constantly mixing in Americanisms which bewildered her hearers, and she did not know which words were which.

Another character said of her, "Poor Petronella, like all others born in America of foreign parents, she was placed on the boundary between two worlds, uncertain as to which she belonged in spirit and soul."[73] She underwent the same experience in the Old World as immigrant parents in the New, when her children grew away from her into Swedish life. Finally the family returned to the United States.

Most authors agreed that their special culture in America could and should exist as long as the influx of immigration from the home countries continued. Some saw the main function of the hybrid communities as providing a transitional environment for the first and, to a lesser extent, the second generation, until the young people were prepared to draw wholly on American culture. A Danish speaker at a Fifth of June festival argued that the only remedy for immigrant homesickness was the creation of a little Denmark in America.

We shall not, as though we were a dead mass, let ourselves be poured into the Melting Pot, where all differences are destroyed, to be molded over into something else from what we are. Let time and the coming generations bring about unity, if they can, and let it happen in a natural way. But we who have migrated here, we are Danes, and we shall not delude ourselves that our mother tongue is too insignificant to sound here along with the English tongue. . . . Only by being our true selves can we become good American citizens.[74]

But there was marked disagreement over the question of whether or not the distinctive immigrant environment could be maintained after the renewing influx ended.

Naturally enough, the first generation wished to make and keep their new environment as much as possible like the old. They succeeded on occasion, only to find they had lost their own children in the process. In a Swedish-American play of 1919 a farmer explained to a visitor why the local Lutheran church was so poor. The old minister's goal had been to make their new settlement just like home in Sweden. He dreamed of the good old days he remembered from the Old Country, and made no effort to find out about conditions in the New World. He got what he wanted, but the younger generation did not care a fig about having two bells in the church tower, like in Sweden. And now most of the old folks who wanted everything Swedish lay in the graveyard, and most of the young people had gone their own ways.[75] A late (1945) Danish story showed how the leader of a Danish-American settlement learned the same lesson. Some Irish moved into the Danish town and built a Catholic church; his daughter almost broke his heart by marrying a Yankee. But he finally accepted the breakdown of his group, saying, "I don't know if there ever will be that good feeling of all belonging together in this country, as we felt it in the communities in Denmark.

But I have begun to see that we can't build a community if everyone stubbornly sticks to his own."[76]

The authors realized that any Scandinavian-American culture capable of surviving beyond the first generation had to be a hybrid affair. Whenever characters argued for trying to cut themselves completely off from American influences they were quickly refuted. The question was how and how long the composite culture could be maintained.

One school in all three national groups held that immigrants should be able to maintain their distinct form of life indefinitely, though they would have to continuously adapt it to changing conditions. A minister in a Danish-American novel compared America not to a melting pot but to a symphony orchestra, "where the different races and national types play their own special instruments, and where the tones some day will blend in a rich harmony."[77] The tones would merge, but not the instruments, so that America would become a land of cultural pluralism in which the English-speaking majority set the key and determined the dominant melody, while any number of minorities added their own variations.

Danish, Swedish, and Norwegian writers, however, tended to consider only their own fight to preserve their heritage, without extending the same argument to other national groups. In fact, they often looked down on other immigrants, especially those from Catholic lands. Swedish-American culture would disappear as a separate stream when immigration from Sweden ended, wrote one author; but Nordic personality traits, rightly evaluated, *could* be assimilated into the general American *Weltanschauung* and there do much to counteract what had been brought over by other nationalities intellectually inferior to the Swedes.[78]

VI. Attitudes toward American Culture

Attitudes toward American culture differed considerably among these authors. Those writing before the turn of the century often denied that the United States had a culture at all. An article printed in a Swedish-American newspaper of 1895 illustrated this reasoning: the United States is not a nation in the European sense. Politically, yes, but not culturally. We have no common type either physical or mental. Our official language is borrowed from England, our customs from all parts of Europe, our appearance reminds one of the whole world. Therefore, if we are told to Americanize ourselves, we can freely answer that there is no particular and characteristic American literature, language, art, customs, religion, or human type. And therefore each national group should preserve its own heritage, so that as a composite of many

107

cultures this may become the most cosmopolitan and highly civilized country in the world.[79]

Other authors in the same period drew an opposite conclusion from the same premises. American culture did not yet exist, but was in the making. When all the best elements brought by immigrants from many lands were melted down together, then a totally new compound would emerge. It was the duty of Scandinavians like others to donate the best they had to the United States in gratitude for all their new home had given them, even though they must disappear as a group in the process. These assimilationists argued that they could not make any contribution to American civilization without becoming an inseparable part of it; they must be satisfied to serve as stones in the foundation of the new nation, timber in the walls of a great new house, yeast to lift the whole bread dough—to cite some of their metaphors. An excellent late (1932) poem in Swedish summarized the viewpoint of the assimilationist:

> We come here:—a Babylon's confusion
> of different tongues, and no one understands
> the other's view of life and God and man.
> We live for years in the selfsame house,
> and remain strangers to one another still.
> No one shares the silent longing of our hearts.
>
> But there on the street our children shout,
> light and dark they make a motley train
> where their hands touch readily in their play.
> No one asks where their fathers first saw
> the light of day—near the Baltic tides,
> by the sands of the Volga or the Mediterranean.
>
> Thus they grow, and thus they blend their blood
> one day together. New generations are born.
> Only a second in time, no longer,
> we exist, who are poured into the cauldron
> that some day a unity may be smelted together.[80]

Many tales contrasted the attitudes of preservation versus assimilation among their characters, the authors weighing the scales in one direction or the other, but at least presenting both sides of the argument. Neighboring families might take opposing positions, one teaching the children Norwegian and keeping alive all possible traditions from the Old Country, the other speaking only English at home and adopting American ways as fast as these could be discovered.[81] Or the conflict took place in a local church, between those who wished to introduce sermons in English and American features like church suppers, and those who viewed such innovations as sacrilege.

Typical of the theoretical debate often introduced on such occasions

108

was that in a Danish-American novel of 1904, which put in opposing camps two well-educated friends, one a minister, the other a drifting dreamer who became a successful businessman. "Should all that the old nations have won of spiritual wealth through centuries of toil and struggle be used only as fertilizer for this new land's harvest of money and worldly gain?" the minister asked in the opening sally.

No and no again!—This land has a greater destiny than just to give us better food and clothing—and we have a greater task than to cultivate that kind of field.

We have the task, which is both a duty and an honor, of preserving all the best of what our homeland has given us: the golden language, the treasures of art, the philanthropic fruits of science, in order to impart them to our new fatherland to aid its moral edification and eternal progress.

But the minister's newly arrived friend listened more sympathetically to his opponents, who explained that this preservationist attitude had divided the Danish immigrants into two factions.

Our opposition party believes that we should shut ourselves off from everything non-Danish to preserve our distinctive characteristics as a nationality pure and undefiled:—I believe that leavening can do nothing unless it is kneaded into the dough and merges with it.

We *can* undoubtedly introduce worthwhile elements into the civilization of this country, but how, unless we ourselves are assimilated with it?—Spiritual values are universally human; they do not depend on certain languages.

And to this must be added that no one can be enough for himself alone. . . . We *must* have renewal—we cannot live on only memories; but where can it come from, if we shut ourselves off from the only living civilization that surrounds us, be it rich or poor—the American?

Step by step, Danish youth will be Americanized. It is useless to try to stop the process; what must rather be done is direct it, to make young people aware of what is worth adopting and what not;—but to live at enmity with the cultural life of the nation which has offered us hospitality shows neither wisdom nor gratitude and cannot be reconciled with our great purpose.[82]

Both sides thus agreed that as Danes they had a purpose, but they proposed—in the abstract—contrary means of achieving it. In the concrete plot of the novel, the hero did become a successful part of American society, without however contributing anything to its cultural life. On the contrary, in the end he returned to Denmark—to take back as much as he could of the dynamic business philosophy of the New World. Judging by the internal evidence of such books, it was easier for immigrant writers to talk about contributing the treasures of their heritage to America than to show it being done.

Authors who had less to say about direct improvement of American culture, on the other hand, and emphasized rather preservation of their birthright for their own benefit, were generally more successful in embodying the effects of their argument in characterization and plot. Rølvaag was the master here, portraying the day-by-day conflicts and misunderstandings that arose when a Norwegian Lutheran married an Irish Catholic. He prepared for the resultant tragedy so convincingly that the reader accepts what had been the Norwegian mother's warning: "We don't keep wheat and potatoes in the same bin."[83]

A Swedish-American tale showed the positive value of what ethnic identity could mean. In the 1850s, a Swedish girl had come to Kansas at the age of ten with her parents. Now she was over sixty, half-blind, prematurely aged by a lifetime of toil in the heart of a Swedish community. She had seen the barren prairie blossom into handsome farms; she had seen the congregation grow, the church built, its bell finally hung—the bell which had rung at the most solemn events of her life: confirmation, marriage, and her husband's funeral. Now as she lay dying on a Friday afternoon, she told the minister she wanted only to live until Sunday so that she could hear the church bell ring for the last time. The minister knew that she could not hold out that long, and rang the bell for her at five o'clock Saturday evening, in accord with the old Swedish custom of ringing in the sabbath eve at that hour. She died during the night in peace.[84]

Rølvaag also introduced more theoretical argument in favor of preserving the Norwegian heritage, through the mouthpiece of a new minister who traced the highly vaunted American institutions and tradition of freedom back through British history to the influence of the Viking invasions in England and Normandy. He pointed out that the Jews had preserved themselves as a distinctive race through all their migrations, and had been able to make their priceless contributions to world culture for that reason alone. Yet they were nonetheless good citizens. This should be the course of all nationalities in America.

One thing I see clearly: If this process of levelling down, of making everybody alike by blotting out all racial traits, is allowed to continue, America is doomed to become the most impoverished land spiritually on the face of the earth; out of our highly praised melting-pot will come a dull . . . smug complacency, barren of all creative thought and effort. Soon we will have reached the perfect democracy of barrenness. Gone will be the distinguishing traits given us by God; dead will be the hidden life of the heart which is nourished by tradition, the idioms of language, and our attitude to life. It is out of these elements that our character grows. I ask again, what will we have left?[85]

No counter-argument being provided, the minister won hands down —as Rølvaag allowed nothing good to come of the disastrous mismarriage in his plot. However, evidence that another outcome of such an alliance was possible was offered by other books in the same tradition. A serialized Norwegian-American novel from 1931-32 showed two successful marriages between Lutherans and Irish Catholics.[86]

Throughout the entire period of this literature, all authors recog-

110

nized many aspects of the life about them as distinctly American, whether they were willing to call the sum of these a culture or not. In many discussions of the problems of cultural transition, even the most conservative preservationists praised some American characteristics as distinctly preferable to the Scandinavian counterparts: admiration for honest labor, and judging an individual for what he does, not what he is; egalitarianism and lack of class distinctions; respect for and courtesy toward women; the economic opportunity which usually rewarded hard work; a certain youthful optimism, energy, attitude of never-say-die and the-sky's-the-limit that was in strong contrast to the closed society these immigrants had come from. Other elements in the United States were consistently criticized: materialism and ruthless competition for the almighty dollar; lack of respect for human life; business ethics which threatened to destroy standards of right and wrong; rootlessness, shallowness, lack of culture, and the eternal hustle and bustle that marked the American tempo of life. Whichever side of this scale of characteristics a given author judged to weigh heavier helped determine his attitude toward the forces and process of Americanization.

VII. Decline of the Preservationists

Through a half century of development this literature not only reflected the major changes of American economy—the closing of the frontier, declining economic opportunity, growth of big business, recurrent depressions—but also the massive solidification of American culture. As the twentieth century progressed, the diehard preservationists declined in number and strength. World War I dealt a terrible blow to their cause. Many stories recounted how a person who so much as spoke a few words in a foreign language was treated as a traitor. The excesses of jingoism produced their own reaction after the war; there was a short-lived revival of the hyphenated culture, as indicated by increased book publication by Danish- and Norwegian-Americans in the 1920s and the early 1930s, before all three Scandinavian immigrant cultures continued on their normal curves of decline.[87]

These changes were marked by the regret characters expressed for the good old frontier days when Norwegians were more pious and more Norwegian, and Swedes more hospitable and more *svensk;* by poems of sorrow over the inevitable disappearance of distinctive traditions, rather than militant calls to rally for their preservation; by significant modifications in the definition of the heritage to be saved. A Swedish-American short story from 1905, for example, was based on sanguine early hopes. Two third-generation immigrants met at a concert of the

Lund Student Choir at the St. Louis Fair on Sweden Day. The young man claimed to be Swedish-American because one of his grandfathers came from Sweden, and he had visited the country; but the girl, who knew the Old-World language, literature, and history, contradicted him.

He had often thought and talked about his Swedish extraction, had been proud of his descent from a people with a long, glorious history, and now a young girl suddenly let him know that he had no right to boast of his Swedish birth. He admitted to himself that she was right, that what he had been so pleased with before was dead capital, which for her had borne rich interest, and from which she would always profit.[88]

The two fell in love and married, but first the hero had to learn Swedish and study Swedish literature, so their home could be truly Swedish-American. The other, Irish part of the hero's parentage was only mentioned in passing and then ignored by all. By 1926, on the other hand, an author related approvingly his meeting with a young man of Swedish name who held a high post in a Chicago business house. When asked if he was Swedish, the man replied no, American, but he was descended from Swedish immigrants and proud of it. No mention of this man's knowledge of Swedish or of anything but his pride, but the author concluded that all Swedish immigrant children should be taught thus.[89]

Claims that there was no American civilization had disappeared by World War I; all recognized the mounting power of its pressures toward conformity. The argument between cultural pluralism and assimilation slowly shifted ground and turned into contention between assimilation —implying a positive influence on the emerging cultural compound— and Americanization, or disappearance into the overwhelming mass without a ripple.

Even among those who accepted Americanization as inevitable, there were considerable variations of attitude. A number of authors—mostly those writing in English—embraced the process without qualification. They portrayed first-generation immigrants as rightfully proud of every step made toward becoming Americans, whether they hated the Old Country that starved them out or loved the land of their birth. Or the parents strove to adopt American ways to keep up with their children, and the tragedy was that they could not. For the second generation was portrayed by most of these authors as American already, whether they retained any special feeling for their forefathers' homeland or not. Thus the first-generation hero of a Swedish-American novel in English learned the ways of his new country so rapidly that his fellow Swedes called him "Yankee Andreen." He took an American wife, and seldom indeed did he lapse into his native language, so long left behind. "Memories of it were like the last wisps of drifting smoke in the long wind of the prairie." In the whole Swedish Lutheran settlement, "The older people used the old language volubly, but admitted no reservations in their loyalty to their adopted country. The young folks, growing up in the public school environment, shed Swedish like an old coat, and thought only in terms of the new."[90] Yankee Andreen's son, when he went away to college, fought fellow students who teased him for being a Swede, and his American landlady had to comfort him by reminding him that all Americans were immigrants, and by awakening his pride and interest in the old Vikings.

A large number of tales portrayed their characters as indifferent to the issue of assimilation. They took the line of least resistance, which inevitably led them into rapid Americanization. Typical was a Danish-American short story about Jacob Johansen, who homesteaded in Montana, married a second-generation Danish wife, and became a rich cattleman, known as "Hardy Jim."

> Cultural interests? No, there was no time for such unnecessary luxuries. They took "Decorah-posten" and got a Danish-American almanac with stories in it each year at Christmastime. But there wasn't much Danish spoken in Hardy Jim's home. What—the children went to an American school, and Mette had been born in America—"the American language" should be good enough for them.
> The father of the house was indifferent. He thought it was the ladies' business, all that. They had more to do with emotions and suchlike.
> Of course it wasn't a matter of his having forgotten his mother tongue or being ashamed to speak Danish. When the Danish farmers gathered for a social evening once in a while—also at his own home—naturally he spoke Danish with the others and enjoyed hearing their old songs.[91]

The frequency of such descriptions of indifference was evidence that this was probably the most widespread attitude toward cultural acclimatization among the members of this immigrant group. Their major interests and efforts were shown directed on other levels toward quite different ends, to which cultural matters were irrelevant. Most authors, however, described this tendency of their countrymen only to attack it.

A third attitude among those who accepted the inevitability of Americanization was regret. A Swedish minister in a novel from 1925 told how he found responsive hearts among the older immigrants in the Middle West, but somehow could not reach the younger generation, "who cannot conceive or understand the trembling strings of emotion in their Swedish-born parents. I do not censure them for this state of affairs, in which the youth make use of their birthright in the land of the future, and undergo a process of amalgamation which is easy for them but painful indeed for the Swedish-born stock. . . . Many a time, standing in the pulpit before a church full of Sweden's sons and daughters, I felt a quiet sadness. 'A dying nation, offered on the altars of the future,' I thought, deeply moved. An emigrant remains always an emigrant, with his heart divided in two directions: towards his father-

113

land and his adoptive land. . . . In the next generation the transition is completed, and the Swedish element has died out forever."[92]

This regret over the inevitable, a common theme throughout the immigrant literature, was by no means limited to the later period. A poem published in 1900 expressed the feeling of a woman who continued to write in her native tongue although she knew she was doomed to a small and short-lived audience.

> You ask me, why we go on singing
> in our mother tongue at the prairie's rim,
> why not forget like those who come after
> that Sweden was our first fatherland? . . .
> Once abandoned, then first we see the value
> of our mother's language and our father's home.
> Longing is the love which sings in our songs,
> and memory colors softly our childhood's tale.
>
> Therefore we sing—however few who listen—
> our harp strings sound unheard, and die away.
> Soon, soon our song will be silent,
> the bard lie unhonored and forgotten.
> No matter! Let the water of oblivion flow over,
> Our dreams would still be luminous and glad. . . .
> Our songs relieve a little suffering and sorrow
> and waken hope and courage in a few hearts.[93]

Perhaps the most significant attitude toward Americanization was that expressed by characters who struggled against it, tried with all their conscious might to preserve their original cultural characteristics—in vain. The best books in this classification were written by Danes in the 1920s and 1930s, and all laid in cities. Enok Mortensen's two novels, *Saaledes blev jeg hjemløs* (Thus I Became Homeless) and its sequel, *Jeg vælger et land* (I Choose a Country), were built around this theme. The hero, Niels Nord, was the only son of landowners, and planned to come to America for three years and then return. Through a rich uncle in Chicago, Niels got a job in a factory and was introduced into the best Danish-American local society. In his *Wanderjahre* he learned about many sides of American life, meeting people who represented a wide range of experience: the rich and successful, the disappointed artist, the embittered radical, the suffering poor. He perceived that many immigrants had done poorly in America, in spite of their struggles, and even those who had done well were far from happy, living dull and colorless lives.

Yet, as he wandered about Chicago seeing both the ugly and the beautiful, slums and the sparkling lake, he felt himself drawn to it all. Time and again he tried to define this force of attraction, which was certainly more than the chase after dollars:

No, it was rather the adventurer's indomitable optimism and lust for life which still floated in the air, and hung a romantic veil over the materialistic and prosaic. There were still people who . . .believed in America as the Promised Land. There was still something young and untouched, which drew the wanderer. Longing still lived in people's souls, and it was longing which had made America![94]

So Niels found, when he went home to Denmark, that he was no longer satisfied there either. The different dining customs annoyed him, the slowness of the horses, Denmark's neutrality when World War I began. He found himself always looking for "News from America" in the newspaper, and discovered that he longed to return.

But you're mad! he reasoned [with himself]. . . . Now you have fallen into the same trap as all other emigrants. Your home is noplace, and you will always long for whatever seems distant and unattainable, whatever lies on the other side of the sea![95]

However, on reading Jacob Riis' autobiography, *How I Became an American,* Niels lost his doubt once more, and hurried back to his fiancée in America.

The sequel novel traced the renewed inner conflict in Niels' life when he settled down as a successful contractor in Chicago. Sparks of energy flew from him at his work; he loved to see walls rise, as he built for his home and family.

The future—yes, that was the great thing about America, which drew and bound all emigrants; even the poorest wretch here could dream of a bright future and win a man's strength with its golden promise. In the Old Country all was arranged and insured, no one went hungry or suffered need, few had too much and fewer too little. Sons walked in their fathers' tracks, but as a rule never went further. . . . Here in America was the opportunity, which always tempted and spurred on, always excited one's mind, always pushed with feverish tension.[96]

Yet he was periodically overwhelmed with homesickness for Denmark. He burned with the desire to preserve *danskhed,* enthusiastically joined a Danish lodge, but had to admit the justice of a friend's attack on it when the cynic asked how the lodge worked for the preservation of Danish culture.

Do they read a single book up there? Is a Danish song ever sung? Can one listen to an informative lecture? Or discussion? Politics and religion are forbidden topics, and what is left to discuss? At any rate, *they* have no idea of anything else . . . And their eternal sentimental fiddle-faddle about Denmark! . . . Good sandwiches and a cold mug in the shade of a beech tree—that's their dream of Denmark! Some of them are honest or naive enough to admit it, but most of them drivel at every opportunity about language and memories and Danish culture. Do they teach their children Danish, or do they—in spite of all their bombastic banquet speeches—keep the sluices open for new streams of impulse from home?[97]

In Niels' own family, his wife (a second generation Dane) agreed that they should try to preserve their Danish ways, but she constantly

115

forgot and spoke English with the children. After a church discussion, Niels was struck with how Americanized he had become himself. A new minister had been hired who spoke good English, and wanted to introduce English as the regular language of services. Niels was opposed, but made no protest. On the way home, "what filled his mind was more melancholy than anger. Was it then impossible to live as a Dane in America? . . . Couldn't even he live together with his own children in his mother tongue? Was there no such thing as a Danish-American, after all—beyond a single generation, and perhaps not even then?"[98]

Niels' character demanded harmony in his life, with his goal before his inner eye.

But when one was an emigrant—hadn't one given oneself over to laws which were greater than oneself? Hadn't one strayed from the familiar childhood swimming hole in the placid stream out into more dangerous waters, where the current and bottom were unknown and dangerous? Was there nothing to do but let oneself be carried by the tide, in the hope that everything would come out all right in the end?[99]

He finally had to give up trying to reason his way out of his endless homesickness for Denmark. The longing stayed with him like internal bleeding, which could suddenly start again at the slightest impulse—the few notes of a melody, a smell of damp earth. But he saw that his children were growing roots in America. His son would soon have forgotten all the Danish he ever knew; wasn't it the boy's right to live as an American? We must sacrifice, the minister had said. Life demands life. America had taken thousands into her embrace, hugged the pioneer to death, and in compensation had given his children prosperity and comfort. Was there no way around the sacrifice? What if he voluntarily laid himself, his past and his heritage, his language and his memories, on the altar of life? For his children's sake, and his own.

He decided to withdraw from the Danish lodge, quit going to the Danish church. After a time the minister called to ask why. Niels tried to explain:

"Homesickness is not bound to a certain person or anything concrete; it concerns the nonphysical, the untouchable, a mood, a smell, a melody, it is the sum of all longing for what is irretrievably lost—I don't know if you understand? And when a person is bedeviled by such a feeling, it's as though some disease were eating away his strength, shattering his soul, destroying his life; then there's only one thing to do, or shall we say two ways out: he can either return and live the rest of his life in the eternal unsatisfied search for the lost land of the past, or he can plunge himself into the life of the New World, cut all ties, forget the past, murder his memories, and then maybe, maybe—?"

"And you have chosen the last?"

"Not chosen," said Niels, "I have fought against it with every nerve, but something in me has driven me in that direction; perhaps it will succeed some day, I don't know."[100]

116

The struggle within him lasted out his story, through the failure of his business in the depression and his decision not to return to Denmark even then. The book ended with his hope that some day a new people and a new culture might arise in America, though he would not live to see it. "Here still lay the deep snows of winter, but spring was not far away. Then the sun would rise again over this land—his children's country, but also his own."[101]

Within the two major groups of immigrant authors, those who wished to preserve their Old-World culture and those who advocated abandoning it, there were thus a number of subdivisions. Among the preservationists who argued for cultural pluralism, a few hoped for awhile to keep their European heritage largely intact, while most saw that even as a distinct group they would have to adapt to American conditions—and then argued over how far they should go. They could not remain Danes or Swedes in America but had to become hyphenated citizens with one foot in each country. Some saw this as highly desirable, enriching individual personality with the best from two worlds; others felt it as tragic, dividing hearts and loyalties so that an immigrant became forever a stranger, never at home.

Some assimilationists sided with the preservationist school, arguing that they could contribute their ethnic virtues to the general American character only if they maintained them through several generations of distinctive group life; some assimilationists sided with the school of relinquishment, contending they must give up their European distinctiveness whether or not they proved able to influence American development, and without ever knowing which. Even those who advocated the throwing down of walls and casting away of baggage, who held that New World culture was or would become something entirely new, even those who accepted Americanization one hundred percent differed drastically in their attitudes toward the process. Some welcomed it, some regretted it, and some cared not at all.

These attitudes existed side by side without clear demarcation; sometimes a given author not only failed to distinguish between their variations but was not sure which he preferred. In other cases a writer changed his attitude toward the issue throughout a long life, giving up his effort to preserve the old and accepting Americanization as inevitable. None ever developed the other way.

This literature came into being when the flood of Scandinavian immigration and the development of exclusive settlements were at their height, and it looked as though both might continue forever. But many forces were gathering strength to cut them off: economic development in the home countries which brought population increase and possibilities of absorbing it into better balance; the closing of the frontier and decline of economic opportunity in the United States; improvement of transportation and communication to make the isolation of distinct groups extremely difficult; pressures of the developing American culture, expressed in institutions like the public school and in the myriad compulsions of job environment and neighborhood; ultimately, official immigration policy, which in the 1920s cut movement from Scandinavia to a mere trickle.

The literature reflected faithfully the declining hopes and activity of the hybrid culture which produced it. After World War I advocates of preservationism virtually disappeared—with the exception of a few undaunted leaders in the Norwegian camp who fought on until the day they died. These, like Rølvaag, were all late-come first-generation immigrants. After the 1930s, most of the literature which can be classified as belonging to this tradition was written by the second and third generations, almost all in English. The problem of cultural adjustment disappeared from these later works as an issue, as it had from the life of the group in fact. They were fully integrated Americans, and the few who preserved their language, studied their literature, made pilgrimages back to the Old Country, felt themselves none the less American for that. The immigrant should love his homeland as his mother, his adopted country as his bride, said a Swedish-American journalist often quoted by his countrymen,[102] but feelings toward a grandmother or great-grandmother had become too tenuous to occasion any comment at all.

Chapter Five
The Theme of Success

While arguments about the preservation of Old-World culture clashed above their heads, most immigrant characters in this literature led their daily lives concerned with more immediate and practical problems: how to find work, make money, win social betterment and success. All took for granted that to exploit the possibilities of the new environment they must enter its economic structure as individuals or separate families, not as an ethnic group. Only during early pioneering years were immigrants shown undertaking cooperation for mutual assistance in the wilderness—the period of "neighborliness" and "sharing" which inevitably passed, however much all deplored its end. Otherwise it was every man for himself in the economic sphere, where American requisites precluded all others.

I. Economic Betterment

1. FARMERS

The means by which most characters sought to achieve their goal of social betterment was in accord with their agrarian background: ownership of land. "It was hunger for land which drove the first and the most to America," wrote a major Norwegian-American author in 1914. "They threw themselves at the earth and slaved on it and never could get enough. The history of the first settlements shows how they rushed from place to place always looking for land, and when they had found some, they left it to look for something better."[1] Because strong expulsive forces in Scandinavia coincided with the opening of the midwestern frontier, a large majority of fictional accounts of immigrant experience dealt with farming people from Illinois to Dakota. Acquisition of free homesteads or cheap railroad land in this area did enable most Scandinavian farmers portrayed in the literature to achieve their major goal: improvement of their status and standard of living.

Typical of this large group was the dominant figure in a Norwegian-American novel, who wandered about his prosperous prairie farm one evening remembering the hopeless poverty of his family for generations back in Norway:

All this: heavy, fat horses, great barns, the bulging hayloft—peace, satisfaction based on enough food and enough power—this was the way he liked it. . . . And it was all his work and bore the mark of his hands. . . . His chest swelled, his beard bristled, his right hand clenched to a fist. For he remembered a boy who had stood beneath the moon and longed to get ahead and get out. . . . How he burned to get ahead and how he suffered torments because all roads were closed to him! . . . Every way he turned, the "better people" stood in his way. . . . Held down, he was. Nobody gave a damn for him. Didn't even look his way. Respected him no more than a worm in the mud. . . .

He would have liked to point to everything on his beautiful farm—at everything that was *his*—and read them a lecture . . . small landholder, big landholder, sheriff, bailiff, district judge, politician, and all the others who grew fat on the toil and simple-heartedness of ordinary folks—they would all have fallen to their knees before his wrath.[2]

In many tales this rags-to-riches theme formed the basic plot; in others it was the background against which a love story or a case of mistaken identity took place; sometimes the rise to economic security entailed moral decline, as the hero trampled all else underfoot in his rush to make his fortune. But most immigrant characters did get ahead, both because they worked so hard and because they benefited from the general increase in land values as the frontier was settled, railroads spread, and towns grew.

Those who acquired their own farms prospered most, especially when they had pioneered on a homestead. In giving them land, America had offered them their golden opportunity, and gratitude for this became a dominant theme in poems and fiction by immigrants of all three nationalities. A mother reminiscing for her daughter about the terrible hardship of pioneer days assured her there was nevertheless one great difference from the poverty the same people had suffered in the Old Country: "Cotters in Norway could never become anything else than cotters, they were condemned to be poor and oppressed for all time. But here they felt they were free. They had opportunity. And when you look at the many beautiful farms out here on the prairie today, then you realize they were right."[3] A Danish-American short story made the contrast concrete in the figure of an old father brought over to spend his last days with his daughter and her husband on their American farm. All his life he had loved to work with animals, but he had never owned so much as a pig back home. On the big American farm, his daughter's barns were full of horses and cows, fat pigs and chickens; and within two weeks he was a friend to every calf and chick on the place.[4] Time after time newly arrived characters remarked on the prosperous appearance of countrymen who had preceded them, or an author compared settled immigrants to their counterparts back home. Thus a

Swedish-American minister described solid citizens flocking to their prairie church: "If genuine Swedish eyes could have seen them in the churchyard that Sunday morning, they would certainly have taken them for gentlemen farmers instead of tillers of the soil; and yet they had all been cotters and small freeholders in the Old Country."[5]

2. WORKERS

Although immigrants who became landowners were generally credited with having done best in America, workingmen were also portrayed as better off in the New World than their countrymen back home—provided they would get jobs. Characters who compared living standards of workers in America and in the Old Country invariably concluded that the immigrants' were much better. A Swedish student who had come to the United States at the turn of the century to study home-ownership was impressed with how many workingmen owned their homes; they had saved the down payment and were allowed to pay the balance on time. An old friend he met assured him that life was much better for a worker in the New World because wages were higher, and a reliable workman could almost always save part of his income. "Here it really pays a manual laborer to work, but in Sweden he doesn't have very bright prospects."[6]

Above all, the workingman's social esteem was much higher in America than in Europe, both because physical labor was considered honorable and because the fluid class structure enabled him to move into the middle or business class without carrying along any stigma from his lower origin. Agricultural folk who won esteem through land ownership went through no reversal of values in the process; but ordinary workers were constantly surprised and gratified to discover that labor was not looked down on in America as it had been back home. A Danish story recording how a little seamstress made good with her own dressmaking shop concluded, "There could be no doubt that small virtues like cleverness, industriousness, and order were valued more highly in Milwaukee than in Nykøbing."[7] The poor-immigrant-makes-good plot appeared in stories about laboring class characters too, and many a ditchdigger or factory worker ended as the well-to-do owner of his own concern.[8] The authors regularly supplied their most successful business characters with a lucky break, in addition to their Ben Franklin virtues; but in the New World anyone might profit from a fortunate chance, not just members of privileged families.

Immigrants of the working class thus felt their position in America superior to that they had left behind because of their larger material rewards, the greater honor accorded honest labor, and the real possibility of moving into a higher class. The aim of social betterment held by both farmer and town-dweller was pictured in this literature as largely fulfilled, and immigrants from all three countries could join in praise of the land which had received them:

> Thank God that luckily you have escaped
> life in browbeaten, class-ridden Sweden!
> Here you easily can win your ambition's goal
> with an iron will and a steadfast soul.[9]

II. Social Advancement (Up from Peasantry)

1. FOOD

The theme of "up from peasantry" appeared in a multitude of forms throughout the literature. Class distinctions in the matter of food, for example, so marked in the Old Country in both kind and quantity, disappeared almost at once in America. Children of a party of Norwegian peasants tasted their first oranges in New York, and on the train west a mother was dumbfounded to learn that pigs were fed milk and corn in this Promised Land. Cornmeal porridge had been holiday food for her family at home, but here they soon got used to milk, pork, and wheat bread every day.[10]

Especially in books following pioneers to the midwestern frontier, the characters were pictured getting enough to satisfy their appetites to the full for the first time in their lives after their first (or second) harvest. At Christmas peasant children stuffed themselves on rich rice pudding and traditional cakes, many of which they had known only by hearsay back home. Typical was a Dane who had slaved for years on his plot in the Old Country without ever getting enough to eat; but after eleven years in the United States he carved his own huge turkey for Christmas dinner.[11]

Those who at least for a time maintained their food customs from Europe were thus soon able to eat like the gentry at home; while those who adopted American food found it much more varied and plentiful than they had ever known before, and as far as they could see prepared much the same way by all classes. No small number of immigrant daughters who hired out in Yankee families brought home methods of cooking and serving new foods which their mothers adopted. Inability to procure the ingredients was never mentioned, for food was cheaper in the New World in relation to both wages and the work required to produce it.

2. CLOTHING

Unqualified approval was accorded American clothing customs. Servant girls dressed as stylishly as their mistresses, and young factory hands

122

sported ties and polished shoes. Home in Norway a peasant girl who had attended a "folk high school" for a few months caused much unfavorable gossip when she returned home with her hair and clothes arranged in good taste and city style. "She even used a hat, which gave occasion for many jeering remarks from the local gossips; because it was regarded as a transgression for a woman to use a hat unless she had the rank of lady." This girl emigrated to Chicago, where the only job she could get was as a maid, although she had always refused to do such work at home. There was an essential difference in America, however, "because here at least one is paid well for one's efforts, and can live and dress decently without being forced to show an ancient family tree of nobility or gentry for the privilege."[12]

Until late in the nineteenth century, so sudden a change in clothing habits was limited to characters who went to town or city environments, or who came in contact with Yankees. In isolated settlements during the poverty-stricken early years, immigrants wore out the clothes they had brought along because they could afford no others, and it made no difference where all did the same. Even at Sunday gatherings, "Both men's and women's clothing was shabby, for the most part 'America-chest' clothes many years old, which had been brought from the fatherland. Some of the men had made no effort to dress up, perhaps because their 'America-chest' suits were completely worn out, perhaps from indifference. They wore their 'overalls,' as they were called, the usual brown or blue American work clothing."[13] One midwestern Swede wrote back to friends planning emigration that they should plan on working on a farm first, for there they could wear out their Old-Country clothes unnoticed.[14]

As soon as immigrants came in contact with other Americans, however, they felt the need of adopting the others' style of dress. "The vivid colors of national costume are gradually toned down to a demure soberness, and soon utterly vanish. There were no silver brooches of elaborately fantastic design, no scarlet bodices, no red-peaked caps to be seen in Hardanger [U.S.A.]. The immigrant instinctively felt that these picturesque details of dress alienated him from his fellow-men, and who, with all the pride of nationality, wishes forever to remain a stranger?"[15]

Those who remained more isolated, especially farm women, retained their old-fashioned styles longer. In several stories the husband, who had more contact with the surrounding society, adopted American suits, while his wife contained to wear her conservative dresses and peasant scarfs. But even the most remote modified their clothing habits as their isolation ended. "The heavy woolen plaid dresses of the women were gradually changed to American calico dresses. Instead of a colored kerchief tied over their heads they wore sunbonnets on week days and

123

shakers on Sunday."[16] Indeed, sometimes the husband thought the transformation too fast. "Mama's clothes changed also through the years, and instead of long, high-necked dresses she took to low-cut, transparent shirtwaists and skirts that ended nearly a foot from the ground."[17]

By the last decade or two of the century, it was commonplace for characters to remark how they could not tell from a person's clothing or manners what work he did or where he ranked in the social scale. Only an occasional upper-class figure reacted against this situation, as a newly arrived Danish character admitted he had not liked the young Danes he had seen because of their loud clothes and free ways. "Were these stylish gentlemen of fashion and decked-out young ladies really ordinary fellow-countrymen of the laboring class? Didn't they have tact enough to dress in accord with their position?"[18] Long before the end of the book, however, this aristocrat too was weaned from such Old-World prejudices. The authors of this literature unanimously approved of the disappearance of European class distinctions in clothing, as proof of social equality in the New World.

3. SOCIAL CUSTOMS

Customs of social intercourse likewise changed rapidly and drastically in the direction of equalitarianism. Former peasants abandoned behavioral distinctions both toward superiors and toward equals in a general levelling informality that was typically American.

Most marked was the almost universal use of the familiar second-person pronoun rather than the polite one even to strangers in Scandinavian immigrant speech, to be found in the direct discourse of all the books. Many an author took the practice as much for granted as his characters and made no comment; but sometimes a newcomer reacted with surprise or was even offended when addressed at sight with "du." Those writers who called attention to the matter always explained it as the custom of the new country, evidence of the informality and friendliness of American life. In a Danish-American tale, a young man who met a family of fellow immigrants out walking immediately addressed the mother as "du." She not only approved, but advised him "to put away all such formal language, we have no use for it here in America. A few places in cities Danes still use it, but for us who were born over here it sounds silly. . . . For my part, I think it sounds as though one were saying: 'Keep away from me'!"[19]

Characters in a Norwegian-American novel discussed the origin of this language custom: One pointed out that peasants in the Old Country used only "du" for "you" in their dialects, addressing superiors not with the formal "you" ("De") but in the third person; naturally they carried this usage with them, but soon dropped the stiff formality of third-person direct address. On the other hand, upper-class Norwegians spoke the official or city language in which the polite "De" was the normal form; but there were so few of them in America that they followed the custom of the peasant majority. Another character pointed out how much "du" sounds like "you"; immigrants might be mixing the two languages here.[20] Whatever the cause, the phenomenon was universal within the immigrant group, and sooner or later even those upper-class characters who were initially offended by the practice adopted it in self-defense.

However, another Old-Country linguistic custom was recorded continuing in several immigrant communities: use of a descriptive prefix attached to a person's given or family name. A book in English describing the life of Swedes in a Michigan mining town mentioned Mrs. Gråt-Peterson, who cried so much for her dead children that her weeping became an appellative, and Mmes Värmlands-Larson and Skånings-Anderson, whose provinces of birth had obviously been added to their names to help keep them apart from others with the same surname.[21] These prefixes were not used in direct address, but in reference to the persons when they were absent.

Polite customs showing deference to superiors by a curtsy, a bow, removing the hat, likewise measured degree of Americanization when described in this literature. Long-lasting survival of such behavior was recorded exclusively in closed communities, and mainly towards ministers. In a Norwegian-American story laid so late that the minister arrived at the church in a Ford, the men still took off their hats when he drove up.[22] Even in an urban colony, a woman was described curtsying as she backed out of the presence of her minister—although she had just withdrawn her church membership in anger.[23] The most effective contrast between Old- and New-World customs of behavior toward superiors was given in stories where an emigrant returned to his home country after having lived some years across the Atlantic. A Norwegian novelist best described this contrast in a classic scene:

Outside the church next day the returned American, Erik Foss, had gathered a little crowd around him. . . . The newcomer was tall and fair, with a brown mustache; and he wore, like the gentle-folks, a collar and tie, a brown frock-coat, and a top hat and shiny boots. But you could see from his hands that he knew what work meant. Seven years he'd been out there; and though he was only the son of Scraggy Olina, he was a big man now. . . .

He was quite the center of attraction today; when the clergyman appeared, the hats did not fly off so quickly as usual. Erik Foss had just been saying that there were no class distinctions in America; a laborer or a parson—one was just as good as the other. His audience could hardly believe their ears. They looked round at Brandt from Lindegaard,—who was so much finer than the other folks that he had to have a special pew with a gilded grille, like a little private paradise, at one side of the church—and they looked at the sheriff, taking off their hats as in duty bound, but all thinking: America . . . no class distinctions . . . just think of that! Then they saw the Colonel from Dyrendal coming; and he was the greatest man of the lot, so they had to make way for him. Hats off, hats off! But strange to say, Erik Foss took no notice of any of these great personages. "Why don't you take off your hat?" one man asked in scandalized tone. "I only take it off to people I know," answered Erik. Ah, it was all very well for an American to talk like that! Then something singular happened. The colonel stopped, looked across at the stranger, and went right up to him in the sight of everybody! The others all stepped back, leaving a clear space around the two men.

"You've just come home from America, haven't you?" the Colonel asked. (Mercy on us! he was talking to Scraggy Olina's son as politely as if he had been at least a captain!) [Including, in the Norwegian original, the polite form for "you."]

"That's right," said Erik; he had raised his hat slightly when the Colonel addressed him, but had put it on again at once, and now he stood there looking quite as tall and composed as the other. The bystanders heard the Colonel say: "It would interest me to hear a little about the conditions over there. If you can spare the time, you might look in one day at my place."

"Certainly I will," answered Erik Foss, in the tone of one doing a service to an equal.

Then the colonel passed on into the church, but the others quite forgot to follow as long as Erik Foss remained standing there. Who would have thought it! When he left the country he was only a young good-for-nothing, one of Scraggy Olina's mongrel brats. And now America had sent him back again as the equal of the Colonel at Dyrendal.[24]

Even when such gestures were acts of politeness to equals, rather than deference to superiors, characters came to realize that they revealed non-American origin. A Danish newcomer out hunting on the prairie one day met a girl who said hello in English. He lifted his hat as he replied in the same language, and she immediately switched to Danish. The newcomer felt that she was amused at his gesture. "He would have to break himself of that habit of lifting his hat. It wasn't American."[25]

American pressure toward greater simplicity and familiarity in customs of social intercourse was shown successfully overcoming more elaborate European courtesies at every point of contact. Many stories portrayed a newcomer invited to table by an earlier-arrived countryman, when the guest went hungry because he could not respond to the informal American invitation to "help yourself." Back home, a hostess was supposed to urge food on a guest many times before he accepted; to reach or ask for something he wanted would show the worst possible manners. In exclusive settlements where immigrants had little opportunity of observing American ways, old patterns were continued: "When all had eaten and been satisfied—they had been urged again and again, of course, for good old Custom's sake—the fun began."[26] But everywhere that Scandinavians had been in contact with Yankees, newcomers immediately noticed the absence of many other habits they were conditioned to regard as signs of good breeding. Host and hostess often began to

126

eat at once, for instance, finished and left the table before the guest had well started; even hired men got up and went out one by one as soon as they finished eating, instead of waiting to be dismissed all at once by their employer—who would not have sat at the same table with them either, in the Old Country.[27] No one said *"Vær så god"* when he offered something to somebody, as he should according to Scandinavian custom, and no one thanked the hostess for the meal when he left the table. An amusing poem addressed to Danish-American children admonished them that they could say *"Tak for maden"* ("Thanks for the food") on the way out if they were quick enough.[28]

This poet regretted the disappearance of such Old-World customs of courtesy, but most immigrants cheerfully accepted the simpler ways of Americans. Thus a young minister direct from Denmark, who offended some of his parishioners with his European manners, tried hard to change:

Pastor Kampmann used the formal second-person pronoun to everybody; he lifted his stiff hat punctiliously every time he greeted a person, and bowed politely when he shook hands in saying good-day and farewell! People do such mechanically in Denmark,—but the Danish-Americans in Peace Plain, as in most other places in the New World, had long since put such "antics" aside—, and now there were some who even were embarrassed by them. Others naturally said the familiar pronoun to the minister, and took for granted that in Rome *he* would have to do as the Romans did.[29]

4. ATTITUDES TOWARD THE UPPER CLASS

Attitudes toward compatriots who had belonged to the upper class back home were somewhat mixed. The dominant sentiment was disapproval toward aristocrats. A "better" Swede newly arrived in America, for instance, was wounded by the unfriendliness of his fellow-countrymen when he applied to them for aid.

He had no idea it was the class he came from which people wanted revenge on, in his person. . . . He came of "better people," he belonged to the more fortunately situated class which never did anything but oppress the laborer. . . .
Now they would repay with interest everything that they had suffered, all that their class had suffered. Now they would exact revenge.[30]

General suspicion toward upper-class immigrants was shown to be well-founded on other grounds as well. People awarded social privilege by birth seldom leave it unless they are driven to by disgrace or wrongdoing. This was almost universally the case with the better-class emigrants in this literature, who often hesitated to leave their homeland because they realized that their departure would be judged as a sign of guilt. "Meinhart didn't think much of America, it was only people who had 'done something' who went there," a Danish-American tale related;[31]

127

but this character was so sure his superior background would enable him to take advantage of the simple folk who were his countrymen "over there" that he just deserted his little store with its load of debts, and removed self and family across the sea. An occasional exception to this rule was introduced as such: "Henrik Krog had taken his legal degree with honors and owned a nice little fortune. And nevertheless he went to America."[32]

The general run of working-class immigrant also looked upon his countryman from a higher level with a suspicious eye because he knew that the well-born were unfit for the hard physical labor required of newcomers. A Danish uncle, for instance, was disgruntled when he discovered that his newly arrived nephew had taken a university degree; a student wouldn't be any good on the farm! But this boy had been forced to study by his father, who wanted a parish clerk in the family; and the young man had emigrated to avoid such a job, preferring work in the open air. Now he studied agricultural implements inside and out, and soon made an excellent farm worker.[33]

Higher-class characters who could not adjust to physical labor consistently came to grief in America. An aristocratic Norwegian businessman who emigrated because he had gone bankrupt found it not so easy to get ahead in the United States as he had thought.

His culture and talent were not appreciated at all. One asked only: "Can you work?" but Mr. Holm could not. What little business ability he had was of no use whatever, since he did not know English. . . . He lacked the capital to start a business for himself. . . . He had only the choice between physical labor or a saloon.[34]

Most of the drunks, panhandlers, and bums in the literature, in fact, had been "better people" in the Old Country. Like the young man in a cheap flophouse in Chicago, whose name was that of a leading scholar in Denmark. Yes, this was his son. He had joined the professional army against his father's will, had been dishonorably discharged after a fight with a superior, and of course was sent to America. "Sent to America! The Lieutenant, who had never had a worktool in his hand!"[35] Naturally he failed, tried many jobs but always failed, until at last he could not get any work at all, wandered about the streets, caught pneumonia, and died in the arms of the Danish minister who related his sad story.

Upper-class immigrants who succeeded did so not because but in spite of their privileged background. In one tale, the only daughter of a rich Swedish-American factory owner was courted by two Swedish noblemen. One had neither money nor a job but thought his title should win him the girl hands down. He was shown the door in short order. The daughter warned the other to get a job in her father's factory under an assumed name. She would wait for him if he proved he could do honorable work. "If you only sweep floors to begin with, I'll still respect that more than your title, because I'm a real Swedish-American, you see. But don't tell papa you're a nobleman, because he'd run you out."[36] The theme of several novels was how the trial by fire they met in the New World made men out of spoiled, incapable upper-class individuals. Then, of course, they earned the respect of their fellow immigrants on the basis of their achievement—and American won out over European standards here too.

Although generally disapproving of aristocrats, occasionally characters expressed a sneaking admiration for the well-born none the less. The daughter of a rich landowner in Norway, now in financial difficulties, turned up at a prairie settlement. In his heyday her father had been one of the worst oppressors of the poor, but now his former cotters vied with each other in offering his daughter hospitality. The son of one family decided to court the young lady, to his parents' delight. "In spite of their apparent contempt for the 'better people' in their home valley, the parents thought this was a marvelous opportunity to establish a relationship with one of its leading families. It was an old dream which could be fulfilled."[37] Many stories showed former servants and cotters now established in their new homes, extending all kinds of assistance to later arriving relatives of their former masters. Not only did ties of personal acquaintanceship outweigh abstract hostility toward a class, but also there was considerable pride and self-justification in seeing the tables turned. Being able to play the benefactor to one's former superior was proof that an important aim in emigration had been fulfilled. It was also a boost to one's self-esteem to associate in America with better-born countrymen than one could have met as equals back home. "Isn't it wonderful that these well-educated fine folks will drink a toast of friendship with us, who never learned anything but common labor?"[38]

Despite abstract enmity toward the upper class, most marked in rural settlements, many stories recorded that individuals with better breeding and education in the Old Country usually became social and cultural leaders of the groups they settled in, even if their stay was only temporary. Reporters and editors of Scandinavian immigrant newspapers were usually described as having been educated in Europe; until late in the century many Swedish and Norwegian ministers had been ordained in the Old Country; and several tales focusing on upper-class individuals among the crowds departing from the homeland recorded that they were looked up to in envy for their fine manners and social aplomb. "Such folk become the notabilities of the emigrating party, as they later often become leaders of Norwegian society in cities over here."[39] Only rarely did these city-bred individuals turn up in rural communities, however.

129

There the local minister as a rule remained the sole representative of higher education and culture, as he had often been back home.

5. ATTITUDES TOWARD MINISTERS

Clergymen were unanimously regarded as belonging to a special category within the upper class. In the Old Country they partook of all the characteristics of the privileged group. They were important government officials, held considerable power over their parishioners at crucial points in their lives, were usually the most highly educated men of the community, and as a rule lived, if not in luxury, at least in much greater comfort than their underlings.[40] Considerable resentment against the local Lutheran minister was expressed both directly and indirectly by a number of characters before emigration. A Norwegian peasant, for instance, rushed home from church after the first time he had ever talked with a returned American, and when his wife finally made out what he was so excited about, she asked if the minister had preached about America. "Oh, no, far from it," the man replied, "the minister and the other swells take care not to mention America or anything else that could help a poor wretch out. They want to keep us here to slave for them."[41]

On the American frontier, however, veneration to the point of obsequiousness was the normal attitude toward the clergy. Every first visit of a Lutheran minister to a Scandinavian settlement was greeted as the most important event in its history. The best the settlement had to offer was freely given him. The most affluent family was chosen by unanimous consent to be his host; the best food they had was pressed on him; the best bed in the house was his; linen still packed in the emigrant chest was brought out for him to use. Yet there was an essential difference in the honor thus freely accorded him from that which had been his due back home. There he belonged to the upper class whose power and privilege had been bitterly resented; here, although much of the prestige of his former position lingered about his person, it was recognized on both sides that he was only the man of God.

As a rule the minister was paid such great deference only in the early settlements, while he was still a guest; and even then he was shown to be aware of his changed relationship to his flock by the way he treated these humble people. To their surprise, even embarrassment, he treated them as social equals. "She grew more and more amazed. She would have liked to see the minister back home offered a slice of bread spread with cream and then talking with a common peasant wife as though they were equals."[42] When a congregation had been formed, however, and a minister hired at a wage the church members paid, then they

130

developed quite a different attitude—another measure of their Americanization. He became neither their master nor their guest, but their servant. An early (1879) Norwegian-American novel, for instance, showed the heroine's dismay when the local Lutheran minister began to attack the community leader.

To her, the minister before the altar or in the pulpit was quite a different being from the minister in private life. . . . She was not American enough yet . . . to look upon the church as an institution which stood in need of her patronage and support, and the minister as a prosy or interesting fellow-mortal toward whose salary she had paid her share, and whom she had, therefore, the privilege to censure and to inflict herself upon, at pleasure.[43]

Several books recorded that the most devout faction among the immigrants long continued in most humble respect toward ministers. Reminiscences of a Dakota childhood published in 1954 recalled a Norwegian grandmother's "devotion to the clergy" and "obsequious politeness to the cloth." "The minister was universally believed in small Lutheran communities to be the vessel of all knowledge, both secular and religious. The problems inherent in the sale of a farm, the courtship of one's oldest daughter, the flirtatious smile of a wife—all could be brought to the door of the parsonage."[44] Many clergymen won such devotion from all factions in their congregations by selfless dedication and service, but in these cases the basis of the esteem accorded them had changed. In America they earned respect as individuals, whereas in the Old World it had followed automatically from their rank.

The dominant attitude among laymen came to be that a clergyman was no better than other people. This conviction was shown in a variety of ways. It was consistently expressed by emigrants who returned to the home country, often being used as culminating evidence of the social equality of the New World. Newcomers who tended to bow and scrape before a minister in America as at home were admonished not to do so. When former peasants saw their own sons ordained, they could no longer believe that clerical garb made a man a different sort of being. The later literature bristled with examples of men of the cloth subjected to mortifying gossip and criticism.

It was simply impossible for them to distinguish between Eckman the clergyman and Eckman the human being. If he laughed like other people, then the minister was worldly and lax. If he joked and was witty, then the pastor was frivolous. If he played croquet or ball with the young people, then Pastor Eckman was setting a bad example for the young. . . .[45]

In America, the fact that many men of God both could and did undertake practical physical labor marked an essential difference from their position in the Old World. A newcomer was dumbfounded at finding

131

a Lutheran bishop out haying in the fields, for instance, while his wife washed dishes in the kitchen.[46]

Yet a certain ambiguity toward clergy resulted from the survival of old attitudes in a new setting. In a Danish-American novel the ambiguity was well illustrated in the attitudes of marriageable girls toward the bachelor minister. One he courted refused him, to her mother's horror, for the young lady already had a sweetheart; but many others wanted dreadfully to marry him. "For although everyone agreed that a clergyman wasn't worth a crumb more than anyone else, still the idea haunted many a little maiden's head that to be a minister's wife was an uncommon honor, which befell only a few."[47] Marriage to a pastor was time after time portrayed as the highest distinction a girl could aspire to. Regardless of the social level she came from, she was lifted to her husband's rank and maintained a special status, like him, in spite of all the menial toil and even poverty she might be called upon to undergo. For it was not easy to be a parson's wife in the United States, several stories pointed out: "the servant of all, without the economic means to hire help."[48]

Within their special status, both clergymen and their wives felt subtle distinctions made according to their level of origin. "Norwegian farmers as a rule differentiate between what comes to them from their own kind and what comes down to them from a higher, more aristocratic sphere," wrote an immigrant novelist. "If the minister has taken his wife from their own level, she can win both their affection and respect, but she usually becomes 'prestekonen.' If she is from a higher class, however, she immediately becomes 'prestefrua.' "[49] (The two different terms for "minister's wife" have about the same connotations as "woman" and "lady.") Several stories related the trials of clergymen's wives who were "ladies." "The parson's cultured little wife strove hard not to give offense with her refined manners, for there were a few formidable dames among the women of the church who gave her to understand that in this country all are just 'common people.' "[50] She was finally accepted by the community when she presented her husband with a twelve-pound son—when she surpassed the other women as a woman, in other words, not in social class or breeding.

In matters of social prestige ministers and their wives were required not to feel themselves any better than their parishioners; this attitude appears to have been adopted by members of the immigrant group from their American surroundings. The feeling of equality between religious leader and church members no doubt made possible "the intimate affectionate relationship which as a rule is to be found between minister and congregation in America."[51] Yet because the clergyman maintained his position as community leader, those who associated with him

132

as social equals deemed themselves elevated in standing by the relationship. Thus the continuing ambiguity in attitude toward the local pastor which was recorded in many immigrant tales, lasting at least as long as the Scandinavian language.

III. Social Classes in America

The stand of many authors on the matter of class structure was equivocal also. Their characters unanimously rejected the rigid class system of the Old World, and praised the United States for its social equality. Yet social rank was absent only in the early years of pioneer settlements. A Danish-American author reminisced,

Old folks often say now that when they were young, people helped each other much more than nowadays. There were no class distinctions. Now, of course, there are rich and poor;—back then they were all poor, and therefore all equally rich. . . . It was natural for them to help each other.[52]

The main theme of several novels tracing development in a Scandinavian community from pioneer to settled times was just this transition from mutual poverty to different degrees of wealth.[53] All improved their standing, but some gained more than others. By the time the second generation reached maturity, this differentiation in wealth had produced class distinctions which were taken for granted at the same time that many characters denied their existence. For instance, a Norwegian-American salesman who was an enthusiastic Mason declaimed to a newcomer, "Yes, that's the great thing about these lodge dances. Genuine American democracy. All are brothers, from the boss of one of the biggest factories in town down to the lowest common worker—no, that's right, here in America nobody is common."[54] He insisted that the hero could even marry the boss's daughter; nothing was impossible in America. But the greenhorn realized that all was not such golden opportunity as his friend claimed. The time was already past when most rich men worked themselves up from the bottom.

Classes did exist everywhere except in the most primitive pioneering years. In a prairie farming community, the son of a poor Norwegian farmer despaired in his love for the daughter of a rich one;[55] in a Dakota town clear lines were drawn between the leading businessmen and their families, respectable workers of one kind or another, and the town drunkards and their charwomen wives;[56] in a small city children dismissed from school disappeared into their homes—the wealthy up the hill, slum children beside the river, middle class in between.[57] In Minneapolis and Chicago immigrants moved from multiple-family semi-slum dwellings

133

to ramshackle wooden houses in workingmen's neighborhoods, from there to middle-class districts with lawns and bathrooms,[58] and once in a while an immigrant tycoon achieved a stone palace on the lakefront;[59] second-generation Norwegian young people with a high-school education and white-collar aspirations were shown feeling superior to and holding themselves aloof from newcomers of the same age from the same country, who were limited to manual labor but made much more money at it.[60] Country people were portrayed feeling embarrassed and awkward in confrontation with people from town.[61]

Occasionally European class pride was transplanted to the new setting too, as in the tale of a Norwegian from a remote valley who came to relatives in Minneapolis. Because his father had assisted in the church service held once every other month back home, he was used to holding himself a little above the common herd. Therefore he chose a boarding-house which was not connected with a saloon, and even attended an evening concert or lecture once in a while. When a girl he grew interested in turned out to be the daughter of a member of the Norwegian parliament, he was delighted—good enough even for him! They were happily married over forty years.[62]

All class distinctions mentioned here were made within one and the same national group as it was distributed along the scale of American society, but they were vastly complicated by differences felt in comparison with other immigrant groups and native Americans on the same economic level. Irish and Swedish workmen formed rival, hostile gangs.[63] A successful Norwegian-American businessman discovered that his economic equals from other groups were glad enough to do business with him during office hours, but would have nothing to do with him socially.[64] Indeed, class lines and distinctions were everywhere.

The immigrant characters made clear, however, that they found the American class structure quite different from the one they had left behind. In person-to-person contact between superior and inferior there was neither overbearance nor subservience. A Danish upper-class immigrant was struck—at first unpleasantly—by how the behavior of his fellow countrymen lacked the timorous servility he was used to meeting in the "underclass" at home. "They seemed to want to revenge themselves by showing affrontery towards his education and descent."[65] The majority who came from the lower class, on the other hand, were delighted at how well their superiors treated them—hired men and girls who ate with the family, lowly employees spoken to as equals by the big boss. A Danish-American businessman on an automobile tour saw the spirit of America exemplified in an incident when a Rolls Royce stopped to help him with a puncture. Both the millionaire and his chauffeur climbed out, rolled up their sleeves, and got their hands dirty. He praised "this fresh, natural *helpfulness* of Americans, who were so happily free from sulkiness and snobbish class feelings."[66]

Furthermore, the social classification these immigrants attained was accorded on the basis of their achievement, measured in external and largely materialistic terms. There were exceptions, men who sought to earn their status through service as clergymen, doctors, teachers; but most of the characters in this literature believed—and many experienced —that if they only worked hard enough, and got a few lucky breaks, they could be able to acquire whatever property was necessary to improve their social standing indefinitely. In a Danish-American short story, a justice of the peace planned to take to wife a lovely immigrant girl whose family had the worst possible reputation in the Old Country. An enemy tried to spread evil rumors about her mother, but the judge took it calmly, saying to the local doctor's wife:

"Strange that nobody has asked about *my* origin; my mother was a dairymaid. I never knew my father, and I grew up as a ragamuffin and beggar. It's really this which is so incredible in America, that one can put one's ability to use—if one has any. And by the way, I seem to remember that your own husband, the doctor, has said that his father was a poor cotter, and that he ran around as a barefoot herdsboy. . . ."

"But my dear sir! You're reducing us all to paupers!"

"No, our parents were; we're not paupers—far from it—I'm about to build a house costing 6000 dollars."[67]

Finally, the fluidity of American class structure was seen and recorded by all. Scandinavian immigrants tried not to escape from a stratified society but only to move upward in it. A recurrent theme in many stories was the comparative speed and ease with which such advance could be achieved. A young Swede, who had taken a job as office boy in a musical instrument store, soon found himself a much better post as a laboratory technician. "This was absolutely unheard of! One day an office boy, the next chemist for a large gas company. Such a change would have been completely impossible in Sweden. Once an office boy, advancement higher than to janitor would not have been worth considering."[68]

Movement in the opposite direction was not accompanied by the same loss of prestige as in Europe, either. A Dane who had worked himself up to a good position in a lumber company observed the bankruptcy of a big rival company. The following day, the bankrupt owner turned up working as a lumber-grader in the competing firm.

Høg had to smile. *That* certainly could be called American—one day owner of the largest lumber company in town, the next off with your jacket to go to work on the other side of the street! . . . "I take my hat off to *that,* Mr. Knox," exclaimed Høg. . . .

"Don't people do the same in your country?" the other asked.

135

"Certainly not very often;—if things go wrong, people just leave the whole mess and come over to you," muttered Høg.[69]

A Norwegian named Peter Smith (at home he had been Per Smie-haugen) summed up the universal immigrant attitude when he urged a later comer to Americanize his name. The latter argued that he was on the lowest rung of society and would remain so regardless of how he doctored up his name. "To heck with the levels of society!" Peter Smith burst out. "It was home in the Old Country that the levels were kept so completely apart. Here the main thing is just to push upward, the whole ladder is open."[70]

IV. Personality Changes

The effect on personality of this challenge of the open ladder was a common theme in Scandinavian-American literature, part of recurrent consideration of the educative effects of immigrant experience. Practically every writer showed his characters learning, growing, changing—not always for the better—under stimuli from the new environment. Evidence that readers took such change for granted was presented by a short story which introduced a peasant in a Danish community in Iowa. He still spoke only his native tongue, wore exclusively European-style clothes, ate all Danish-prepared food. The whole removal had happened so fast, when he had never been more than a few miles away from his birthplace before, that it seemed to have left no trace on him. The only difference was that now, instead of farming his fifteen-acre inherited holding, he plowed and harvested a farm over ten times bigger. The joke was that every reader would recognize as absurd the premise that such a peasant could go through the experience of immigration unchanged; and a comic background was just what the author wanted for his amusing tale.[71]

A Swedish-American novel published in 1899 described well the narrow and ignorant lives many peasants led before emigration. The story opened in a remote province of northern Sweden, where conditions were still as they had been earlier all over the country. The young hero, Adam, had been taught to read by his mother, and in a few months of school for a couple of winters he learned to write and figure a little and to recite his catechism and Bible history by heart. He read over and over the only two books his family owned: Luther's postille and the Bible. No member of the family had ever seen a newspaper, but they did not miss it. "The struggle for existence claimed all their time, from early morning to late at night, and what happened in the rest of the world did not concern these everyday folk."[72] A public market was held three times a year some distance away, and when Adam was taken there as a teen-ager, he saw a crowd for the first time in his life. Two men had emigrated to America from the district, but nobody believed the nonsense they wrote back, that there was no nobility or upper class, for instance, and American pigs got better food than poor laborers in Sweden. But one spring day an emigration agent turned up and began to tell about the 160 acres of free land anyone could claim over there. At first the peasants laughed at him, but gradually became convinced that his story was true. Then all wanted to go, but only a few had money enough; among them, of course, was Adam. The author only mentioned in passing Adam's surprise at everything new on the long trip, failing to carry through the contrast between Adam's background and the American environment to which he came. Once the hero entered the New World, he moved through one experience after another with as much aplomb as if he had been born in Chicago.

Better authors of all three nationalities often commented on the broadening and uplifting influence on peasant personality of immigrant experience. A Swedish-American maintained that the character of his countrymen was developed in their new home much better than in the old. For insofar as the Swede in America lived under the influence of higher intellectual and spiritual forces as a pioneer in the open West or a breadwinner among the motley swarms of a big city, "he can hardly avoid being lifted several inches, figuratively speaking, above the general level of those who stay in the Swedish province which was at first the entire world of both. . . . What is uniquely *small* in a bad sense in the Swede as such . . . loses its foothold in his character . . . and is replaced by something bigger and better, in harmony with the republic's institutional structure and accepted goals."[73]

A Norwegian-American author, after remarking that better education had slightly lessened the gulf in Europe between peasant and townsfolk by the turn of the century, maintained that the annual spring crowds of emigrants from Norway were still what they had always been —almost all people from the lowest classes, with a minimum of education and experience. He attributed the transformation they underwent in America to social influences there.

It is quite remarkable how fast the emigrated cotter's boy and hired girl under this country's larger and freer circumstances develop into comparatively well-brought-up and cultured individuals, by coming in closer contact with "the world." . . . The modern cut of their clothes has something to do with it, but it is not everything. Greater straight-forwardedness, cordiality, naturalness, and tact are soon evident in the behavior of most. Intercourse with many kinds of people wears down the sharp edges and removes coarseness and awkwardness. The serious, almost sad faces take on a lighter, more friendly cast. The shy reserve and stiffness is replaced by friendly, courteous willingness to oblige.[74]

Showing this change in terms of individual characters, a novel of pioneer life in Dakota described boys from a poor family, who had never read a page of their own accord in the Old Country, dropping into a neighbor's hut time after time to read the old newspapers covering the sod walls. "Was it the journey, or the winter they had spent in the little lumber-town in the East, or the life on the prairie, that had made them so wide awake?" the Norwegian author asked. "Maybe it was due most of all to their memories of the Old Country, contrasted with the life out here—the mountains and the fjord which were still so fresh in their minds, and now this desolate prairie. It gave them so much to wonder at, to compare and think out for themselves."[75]

Learning to think for oneself was pictured as a common by-product of immigrant experience, not only in judging practical matters like new farming techniques, but also in developing a philosophy of life. In a Danish-American novel a newcomer and his wife found the local minister ruling a settled rural community like a dictator, imposing on all his own hellfire brand of Christianity. In opposing this, the couple learned both to define their own principles and to fight for them. Home in Denmark they had lived in the shelter of like-thinking friends, where all shared the same beliefs. "Now they had to stand on their own feet, like a tree in an open field, and must thrust their roots so deep that they could withstand the storm!"[76]

A goodly number of weak personalities learned self-reliance from their adventures in the United States. Many went to the bottom, but those who survived were pictured as growing into men of strength and purpose. Many short stories outlined, as several novels traced in detail, the redemption through hard work and responsibility of a personality which began by drifting. "Why hadn't he been brought up to be self-reliant, to stand on his own feet, over there in the Old Country? Over here, he had to accept his responsibility or be pushed to the wall. . . ."[77]

The social advancement and material security which the majority of Scandinavian immigrants achieved also improved the morals of many a poor wretch who had to lie and steal in the Old Country to keep body and soul together. In a Norwegian-American novel a destitute fisherman toiled in vain day and night to feed his children; he often bought on credit and promised repayment he was by no means sure he could make. "There is many a poor but honest soul at home who will promise anything when it is a matter of life and death for his beloved children!"[78] First in America did the fisherman's inhuman toil bring returns, and at last he became known as and could feel himself to be an honorable man. Another author wrote of the "personal self-reliance and confidence in behavior which material independence and security confer as refuge and gift."[79]

138

All authors thus agreed that the effect on immigrant personality of the challenge of American opportunity was to quicken and stimulate people previously bound by tradition. A Swedish-American storyteller even advanced the theory, only half in jest, that there must be something in the very air of the United States which caused such a radical change in immigrants' character.

Take the most morose, the most stoical, apathetic, and indifferent rustic from the Old World and transplant him to American soil, and even after only a few days one can see a remarkable transformation. At least he will immediately develop an irresistible zeal to earn money, his eyes take on a more lively, audacious, searching look, on the street he begins to move at a faster pace, he becomes unconsciously prone to unrestrained boasting and bombastic exaggeration. It actually seems as though the climate or even the very air makes this change possible. A little later one assumes it as a natural consequence of a richer supply of nourishing and varied food.

If one includes a certain feeling of independence, more or less justified, . . . together with the hope, one might almost say certainty, of material betterment, then it is easy to understand how the whole nation is pervaded by enthusiastic ambition, and why a worker west of the Atlantic can accomplish a good deal more than his brother in Europe.[80]

V. Educational Opportunity

Listed high among the greater opportunities available in America was better education for all. Sometimes an ambitious boy emigrated mainly in order to go to college. "There will be a chance for you to attend a church school," a visiting Norwegian-American character urged a lad in Telemark. "Hundreds of young men have worked their way through, and now are ministers, teachers, businessmen. In this country most of them would have remained common laborers."[81] For in the Old World normally only upper-class sons got a higher education; very seldom could a peasant youth win the patronage of some aristocrat to support him through university study.

During the latter part of the nineteenth century another type of school did spread throughout Scandinavia: "folk high schools" founded by private philanthropy and patriotism. Here rural youth could spend a term or two beyond elementary school reading history, literature, and other subjects. Occasionally a young emigrant had such an additional dash of education in his background. Indeed, upper-class characters sometimes complained that it was the peasants with most education who emigrated, as though greater knowledge made them more dissatisfied to stay at home. This type of high-school education, however, was miles apart from the classical training of the Gymnasium, which alone led to the university. The gulf between the two reflected that between upper and lower classes. Both types of schooling were enjoyed by only a minority. The vast majority of peasants and laborers had no more than a minimum of education, and could expect no more for themselves or their children in the home country.

The United States, however, offered higher education to people of every class; and although not many first-generation immigrants were able to take advantage of the opportunity, their rise in status both permitted and entailed more schooling for their children. For the Old World had taught them to value education as a symbol of social rank. A Danish farmer struggling on a rented farm in Nebraska maintained through hardship and heartache the typical hope that his sons might become what he was not—educated men.[82]

Under the influence of such value orientation, the children of this ethnic group usually completed the highest education available in their area. For about twenty years after the Civil War, this meant graduation from the local elementary school. When high schools spread even to small towns, Scandinavian-American boys and girls almost always were pictured attending them. Only occasionally did a story mention that a father did not want his son to continue beyond the eighth grade, or that a boy had to miss classes spring and fall to help with farm work;[83] rare indeed were pietists so strict that they forbade a daughter to go to high school because a woman's place was in the home.[84] In a story published in 1903, a minister boasted in a letter home to Sweden that his little town had a high school from which not only all the town youth graduated, but also most of the boys and girls from the surrounding farm region.[85] Clearly this was not the case in contemporary Sweden.

The most striking change in educational achievement resulting from immigration was the frequency of college and university attendance by young people from this group of largely peasant origin. In Norway the son of poor fisherfolk who had narrowly escaped death at sea longed in vain to serve God, until finally one day he made such a big catch that he could afford a ticket to America. There he earned enough from summer farm work to go to school winters until his ordination.[86] Another laborer first felt himself called to the ministry after immigration, when he found himself stopping fights and drinking bouts among his fellow workers in a sawmill. He went to Augsburg Seminary and became a dedicated pastor.[87] The highest aspiration of many a fictional family was to give a son to the Lutheran church; and the goal was reached whenever the lad made an effort, regardless of how low a point he started from. Sometimes his family could help a little, but whether they could or not the honor to them was so great that they gladly dispensed with his work at home. Most often the aspirant began the long course of studies without a dollar to his name and, like American students, earned his own way. All the summer religion schools sponsored by Lutheran churches in these stories were taught by theology students.

140

From the mid-1880s on, a few immigrant children continued non-theological education after or even without high school; for many church-supported schools had both an academy and a college department. By the turn of the century it was common for both sons and daughters of businessmen and more prosperous farmers to go at least a year or two to college, and not uncommon for the children of the less successful. In a Danish-American novel of 1892 the eldest son of a poor farmer studied to become a doctor and the eldest daughter attended teachers' college, although the family had a terrific struggle to help pay their way.[88] A rare tale voicing opposition to higher education for women gave evidence of its increasing frequency, when Swedish-American neighbor women discussed this subject in a humorous story from 1903. One would not let her daughter go to college because the girls got so stuck-up there. The other pointed out that some might, but not all. Their minister's wife, for instance, was still "nice and common" even though she had attended college for many years.[89] By the time of the First World War, going away to college had become so usual for both sexes of farm, town, and city children down to the lower-middle-class level that both authors and characters took it for granted. In a short story from 1930, only one daughter of a large family stayed on the farm instead of going to college, and she felt herself anomalous.[90]

The image of success won by Scandinavians in America was thus drawn with many facets. The authors pictured most plainly the material improvement in standard of living made possible by migration westward. Not only did the United States possess richer resources than their home-land, but its wealth was distributed on a different basis. Most writers were convinced that hard and honest labor would win anyone his fair share. The poor-immigrant-makes-good plot was ubiquitous in their fiction, and poems in praise of the great material opportunities of America spangled the pages of Scandinavian-language newspapers every Fourth of July.

With economic followed many-sided social betterment, flourishing in the free and equal air of the New World. Countless poems and comments by authors and characters lauded American freedom from class restrictions, inherited prejudices, formalized snobbery in social inter-course. Former peasants, escaped from inherited positions at or near the bottom of society, fully appreciated a land where social position depended not on birth but on vocation, and where occupational choice was free. Anyone who aspired higher than his ability made possible could improve it through education or training, open to all. Moreover, although some types of work carried more prestige and material rewards

141

than others, a good worker in even a lowly position was respected as a man much more than his counterpart in Europe. Approval of this social order lay beneath the praise of American liberty and equality which recurred constantly in both poetry and prose. As long as they felt that this state lasted, most immigrants asked no more.

Chapter Six
Change in Immigrant Institutions

Principles of competition and self-reliance which the immigrants developed in economic life inevitably carried over into other activities. Members of a group selected largely on the basis of personal ambition were already predisposed toward pragmatic individualism. A Danish-American, for instance, praised the energy, will, and self-confidence of Americans:

Each individual knows what he wants, and what he wants he believes he can get. And what's so wonderful here, is that we don't have a lot of stupid prejudices to drag around . . . we don't have hobbles on our feet in the form of tradition and bias. . . This is a side of the Americans' practicality and healthy common sense.[1]

Such emphasis on individual ambition and achievement was part of the strong pressure which the American environment exerted on patterns of behavior brought from Europe.

Distinctive immigrant institutions developed only where people of the same national background stayed together in sufficiently large numbers to form their own community; for when they partook in activity of wider scope, as in politics, the terms of participation were dictated by others. Even where they maintained full control, their organizations were limited and molded by their bicultural situation; ways of thinking and acting formulated in one society had to be adjusted to another. Old-World models survived longest in institutions rooted in the local neighborhood: family, church, local clubs. Associations based on a larger area usually grew from New-World precedents: newspapers, colleges, fraternal societies, synods. Elements from each culture were present in both types of social organization, but the direction of their development was regularly away from European and toward American models. This movement was most rapid where the institutional activity was regulated by American law, as in the case of schools.

I. The School

1. PUBLIC SCHOOLS

All stories about exclusive frontier settlements recorded that Scandinavian pioneers founded schools as soon as possible after their arrival, often during their first winter. All these newcomers had had some form of schooling in their homeland; all could read and most could write. They took for granted that instruction in such basic skills was essential for their children. Where government aid was lacking, they took the matter into their own hands and promptly founded primitive schools, as naturally as they held their own prayer meetings until a minister came.

Such early schools were modeled exclusively on European prototypes. The children met in private homes, the largest in the community or at each home in turn. This had been the form of the *omgangsskole* (ambulatory school) with which the immigrants were familiar from recent history back home. Until a real teacher could be hired, the schoolmaster was regularly the man among their number who had most education—not a woman, for teaching was long an exclusively masculine prerogative in the Old Country. The chief subject of instruction was the Lutheran religion. All accepted that in their new home as in their old the most important function of the primary school was to help prepare children for a Christian life.

The intimate connection between church and school in Scandinavian immigrant communities appeared clearly in the first Norwegian-American novel, "Alf Brage, eller skolelæreren i Minnesota," published in 1874 but laid a decade earlier.[2] A Norwegian-Lutheran congregation hired the schoolmaster-hero to teach a term of two months in each of three districts, for a salary of $20 a month; later he also was appointed church precentor without additional pay. He boarded and held school for a week at various homes in turn, where the parents often listened with interest to his explanations of theology. Under his firm direction the children memorized the catechism and answers to the questions they would be asked at confirmation. If anything else was taught or learned in Alf Brage's class, the author neglected to mention it.

When tax-supported schools were founded after the political organization of the territory, church-affiliated schools were often continued awhile parallel to and competing with them. This solution to the problem of religious education caused other problems, however. Many of these were defined in the Alf Brage novel in a conversation between the minister and the schoolmaster: how the American school was held at the same time, and all citizens had to pay taxes to support it whether they made use of it or not; how impassable roads in spring and fall, and severe cold in winter, kept the children at home, and they were needed for farm work in summer; how the Norwegians owned no schoolhouse, so the children had to meet in private homes; how as immigrants they had to learn two languages; and how many parents unfortunately considered the parochial school of secondary value. They thought it more important for their offspring to learn English than to learn about God.[3]

The struggle of the pious against such parental worldliness was reflected in two or three other early tales, where the local clergyman sometimes went so far as to forbid members of his congregation to send their children to the godless public school.[4] Threats of damnation for the disobedient proved ineffective, however; they either fired the minister or withdrew from the church. Once public schools were well established, the Lutheran parochial ones rapidly dropped away. The cost of maintaining a double school system proved too great. Only a couple of Danish-American novels recorded a sporadic counter-movement, when communities of Grundtvigian Danes, disappointed in the poor training given by public schools, were pictured founding small *friskoler* (free schools) for their own children.[5] Otherwise the struggle between the rival forms of education was over by the time that this literature got well under way, and from the 1880s on almost all stories showed children attending public schools as a matter of course. Occasionally a newly arrived adult squeezed behind a desk and sat with the youngsters a few weeks to learn some English.

Although religion was banned from the public school by custom and Constitution, American law gave control over the institution to a school board elected by the local community. It was therefore possible for exclusive Scandinavian settlements to maintain some other aspects of Old-World tradition in teacher appointment and curriculum. This opportunity was seldom taken. The few stories which described the efforts of preservationists to work for conservation of European culture through the local school recorded their defeat by their own countrymen. In a Danish community in Nebraska, for instance, a local leader who argued that a well-qualified Danish schoolmaster should be hired was out-voted because the majority of immigrants were not interested in their cultural heritage. They wanted an American teacher even though he was a Baptist, because he could instruct their children in proper English.[6] In this community the tradition of male grade-school instructors had survived, but most other stories recorded that the American practice of hiring young women as teachers soon predominated. Occasionally an author mentioned the reason for the change: the low salary. Where some lingering Old-World influence appeared in the school system of an exclusive community, it was usually negative— directed not toward preserving European values so much as against innovation. In a Norwegian-American novel a second-generation teacher was shocked at the backwardness of the one-room high school she took over in a Norwegian town in Minnesota. The stinginess of the local taxpayers was the main reason for the shabby room and desks, the few tattered texts, the absence of a library and other facilities; but the local leaders, mostly churchmen, also expressed their moral opposi-

145

tion to the folderol of a modern high school and resisted the new teacher's efforts to introduce amateur drama and a library.[7]

The literature reflected considerable criticism of a system which assigned education of the young to inexperienced misses who were less interested in their charges than in finding a husband, and who rarely stayed more than a year at any school. Sometimes the reference was humorous, as in a Danish-American tale about a slow-witted boy who attended public school; since the teacher was new every year, the boy succeeded only in getting through the first half of the first reader eight times.[8] More often the criticism was hostile. A Norwegian-American novel contrasted young American schoolmarms, empty-headed under their marcelled hair, with a dedicated Norwegian schoolmaster who had labored all his life at teaching values as well as the three R's. In a painful twist of plot the old man was forced by a local politician to give up teaching altogether.[9]

2. RELIGIOUS INSTRUCTION

Although the European model of primary education lost out in competition with the American public school, first-generation parents continued to feel responsible for providing formal lessons in religion for their children. As the leader of a Norwegian prairie settlement pointed out, of course the children had been baptized by visiting ministers, and their parents had tried to teach them the catechism, but to little avail. Soon some of them would be old enough to be confirmed, and for that vital ceremony they *had* to be prepared by a trained teacher or clergyman, like back home.[10]

To solve this problem the individual congregations founded part-time summer schools to give instruction in Lutheran doctrine in the European tongue. The prototype here was evidently the summer Bible camps of American sects, for nothing similar had appeared in the Old Country. Reference to these church schools was so common throughout all three branches of the literature that the institution must have been practically ubiquitous throughout the Scandinavian settlements of the Middle West at least from the 1880s until the first World War. It was notably a rural phenomenon, however. Lutheran Sunday schools based on American models were usually mentioned as the source of religious instruction for child characters in cities and towns. A Norwegian mother who sent her children to a Methodist Sunday school because that was the only one available in a Dakota hamlet maintained that she was incapable of teaching them herself. "Yes, I know that's the way it always was in the Old Country; but we're not in the Old Country now. When we have a Sunday school right under our noses, I'm certainly not going to struggle

146

with trying to teach the children at home."[11] The problem in this story was not solved until the Norwegians started their own Lutheran Sunday classes.

American-style Sunday and summer schools were conceived as substitutes for the many years of religious education no longer provided by schools and home. Special preparation for confirmation, on the other hand, remained in the Old-World tradition in both rural and urban settings. The minister instructed the children once or twice a week for six months before the annual public hearing in church at which they were examined about doctrine. This was usually a formality, for the pastor distributed the questions judiciously and as a last resort held back from the line-up any he thought could not answer even the easiest query. To have to "lese for presten" (study with the minister) two years in a row was considered the worst shame which could befall an adolescent, and more than one clergyman was pictured passing children he knew to be unqualified for fear of the uproar which would result if he failed them.[12] For all who professed to be Lutherans had to pass through that ceremony. Practically every story with characters aged fourteen or fifteen took for granted that confirmation was part of the universal experience of that age-group. The minority of irreligious parents who neglected this responsibility toward their children were condemned by their neighbors. In one story Norwegian women gossiped about an old man whose American-born children had been neither baptized nor confirmed, and who had told the minister to mind his own business. No law in this free country forced him to submit to such nonsense, he said. A neighbor commented, "No, that Norwegians can be turned so topsy-turvy seems almost unbelievable. We know well that other nations can behave so—they don't know any better; but how people brought up strictly in fear of the Lord can fall so low and get so hardened, it beats me."[13]

The language of all types of religious instruction remained European longer than might be expected, considering the innumerable complaints throughout the literature about the rapid Americanization of the young; but since this was the only regular training in their parents' native tongue that most children received, and their elders tended to attribute moral worth to the language in which *they* had learned Commandments and catechism, the Old Guard of each community long resisted the introduction of English in this area. Sometimes they opposed the change too long, and brought about the opposite effect from what they intended. Several second-generation characters learned to hate their parents' native tongue because of the abstract and incomprehensible terminology they were forced to memorize at religion school.[14] A Danish-American novel of 1928 recorded the transition to English in midstream: use of both languages in parallel Sunday school classes, so that parents could choose which tongue they preferred.[15]

3. SEMINARIES AND ACADEMIES

Both seminaries and academies founded by Scandinavian-Americans also appeared with considerable frequency in the literature. In most stories laid before 1890, minister characters had immigrated after training and ordination in the Old Country. This depiction grew less common toward the end of the nineteenth century, and from about the time of World War I a newly arrived immigrant minister was a rarity. High-church synods of all three national groups continued to call their pastors from the mother country longest. Fictional clergymen in low-church synods, on the other hand, who tended to come from families of lower-class origin, almost always were inspired to the service of God in the New World. Hardly ever did a theology student once in the United States return to the Old Country for training. Instead, when a young man decided to prepare for the ministry before his group had established its own seminary, he attended an American school or one maintained by another immigrant nationality. Thus a Norwegian-American novel, copyrighted in 1893 but laid a quarter century earlier, pictured its hero studying theology at the German Lutheran seminary in St. Louis.[16] Contemporary readers would immediately recognize which synod he meant to serve, for its ties with the conservative German-Americans led to major splits among Norwegian-American churchmen. The passing mention in later stories of one seminary or another immediately identified the character's synodical affiliation for readers of the time—as when in the same novel one Norwegian-American boy attended Augsburg Seminary, another Luther College.[17]

Private academies received more attention from immigrant novelists. Occasionally a preservationist leader was pictured founding his own school to help indoctrinate later generations with Old-World culture; more often the main aim was to provide Christian, specifically Scandinavian Lutheran education as an alternative to the public high school. For criticism of American high schools grew along with their number. Not only did immigrant authors object to them as shallow and godless, but some pictured them actively misleading second-generation youth away from the moral values of their ethnic group.[18] Combining the models of the American preparatory school and the Scandinavian "folk high school," Swedes, Danes, and Norwegians founded many small academies supported partly by student tuition, partly by church and synodical contributions; for the aim was to attract young people not only of the local community but also of the same brand of Lutheranism wherever they might live.

Instruction was in English, although classes in the appropriate Old-World tongue were offered and often required. Other courses resembled those in American high schools. A Norwegian boy took American history, reading, spelling, and grammar in English, arithmetic, Norwegian, and religion in his first year; Latin, algebra, world history, American literature, geography, physics, Norwegian, and religion in his second.[19] Not only could second- and third-generation adolescents learn about their European roots at such an academy, but also young newcomers sometimes attended a term or two for an introduction to the life and language of their new country. Such institutions were thus two-way bridges between the Old World and the New.

Regardless of the curriculum, the emphasis of instruction was always on morals and values. Alumni of a Danish-American academy, founded to promote the Danish reformer Grundtvig's "happy Christianity" in Wisconsin, enjoyed all their lives the Danish songs, dances, and social games they had learned there. Most of the young people of the community went off to this *høiskole* for a few terms; one was inspired there to become a minister, another to write a book and become a "real author."[20] However, the efforts of the faculty to interest stolid farm youth in higher values were not always successful. A Norwegian newcomer remarked how an academy teacher's labor to awake enthusiasm for "the great ideals in life" had about as much effect on his pupils as squirting water on a duck.[21]

4. COLLEGES

Scandinavian-American colleges also appeared often in the literature. These were of course based on American prototypes, since no similar institutions existed in the Old Country. All were church-supported schools, but the financial aid which the parent synod could give was often insufficient. A book describing the early years of Bethany College in Kansas told how it depended on Swedish settlements throughout the state. Appeals for contributions met with gratifying response: "Ten sacks of flour from New Gottland; two quarters of beef from Johnstown; 24 dozen eggs from Fremont. . . ."[22] The finances of these early schools were so uncertain that no student's proffered tuition could be refused; therefore many members of the student body had had insufficient preparation for college or none at all. Before high schools became common, the colleges often had an academy or high-school department for students unqualified to take more advanced work. Otherwise they signed up for few and easy courses. A cowboy from Arizona, for instance, came to Bethany College with the aim of learning to "talk and say things without a hitch, and bow and be polite, and laugh in the right place."[23] He decided to take spelling and cornet.

Throughout the fiction, most of the colleges mentioned belonged to the Scandinavian-American tradition. Naturally each character elected one of the same nationality and religious bent as himself. Norwegians usually attended Luther or St. Olaf College; Danes, Grand View or Dana; Swedes, Bethany or Augustana. The literal realism of these immigrant tales appeared not only in the naming of such schools, but also in the introduction of actual teachers and administrators as characters. Fictional accounts of events at some colleges dated their settings practically to the day. In volumes of poetry, occasional verses written to celebrate one or another occurrence at such schools were commonplace. "Den ny fløj til skolen i Des Moines" by a Danish-American minister, for instance, celebrated the opening of a new wing on the main building of Grand View.[24]

The expressed aim of these colleges was the same as that of the immigrant-sponsored academies: to provide a higher education adapted to American conditions but including something of Lutheran values and Old-World culture. According to the evidence of a number of stories, good teachers did inspire some second- and third-generation students to genuine appreciation of their Old-World heritage. In a Norwegian-American tale, for instance, the granddaughter of a prairie family decided to go to college for teacher training. The suggestion of her Norwegian grandmother that she attend a Norwegian-American school was derided by parents and children alike. "Why should this Norwegian business be mixed in? . . . She had no use for Norwegian in an English-language school! They were in America now. And therefore they should be wholly American, without any hyphen." But the grandmother persisted. She reminded them of the choir from a Norwegian-American college which was known all over the country, of a professor at the same school who was a famous author. The family finally sent for a catalogue, and were so impressed that the daughter went there after all. She didn't like it when she discovered that she had to take Norwegian, but she grew interested when an assignment required the drawing up of her family tree. Only the grandmother could help her then. At the end of the year the grandmother was invited to visit the college and stay in a dormitory to talk Norwegian with the girls there. Drinking coffee with the professors and college president, all speaking her native tongue, she was led to tell about her life in the Old Country. One teacher finally praised her for her "right kind of family feeling, which keeps people from forgetting their ancestral ways." When the party was over, her granddaughter proudly showed her a hidden microphone; the conversation had been broadcast.[25]

These institutions of formal education reflected varying degrees of pressure from the surrounding society. Because public schools were directly regulated by law and administrated by the American political system, the immigrants had little influence over them. Individuals in the fiction were rather shown accepting the completely American character of tax-supported education and adjusting to it as best they could. Seminaries, academies, and colleges founded by various segments of the group, on the other hand, remained under the control of those who supported them. Once such institutions had been properly incorporated they could be run as their founders pleased. Nevertheless these private schools differed little from their contemporary American counterparts. In organization and administration they faithfully followed New-World models, including all the paraphernalia of courses, grades and credits, graduation ceremonies and diplomas. They differed only in that they created an atmosphere of respect for and offered special classes in the language, literature and history of a minor European nation.

Education carried on within individual churches of course remained free from outside control, but even here the influence of American examples was strong. Summer and Sunday religion schools were copied from churches in the United States. Preparation for confirmation, however, long remained in European forms, for in this field Old-Country prototypes were protected by American respect for religious freedom. Almost all formal education thus came to be conducted in American patterns, even when these were used to further deliberately non-American ends.

II. Cultural and Social Organizations

Institutions of informal education developed along the same lines, proliferating in bewildering variety from both European and American models but gradually losing their bicultural characteristics as they moved from the first toward the second. In the field of music, for example, the inspiration for amateur choral societies was credited with having been brought from the Old World.

> They came from the high Northland . . .
> and brought with them on the journey long
> their sweet and happy Swedish song . . .
> and many a noble melody
> was carried over land and sea
> by Svea's heirs to this country.[26]

Several novels described the founding of choral societies in midwestern farming communities in the 1870s and 1880s. Now the suggestion came from an ordinary farmer who hoped to improve the spirit of the neighborhood, split into factions by church feuds.[27] Now a minister brought the idea back from a synodical convention, to brighten daily life for the young people. Gathering regularly from the wide-spread farms, they learned more than voice training. The poetry of the words they sang taught them to see beauty in the nature around them, in the change of the seasons, even in the memory of the Old Country which their parents seldom mentioned.[28] Urban choral societies of ordinary laborers and clerks gave regular concerts and dressed in uniforms or folk costumes to parade on their Constitution Day. The groups met in singing competitions which were fully reported in the immigrant newspapers, even to titles of the songs sung. These were naturally Scandinavian, though a Norwegian group might well include songs by the Swede Bellman, and Danes music by Grieg. Many poems in collected volumes by Scandinavian-Americans carried a note that they fit a given melody, or that they were first sung by such-and-such a chorus on a given occasion.

No book mentioned church choirs in the Old-World rural districts from which most immigrants came. In a few descriptions of European church services, the liturgy was sung or chanted by the minister, with responses and hymns by the precentor and the congregation. Choirs were never mentioned in frontier churches either, although the singing (or lack of it) by pastor and congregation was often commented on. When church choirs did appear, it was in stories dated after the turn of the century, and mainly in town and city congregations. No tale recounted the founding of such; they simply appeared in full swing in churches which had progressed quite far in Americanization.*

The literature recorded many other kinds of cultural effort in Scandinavian rural communities after the frontier had passed. When the local teacher was of the same nationality as the inhabitants, she often took the lead and made her schoolhouse the center for community-wide spelling bees, singing schools, debates, even amateur drama. A doctor was the father of cultural life in a Danish town in South Dakota, seeking to brighten the drab toil of everyday life which had driven four housewives insane within two years. He suggested celebration of the Danish Constitution Day every June fifth and the founding of a library and reading club; but the community went further. It built a meeting hall and founded many other clubs too: for prohibition, for young people,

* Historical sources contradict the implication that immigrant church choirs might have developed from exclusively American models. See for instance Carl L. Nelson, "The Sacred Music of the Swedish Immigrants," in J. Iverne Dowie and Ernest M. Espelie, eds., *The Swedish Immigrant Community in Tradition* (Rock Island, Ill., 1963), pp. 51-57.

for gymnastics, for charity, for school support, for political parties, even a "Dilettante Society." "It was almost impossible to live in Hartland without being a member of three or four organizations."[29] Here the American pattern of "joining" was adapted to serve other ethnic ends. Similar organizations flourished in the Scandinavian neighborhoods of cities. A Norwegian-American novel described celebration of the Seventeenth of May in Chicago when such societies were out in force:

We thought it was glorious and wonderful to see the big American and Norwegian flags come along Milwaukee Avenue, and hear the bands play "Star-Spangled Banner," "Sons of Norway," "Yes, We Love," and "Yankee Doodle" almost simultaneously. And how smart and handsome they all were! There were the "Northmen's Song Society" with their picturesque red cloaks over their shoulders, Turnvereiners in their neat white uniforms, besides all the other societies with their flags and bands.[30]

Some immigrants had been familiar with certain of these types of organization in the Old Country: prohibition societies with alcohol-free parties, young people's social organizations, clubs devoted to gymnastics. The prototypes of others were distinctly American: spelling bees, debates, parent-teacher associations. A good number were indefinite in origin, growing up on both sides of the Atlantic at about the same time in response to similar conditions—although many immigrants living in comparatively isolated communities had no contact with them before coming to the United States. Such were amateur drama groups and reading circles, which were recorded in Scandinavian-American communities from the 1880s well into the twentieth century. Amateur drama was distinctly an urban phenomenon, while reading circles with small lending libraries were common in rural and small-town settings; both expressed an attempt to keep in touch with developments of formal culture in the homeland. Most plays produced and books bought had been written in the Old Country, but occasionally titles written by fellow immigrants were mentioned. Both these cultural activities were carried on in the European tongue.

Purely social clubs based on national origin also appeared constantly in this literature. Some were modeled on American secret societies, with initiation ceremonies, passwords, and dire oaths of secrecy. These usually offered life insurance and sickness benefits to their members. Some were founded in response to a specific situation in a given community: a Danish society to preserve cultural heritage—and incidentally to provide its members with liquid refreshment free from official closing hours and a snooping minister; a marksmen's club meeting on Sunday afternoon to challenge the power of the dogmatic pastor.[31] Others grew directly out of immigrants' sense of being rejected by the larger community. Such was "Foreningen Norge," started by the leading business

153

man in a prairie town, after the doors of local American society had been shut in his face. This club held meetings, parties, and dances in its own hall above the bank, to which only those of Norwegian blood were admitted; it brought many lecturers and a few musicians to town.[32]

These social associations flourished in both urban and rural environments, clearly in response to a variety of needs. A Swedish-American satirist claimed that his fellow immigrants lived together in a country town in peace and harmony during the early years, but then first one and then another began to get ahead of the others. "The number of societies grew in competition with the number of churches, and associations were founded to pursue all possible goals, but mostly so that everyone could be a little better than anybody else."[33] A Dane who began by being very active in the local lodge "Denmark" finally turned his back on it as worthless. He saw his countrymen as so dull, "their horizon so narrow, their world so limited, the physical was primary and everything else of less importance. . . . And they crept together . . . certainly not to preserve their mother tongue or the Brotherhood of Fellow Countrymen, but simply from fear . . . of loneliness."[34] The educative influence of these organizations, however, must have broadened the personalities of former peasants from isolated areas where all organized social activity had been monopolized by the local aristocracy. Only in America could a saloonkeeper become treasurer of the Danish club, doorguard of the Masons, and twice elected to the town council.[35]

The rapid decline of these immigrant associations was also recorded in the literature. A group of older immigrants discussing the second generation in a Norwegian-American novel could not understand what was wrong with the young people. One recalled,

When I came here, we were nearly all newcomers, we were young and we were poor. We worked hard, and most of us had not had much schooling. But we started reading circles, we had a big men's chorus, and there was even a Norwegian band here. We founded our own health insurance society, and now and then we got together and hired some well-known man to come and give a lecture for us. We held discussions on everything under the sun and we even acted "To the Mountains" and it wasn't so bad. But we were only simple workers and hired girls nearly all of us. Young people nowadays never organize anything. They go to school until they are grown and never seem to have much to do; but they complain about being more tired when evening comes than we were who toiled at heavy physical labor.[36]

Late-arriving immigrants complained constantly that they had nowhere to go and nothing to do in their free time. Those who investigated the surviving libraries of reading circles and lodges found the book collections thirty years behind the times, or locked behind glass doors to which the key had been lost years before and no one had missed it.[37] In a novel published in 1938, a young man found a Danish society still in existence in the city he came to, but the heart had gone out of it

154

and only a shell remained. "Yes, Danish culture and Danish language had lived here once, green and fresh, but now they danced their last autumn dance like the dying leaves of the park, and soon all would be covered over by the white snow of winter, and no trace of them on America's earth would ever more be seen or remembered."[38]

No author discussed the reasons for the deterioration of these organizations, but a reader can see that they declined as Americanization developed within the ethnic group. As the immigrants grew to feel more at home in their environment, most joined American clubs and societies. Those who maintained membership in Scandinavian fraternal organizations complained that even these were all too like their New-World counterparts. "The whole idea of such clubs is based on American patterns . . . we go to Danish meetings and think and act too much according to American custom and usage and spirit."[39]

III. The Press

European authors seemed more aware of the significance of the Scandinavian-American press than immigrant writers, who tended to take their newspapers so completely for granted that they seldom referred to them in more than asides except for criticism and caricature. No one expressed surprise that literally hundreds of weekly and biweekly journals had sprung up for a reading public the majority of whom had never subscribed to papers back home. In Europe until fairly late in the nineteenth century newspapers had been a luxury written by an elite for an elite, and ordinary people whose mental and physical horizons were practically identical paid them little attention. But once these people had emigrated, they found that they wanted regular news from the Old Country they had left behind, and practically all could soon afford to pay for it. Here there was no conflict between old and new patterns of behavior; the entire group rapidly adopted the American practice of a newspaper subscription for every family. Because of the language difficulty, however, the first generation were almost always pictured subscribing to their own special journals.

1. FUNCTIONS AND CHARACTERISTICS

Both the Swedish novelist Vilhelm Moberg and the Norwegian Johan Bojer pointed out the dual educative role of the Scandinavian-American press. Long columns of news from the Old World, often printed province by province, kept immigrants in touch with the most important events in their former homelands; while at the same time news from all over

America helped to make them aware of the problems of their vast new land.

> But after the post office had moved so near, people begin to take newspapers, mostly Norwegian-American ones with all the news from the Old Country. Now there is something to read aloud on Sunday evenings, it's like getting a letter from home in every number. But here is a lot about America too, from every part of this big country. Isn't this important for the settlers here? Don't they live in America? Hmm, they've got politics and parties and conflict here too, looks like, who'd thought of that? These pioneer settlements have been so isolated, thoughts and feelings have stayed in the Old Country, people were here in this strange place only to cultivate the earth and get rich. But the newspapers teach them to be concerned also with the country which gave them the earth and the scope to get rich some day, if they only willed it.[40]

The one immigrant author who pictured the founding of a newspaper also emphasized its assimilative function. "*The Hardanger Citizen* was primarily the organ of the Scandinavian immigrants; it contained weekly reports of the political and social news from the mother countries, but in its editorial comments it assumed a distinctly American point of view and was throughout its columns strictly loyal to the institutions of the grand republic. Its first aim was not to keep up the immigrant's connection with his fatherland, but to make him an intelligent voter, and a useful American citizen."[41]

Newspapers served as organs of education in other ways, too. They played an important role in religious strife; many served as the mouthpiece of church leaders, whose arguments on dogma and the true faith were quoted by characters against each other. In political matters both local and national, the press was shown as the primary agent of defining issues to immigrant voters, not always truthfully. No lie was too black for the newspaper published by a Norwegian businessman who practically owned the prairie village he founded, when it came to the momentous issue of moving the county seat.[42] These periodicals often furnished the only contact rural residents had with literature. In a Danish-American novel a farm wife cut out of her paper poems which she read over and over as the only literature she possessed.[43] References to one newspaper or another, often by actual name, were in fact so frequent and so casual in the immigrant literature that one must conclude they were an essential part of immigrant life.

The press also helped bind together the members of a far-flung group. In one tale, a news story about a deserted Norwegian wife landing in New York with her brood of children was read by a neighbor of the previously immigrated husband in the West, who revealed where he was.[44] Settlers in a prairie town drew other Danes by advertising land in a Danish-American newspaper, and then attracted a doctor, dentist, banker, and other specialists by the same method.[45] A family of Norwegian newcomers advertised in *Skandinaven* for their missing father, a sailor on the Great Lakes.[46]

The immigrant press was shown to be unlike that of the homeland in one way emphasized in story after story: readers contributed much more of what was printed. An educated Norwegian immigrant who decided he wanted to become a journalist sat down to study the newspapers of his group, and concluded that they were very different from those at home in this respect.

The need to communicate was irresistibly strong in lonely farmers on the frontier, and found its release in the press. Large and small of whatever happened or impressed them in their daily lives, was reflected in the neswpapers. And in this way the journals came to record the immigrants' history more vividly than any writer of history could.[47]

This characteristic was often satirized by writers plagued by it in their work as journalists. The Norwegian-American editor O. S. Buslett, for example, quoted in a short story a typical unsolicited communication from a subscriber:

Inasmuch as it is now so long since anything appeared in your paper from these parts, I will now take pen in hand to tell my fellow-countrymen and countrywomen that all goes well at this point of the earth's surface, which goes by the name of Nordheim. . . .[48]

Another leading editor, Waldemar Ager, wrote a short story about a typographer in charge of his small-town paper while the editor was away. The young man tried in vain to discourage a would-be contributor:

This of yours would be a bit too long, I'm afraid. It keeps piling up, piling up —hardly know what we can do with it all. Folks are just too bright nowadays, you see—everyone who pays for the paper wants the space for a three-column article about the hole-in-the-wall where he fetches his mail. And poems—well, if you could see all the poems we use as fuel for the stove, you'd hardly believe it. And a lot are so bad that they almost won't burn. Of psalms alone we've burned up enough for two psalmbooks as big as Landstad's, just since I came here.[49]

2. PROBLEMS

A Swedish-American novel digressed into a long account of the problems of immigrant newspapers when its student hero ran into an old friend who worked on a comic weekly in Chicago. A newspaper aimed at an ethnic group, he learned, had not one reading public but many, and more varied than a layman could imagine. Subscribers were spread from New York to San Francisco, from Canada to Florida. Before emigration they were already a motley mixture from city and country, educated, half-educated, and uneducated; and the different environments they settled in continued their development in opposite directions. The Swedish church was so important to many immigrants that it must never be offended; but

157

many others were so glad to have escaped the state church that they wouldn't have anything to do with religion at all, and a newspaper could not give too much space to the Augustana synod for fear of offending them. A journal had to take sides in political issues, but no matter which side it picked the other would be furious. Subscribers demanded *all* the news from both Sweden and America, but didn't understand they were interested in only their own home province, and complained about so much news from other provinces too. They objected to the cost of immigrant journals, compared with American prices, not realizing the mass economy of the latter. As for language, the papers were criticized by recent arrivals for defiling Swedish, but they had to use Swedish forms of English words in daily use by their readers because Swedish lacked such words.

Nor could immigrant editors afford to pay adequate wages. They got much material free, reprints from both American and Swedish sources and unsolicited contributions, and the price to subscribers had to be held as low as possible. Therefore good men would not stay in journalism. (Most Norwegian reporters in Chicago, declared a well-known author in another story, were actually drunken wrecks the editors could hire cheaply—men educated in Norway, often with considerable talent, who had gone wrong one way or another and been shipped off by their families to get rid of them. Unable to do the heavy physical labor required of greenhorns, they were driven by bitter need to work for less than living wages, and slaved until they died in harness or were carted off to a drunkard's hospital.[50]) To be a successful immigrant journalist, the Swedish-American novel concluded, a man must possess universal knowledge, be at once both churchly and irreligious, conservative and liberal, never offend anybody but satisfy everybody's widely different tastes—and have no personal needs or false hopes for a secure old age.[51]

An amusing short story related the trials of a young Swede who tried to be this perfect reporter, but who angered subscribers right and left. A Swedish Methodist minister raged at a reference to himself as a peasant lad; all the members of his congregation withdrew their subscriptions and advertising. Omission of the name of a wife who prepared food for a lodge meeting offended the members of this organization. Misprints went from bad to worse until finally the town grocer was insulted. He announced he would refuse credit to anybody who read *Svenska Posten,* and that was the newspaper's death knell.[52]

3. TYPES OF CIRCULATION

Two widely different types of immigrant newspapers were described in the literature. The authors credited only those of nation-wide circulation with serving as an educative or unifying force. Small-town local news-

158

papers, on the other hand, were often described springing up like mushrooms in a multitude of Scandinavian centers, but dying again just as fast. These were the butt of most of the satire in these stories, which portrayed them as veritable scandal sheets, their editors eager to print any scare headline or gossip which might sell five extra copies, their reporters more expert with scissors and pastepot than with the pen. A Danish-American tale showed the reason for their poor quality, in telling of two rival newspapers in one small town with about 8000 Danish inhabitants. More than half took English-language papers, and over half of those who read their native tongue preferred a much better Danish-American journal published far away. Neither of the local weeklies had over a thousand subscribers, so they were engaged (almost literally) in a duel to the death for the few readers they could attract.[53]

IV. Politics

In political matters the literature showed Scandinavian immigrants maintaining for a time patterns of interest (or lack of it) brought from home, but gradually abandoning these in favor of American issues and ways.

1. CITIZENSHIP

Citizenship was a special point. Many authors did not mention it at all, taking for granted that their characters had adopted the citizenship of their new home. Many others only referred to it in passing, as when family heads took out first papers to qualify for a homestead. Some writers, however, emphasized the emotional significance of the act by portraying their people either proudly acquiring citizenship as soon as possible in glowing patriotism for their new country, or delaying many years tormented by the finality of the step in cutting themselves off from their homeland. In no book did the characters *not* become American citizens sooner or later. Either it was definitely stated that they did, or the matter was not mentioned at all.

The right to vote acquired with citizenship came to many in the early years as a marvelous surprise.

The next summer there was a presidential election, and speakers came to hold openair meetings and orate in both English and Norwegian. . . . But could it really be so important what people around here think about government in the great United States of America? Does it really depend on the fellows out here who is to be president? Ordinary workers do not have the right to vote in the Old Country, but here both Ola and Kal are as important as millionaires, believe it or not! That's the way it is in America, they must write to tell relatives and friends home in Old Norway.[54]

Here was social betterment indeed, for universal male suffrage did not come in Norway until the very end of the nineteenth century, and office-holding was often limited to the local gentry. On the Dakota frontier Rølvaag showed Norwegian peasants and fishermen establishing the government of their township themselves, electing the officers prescribed by American law from their own number. The new justice of the peace was terrified when he had to marry a couple, however, because so important a ceremony could be performed only by an ordained minister back home.[55] Once political reform got under way in Scandinavia, however, it developed with a rush. In a Norwegian-American novel published in 1917 the heroine politely informed an American patriot that Norway was not an oppressed land, and she was not a bit more free in the United States than she had been at home—in fact, women had the right to vote there, while here they were accounted like criminals and the insane, as unworthy of that duty.[56]

2. INTEREST IN POLITICS

Those later arrivals who had had political interests before emigration often continued these for a number of years and ignored the American politics around them. It would appear that concern over politics in the Old Country inhibited attention to the same in the new environment. An old pioneer in Nebraska who followed every involution of Danish parties recorded in his weekly papers sent from home did not know even the names of American parties.[57] Around boardinghouse tables in city and town newcomers discussed the veto question that roiled Norwegian political waters in the 1880s, or the issue of the "clean" flag; some were peasant boys who had paid such matters scant attention at home.[58] A passionate topic for several years was the impending separation of Norway from Sweden, in many stories erupting into both individual and street fights between representatives of the two nationalities. Swedish resentment of the Norwegian demand for independence was reflected in many contemporaneous Swedish-American poems.[59]

Interest in American politics was depicted as developing when immigrants had settled in a community where they expected to stay. Problems arose in their relationship to law and government, or to other groups, and they learned to manipulate the political means to deal with such matters provided in American institutions.

An American novel about Swedes in Minnesota gave an excellent picture of people who had previously been politically illiterate gradually awakening to the power of their ballots. When a jealous Yankee neighbor dynamited a new Swede porch—the first in the settlement—and the Yankee sheriff did nothing, the Swedes began taking out citizenship papers; only a few at first, but within a couple of months the clerk of the district court was swamped with business. The new citizens attended

160

the nominating caucuses, but were too inexperienced to take part; so the Yankee sheriff was renominated. When the ballots were counted, however, every Swede in the county had pasted over his name "For sheriff, Gustaf Moberg." The Swedish candidate won by a comfortable majority, and from then on there was no stopping the political power of his countrymen. "These foreigners had learned how to act together and acting together they were a force to be reckoned with. From that day forward no party with its wits about it put a ticket in the field without giving the best places to the Swedes."[60]

3. POLITICS BY ETHNIC GROUPS

Such politics by ethnic groups appeared often in the literature. A novel laid at the beginning of the 1880s had the young suitor and the old father of the heroine end their quarrels over theology by agreeing it was high time for their group to take a hand in political matters. The idealistic young man expatiated on the lust for freedom in all Norwegian souls, and how the sterling Norwegian character ought to have greater influence in American politics. The older man argued that the Irish had run things long enough; it was time for the Norskies to have a turn. Both were very interested in a young Norwegian lawyer already active in politics; the reader could take for granted that they would vote for him at every opportunity.[61] In another tale a young man entering politics found his sturdy, typically Norwegian name a distinct advantage in drawing votes from Norwegians all over his district.[62] An English-language novel published in 1943 recorded candidates filing early for the campaign of 1936 in Minnesota. "Everything depended on the name of the candidate. Since many people in Minnesota are of Scandinavian birth, a candidate whose name ended in 'son' or 'sen' had the advantage."[63] Even campaign verse was not argumentative but confident. Now all of us who call ourselves both Swedes and Americans will join forces to support this candidate for governor of Minnesota because he is Swedish and therefore honorable, a versifier declaimed at length in "Kampanjsång för John A. Johnson."[64] Politics was one field where pan-Scandinavianism seemed to have been the rule. No book recorded election rivalry between two of the three nationalities; on the contrary, they stood united in politics against the Yankees, the Irish, or any other ethnic group.

The immigrants' political interest was pictured growing out of immediate local problems and only gradually extending to state and national politics. In pioneer settlements, people who had previously been governed from above showed little concern with politics beyond the county level. For instance, a novel pictured a Danish frontier community as the most peaceful place imaginable.

161

One sees no trace of the restless, stormy America. Each lives in his own work and his memories of home, and lets *those* govern who are born to rule; a man has done his duty for the good of the republic when he has read his newspapers well enough to be able to vote according to his convictions, and any urge to take part in public life is satisfied by a county office.

If Congressmen make a deal with one "ring" or another to cheat the national treasury out of a million or two, that is regarded as a dispensation of Providence which must be accepted.[65]

4. ELECTION TO OFFICE

Many of those elevated to office in early local elections were immigrants who had pushed ahead of their fellows financially. A Norwegian-American political novel recorded that the first Norwegians in politics were usually merchants from the small towns, agents for agricultural machinery, men with a little capital they could loan out at high interest, those who knew some English so they could interpret between their ethnic group and others. Except in the most closed communities, where one voted for one's neighbors, it was the American party system which first put these men into office in order to manipulate the votes of their group.[66]

Not until the body of immigrants in any one place had adapted to their new environment and learned the language did such petty politicians lose their power. "When the immigrants had acquired more of the language, they got a taste for politics. Town officers must be elected, and from that to taking part in county and state politics was not a long step."[67] The main force for widening interest in politics was growing economic problems as the immigrant farmers went over from subsistence to profit farming. One sterling character refused the office of county treasurer on the ground that he was not interested in politics and could not neglect his farm; but he let it be known he was interested in nomination for the state legislature, where new laws should be passed to regulate usury, grading of grain, railroad rates and rebates, etc. Later this Norwegian was elected governor as a compromise candidate on the Republican ticket.[68]

5. REPUBLICAN PARTY LOYALTY

Throughout the literature the overwhelming majority of Scandinavian-Americans were portrayed as loyally Republican in party affiliation. A few writers remarked on the origin of this unanimity in the revulsion these Northmen felt against slavery, or in the fact that there were almost no Democrats around to present counter arguments in the crucial decade of the 1870s, when this group was awakening to political activity. Most writers, however, took this Republican affiliation for granted, and depicted only comic characters or Irishmen as Democrats. All exciting political struggles in the fiction were fought on the caucus or primary level, for whoever won the Republican nomination would automatically win the election.

6. POPULISM AND AGRARIAN RADICALISM

In the 1890s, however, the solid Republicanism of this immigrant group cracked a little. The growing economic problems of western farmers were reflected in increasing criticism by fictional characters of Wall Street and The System. Yet the Populist revolt was portrayed as too radical to win a large following among such traditional conservatives.* Comparatively few writers mentioned this political development. A handful pictured its widespread but short-lived popularity, but none argued in its favor.

Two major Norwegian-American authors gave extensive consideration to the Populist movement, although their common rejection of it was based on unlike grounds. Rølvaag had the hero of *Their Fathers' God* begin his political career by seeking a Republican nomination, but he felt himself most attracted by the sweeping reforms proposed by the Populist party in the election of 1894. An old Democrat, warning that the Republicans were bound to win, told the young man that "The great progressive ideas never win out overnight; they must fight long-drawn-out battles. . . . When a progressive measure wins out it is usually being pushed through by the conservative cud-chewers; by that time the idea is no longer new."[69]

Simon Johnson based his condemnation of Populism on moral grounds. In a long novelette describing the growth of the movement in a Norwegian settlement in Dakota, he argued that the farmers of the region were not really so badly off. Compared to their own parents, they were all comfortable, even rich; only in contrast to city folks with white hands and shirts could they feel themselves downtrodden. Outside agitators had to work hard to convince them they had been robbed by eastern money barons. Johnson held that these agitators were crooks and scoundrels, working only to increase their own power and fortunes by any means and incidentally undermining the honor and honesty of the Norwegian group. The rich farmer who became a Populist candidate found no trick too vile in his campaign to crush the old schoolmaster who led his moral opposition, though both were Norwegian and had been good friends before.

Most important, Johnson accused Populists of focusing on material-

---

* A recent historical study argues the opposite, that at least "Norwegian-Americans have stood consistently left of center in their political outlook and action." See Jo Wefald, *A Voice of Protest, Norwegians in American Politics, 1890-1917* (Northfield, Minn., 1971).

163

istic values only, claiming that if farmers could get more money out of businessmen and bankers, they would automatically solve all the problems of society, and live in peace and happiness for evermore. The old schoolmaster rejected Populist propaganda because it "tried to build an uprising of the people solely on a slight material improvement, which is still doubtful, by the way. I have myself hoped for an uprising of the people . . . but I wanted it to concern their souls and not just their pocketbooks. . . . The dissatisfaction which has been worked up is false. This way of thinking that prosperous people must constantly have more and more protection from the government, leads them ever further from themselves and the growth of their character, which alone can be the basis of the future."[70]

Johnson was the only author who depicted the similar agrarian political movement in Dakota shortly before World War I. In a later book he described how hoodwinked voters laid the future of an entire state in the hands of radical politicians and idealists, who planned to change the governmental and legal structure, socialize much of private business, and found all kinds of cooperative banks and firms which would be so profitable that taxes could be abolished. The war intervened before these reforms got under way, and when the politicians could no longer deceive the voters with postponements and promises, they absconded to greener pastures with the public funds. But the moral damage had already been done, the novelist lamented.

The old Norwegian integrity was no longer to the same degree considered a virtue. Alien agitators rushed from farm to farm, strange speakers held forth in the towns, they used every possible trick to arouse the farmers and keep them stirred up. Those who understood that tricks were being used comforted themselves with the thought that the opposing party did the same, it was an eye for an eye. . . . But the majority floated with the current and were dominated by the agitators' poisonous tongues. . . . They forgot the old ways of thinking and the old peace, the spirit from agitators' circles in the large cities moved in and lived with the freeholding farmers, they were no longer the same people.[71]

7. POLITICAL CORRUPTION

Nowhere did Johnson present other politicians for comparison with these, but practically all the writers portrayed American politicians of any party as scoundrels and crooks. Sometimes an immigrant who was introduced to political corruption recoiled in moral condemnation, like the Danish-American contractor who entered his bid to build a public building. A member of the city government demanded a healthy cut of graft first, and when the Dane refused in shocked surprise, he lost the contract.[72] More often, political corruption was taken for granted. In a Norwegian-American prohibition novel the question of closing the local saloons was put to a vote. The tactics of the saloon party were calmly described as the usual thing: buying votes with drink, repeater-voting, outsiders brought in to swear they were local residents, stuffing the ballot box, and the rest.[73] A satirical novelist was thoroughly amused at the dirty politics his Norwegian hero learned to play against his archenemy, an old Yankee named Ward. Political agitations of the nation at large appeared only as a background for their squabbles. Ward was a Republician, of course, but while the reforms of the Free Silverites were the last thing on earth the Norwegian wanted to see enacted, he pretended to be one of them in order to oppose Ward. He even made a deal with another corrupt Norwegian businessman whom Ward had brought into politics as *his* tool long before, and this ex-saloonkeeper went to the state legislature on the Populist ticket while the hero got his courthouse and county seat. Thus the will of the people was carried out at the grass roots, this author ironically concluded.[74]

Occasionally an immigrant writer reacted to political corruption with righteous indignation. A novelette published in 1910 seemed to be a thinly disguised attack on Wisconsin politicians of the time, although a half century later all that the book communicated was disgust for voters in general because they were so easily misled. The villain, Jacobus, won election to the state legislature by making the most stupid contra-dictory promises, but even when he was exposed as a scoundrel the voters did not throw him out. After he had finally shot himself they *still* elected him posthumously in obedience to the orders of the chief boss, who wanted to appoint a substitute. The good character, on the other hand, never won an election.[75]

Few heroes in these stories ever ran for public office. At best, a good character who was elected to the state legislature discovered that it was a farce. No one paid any attention to law proposals, representatives of greedy corporations bribed openly, legislators bargained for each others' votes in cynical horsetrading. The Dane's proposal for a food inspection law was buried in committee until a clever older politician dug it up and got it passed for the job appointments it would provide. Little by little the hero realized that "the Northwest was too young, too uncivilized for lawmaking. The life to be regulated was still with-out fast form."[76]

Although not very interested in public office, a considerable number of Scandinavians were shown to be eager voters. The Populist movement taught them that the ballot could be used as a tool to protect their economic interests, and they continued their political activity in the American pattern of flaming excitement at election times but indifference in between. "The Danish political club regularly went to sleep im-mediately after the election every second year, but awakened to violent activity every other year for the gubernatorial election. And every fourth year at the presidential election for a month it overshadowed all other organizations."[77]

Politics and religion were often named as the sole interests of immigrant men outside the round of their daily lives. On the other hand, a large number of characters were pictured as indifferent to political issues. Women were rarely interested in matters of government, and many stories following the daily life of immigrants through long periods never mentioned the topic. The theme of religion, however, was present in almost every book, and concerned not only men and women alike but also children. A reader who weighs what these works of fiction revealed of their characters' lack of contact with politics before emigration, in contrast with their dependence on and interest in the homeland church, is inclined to conclude that patterns of behavior rooted in the Old World were in this respect firmly re-established in the New.

V. The Church

The divorce between religion and government in the United States presented Scandinavian Lutheran immigrants with a new situation. In the Old Country most had been passive church members; they were born into a state church directed by a pastor educated, appointed, and paid by a distant authority. Only in Sweden did the congregation have a limited voice in the appointment of its minister. One novel published in 1899 recorded trial sermons preached in the local church by three candidates for a vacant post. The land-owning peasants wanted one man, the gentry another; of course in the voting the gentry won out.[78]

In all three countries the rules and regulations of organized religion were dictated by central authorities. The local people paid for their church both through general taxes which supported the entire system and through payments to the local minister for special services, offerings at Christmas and Easter, and work donated for maintenance and repair of local church property. Otherwise they had nothing to do or say except attend church regularly and profess the doctrines taught there. Indeed, when pietistic Lutherans undertook more active expression of their faith, they often suffered both persecution and ostracism. When a pietist in a Norwegian valley lay dying, his minister refused to administer the Lord's Supper to him. "Rev. Hjort did not like the pietists. . . . Instinctively he felt they questioned his conversion and his inner call to preach the Word of God. . . . Both in public and in private he ridiculed them, and the only times he became eloquent was when he denounced pietism and fanaticism."[79] Pietists often organized their own

166

extrachurch forms of worship, but with only lay readers and preachers; few withdrew from the sacraments and service of the state church. It was an eloquent commentary on the devotion of this group to their traditional faith, that in spite of the passivity of their previous relationship to the formal church, they nevertheless promptly accepted the responsibility of establishing their own religious institutions in America.

1. ORGANIZATION

The pattern on which these churches were organized combined models from the Old World and the New. Newly arrived immigrants attempted to set up this important institution as much like the one at home as possible, if only because they knew no other way. But their knowledge of the inner workings of the state church was extremely limited, and its structure could not be fitted to the drastically different circumstances into which they came. No direction was offered or expected from the Mother Church, either, bound as it was to the nation on which the immigrants had turned their backs. Individual clergymen might feel called to follow these flocks to guide them, but no hint of concern for such renegades ever escaped official circles as pictured in this literature. Therefore European models were shown dominating only in external characteristics and internal doctrine—the aspects of church life farthest removed from American conditions and law.

To keep their church as much as possible the same, these Lutherans had to introduce a drastic change in the matter of membership. At home, because every person in the community had been born a church member, no formal definition of the congregation beyond geographical delineation of the parish was necessary; but in the United States those who wished to be accounted parishioners had to stand up and say so. A Norwegian-American novel, recording the foundation of a congregation by the historical personage Pastor Preus, had one man object to signing the register. All in the settlement were Lutherans, he argued, so all belonged automatically to the church. Preus had to convince him that this was like the "free church" at home: each member must join individually.[80]

Occasionally the most pious discussed the further problem of refusing church membership to the "unsaved." A Swedish Lutheran Colonization Company in Kansas tried to drive away all would-be settlers who would not subscribe to their strict creed—and they picked and chose among the applicants.[81] Usually, however, characters who considered this issue concluded that they could not judge who were true Christians in the sight of God, and that they must therefore follow the Old-Country precedent of admitting any and all applicants into the shelter of the church.

167

Any and all, that is, with the same profession of faith and ethnic background. In the many stories which followed the fates of Scandinavians living together with other nationalities, the latter were automatically excluded from the church as from the social life of the others, provided that the former were numerous enough to have their own. The different tongue not only served to hold those of the same national origin to their traditional church but also effectively excluded others, so that even after the language of service had become English the members of the congregations referred to in this literature seemed still to be largely of the same branch of Scandinavian descent as the founding fathers. A handful of exceptions were married partners who joined the church of their Swedish or Danish spouse; but mixed marriages were also recorded where the Methodist or Catholic wife continued to attend services in her own church, while the Lutheran husband went off to his.

2. DISTINCTIVE CHARACTERISTICS

When church membership was restricted to people with the same language and traditions, they could more easily agree to establish their religious institution on the basis of the European model in all respects not affected by American law. Therefore whenever a congregation was formed in this literature, everything possible was done at first as it had been at home. "The church buildings stood 'in a high place,'—that idea the founders had surely brought from Norway"[82]—preferably where the first graves of the community had been dug; for those who had gone to God should lie in the shadow of His house. The builders were too poor to imitate the beautiful old churches at home, but they could copy the plain four-square meeting houses of pietists and dissenters in the Old Country, with the addition of a tower and bell. The altar was toward the east, with an embroidered altar cloth, candles, and Bible, and if possible an altarpiece hung behind. In one novel a Norwegian donated the cover his mother had woven for his marriage bed to this higher purpose.[83] In others the bare wall behind the altar was commented on unfavorably, for the absence of adornment in the house of God was felt as a fault. There were low benches to kneel on during communion, and a high pulpit for the parson when he preached. Men and women sat on opposite sides of the church, separated by sex just like at home. Several books mentioned continuing the Old-Country custom of ending the ringing of the church bell as the minister stepped out in his robe and ruff, so that the last ding-dong was the opening of the service.

The ceremony itself remained the same, with identical hymns sung out of familiar hymnals, the selfsame prayers and confession of faith and order of worship. The precentor still led the congregation in chanted responses; communion, baptism, confirmation, marriage, and funeral ceremonies remained unchanged. There was the same procession of worshippers to lay special offerings on the altar for the minister at Christmas and sometimes Easter—the only regular cash donations he got from his parishioners back home. Prayer meetings and mission societies were soon established, for these activities were common in the Old Country. Even old-fashioned functions like the churching of women to cleanse them after childbirth, and public church discipline applied to such wrongdoers as sabbath violators, occasionally turned up in tales of the early days. All these characteristics appeared as background descriptive touches in story after story in all three branches of the literature.

In later fiction, however, many of these distinctive features had disappeared. Sometimes a plot chronicled the change in action, like a fight within a congregation over the site of a new church—whether it should be near the resting place of the dead in the old tradition, or with the restless joy of life around it, in the American way. The young Danish-American minister, who preferred the latter alternative, also wanted a kitchen and serving room in the basement of the new structure; but some of his flock reacted in horror: " '. . . wouldn't this take away the atmosphere of holiness which should be everywhere in the house of God? . . . Cooking and coffee-drinking in the church!' '*Under* the church,' corrected Karoline," who clearly supported the minister in such American innovations.[84] Sometimes one old characteristic hung on in a given church where the others had disappeared. In a Norwegian-American tale an elderly wife and husband sat side by side at Christmas service (separation by sex had ended) but both filed up to the altar to lay their offerings on it.[85] Most often, however, the Old-World customs simply disappeared from later stories. Since their presence had previously been worthy of notice, the reader infers that lack of mention indicated their absence—especially when incompatible customs, such as regular passing of collection plates, were described instead.

On the other hand, a host of new characteristics akin to those of American churches made their appearance in books published in the 1890s and after. There was occasional reference to their inception. A character commented how American churches went to much trouble to capture the interest of the children with parties and festivals, unlike the Swedish state church, which required dull memorization of dogma;[86] or a conservative congregation objected to a new minister who was always trying to improve things, and who even defended young people's organizations, prohibition societies, and such, "which people weren't used to from the old days."[87] Sometimes the clergyman was the agent of innovation, sometimes he opposed it with all his might; but its

169

origin and cause can be seen in the complaint of an old Swedish farmer that *his* pastor kept their church just as it was in the Old Country, but the young folks had all deserted it.[88]

Most immigrant churches avoided this fate by the introduction of extraneous activity into the religious organization. Many kinds of uplifting entertainment were instituted for the benefit of the younger generation—debates, readings, lectures, music, decorous parties with innocent games. The minister who had noticed that Thursday-evening prayer meetings were almost deserted except when refreshments were served at 25 cents a head (whereupon the place was crowded) only heeded the signs of the times when he arranged much coffee-drinking in his Swedish church.[89] These immigrant churches gradually adopted all the American appendages to religious activity in response to a dual challenge: the need to provide a counter-attraction to all the interesting doings in native religious institutions when language was no longer a barrier, and the need to earn money for church support. Because the church was long the only organ of social activity in many immigrant communities, it developed many new enterprises: Sunday schools and Bible camps, annual church conferences, young people's clubs, ladies' aid societies, sewing circles, church suppers and socials, bazaars and picnics. It might be a *lutefisk* supper instead of an ice cream social, and handicraft work of knitting and embroidery in Old-Country style might be sold at the bazaar, but both the end and the form of raising money were American.

Formal church organization received comparatively little attention from the immigrant authors. Evidently the matter was so familiar to their readers, or so irrelevant to their plot, that they seldom found it worthy of mention. Prior to formation of a congregation, those characters who wished to worship in social forms held informal Bible readings and prayer meetings modeled on Old-World pietistic practice, and for the services of a minister were dependent on the "buggy-priests" described in many pioneering tales. These operated on the American pattern of the circuit-rider, circulating through frontier settlements looking for Lutherans of their own ethnic group. Normally one of these initiated and directed the fictional founding of a congregation, so that inexperienced laymen received the guidance they needed.

American legal requirements caused a number of radical differences in the structure of this daughter church. The congregation was still the basic unit, although now defined and recruited in quite another way, and it still issued a call for its minister; but from there on the immigrant authors pointed out dissimilarity at every point. In the first place, the parishioners had to do everything for themselves. "Our misfortune is that we were brought up in the state church," a pious

170

Lutheran harangued his fellow Danes. "We are used to having everything done for us by bishops and ministers. All this care by the State . . . has held our initiative down. . . . But fellow-countrymen and comrades, we must learn that if we are to get anywhere in spiritual matters, *we* have to take hold. If we are to have a Lutheran church, we must build it ourselves."[90]

To be recognized as a church under American law, a group of individuals had to incorporate itself: define the body of members, specify their powers, structure their functions. Registers of membership were signed, constitutions drawn up, congregational councils elected to take charge. Since none of this had occurred in the Old Country before they left, the immigrants must have followed American models here.

When they had organized themselves as a congregation, then they must call a minister; but now *they* decided who should serve them, instead of meekly accepting the decision of higher authorities. A Norwegian pioneer held his head high on the way home from a meeting where the settlers had decided to organize a church. "He pictured the time to come when he would sit in the congregation council and help appoint a minister. For it was certainly not the King who did that here. Per was in America now."[91] Often several churches had to share the services of one minister and divide his cost. A pioneer clergyman in Dakota found his pastorate larger than the whole area of Denmark. In his first year he drove 18,000 miles to give 150 Sunday sermons, and at least equally many services on weekdays.[92] In time, however, every congregation pictured in the fiction achieved the goal of having a minister of its own.

When the congregation was formed and the preacher hired, the next problem was to provide a place of worship. In settled communities the characters usually began by hiring a hall or sharing a church with another sect; on the frontier the first services were held in the largest house, a barn, a school, even under the open sky. But everywhere, at the earliest possible opportunity, all pitched in to build their own church. Several authors described the pride of those who took part in the work: sawmill workers carefully putting aside the finest planks for this purpose, local bigwigs submitting to the orders of the one trained carpenter in the settlement.[93] And the sense of achievement they felt sitting in a house of worship they had built with their own hands —this none of them could have dreamt of in the Old Country.[94]

3. FINANCIAL SUPPORT

When congregation and church had been created, and minister and parsonage provided for, who was to pay the bill? Donations in the spirit of sacrifice for God had often made possible the initial achievement. For a Danish church one settler gave land for the building, another a lot for the graveyard hard by, a third a gravelpit for material to make cement, and all pitched in to work for nothing until the structure was completed.[95] But sooner or later permanent financial arrangements had to be made. Story after story emphasized the great difference this economic responsibility for their religious life made to immigrants who heretofore had paid so indirectly for their church through taxes that they had never given the matter a thought. Now the congregational council figured out how many bushels of wheat they must contribute per man per year; later members pledged annual donations in proportion to income. Still later a church treasurer or financial committee tried to collect tithes from a recalcitrant tightwad, or saw with dismay how pledges declined when a minister offended a wealthy group or individual. Here of course lay the source of the power of each congregation over its own affairs; with the responsibility they accepted for church matters followed authority over the whole.

Mentioned from time to time in the literature were higher organizations to which local churches belonged. These synods were already present in the earliest stories, with no indication of their original formation—although later splits and splinterings were recorded. District meetings and general conferences held in each synod appeared in several stories, attended by both clergy and laymen. In a Norwegian-American novel laid in the 1880s a pastor pressed a devout farmer to attend a conference meeting; people were criticizing the organization as being too much run by clergymen, as of course it must be if laymen did not take part.[96] A generation later, June was described as the great month of church meetings, when "Farm and business are put aside for awhile, and great bands leave for the annual conferences, as the children of Israel in olden times traveled to Jerusalem for the great festivals."[97] These were clearly American institutions, for no laymen in the Old Country had attended such congresses. The bishops who occasionally appeared as background figures in stories were familiar enough from the Old World, but no author indicated their method of choice or function; clearly their power over member churches, like that of the synods, was limited. The whole structure was thus thoroughly democratic, under the control of lay as well as clerical elected leaders, dependent for financial support and ultimately for power on the individual congregations.

The changed status of the immigrant church had the dual effect of eliminating those who had no interest in it and stimulating those who were concerned. In many stories indifferent churchgoers in their old homes were awakened to religious enthusiasm in the new.

Endre had become a diligent churchgoer since he came to Chicago. His disposition and whole temperament was religiously inclined. As long as he had remained in Norway, it had drawn nourishment from many sources. The local young people's society with its patriotic life . . . the early awakened love for a young woman. . . . The church was the center and summit of it all, but this he had not consciously realized. He had gone to church only when it was convenient.

Here in Chicago he had only the church to turn to, and it attracted him with constantly stronger force.[98]

Author after author recorded his characters' impression of how much more lively church life was among Scandinavians in America than back home. A minister who had resigned his call in Denmark because there were so few true believers among all the members born into the state church, was delighted by the energy and blooming health of the Danish free church in the New World. He estimated that towns with the same number of Danish inhabitants as at home supported three times as many churches, at least.[99] A devout young Swedish clergyman, who emigrated because his homeland had become so ungodly, found his ideal in Swedish-American Lutheranism, which he vowed to serve until death.[100]

4. CHURCH CONTROVERSY

Yet this new, free status of the Scandinavian-American church had unexpected consequences which were less welcome. A group of people who had worshipped God under a common theological roof for centuries might be expected to establish the same unified religious institution in the New World. In fact the opposite took place. This literature reflected Scandinavian-American church life not as harmonious whole growing out of a shared past, but as a clamorous battlefield where Norwegian fought Norwegian and Swede strove with Swede as bitterly as either national group ever opposed outsiders.[101]

A number of fictional accounts of this conflict traced its origin to dissension within Lutheran state churches in Europe. The story was the same whether laid in Sweden, Denmark, or Norway: how the state church had long since lost its living soul to formalism and rationalism, so that holy worship became a social gathering which began with a sermon and ended with buying and selling. In reaction to these conditions, pietistic movements spread through the rural districts late in the eighteenth century and into the nineteenth. "It was a deeper and warmer spiritual life which these new movements emphasized, a more personal Christianity, more serious and living faith in God, a more holy life," explained a Swedish-American novelist; if this awakening concern for a more emotional belief had been accepted and properly directed within the state church, it would have done only good. But instead it

173

was repressed—people forbidden to meet for private worship, thrown into prison as troublemakers.[102] A Danish-American novel indicted the Danish state church on the same grounds, but recounted how the opposition led by such great reformers as Grundtvig and Kierkegaard finally brought reform, so that even lay preaching won a place within formal church organization as the "Inner Mission."[103] Norwegian-American tales often mentioned pietists or Haugeans among immigrant Lutherans, followers of the Norwegian lay preacher Hans Nielsen Hauge, who emphasized evangelicalism and spiritual awakening but always within the state church.[104]

Once removed from the control of that institution, however, the warring factions transplanted to America split off in all directions. A minister discussing the inner conflicts of Norwegian-American Lutheranism in a novel explained, "Besides human depravity, according to which each seeks his own and not what belongs to Christ, the basic cause must be sought in the different views on what makes a true Christian and also somewhat in the different kinds of upbringing our people received in Norway. There we have the high-church party with the majority of ministers at its head, but there we have also the low-church party with revivals, lay activity, and inner-mission organizations on its program. . . . The former stresses the importance of the sacraments, the forms of worship, and everything which might be called churchliness, the latter conversion and the life of the soul first and last."[105]

Both types of minister were recorded in one parish in Norway, where three local men were called "readers" in ridicule because they read the Bible aloud to each other. The old pastor viewed these three as dangerous fanatics, and warned the people against such vagary so often that he seldom had time to remind them of their own vices. Then a new minister came to the parish, who appointed the three "readers" as his advisers. He preached not only in the church but also at prayer meetings in private homes. Person after person underwent conversion, and the revival this pastor stimulated lasted a long time.[106]

Most immigrants, however, had experienced only one of the warring church camps before leaving their homeland, and carried along predilections in favor of that one which they expressed in founding their organized church activity anew. Fiction often recorded the very moment of planting these seeds of discord from the Old World in new soil. A tale of Norwegians in Minnesota before the Civil War described their first devotional service when Elling Eielsen (a historical figure) visited the little settlement. He preached standing in a doorway, so that everybody both in the house and outside could hear. But the weather was very hot, and the man of God removed his coat. This human gesture

174

horrified his listeners; no true minister would do such! He preached much too movingly and plainly to be an ordained clergyman, and he did not wear the traditional black robe and white ruff. Some of the settlers were afraid to have him pronounce the marriage and baptismal ceremonies. At home no one had ever preached so well except pious laymen, and they certainly couldn't marry people! The dissatisfied and suspicious sent for Pastor Preus (also historical), who organized their congregation and suggested for their first minister a young man just ordained after his training at the University of Christiania (Oslo). This high-church advocate turned out to be a tyrant, insisting that all confess their sins to him, especially the sin of setting oneself up against the Lord's anointed. In the end, the truly devout sent for a genuine revivalist minister from Norway.[107]

Under this plot lay a great deal of church history which would be common knowledge to contemporary readers. They could place the author by his rejection of both the anticlerical Eielsen, the validity of whose belated ordination was subject to much dispute, and the high-church, Oslo-trained party. When the author applied the metaphor of "grubbing" a claim before it could be planted—cleaning out stumps and underbrush—to the Lutheran church in America, which must be cleansed of centuries' overgrowth of conceit, superstition, and prejudice, he clearly took his stand with the low-church, evangelical faction of state-church supporters, who wished to transplant only this portion of the European model to America.

Before long an immigrant could choose exactly what part of the Old-World tradition he wished to uphold; there were churches to represent them all. A Norwegian settlement in the Red River Valley of Minnesota received its first pastoral visit in the summer of 1870, a novel recorded. Before a meeting was called, however, a committee was elected to investigate whether the visitor was a true Lutheran minister. They wanted no false learning brought in. This man claimed to have been ordained by Elling Eielsen, and he did not have and would not use the black robe and white ruff. The committee denied him the right to speak, but he held services anyhow, and the community split over the issue of whether or not he was a true clergyman. Not long afterwards another Norwegian Lutheran minister came, this one outfitted with full clerical garb. More believed in him, and many brought their children for him to baptize. The following year the local Haugeans formed a congregation and called a minister. Then a Synod-pastor came through and organized another church; and finally even a Conference-preacher. (Contemporary readers would immediately recognize the three leading rival synods within Norwegian-American Lutheranism.) First the local ministers and then the people began arguing bitterly over questions of doctrine. Within a decade the members of the different synods would have practically nothing to do with one another, but this author noted thankfully that the bitterness lasted only some twenty to thirty years.[108]

The literature reflected this church conflict mainly within individual congregations. It usually caused the partition of the congregation, although according to these authors many more such divisions resulted from "human depravity" than from genuine difference in belief.

A typical example was the fight in a Danish-American community over a gravel-pit. This had been donated to the local church at the time of its founding; but the donor had never formally transferred the title, and continued to pay taxes on the property. His idea was that all members of the church should help themselves to gravel as a symbol of mutual cooperation and friendliness. But the old man died, and his American-born son, discovering he had inherited legal ownership after all, accepted the purchase offer of the state highway department. At a church meeting called to discuss the problem, the minister spoke his mind. The sale might have been legal, but it was morally wrong; it was against God's will. Shortly afterwards the American-born son was killed in an accident, and at his funeral the minister preached from the text, "As ye sow, so shall ye reap." Those who had supported the young man in the conflict were mortally offended over what looked like a hint that God had killed the young man over the gravel-pit affair, and a good number withdrew from the congregation to form their own.

Now over twenty years have passed since this happened. The two churches in Peace Plain are still standing. But there is no minister there, and no services are held in either.

It cost too much for the two small congregations to keep the work going; and they could not bring themselves to offer a brotherly hand and ask forgiveness for the many bitter words which had been said on both sides in the course of time.[109]

In a factory town, the Swedish colony numbering a few hundred souls had originally one Lutheran church, which they could well afford; "but after typical Swedish jealousy had been given free rein a few years, three spires pointed towards the abode of peace on high."[110]

The height of ecclesiastical pandemonium based on personal animosity was recorded in a short story where a local "parish king" tried to run the church like everything else to suit himself. When the other settlers elected his archenemy as president of the congregation, which belonged to the Norwegian Synod, Lars sought revenge by bringing in another minister from the Conference. He could not get control of "his" church building for the new pastor, however, for the old congregation legally owned it—and men stood guard day and night to keep him out. Finally Lars built a second church in the same style as the first, and so near that worshippers in one could hear the service in the other. A long series

176

of conflicts followed, as when Lars was refused permission to bury two children in the Synod graveyard with his Conference minister; he buried them anyway, and the next morning the caskets were standing outside the wall. After several years of spiteful tricks on both sides the two ministers finally came to an agreement, and Lars withdrew from association with both. A Yankee came by once when both churches were in session and asked what all the racket was about. Were the two congregations fighting? No, said Lars, it was only the Norwegian Lutheran church in America.[111]

This story was a highly exaggerated account by an author who attacked everything Lutheran, but its caricature reflected an important result of the removal of effective control over individual congregations in American Protestantism. "What the state church had molded, the free church could not preserve," wrote a more objective novelist; "what the first could command, the second failed in requesting. 'In the congregational councils, every little parish king and bookworm bigot has his hobby-horse to ride, and they ride through the congregations so they are split into splinters over a hair's breadth of abstract interpretation,' an old sexton said."[112] Indeed, many intrachurch conflicts supposedly over doctrine were shown by these writers to have been inextricably involved with local personality conflicts. A trilogy of novels by Johannes B. Wist about an immigrant named Jonas Olson described many years of rivalry between neighboring Norwegian Lutheran churches in Dakota, including doctrinal argument between Missourians and Antimissourians; but the local schism was shown really to be based on Jonas' lasting resentment over having been thrown out of the first organizational meeting held by the majority group.[113]

Even the ultradevout first novel published in this literature, laid during the Civil War, pictured the initial schism among Norwegians in a pioneer community in Minnesota as a mixture of religious and worldly concerns. An ignoramus who had failed his teacher's examination in Norway came through as a traveling parson, preaching conversion and economy. He attacked Norwegian Synod ministers as false prophets and hardhearted tyrants because they maintained that the Bible did not declare slavery a sin. Many settlers wanted him for their regular clergyman, even though he was not ordained. "Some agree with him because he preaches conversion, other because he prates against Norwegian state church ministers, and still others because he could be hired so much more cheaply, and all congregational expenses would be much less with him as parson."[114]

Yet the literature recorded many a conflict over genuine belief also, on both local and synodical levels, not always resulting in an open break. Danish-American authors especially tended to show opposition

177

between Grundtvigian "happy" Christianity and the moroseness of the "saved" ending in reconciliation. In an Iowa community where nearly everyone belonged to the one Danish Lutheran church, "some from habit, some in earnest, and some because it was good business," a revival movement had split the congregation into two camps. The "saved" became very puritanical, rejecting as the work of Satan all joy, song and dance, even politics and cultural activities. The way to God, the stern and relentless judge, lay through sorrow. In this novel the "happy" Christianity won out and the "saved" were brought to see the error of their sullen ways through the death of an innocent child, without schism in the formal church.[115] In another Danish-American novel the domineering minister represented harsh orthodox Christianity, preaching only about the misery of life, the sufferings of Christ, the sinfulness of man. But the newcomers who opposed him with their Grundtvigian views had flaws in their Christianity too; they felt hate for their enemies, lacked sensitivity for the tragedy of human life. The credible plot in this novel developed slow inner reform on both sides, until they finally met in a compromise based on Christian love and including both joy and sorrow.[116]

Not all accounts of revivalism had such happy endings, but most authors agreed in rejecting the morose moralistic attitudes of "saved" characters. In a Norwegian-American tale, for instance, husband and wife belonged to a pietistic circle led by a lay preacher, which met in private homes or a rented hall; "they sang long Swedish songs to guitar accompaniment and talked about the Worm which never dies, and the fire which is never quenched, until they hardly dared set out in the dark for home. There was much crying and much prayer in an atmosphere wet with tears and soggy confessions."[117]

Alignments of conflict both within and between local churches remained in constant flux, however. Sometimes the "saved" were arraigned against the Grundtvigians, sometimes against the orthodox; occasionally the last two were pitted against each other. In other accounts the combat was between high-church formalism and low-church emotionalism, or between the laity and the vested interests of the clergy. Some ministers opposed lay preaching, prayer meetings, and confessional gatherings, while others encouraged and led them; but although many clergymen were presented by their authors as misguided, practically all were adjudged sincere. Typical was a long tale about a devout minister who had kept his congregation united and growing for over ten years. He got a large, fine church built and paid for, and always taught only the pure truth from God's word as he had learned it in school. He recognized that few had been won to his ideas, but he did not realize how dull and dry his sermons were. When a traveling preacher from a rival synod appeared and held services in private houses, converting in good old emotional style, the elderly minister underestimated his appeal and did nothing until too late, when the majority of the congregation withdrew from the synod and took the church with them, under American law. The author convinced the reader of absolute sincerity on both sides: the new preacher seeing the old as fallen asleep in sin, the old viewing the new as a wolf among sheep, a tool of Satan, misleading the ignorant into eternal perdition.[118]

References to doctrinal argument were numerous in all three branches of the literature, but most authors gave more attention to its social effects than to its content. Seldom did they even mention the issues at stake, summarizing rather a character's reaction: "At first he had followed these theological duels fought in the newspapers by laymen and clergy, but he had never been able to find out what the controversy was about. It had however made him disgusted with the whole of church life among the battling Norwegians."[119] The theoretical argument over whether or not slavery was sinful in and for itself was mentioned in a few early Norwegian-American stories; all agreed that its effects were bad, but the orthodox held that God justified the institution in the Old Testament. Doctrines of the sanctity of the "saved," of atonement and the basis of salvation, turned up in a few scattered references. But only the early labor leader exiled from Norway, Marcus Thrane, listed major issues satirically in *Den gamle Wisconsin Bibelen:* "The Lord gave this synod a still more perfect word than He had given the Mother Church, so that the People of the Western Home received the true, unfalsified dogma on slavery and on sanctification and on predestination and on interpretation of the Fourth Commandment. . . ."[120]

Such doctrinal disputation, however, was highly serious to those who took part, and these were not the clergy only. One incident related the homecoming of a devout old farmer from a district meeting where he had seen that the coming split in his synod was unavoidable. With tears in his eyes he told his family how the ministers had debated for hours trying to clarify exactly what their disagreements meant. He had dreaded a break in the synod before, but now he realized it was better to have the lines drawn, so that everyone could know where the others stood.[121]

So much controversy helped maintain a whole spectrum of Lutheran institutions within each of the three national groups. Many newcomers noted this range of choice, and some even went shopping from one church to another until they found one to their taste. A recent arrival in Chicago discovered that in the first church he visited he missed the precentor's part in the ceremony, and the minister's robe and ruff; he had never thought about either before, but now he did not feel at home in a Norwegian Lutheran ceremony where they were lacking. The next

179

Sunday he went to a different house of worship and found both the precentor and the ministerial dress, so there he stayed.[122]

Several characters who joined a church on the basis of chance discovered afterwards that they were drawn into theological conflict in spite of themselves. One greenhorn thanked his stars that he had not known there were five different Norwegian Lutheran synods when he came to the the United States, because he would have had to investigate them all; but in his ignorance he simply joined the one in which his brother was ordained. "Although I had not made a choice, I found out in time that I had taken a standpoint. . . . The fact that I had accidentally become a member of Hauge's synod made me a churchly opponent of all the other synods."[123] Another newcomer, who had casually joined a Norwegian Synod church in Minneapolis, discovered himself in the minority when he moved to a pioneer settlement in Dakota.

He suddenly realized that if he was to be anybody out here on the prairie, where people seemed to be so intensely interested in these church matters, he would have to study up on theology. . . . Unfortunately he had neglected to investigate the questions of conflict. They had not interested him before. In his circles of acquaintanceship back in Minneapolis people were concerned about quite other things; and when occasionally he got together with Synod people and they had a chance to talk about churchly matters, he never learned anything because they were all in agreement. Now he realized that he, at least, was ignorant of what he had agreed with.[124]

So he undertook assiduous study of Synod-friendly newspapers, and became such a rabid partisan that he led the split between the Norwegians of the community into two warring camps.

5. SOCIAL EFFECTS OF CHURCH CONTROVERSY

Of greatest concern to the authors of this literature were the social effects of these disputes. Norwegian-American literature contained the largest volume of discusssion of this matter, but the other two branches echoed identical conditions. The only contact between the Children of Light and the Children of Darkness in a Danish-American community, for instance, was in the public grade school; beyond the age-limit required by law for that, the separation was complete.[125] In a pioneer Swedish community divided between pietistic and "separatist" Lutherans, the antagonism of religious differences was "carried into the social and economic structure of the community. Stores owned by Lutherans employed clerks of like faith. The Separatists did the same. People patronized those of their own creed, and lines were closely drawn. Intermarriage between young people of the two factions was unthinkable."[126] Over and over the same story was told in Norwegian tales:

The ties of old friendship broke. Neighbor did not speak to neighbor. The daughter who was married to a member of the other party became a stranger in her father's house. Man and wife turned into dog and cat. Brothers and sisters were sundered from one another.

On the other hand, old enemies became friends and were reconciled, when only they found themselves on the same side of the insurmountable fence which had been raised between Schmidt and Missouri [synods].[127]

A positive effect of all this controversy was "such churchgoing and interest for churchly matters as can hardly be matched in all the history of Lutherdom." The piety of the majority of rural immigrants not only became a group norm but also was intensified far above what it had been in the Old Country. Some of the reasons for the increased importance of this integrative institution have been discussed earlier: it was the only institution (except the family) which the immigrants could reestablish relatively unchanged in the new environment, and so served as the chief bond with their premigrative past. In many communities it provided the only organized social activity available for a long time, and consequently became the center around which all else revolved. Because it was dependent for existence upon the voluntary contributions of its members, these were awakened to new attitudes of responsibility and participation in church affairs. The doctrinal altercation which rose to such heights of bitterness and schism among Scandinavian Lutherans in America thus not only measured how much their church meant to these people but also served to increase their interest in it still more. Who among ordinary folks ever argued so hotly about predestination in the Old Country? But a second-generation character in a Norwegian-American tale recalled how his father and their nearest neighbor disputed this question for years, culling their munition from opposing church newspapers.

Both could get very excited and go so far that they snapped their fingers at each other; but both had enough common sense and self-control not to go beyond a certain point, and then they were just as good friends again. For these two, and perhaps for many others, the conflict certainly was stimulating and of considerable benefit.[128]

When later immigrants with less interest in religion arrived, many from urban backgrounds, they often discovered that they had to develop or simulate enthusiasm for the church before they were accepted as members of the group. A Danish newcomer looking for a job in a midwestern rural community was informed that no one would think of hiring a man who had not been recommended by the parson. This character had hardly seen a man of the cloth since his confirmation, but now he sought out the local minister and soon became a regular churchgoer.[129] Religious belief was thus shown to be an essential aspect of group identification, for many immigrants a more significant one than their language or national origin.

181

Attitudes expressed toward non-Lutheran faiths emphasized the importance to group identity of church alignments. The pious majority among the characters looked upon on other faiths as anathema. Most vehement was the anti-Catholic sentiment of these Lutherans; for those who professed the Catholic faith were doubly outsiders, in nationality as well as theology. "To think of binding oneself in marriage to an Antichrist and devil's helper!" exclaimed a Norwegian-American goodwife about a neighbor girl who had married a Catholic. "Those aren't *my* words. I was sitting reading in *Lutheran Testimony* just now when you came, and this expression is right there. Isn't it terrible? It's the same as throwing oneself right into the arms of the evil Fiend."[130]

Denunciation of Protestant sects was only slightly less forceful in the early literature. In a novel laid in 1852, a helpful Swedish-American minister rescued a party of hapless Swedes upon their arrival in New York; but when it turned out he was not Lutheran, the hero of the story recoiled from him in horror. The sect of this pastor was not identified, but most of the party rejected the material gain he offered them if they would settle near his colony. "I was born and bred Swedish," declaimed the hero, "and Swedish I will remain. My fathers' church shall be planted here in America even if I have only three others with me."[131]

Baptism and Methodism were most mentioned by later authors, whose prejudice against the sects seems to have been lessened by personal contact through time. A Danish-American novel of 1891 recorded the troubles of a prairie community where the Baptists organized before the Lutherans and therefore got a head start; but the community survived, and Danes of different faiths maintained comparatively normal relations with each other.[132] In another book the same minister-author reconciled Methodist children with their Danish Lutheran mother on her deathbed: "I cannot understand that our hearts must be sundered because we belong each to our own branch of the Christian church."[133] A Swedish-American author disapproved of the hatred she recorded between immigrants of common ethnic background but different faiths. A Lutheran family would have nothing to do with new neighbors who they discovered were Baptists. When a sister came on an extended visit, they had to leave her alone in the house for a few days; and on their return they were horrified to discover that she had been fraternizing with the Baptist neighbors.

"But Hulda, you certainly can't believe that they'll get to heaven when they're not Lutherans?"
"Indeed I believe they will, if they are sincere and want to do what is right."
"Now you go too far, little Hulda."[134]

But Hulda convinced the others in the end. Clearly by the turn of the century most of the heat of religious disagreement had cooled.

6. DECLINE OF FAITH

Indeed, there were many complaints in this literature that both the second generation and later immigrants were less concerned about their Lutheran faith than the founding fathers. An old Swedish-American minister lamented that "the second and subsequent generations of our people in America are not what the first generation was. It's as if the Christian spirit has been leached out of them. I'm no pessimist in the real meaning of the word, but I can see very well that much of the old, deep Christian faith follows the pioneers into their graves."[135] A generalized account of emigration from Scandinavia at the beginning of World War I included the author's opinion that "the Lutheran church did not seem to be so dear to all these immigrants. Most of them knew best the non-state church meeting-houses and private devotional gatherings, or perhaps they preferred not to bother about anything Christian."[136]

Elements in the American environment were often blamed for the decline in religious fervor and morality which was observed within even the most self-righteous groups. An aside in a novel of 1874 about "an American of the common sort, who has little respect for any kind of religion"[137] was echoed regularly down the years: Americans were immoral; they stole and lied and murdered, committed adultery and divorce, dishonored their parents, gambled and danced. A leading Danish-American pastor told Danes back home that they should be thankful they belonged to a church protected by the state, for they were spared such trials as the godly met in America:

> . . . where all only laugh at Christendom,
> where no knee is bent to Our Lord,
> where dance and revel replace attending church
> and wordly desire is the only need of the heart . . .
> where fanatics have free play
> and the weak are given no support;
> faith retreats day by day
> while superstition grows strong . . .[138]

Clearly members of each churchly in-group felt themselves morally superior not only to the other factions and sects with the same ethnic background but also to other nationalities.

7. FUNCTION OF CHURCH CONTROVERSY
WITHIN THE ETHNIC GROUP

These attitudes showed that an important function of this church conflict was aiding the immigrants in establishment of a new self-definition. At home the place into which they had been born automatically provided their social definition; in the New World they found themselves defined

183

by their ethnic origin and by occupation. The church which they created and supported helped them conceive new self-definitions preferable to these. Over and over characters declared that first in America had they learned to appreciate their Lutheran faith. Typical was the young man who discovered that "the church and the word of God belonged to him in quite a different way here from home in Norway. In this strange land, among people whose language he did not fully understand, he felt himself insecure. But he had powerful allies in his minister and congregation, and he could lean on God, Whom he knew through his childhood faith but first now really felt close to, as on a wall."[139]

Identification as a member of a given church body also made possible easy classification of others according to their inclusion in or exclusion from the select group. A Norwegian-American short story pointed out how even genius was delimited by church affiliation. "If you are a talented musician, you have no talent outside of the church group you belong to. If you are a poet, you're not read outside it; if an orator, you're not heard beyond it."[140] Standards of judgment were thus provided ready-made to members of the small community, as they had been within the larger society back home. The abundance of conflicting polemic forced ordinary persons to make choices, however, and one function of the whole disputation became to teach them the mechanism of how to win acceptance by a given group, and how to maintain membership in it by behavior in accord with group standards.

A reader who places this conflict within the historical situation of a cultural group in flux sees that it arose concurrently with the developing self-consciousness of that group as it grew strong enough in numbers to assert itself in certain areas at the same time that its strength was challenged by the surrounding society. In this situation of stress, efforts to maintain a larger group definition based on national background failed. "The only thing which all the readers of an immigrant newspaper have in common is their memory of their native land, and that fades with time."[141] As the larger classification lost its primacy for many members of the ethnic group, smaller deliberately chosen associations increased in importance. Within church groups sanctioned by God and the Truth, each individual could find support in the struggle to maintain his identity and uphold his worth against the threatening environment. To condemn its values as inferior to his own became part of his self-preservation. Some explanation of the dogmatic bitterness of Scandinavian-American church warfare can be found in the inner uncertainty and need for aggressive defense which are characteristic of the marginal man.

But by the beginning of the twentieth century this immigrant group was no longer marginal. Scandinavians had proved their worth in many ways fully acceptable to American society, and in doing so gradually adopted

184

its value orientation. As they grew to feel at home, most came to feel that their own values were not so different from those of other people after all. Ministers and lay leaders began to talk of joining again synods sundered in heat a generation before. The majority had lost their interest in fine points of doctrine and were willing to unite again on a broader basis, even with native American and other immigrant Lutheran synods. Thus patterns of conflict formed in the Old Country, after developing under New-World conditions to higher activity than ever back home, ultimately declined to the level of the surrounding society; and Scandinavian Lutherans learned to practice religious tolerance in the American spirit.

The constant flux in immigrant institutions which was pictured in the literature thus expressed the changing forms of social interaction developed by members of the ethnic group during the process of Americanization. Wherever their prototypes may have originated, the institutions steadily lost what European elements they possessed as the individual immigrants discarded behavioral characteristics brought from a traditionally stratified society and adopted those appropriate to a fluid social organization in which status depended on achievement. Within the more relaxed control imposed by the American community, people who had remained passive citizens back home now learned to create and manipulate their own institutions. In the process they also discovered the techniques of social power. The dynamic energy which this discovery released was reflected in many books, which showed characters outdoing themselves in the conviction that when a person knew what he wanted, he could get it if he only tried hard enough.

This challenge to individual exertion, rooted in the American philosophy of individualism, exercised great influence on the development of immigrant institutions, away from respect for tradition and authority toward greater freedom and importance of personal choice.* Over and over this was shown to be the meaning of movement from Old- to New-World models of social behavior: increasing appeal to and reliance

---

* An incident in a Danish-American novel illustrated immigrant appreciation of greater individual freedom in America. A Dane who had almost been run over by a train in Chicago thought of how in the Old Country a uniformed guard would have been on duty to warn all away. Once he had gone out on the platform of a Danish train and been brusquely ordered off. "Of course he had immediately obeyed the authoritative voice . . . he was used to protective authorities in those days. Now it would have annoyed him, he knew. In America, thank goodness, a person could go wherever he wanted on a train, and if anybody wanted to fall off an express or be run over by a locomotive, that was his own affair. It was a free country!" Mortensen, *Jeg vælger et land,* p. 170.

on individual effort, with competition for personal esteem and power both within and between social organizations. The literature showed how in this way principles of competition and self-reliance which dominated economic life also permeated other types of social activity.

Chapter Seven
Change in Immigrant Values

The philosophy of individualism which provided a favorable climate for economic and social betterment also had other effects, which Scandinavian-American authors liked much less. Somehow the ideal of material success tended to change the values of those who pursued it whether they won much prosperity or not. No one had foreseen this development and few understood it, but all the writers realized that some kind of value-transformation was taking place.

I. Home and Family

There was unanimous agreement on the basic values of the group at the time of migration: home and family.

> He believed in God and humanity,
> believed in the joy of having a bride. . . .
> But the croft was little, the hut was mean,
> though he felt that nowhere, in any dell,
> was a place like his home which he loved so well.
>
> And his love for his home drove him far away
> to a foreign land; he could not stay
> where his bubbling hope
> lacked room and scope,
> For in his heart throbbed vigor and life.
> Why shouldn't he too have a home and wife?[1]

Over and over departing characters declared that they had to leave their homeland with all there they held dear in order to found their home. "If we got married, I'd be Hans Jensen's cotter, and you'd have the privilege of sitting in a tumbledown cottage all your life." But in America some day they too might live in comfort, maybe even in wealth. So the young Dane left to get a start while his girl toiled on dreaming of "a couple of pleasant, clean small rooms she could call her own, where once in a while she could sit in peace with a book."[2]

Even after many years in America, immigrant writers at all periods continued to repeat variations on the theme of home as their highest value.

> My home is my end and my beginning,
> my goal, but also my means of winning;
> my hope, which both joy and sorrow does yield:
> my challenge, my risk, my castle, my shield.[3]

A large part of their gratitude to America was for its provision of the material means to build a better family life. Many tales and poems described happy immigrant homes alight with love, shining through trial and sorrow like the lights of a city on a hill.[4]

After the turn of the century, however, a growing number of stories recorded disappointment of many immigrants in their New-World homes. Farm and small-town parents often resented how their children developed interests which took them more and more away from home—not only the organized activities of church and school but also all kinds of social gatherings and entertainment, some of doubtful morality. Especially in urban settings, successful businessmen were often pictured as realizing too late that their struggle for success had cost them something worth much more. In a midwestern town, for instance, a Norwegian-American sat drinking alone in his office night after night, trying to analyze why he and his family had grown so far apart.

> They had fixed the kitchen thus-and-so, because the Joneses had theirs thus. . . .
> The crayon portraits of his parents had to be taken down because nobody ever saw such on the walls of the "better people." Framed pictures of brothers and sisters were put away because their clothes were so old-fashioned . . .
> If he came home when guests were present, and everybody was talking and laughing and having fun, they fell silent when he came in. If he tried to say something, usually his wife or daughter contradicted him. He didn't eat properly either, and whatever he liked nobody else would have. . . . If he talked Norwegian they were insulted, and if he talked English they corrected his vocabulary and pronunciation.
> It wasn't his home any longer. It wasn't a real home at all—it was a counterfeit, a bungled imitation of a lot of other homes.[5]

A big-city manufacturer sitting in his office on Christmas Eve had similar bitter thoughts: "What a travesty this Christmas Eve was compared to those of long ago in his childhood home [in Denmark]. He was alone. His modern American wife, his son and daughter, children of the new crazy jazz era, were seeking pleasure at the country club. When he was a child, home was a sacred thing. Home did not mean much any more. It was only a dumping-place between dinners, dances, and theatres."[6] Middle-class Swedish-Americans felt the same malaise as many other characters in the years after World War I: "Certainly they appreciated having an elegant home, where they ate, slept, and received guests— and that was its sole mission. All the rest in life, plans, goals, work and temptation, existed outside the home."[7]

II. Materialism

Most authors agreed that this unwholesome condition was caused by displacement of the home by goods and gold as the immigrants' central value. Materialism as a disease infecting the whole American environment they saw spreading like an epidemic within their own group. Some emphasized the contagion in the surrounding society:

> Money buys honor, money buys power,
> for money the purest is soiled;
> for money the culprit goes free in an hour,
> for money uprightness despoiled.[8]

Others confined their criticism to members of their ethnic group, as in Rølvaag's book-length analysis of an immigrant man and wife who grew literally money-mad in *Pure Gold*.[9]

1. COMPETITION

Another Norwegian-American author devoted two different novels to consideration of how and why pioneer settlements which had lived their first years in mutual helpfulness gradually developed a spirit of competition which drastically changed the original ideals of the characters. As a philosophical grandfather mused, "It's as though the people were over-eating! They came here, over-hungry, and now one chance after another opens before them, and they can't stand it, after being starved so long."

The first years we were here . . . one was always ready to help the other—they shared trials, as well as joys, together, and this was a blessing in itself. Just one thing, that people were willing to help each other without bothering to keep account of it . . . We didn't figure up then; we hadn't learned the inhuman habit of reckoning people . . . at the value of money. . . . But as soon as the crops began to be sure, and the fields grew bigger—in a very short time quite a different spirit came in among us. Folks no longer had need of each other . . . so that now they never overlook anything they think themselves entitled to.[10]

Endowed with his creator's hindsight, the old man predicted that his people after centuries of poverty would fail the moral test of being suddenly thrown into a situation where they could have all they could grab.

Story after story traced how ambition to seize as much as possible of the offerings of a bountiful nature developed into competition which changed the immigrants' attitude toward each other as well as their life values. Rølvaag pictured vividly how Per Hansa in *Giants in the Earth* repeatedly slipped over the line between his legitimate right to what he

189

could wrest from the soil, and his slightly shady title to what he could gain by being smarter than his friends. He never shared his good ideas until he had gotten ahead of the others by using them first: plowing and planting before he built a hut, putting house and barn under the same roof, netting and salting fish from a distant river, catching marsh ducks with a net, selling potatoes to later comers, whitewashing the inside of the sod walls of his hut. As his best friend pondered, "Was this like Per Hansa, who had always confided everything to him? But here he was going about doing everything alone! When he had learned how a black earthen wall could be made shining white at so small a cost, why hadn't he told the others? There was so little cheer out here; they all sorely needed to share whatever they found."[11]

When it came to a more serious moral issue, however, all the Norwegians but one lined up on Per Hansa's side. On the quarter-sections of two neighbors he discovered claim stakes not their own which he secretly destroyed in the fear that they might have to move away from land on which they had already invested a summer's work. The stakes turned out to be unlawful, for the Irishmen who had put them down had not filed at the land office nor fulfilled residence and cultivation requirements; but this Per Hansa did not know when he committed the act. However, after the Irishmen had admitted defeat and Per Hansa basked in the praise of his friends, only his wife realized the moral degradation involved. "Where I come from, it was always considered a shameful sin to destroy another man's landmarks. But here, I see, people are proud of such doings! . . . In my opinion, we'd better take care lest we all turn into beasts and savages out here!"[12]

2. DISHONESTY AND FRAUD

How Scandinavian honor and honesty were lost in the American environment made many a sad story. Nearly all authors agreed that native Americans were, if not thoroughly dishonest, at least eager to jump at every opportunity to make a fast dollar without a thought for moral consequences; and the immigrants soon learned to do the same. Typical of a hundred incidents was that of a Dane who started a slaughterhouse in Omaha with a Yankee partner. All went well until the Dane ran off with the cash and his partner's wife. However, the immigrant turned out the victim of a double-cross, for it was all a plot by the Yankee partner to get sole control of the business. His wife came back as soon as the Dane had spent all his money on her, and gave out the story that she had been visiting relatives. Another Dane learned of all this with amazement. "Of course he had heard a good deal about Yankee cunning, but this surpassed everything he would have thought possible.

190

'You don't know Yankees very well yet, Mister Tomsen,' said the store-keeper laughingly; 'otherwise you wouldn't be so surprised at what I've told'."[13] Neither seemed surprised at the action of their Americanized countryman.

These writers judged the ethics of both individual Americans and the society at large to be deplorable. There were exceptions, but the general rule of every man for himself seemed to have created a moral climate which infected and subverted the honesty and honor which the authors believed to be the birthright of their group. Incidents in which immigrants were tricked, cheated, and robbed by others were rife throughout the literature, not only during their early years but throughout their lives. Occasionally even one of the better storytellers was so horrified at how individuals could be misused in the Promised Land that he exaggerated a plot to the point of caricature. In a Danish-American tale, for instance, a gifted young schoolmaster, forced to emigrate because of his radical views, found he was physically too weak for farm work and applied for a job on a Danish immigrant newspaper. The editor turned out to be a fraud, who held man and wife to heavy labor with only poor food and filthy lodgings as pay. When the wife grew too pregnant to toil any longer, the couple were thrown out. The husband soon wore himself out at road construction for a dollar a day, and of course his wife and baby died.[14]

Even worse in the view of these writers was the plundering of hard-working, honest people by institutionalized wrong-doing—in frequent bank failures, for instance. In numerous plots the savings of long toil were wiped out overnight by a bank failure; and most bitter to the victims was the knowledge that although the bankers were manipulating the situation to steal the money, they would go scot free. Only one man was ever pictured insisting on his right to get his own money back, and the point of the plot was how badly society treated him. He was a rare exception who arrived from Norway with $1500 in gold. When the bank where he deposited it promptly failed, the Norwegian consul advised him to take accept with gratitude the ten cents on the dollar he would be offered in a few weeks. Of course the bank president would continue to live in his Fifth Avenue mansion, which was in his wife's name; and he would soon be back doing business as usual. Twice the immigrant forced his way in to the rich man to demand not charity but his right—in vain. He got only revenge, for the banker died of injuries suffered when the immigrant knocked him down stairs. The Norwegian was pronounced insane for his impassioned argument that society was at fault for tolerating such institutions, especially those of its members who meekly accepted their ten percent.[15]

American lawyers and the legal system were pictured as corrupt as politics. More than one newcomer hero, for instance, when he rejected the suit of an insistent Amazon, found himself sued for breach of promise. A Swedish greenhorn haled into court on such grounds watched the cases before his own decided in haste by a superficial judge. Evidently distribution of "justice" was as hurried as everything else in America; and the newcomer was shocked to observe in action the kind of moral rottenness he had read about but never dreamed could touch him. He could not believe that he might be found guilty when he was completely innocent, but friends warned him of the power of a girl's tears on any jury, and of the unlimited witnesses she could buy. Rather than face such a parody of justice, he fled.[16] A Norwegian-American novel described at length how whenever the Norwegians of a prairie community tried to bring a dishonest or dangerous American before the bar, drunken Yankees swore to his innocence before a prejudiced judge, and all went free.[17] In almost every contact the immigrants had with lawyers, they were robbed or cheated. The conclusion they drew was inevitable: "these Swedish people had time after time fallen victim to American lawyers' wiles, from which experience the colonists nursed a certain well-founded dread of both the law and its administrators."[18]

3. BUSINESS ETHICS

At the bottom of the general corruption, many authors described American business ethics. No small number of the more didactic-minded inserted long denunciations of the adage "Business is business," always quoted in English. A Danish-American novelist, for instance, interrupted his plot to describe two Yankee businessmen, both millionaires and good friends, who never hesitated to skin each other for pecuniary gain. " 'That's business,' as they say, and the most heartless and egoistic, the worst vampirism is thereby made not only permissible but plainly necessary, yes, almost honorable. With this excuse the most bloody injustices are carried out not only against individual persons but also against the entire society. 'That's business,' one says, and so he not only cheats and swindles himself, but gets public officeholders and legislators to seal the injustice, spreads corruption in ever-widening circles, brings destruction to many a home and disgrace to many an ancient, honorable name."[19] The more sophisticated authors showed American business ethics in action in a thousand different situations, all dedicated to getting the better of the weaker party—who was almost invariably an immigrant. A glib traveling salesman talked new arrivals into trading a gold wedding ring for a photograph of President Garfield and wife,[20] or a Yankee mistress cheated an immigrant maid out of her hard-earned wages.[21] Often a banker or storekeeper rigged a loan or advance credit

192

so that the penniless beginner had twenty or thirty percent interest to pay.[22]

Not only American businessmen were portrayed as operating on such principles. On the contrary, most Scandinavians who made good in business had successfully adopted the same practices. The motto of a Danish-American cattle dealer was, "In business anything goes. If he can cheat his best friend in the sale of a bull, he does so gladly. But if it happens that someone tricks him in a transaction, he holds no grudge. 'I got to keep my eyes open,' he reasons."[23]

A trilogy of Norwegian-American novels traced in detail the business education of an ambitious newcomer. He got his start as a grocery clerk, and from the first day was given strict instructions by his Swedish boss on how to slip a couple of spoiled or overripe pieces of fruit or vegetables into every order, how to manipulate the scales to give less than full weight, and many such tricks of the trade.

Jonas was in doubt over whether this could strictly speaking be honest.
"For the time being it's none of your business what is honest or dishonest," said the chief. "We didn't hire you to pass judgment on the firm. We are responsible for our business methods ourselves. All you have to do is follow orders. When you set up in business for yourself, you're welcome to do as you please, and be left with all the rotten eggs and spoiled fruit you want, if you think that's a better and more profitable method than mine. But here you just do like I say, see?"
"Yessir," said Jonas.[24]

Jonas proved an apt pupil. Before long he was setting up advertising campaigns and bargain sales which attracted many customers, and he even fathered the idea of hiring a scurrilous hack writer to attack the private life of their nearest competitor. This tactic was so effective that the unfortunate storekeeper lost customers right and left, and soon went bankrupt. Later in Dakota, when Jonas matched wits with a crooked Yankee banker over the purchase of a valuable section of land, the excitement of the chase and narrow escapes disregarded any moral issue. Jonas beat the crooks on their own terms and gained control of the whole area on which a railroad town soon rose; but he ran the town to suit his own interests, just like the crooked Yankee. His wife's efforts to improve his character failed. Jonas was clearly meant to be a satirical figure, but the author seemed nonetheless to feel a sneaking admiration for an immigrant who managed to snatch wealth and success from under the noses of the sharpest Yankees.[25]

With very few exceptions, the infrequent immigrant characters who made large fortunes adopted American business ways: abandoning all values but materialism, eliminating all interests except business, taking advantage of every situation without regard to human consequences. The writers agreed that to get ahead in America one must not only work with

193

all his might and main, but be hard, grasping, ruthless. They showed character after character knocked down and trampled on in his "dog years" until he finally learned to use others as they used him. As a Swedish-American poet put the matter in a bitter moment,

> Rake in, rake in all you can reach,
> then you'll get rich! . . .
> You're the one who must make your way.
> Why should you help anyone else?[26]

4. INTERPERSONAL RELATIONS

Some immigrant characters were shocked to discover how American materialism affected interpersonal relations. They found themselves appraised by others not as human beings but as instruments to be used. A young Norwegian recalled his first impression of his boss: "a pair of cold eyes which seemed to take measure of everything. . . . face after face—it was always the same eyes. . . . Everybody tried to figure out what a guy like Lars Olsen could be worth to them—what they could count on to their own advantage from one like him. It hadn't been like this back home."[27]

Numerous incidents occurred or were told to newcomers in warning. A Dane serving as brakeman on a railroad had the job of driving off tramps. He tried not to see them, but his fellow official delighted in throwing them off the train at full speed. One time the engineer stopped the train suddenly, badly frightened. He had run over two men. The trainmen ran back and found one dead, the other dying. Rather than get into trouble over the incident, they threw both into the boiler to burn them up, one still alive. The Dane immediately quit. He would rather go hungry than take part in such treatment of fellow men, but it did not bother the Americans.[28] Accidents to men building railroads or cutting timber were often fatal. At a lumber camp in a Norwegian-American novel, a team of horses hauling logs down an icy incline slipped and they and the driver were smashed flat. "Within half an hour the wreck was cleared away, the icy driveway repaired, and one load after another sped past the site of the accident as though nothing had happened. The traffic at Knapp, Stout & Co. could not stop for such a trifle as this, that a newcomer was sent to eternity and a team worth $500 was no more."[29] In a Danish-American novel a young immigrant tried to cheer up an older one with the hope of more work available come spring. Only for you who are young, the old man said. "America will have new, healthy blood; we old people can only rust or rot to pieces on the junk piles, like worn-out tools or machines. We are rejected and condemned." Later the old man died from poisoning by lead paint. Zinc

194

paint was always used in Denmark, more expensive but harmless. As the widow said bitterly, "Never mind a couple of painters when it's a question of saving a few cents, isn't that right?"[30] On the basis of repeated similar experiences, several authors drew the conclusion which an earlier arrival imparted to a fellow immigrant in a Norwegian-American novel:

Here there are so many people that human life steadily falls in price. If hundreds are killed in fires, railroad accidents, cyclones, tornadoes, floods, prairie fires and the like, which we have an abundance of,—that's nothing! Thousands come to take their places, and it's cheap labor that's wanted. A human life is nothing here.[31]

This attitude toward human life as cheap and expendable did not appear in tales of the frontier, nor in agricultural communities at any stage of their development. It arose only where large numbers of people were collected on a casual and temporary basis: as workers or jobhunters, in labor camps, factories, slums. Where people were few, as a rule even Yankees received strangers courteously and offered them generous assistance. Wherever business relations determined the attitude of a man toward his fellow men, however, these critics saw human values subordinated to the end of making money; and since business relationships came to dominate the lives of all except farmers, and impinged more and more strongly even upon them, the writers tended to impute to the entire American society this indifference to human life, which they criticized bitterly. Or at best they viewed America as a "strange mixture of good and evil, where one did the loving work of the good samaritan with one hand, while with the other dealt the death blow to his brother Abel. Through all this chaos of political corruption and compassionate ideals of reform, churchly piety and devilish hypocrisy, outward propriety and social immorality, imposing works of charity and merciless oppression of workers—ran like a red thread the selfish, limitless lust for money."[32]

III. Social Protest

Business ethics were assumed to be the foundation of the social injustice and oppression of the working class which stories and poems recorded in growing volume toward the end of the nineteenth century. Poets of protest appeared in this literature as early as the 1880s and continued down through the Great Depression, writing both in their European tongues and in English. The Swedes produced the most and the best. A little volume of verse published in 1888 included a "Swedish-American Workers' Song," expressing hope for a day of greater justice for common laborers, and "A Hero's Death," recounting how a factory

195

worker was killed at his job "in the strenuous fight for daily bread."[33] By 1932 a literary critic could claim that several Swedes were to be found among better poets of labor in the United States,[34] including one known to the general public under the name of Joe Hill.[35]

There was also considerable Danish and Norwegian immigrant verse of social protest. The following sample of these differed from the average only in greater vehemence of imagery:

> What is our land? A chaos merely
> of debris-culture and rotten forces
> which think they have scaled the highest peaks
> and despise the entire world.
> But if you look in hole and cranny
> you will see a sight you can never forget.
> Here gold is spun of human bowels,
> here steel is hammered from human arms,
> here pearls and diamonds are cut and polished
> from a mother's tired tears,
> here is woven silk and satin
> from a child's need and misery,
> here blood is tapped from the keg of the heart,
> to be sold by the glass and the drink.[36]

The majority of poems on this theme consisted largely of such generalized criticism, often introducing the personified image of Trusts or Wall Street, but a good number were specifically labor-oriented: celebrating Scandinavian immigrant labor leaders, deploring the Haymarket riot or the execution of Sacco and Vanzetti, attacking the monotony of factory labor.

Although there was considerable incidental comment on the trials of laboring-class life in this immigrant fiction, no novel was primarily concerned with factory or other unskilled workers. Almost all male characters began on this level, but after moving past their "dog years" those who were not farmers tended to become small-time entrepreneurs —housepainters or plumbers, carpenters or storekeepers, garbage collectors, saloonkeepers, masseurs—or go into business. The majority of those who remained wage-earners were employed in relatively small enterprises: a neighborhood store, a sawmill, a lumberyard, a furniture factory. These usually appeared either in short stories or as minor characters in novels, so that the reader saw them at only one stage of their progress. Main characters followed through several stages usually ended up financially on their own. At least until the turn of the century, the majority of the stories were laid in rural areas with their characters involved in agriculture. This occupation remained strongly represented throughout the literature, reflecting the midwestern concentration of the Scandinavian group.

196

In all types of economic activity, whether as independent producers, entrepreneurs, or wage-earners, many characters suffered economic injustice in America. Pioneer farmers staggered under debt, paying exorbitant interest rates on the capital they had to borrow to get started. As a Danish pioneer told his bride, "We have debts, Martha . . . and we must scrimp these first years; I got the land for nothing, that's true; but it costs a lot to build out here on the prairie, and horses and wagons, machinery and tools, it all runs up." When he took his first crop to town, he came back in a savage mood. Nearly all his money had gone to interest and shopping debts. Only a few dollars were left to pay on the principle. "All that toil they had done for others; they had worked until their arms ached, they had gone without sleep until their eyes burned, and then these fine gentlemen who sat there in town behind the polished windows of the bank took it all."[37]

In this story, as in most with a similar setting, the characters finally paid off their mortgage and owned their land free after a lifetime of toil, although often they had sacrificed everything else to this end; but from the 1890s until the first World War the general agricultural depression forced most farmers into economic crisis again. A bit of newspaper verse from 1894 epitomized the trouble: Farmer Per Johnson drove his wheat to town to sell. He took a long shopping list but returned with nothing, because the price of wheat had fallen while the cost of everything he had to buy had soared. The bank took most of what he got anyhow.

> As poor as before on my croft, now I stand
> with greying hair and a trembling hand.[38]

From this time on, the economic movement of characters involved in agriculture was by no means always upward. In spite of toil as desperate as that of the pioneers, some farm characters were ultimately ruined by low prices, and lost their land.

Small-time entrepreneurs also found their fate and fortunes progressively more at the mercy of American business cycles. A Norwegian storekeeper went bankrupt when his bank failed;[39] a successful contractor lost his firm during a depression.[40] In a typical short story, a Danish housepainter came to Chicago planning to earn enough in a few years to start his own business back home. He was so lonely, however, that he married. Children came rapidly, and then hard times, and his dream of returning to Denmark faded. Jobs got fewer and fewer until there were none at all. The family moved to the slums, where halfway through January they ran out of coal and food. Appeals to both the Danish insurance society and the Danish church were refused, for the painter was not a member of either. The wife finally found a job in a laundry and literally worked herself to death for $7 a week. Then charity gave her a big funeral, with the minister and lodge members attending.[41]

From the turn of the century onward, factory workers were consistently portrayed as the worst off of all. They might make more money and feel that they enjoyed more social prestige than their counterparts in the Old Country, but they found the struggle for existence more brutal in America, and themselves more often its victims. A few stories included descriptions of dreadful working conditions in crowded, dirty factories, or pictured unpleasant details of slum life; occasional mention was made of the soul-killing monotony of factory routines, as in the case of a Swedish girl who in ten years of mill work was transformed from a human being to a cog in a machine.[42]

Most authors concerned with the working class emphasized the insecurity of the laborer's lot. This was largely a result of low wages, measured now not against pay in the Old World but against the capitalist's profit. A Swedish-American novel, after portraying the sad death of an overworked and underpaid proletarian, jumped to description of the luxurious castles of millionaires in the same city. "Hundreds of thousands of workers have been necessary to create these prodigious fortunes, that is true, but it is just as true that when their work is paid an average of a dollar a day, the capitalists' profit on their laborers' toil is often a thousand dollars a day. This is called economic justice and republican equality."[43] Another immigrant writer judged the fight against capitalistic oppression to be much worse in America than in Sweden. Many individuals, of course, continued to make good through luck, "but we are speaking here of the great majority. Buried in the suffocating atmosphere of large-city workshops, they must expend the strength of their best years in the service of the corporations. . . . Their pay is always calculated so that they must remain in dependent circumstances. . . . After a lifetime of honorable and strenuous toil, by which each to the best of his ability helped bring this land to blooming prosperity . . . they are rewarded by a dark old age and the poorhouse."[44]

Although workers saved money in good times, when sickness or a strike or a depression threw them out of work their meager savings were soon used up. The capitalists, on the other hand, could foresee when bad times were on the way, and entrench themselves in their palaces until the storm blew over. This was the second basic reason given by Scandinavian-American authors for the insecurity of laboring-class life: complete dependence on wages, which might be cut off at any time; and once discharged, workers were often unable to find any kind of job again. As a Danish farm boy found when he went to work twelve hours a day in an Omaha packing house,

198

He soon sensed that everyone was afraid of losing his job, that the workers spent all their wages from week to week, that there was no surplus of flour, pork and canned fruit in their homes, that sickness in the family was dreaded like the plague, and that no matter how long a man might have worked here, he was never a man, but only worker number so and so, who could be laid off or "fired" with no more concern than was shown to the hogs that were driven to the slaughter pen.[45]

Capitalists, factory owners, and bosses as a class were usually portrayed as villains by authors who dealt with working-class life, just as bankers, lawyers, and politicians were similarly condemned in rural settings. A Norwegian-American novel, for instance, opened with the description of a big ditch being dug in Minneapolis. The workers were watched by many bosses, all ready to curse and shout if one so much as stopped to wipe his face. "What the hell did the bosses care about that? If occasionally a weaker or less experienced digger collapsed, ruined by overstrain or dead as a herring of sunstroke—that these worthy beings took with commendable calm; it didn't pay to be human in their 'business'." The author fulminated against the ignorant and vulgar men, often Irish, used as bosses by American enterprise, claiming "The average Norwegian is by nature too considerate to do well in such a post of command."[46]

Most Scandinavian characters, however, looked beyond the hired foreman and attributed their economic woes to the ruthlessness of men already rich whose only goal was still more money. In a Norwegian-American novel with a factory owner as hero, he got his start by driving his workers to their limit and paying them as little as possible. Not until the great Chicago fire wiped out all he had achieved did he have a change of heart, remember his mother's Christian teachings, and become a model employer. Then he not only paid the best wages in town but also inaugurated a profit-sharing system, reasonable working hours, healthful factory conditions, aid in sickness and death, an old-age pension program. However, this paragon of capitalistic virtue was contrasted with *normal* employers at several points. At meetings with fellow capitalists, he argued in vain against their selfish, evil heartlessness. Clearly the author meant to present a solution to the violent conflicts between labor and capital which he described as demoralizing industrial Chicago; but his hero rejected personal wealth as a life goal, while it was the professed aim of all the others, so this immigrant's influence was limited to his own factory.[47] More typical was the behavior of a Norwegian upholsterer who overworked and underpaid his help and threw out a union organizer who tried to protest.[48] Thus a considerable group of immigrant authors found the root of American economic injustice in the untrammeled greed of the capitalists themselves.

Another diagnosis offered by other authors censured rather the capitalistic system. These were a small but vehement minority: a few lone voices in the 1890s, growing in number during World War I, reaching a climax in the 1930s. A handful of characters were socialists or anarchists in their time, Wobblies a little later; one or two even flirted with Communism during the Great Depression. A pioneering family, for instance, caught socialism from an itinerant carpenter, but they remained political freaks in their rural community.[49] Occasional radical poems proclaimed the coming socialist victory of the working class, or hailed the inevitable Marxist revolution. A few stories pictured idealized cooperative or communistic experimental communities as a solution to the excesses of American principles of private property.

Most criticism of The System remained no more than that, however. The exploited suffered in bitter resentment, but seldom took steps to remedy their situation.[50] Most were like the Danish rental farmer who toiled and figured endlessly in the futile attempt to find a solution to the problem of his debts, "not understanding well enough the whole system under which he lived to know that there could never be a solution for him. The invisible chains that bound him were not so invisible but that he sensed their presence. What he did not know was that there could be no partial escape from his bondage, that for him and the millions who toiled in the black loam of this rich land there would be only one reality and that would be poverty—only this one truth as long as the system endured."[51] Two novels later, when the old man was about to lose the land he had been forced to buy at peak prices during World War I, his son suggested the farmers organize to fight back with guns. The father was horrified at the thought; it was not for him to oppose even an unjust law by force. The young man recognized the soundness of his father's judgment in regard to the farmers of Nebraska. "Earnest workers every one of them, they hated the mortgage companies and the bankers. They believed in their right to their land, but a deeper belief dominated their rebellion. . . . The evils done in the name of the law are as infinite as the stars, and the farmers knew this fact well enough, but open rebellion was something not yet dreamed of in their philosophy."[52]

Scandinavian workers in this fiction usually also turned a deaf ear to the arguments of labor organizers and strike leaders. Most working-class characters opposed strikes on whatever grounds, afraid of the loss of wages and jobs, and many authors represented all such deliberate work-stoppages as foolish and wrong. Nowhere except in the scattered work of a few labor poets did the sense of membership in a proletariat appear. As the immigrants had come to win personal betterment by their own efforts, it would seem, so most clung to this ideal regardless of the odds against them. References to the few radical members of the ethnic group often condemned them for their atheism as well. A rare socialist hero ran up against this hard core of conservatism in his fellow immigrants after a long series of conflicts with the American capitalistic system as both worker and farmer. Everyone he met told him about the trust controlling one particular product—lumber, paper, milk, meat, grain —so that those who toiled to create the wealth got next to nothing for it. The hero came to realize that the only solution was for workers and farmers to organize and cooperate as the capitalists did; but when he tried to persuade some of the complainers, they turned their back on him. *They* were Republicans.[53]

IV. Decline of Economic Opportunity

This author blamed trusts for the scarcity of jobs, but many others saw that the declining economic opportunity which caused the evils they deplored was the result of historical development: the country was filling up. Reflected in the literature was the accelerating retreat of the frontier. Newcomers who stopped in older colonies—first in Illinois, later in Wisconsin, Iowa, and Minnesota—regularly found no suitable land available in the vicinity and pushed on further west to wherever land was then being offered for location. In a Norwegian-American novel opening in the 1880s, two families who had planned to settle in Red River Valley discovered that the two years they spent in Wisconsin had lost them the chance. All good land there had been taken up, and they had to continue two hundred miles further west to where the land had just been surveyed. Within a few weeks most of the nearby claims had been occupied, and a friend who came after them had to go a good distance further before he could find a suitable farm.[54] From the latter part of the 1880s immigrants often had to buy land, starting out then with even larger debts. A Norwegian-American tale deliberately contrasted families which arrived earlier and were already free from debt on good soil with a few latecomers who had to buy in on the "gravel bottom," the only unoccupied land left. These families stayed poorer than the others in spite of much harder work.[55]

Decline in the availability of jobs from the 1880s on kept pace with the disappearing frontier. In a novel published in 1889, a Danish-American writer described his hero's arrival in New York in 1851, when swarms of confidence men descended on him with job offers. The greenhorn knew enough not to trust them, however, and decided to hike westward and find work for himself—as he did within fifty miles. "It was much easier to get a job then than now," the author commented, "for workers were not so plentiful in America as nowadays."[56]

201

Another Danish-American tale described the problems of those "now-adays" (the 1880s) when a new arrival found that his brother, who had been making good money in a Chicago lumberyard, had lost his job through a strike. The two men wandered the length and breadth of Chicago looking in vain for employment; finally they had to go to work on a railroad in the baking sun and blowing dust. "Before his arrival Hans had thought of America as a land where there was enough work for all willing hands, but he soon learned how difficult it was to find something to do. And now every day he saw jobless men on the move along the railroad track."[57] A Norwegian-American novel opening in 1892 summarized the difficulties of a new immigrant from that time on. The public land available for farming was all gone, the rest owned by private companies which would sell only at comparatively high prices; there was no more well-paid work in railroad construction, most of which was finished now; and ordinary farm work was hard to find because of the new labor-saving agricultural machinery. In towns centralized department stores were driving the small shopkeepers in outlying districts out of business. Writing in 1899, the author warned would-be immigrants to think twice and investigate carefully before departing for America.[58]

Yet immigrants continued to arrive with the firm belief that America was the land of golden opportunity. Some still managed to make good, at least until hit by a depression, but many learned from unending years of trial that their expectations were out of date. A Swedish-American tale published in 1905 opened with the remark that "The struggle for existence is always fierce in America, but that of the last two years had been unbearably so. Sometimes, while a man could work, he had enough and to spare, but hard times always returned again, when dollar bills were only a memory and a man walked miles looking hopelessly for a job in order to save a nickel." The three friends in this story finally agreed they had had enough of compulsory unemployment, and signed on a cattle boat to return to Europe. As they went up the gangway, it seemed "a Jacob's ladder, which led from America's misery to Europe's greater possibilities, because if one is *willing* to work there as hard as one *has* to work in America, then it's easier in the Old World both to make a living and to win a tolerable social standing." As the boat steamed out past the Statue of Liberty, one of the Swedes cried bitterly, "—Freedom here, infamous lie!"[59]

Not only newcomers appeared with increasing frequency in these stories as tramps and beggars and petty cheats—never, however, as criminals—but also immigrants who had gotten a good start and were on the way up when a depression hit them. The story was the same whether it was the panic of 1893 or 1907 or 1929, or any of a number of smaller recessions in between. A Dane came to Chicago in 1919, for instance, when it was easy to get work. He did well until the crash, but then there were no more jobs to be had. Down to his last few dollars, he fainted on the street and awoke in a hospital; this experience took his last cent and part of a lung. When the doctor warned him to go to a milder climate, he rode the freights to California. The story left him on the way to the Danish consulate there, hoping for a loan.[60]

A new pessimistic tone developed in much of the literature after the turn of the century. The movement of many plots changed from poor-immigrant-makes-good to good-immigrant-becomes-poor. Honest workers were reduced to begging; bums froze to death in Chicago slums. Something strong but intangible weakened with the decline of economic opportunity: the belief that a man was restricted only by his own limitations, confidence that those strong enough to fight through hardship would win their goal, faith in the happy ending and the American Dream.

> As long as the land lay wild and waste
> and danger from Indians had to be faced,
> our arm was gold in forest and plain;
> we cleared the woods, plowed farm and field
> and gave the Yankee rich harvests of grain.
> Fear or sloth the Swede has never revealed.
>
> But times have changed. Language now has praise
> for native-born only, and Yankee ways.
> The crowds of foreigners turned into white slaves.
> And proud Columbia! That rich, fair maid
> builds her pleasure palace on crosses and graves
> and hears not the prayers of her labor brigade.[61]

V. Loss of European Values

A considerable number of writers, however, blamed the economic woes of latter-day immigrants less on trusts or depressions or social injustice than on their own moral failure, loss of Old-Country ideals of frugality and pride in their work. A Norwegian-American novel, outlining the hard times in the Middle West during the 1890s, recorded how the farmers believed it was all the fault of the government. To fight the power of "The System," voters joined the People's Party in droves; but a measure of local political success brought no improvement. Indeed, the new politicians proved as great rascals as the old ones. Finally farmers began to realize that their harvests were so poor because the soil was wearing out and full of weeds. They had to turn to more scientific methods, go over from wheat to corn and more varied crops, fatten livestock for sale.[62] In another tale, a successful scientific farmer criticized his neighbors: "They toil and drudge early and late without any plan or goal. That's why they don't get anywhere. The other day I heard a man talking about this, after he'd come back from a trip to Norway. . . . He said that if people over there farmed like people here, they wouldn't get any crops at all. Here farmers are so careless that everything just goes so-so."[63]

1. WORKMANSHIP

Characters complained about declining responsibility and workmanship in other fields too. A Norwegian-American farm wife found it difficult to keep maids. "One of the girls quit after she had worked a couple of weeks, another wanted both Sunday and Wednesday afternoons off, a third refused to wash so that most of the work fell on Mrs. Holmen herself, and she felt as tired and careworn as in the first years. . . . 'No, it's certainly not the same now as when I was a hired girl myself back in the Old Country. Then we thought it shameful if we couldn't stay in a post more than a year. Now the girls quit and leave when they've worked a week or two.' "[64] In another novel, a Norwegian painter worked hard at forgetting his training in thoroughness and care, in order to keep up with the fast but sloppy work of an Irishman.[65]

2. THRIFT

Writer after writer concurred in the view that the sturdy Scandinavian virtues of thrift and frugality were all too rapidly lost in America. The pioneers preserved them by necessity, but in the literature these virtues seldom survived the first generation or the passing of the frontier.

On the frontier, pioneers usually sacrificed and suffered to acquire what by New-World standards were small amounts of land. Those who took the 160 acres they could get free aspired to little more in the early years. Rarely indeed did they file on a preemption claim at the same time, to gain title to another quarter section. One reason for such consistent behavior was certainly their poverty. Still governed by peasant dread of debt, they strove to keep their loans at a minimum. Neither did they have money to hire labor, and in most cases the quarter section of a homestead was as much as they could hope to manage with the immediate family. An old Dane in Dakota, recalling that all his fellow pioneers had come from the poorest class, pointed out that "Their desire for property ownership usually was limited to what a man with his family could cultivate for himself. The opinion was often advanced that 160 acres was too much for one family."[66] Even when Per Hansa in *Giants in the Earth* dreamed his wildest dreams of the future, he lusted after only two more quarter-sections to add to his homestead. "These two quarter-sections would make an estate more magnificent than that of many a king of old."[67]

Once the pioneer "dog-years" were past, however, and above all after the second generation had taken over their fathers' farms, the American system of easy loans and buying on credit ensnared all who forgot their old peasant fear of debt. A Norwegian-American farmer watched while the forced sale of a nearby farm was temporarily stopped by an armed group of neighbors. The owner had borrowed $10,000 on his land when prices were high; now it was worth only a third of that. The sheriff got the farm for the mortgage company before long, but the watching neighbor blamed not "The System" but the individual who was so dumb as to take such a loan. He should rather have followed in the footsteps of the neighbor's father, who "was as afraid of debt as of fire. He would never allow anything to be bought on credit. If we didn't have cash to pay, we could do without, regardless of how necessary we might think the thing was."[68] Tale after tale showed characters coming to grief when they were tempted by easy loans to buy fancy machinery or furniture, build big houses, live above their incomes in the effort to keep up with the neighbors.

3. LOVE OF LAND

Another reason for the modest aspirations of newcomers lay in the often-repeated boasts of immigrants about how large their homesteads were compared with estates back home. Coming from lands where a half-dozen acres of tillable soil constituted a respectable holding, their free quarter section seemed to them tremendous. In book after book the pioneer farmer's consuming drive in the early years was to get all his land under cultivation, build bigger and better house and barns, improve his stock—increase the value of his farm, not its size. An occasional individual who was able to claim further homesteads in the names of grown children, or who bought up much land while it was cheap, was usually looked on as taking an unfair advantage. An immigrant in a second-generation novel reproved his wife when she started buying land in her own name:

Magdali! Do you forget how it was in Norway! . . . There was a day when men like me—men who loved the land—were up with the sun and at work as long as there was light to show them the way—and the days were long in that north country of ours. But they labored through the long days because they loved the land. . . . But other men—they were the men of the town—took the land from them and owned it, because it was wealth. . . . One day all the land belonged to the few who had no love for it. . . . You came to America with me because we could not live and have our children work for the big landowners and have nothing for their labors. . . . And now—already you and your brother would forget why we came. You would own more land than you can use. You would turn men away from their land so that the land can be yours to hold.[69]

This love of the peasant for his soil was pictured vividly in a number of tales. In a novel by a returned American, the son of a landowner in Norway gratefully accepted help after his immigration from former cotters of his father who were now doing well in Chicago. At Christmas he gave one of them a picture of the cottage on their croft: "their family home, cleared and cultivated by their forefathers, but owned by someone else. . . . He couldn't help thinking how different life might have been for one of them if he or she had gotten the holding as his own." But the younger generation did not want to rent any longer, even on favorable terms. "The landlord on his side would have felt he was committing sacrilege if he sold any part of his ancestral earth. And so the cotter's children emigrated to America, while the landowner was left with more land than he could cultivate profitably with the machinery available then."[70] Motivated by the possibility of becoming landowners themselves, pioneers were pictured enduring almost unbelievable hardship in order to found their own family estate even larger and richer than those they had served in the Old Country.

To this end many of them sacrificed all other values—according to some authors, even their children. A Danish-American pastor calling on an elderly farm couple drew out of them why their grown children never attended church. The parents complained that evil forces emanating from the nearby town lured the children away—dances, gambling, drinking. One son had been brought home drunk, a daughter had an illegitimate baby. The minister told the parents that the degradation of their children was their own fault. They had bought so much land when they came—as they felt they had to while prices were low, so that each child could have his own farm when he grew up—that the family was overwhelmed with debt. All had to toil constantly to bring the financial success they now enjoyed. But the parents would never let the children have time for innocent recreation with their contemporaries, so that they could learn the difference between right and wrong. Therefore the family had really paid for its land with the moral ruin of its children.[71]

Yet even when bought at such a price, rich prairie earth did not mean the same to immigrant landowners as the cramped and stony fields of their fatherland. The landowner's son who found former cotters on their own prosperous farm admired their achievement and the economic opportunity which made it possible, but remarked that America was still not the homeland. "Can we ever come to feel so much at home here that we no longer miss the life and environment of the Old Country?" This question the transplanted farmer could not answer; instead he began to recall some of his most beautiful memories from back home. "It was almost a tear which glinted in the elderly man's eye. 'I can certainly understand the bitterness of emigrated peasant sons when they talk about the brother who got the family farm. But it's like I say, everybody can't stay home on the farm. We've got farms here too, you'll see.' "[72] Of course landless immigrants appreciated the rich soil America gave them; but the fact that the authors so often used the English word *farm* in the Norwegian or Swedish text indicated that they felt an essential difference between fields plowed and harvested on one side of the Atlantic and on the other. "The earth we own, the house we built,—there is always something alien about it, as if it were really someone else's. It's as though we don't own it in the same way as land is owned in Norway and . . . it is nearly always for sale."[73]

Land *could* not be owned in the same sense in America. All the rich associations of a long and stable history were necessarily lacking in an area which so recently had been wilderness. Even legal concepts of land ownership were very different in the United States. Within the *bygdekultur* of Norway and Sweden not only was primogeniture required, but also an individual's title to his land was conditioned by the *odelsrett* of freeholds. This allodial law regulated the sale of family property. Should a farm be offered for sale, the right to buy followed upon nearness of kinship. Only after nearer relatives declared their disinterest could more distant ones have a chance, and only when no known kinsman wished to purchase could the title go outside the family. Even after it had done so, anyone who could prove relationship was entitled to buy back the property at any time within a set period of years. *Odelsrett* expressed the ancient sense of connection between the clan and its freehold, so intimate that it seemed like sacrilege to sell a croft from the family estate to the cotters who tilled it.[74] Occasionally an immigrant farm owner tried to carry on this tradition in the stipulations of his will, as Rølvaag's Beret Holm specified: "Peder is not to have the right to sell the farm outside the Holm family as long as there is any of them willing to buy."[75]

In Europe the older generation made over title of the land to the eldest son in return for lifetime support, and continued to live on it as honored patriarchs. In America the literature recorded family after family where all the children left home as they grew up, abandoning the old folks to carry on as best they could. When the last of six Danish-American sons broke the news that he too was going to strike out on his own, his father made a terrible scene. The mother told another son, "I know he hoped Karl would take over the farm. In the Old Country it is an honor for a son to take over his father's farm. It stays in the family. That is one reason why your father was so anxious to own land. He wanted a home that would bear his name—but now—well, it is different here in America."[76]

When the old folks grew too feeble for the heavy work of farming, and hired help had become prohibitively expensive, they had no choice but to follow the American practice of selling out to strangers and retiring to town. There they might spend their old age in comfort, but many stories described the loneliness of their idle days. Even when they continued to live on a farm where a son or daughter had taken over, they were more apt to be considered old fogies than honored patriarchs. A Norwegian-American son chafed at his father's objections to newfangled ideas he had learned at agricultural college, and argued that if he could not have and run the farm as his own he would not stay. The crisis was resolved only when the parents turned over the place and moved to town.[77]

Yet the Old-World tradition of love of the land survived longer and stronger than this criticism by the immigrant authors would indicate. They tended to emphasize violations of the older pattern, while taking for granted examples of its continuance. It remained fully as commonplace in midwestern stories for a son (or daughter) to take over the parental farm as for him to refuse. The very setting of many tales involving the second generation—on the family farm in the midst of an enduring Scandinavian settlement—gave evidence of continuing attachment to particular soil. Any number of far-fetched twists of plot, especially in tales for Christmas annuals, saved a midwestern family homestead from sale at the eleventh hour so that some representative of the clan could continue in residence. And those who decided to sell out were often pictured leaving their homes in deep sorrow. "He could not hide from himself that it hurt. When the strangers tramped over the fields and the floors, they trampled on something of his."[78]

The recurring theme of the greater moral worth of rural life may also have been a surviving expression of Old-World attitudes. Many an immigrant poem compared at length life in city and country, always concluding that the latter was infinitely preferable.

> Here all is clean and free and great
> far from the city's darkling gate—
> from the rush, and wrath, and fear!
> The green countryside round house and rack,
> the glossy cattle, the rounded stack,
> the golden grain in bulging sack—
> Heaven's blessing is here![79]

All agreed that country life developed ethical superiority. When an elderly farming couple retired to town decided to adopt a baby, they concluded they would have to move back to the old place because "here in town he'd only be ruined."[80] Scandinavian-American writers consistently insisted that a farmer enjoyed not only higher status but also finer moral qualities than a factory worker or business employee, even one with a much higher income.

This theme was also strong in contemporary American literature, growing along with accelerating migration from rural to urban areas. Its presence in Scandinavian-American literature might be interpreted as a sign of amalgamation with the larger society rather than survival of European attitudes. At least the emphasis of many immigrant authors on *why* their characters were so much better off in rural life seems purely American: over and over they praised the economic security of land ownership. Bankers could not embezzle dirt, and farming provided at least the basic necessities. "Often the times are poor, and a man gets nothing for his work, but he has a home and he always has something to eat."[81] The land itself had a way of increasing in value as a region grew up, providing capital gain even when income remained low. Two Danish newcomers "soon realized that if they were ever to win financial independence it would have to be through agriculture. Work in the cities, on railroads and in factories, was much too uncertain and fluctuating to permit saving much of one's annual wage."[82]

This predilection toward agriculture for its security as well as its prestige motivated many first-generation farmers to try to supply all their children with farms. In the Old Country primogeniture provided land for only the eldest son, although he had to pay his siblings their equal shares in the value of the property. In America it became customary for the youngest child to take over the parent's farm, because he (or she) had stayed home longest to care for the old folks. Meanwhile the parents had often gone into debt to buy land for older children. The ideal pictured in several stories was for each child to be given his own farm when he married. This was certainly the most effective way to get them to settle in the same area, as rural children had often done in Europe. Parents financially able to maintain this pattern were condemned when they violated it. Seeing two sons of a prosperous farmer set out with their outfits for the frontier, a Norwegian-American exclaimed, "That moneybags! Does he need to send his sons out into the wilderness? . . . if he meant anything with his pious talk about 'our children,' he'd give his sons a start here at home. He could well make over a piece of land to both of them without losing his livelihood." The author contrasted this father with another one poorer in worldly goods but richer in moral values, who told his son: "I'd like to have you settle down here.—Well, of course you can't have this property, but there's a lot of land for sale cheap around here. I'd rather go into debt to give you something to begin with than see you start something else and leave."[83] Here the avail-

209

ability of land in America offered a new means to carry on an old pattern.

All too often, however, the lust for land described in many an immigrant farmer's soul was motivated less by concern for his children's future than by his desire to improve his own status. If land ownership was both noble and ennobling, then the larger his acreage the better the man. Gradually what had been an end in itself thus came to be considered a means to produce and evince wealth. As such, any given farm was only real estate, to be sold at a profit whenever the occasion was offered. An effective short story, "And They Sold Out," summarized a theme which appeared frequently in this immigrant literature. It told how a hard-working Norwegian farmer, after toiling to pay off the debt on and improve his farm, twice was forced to accept a good bid and move away because his Norwegian neighbors had all sold out to invading Poles.[84] This destruction of the bond between family and place was charged with causing the increasing mobility of members of the immigrant group, after the American pattern. "Yes, that's the disaster! . . . We're turning into a people always on the go! We never live long enough in one place to learn to love it—long enough so that the landscape can imprint itself on the hearts of a clan. We only stop one place long enough to 'make good' . . . and then the home is for sale."[85]

Criticism of how characters constantly evaluated their farms in money terms indicated that some authors felt a fundamental change of value orientation was taking place within their group. Land ownership continued to be highly prized, but for different reasons. In America acquiring land came to be primarily a way of getting ahead. Characters often discussed how to increase profits, beat the market, make farming into a better business—hardly ever how to make it a better life. "These days Peder toiled like a slave with the fall plowing. Couldn't afford to hire help, the way prices were now. Last year no crops, not a scrap to sell; this year an overabundance on every hand and no prices. He could see no future in this grain farming. The joy he used to get from his work was gone."[86] The majority took for granted such pervasive materialism, but a strong minority of preservationists condemned it. "They came here from Norway with fairytales about great wealth dancing in their heads. Greedy. Now they never can get enough, that's why they clutch so tightly what they have. They can't live, though their thoughts never rise above their livelihood."[87] Many plots were designed to bring poetic justice on the heads of those who overreached themselves investing in land with borrowed money. High interest rates or falling prices brought the sheriff to supervise enforced sale.

210

4. STANDARD OF LIVING

Even those who remained content with smaller farms often grew discontented with their standard of living. No longer did they compare it with the deprivation they had known in Europe, but with their wealthiest neighbors and the folks in town. They built great barns and fancy houses, often on borrowed money. "Some put towers on their houses;—the tower had no use,—it was ugly!—but a tower cost money. And the main thing was to demonstrate that one had the money."[88] Neighbors competed in size and equipment of their barns, number and quality of their stock, even in house furnishings and clothing. A Norwegian who returned to a prairie settlement some years after its founding was puzzled by the coolness that had grown up between neighbors. An old man explained the change: "Wel-l-l, either I'm crazy or the others is. The way they drives, an' want to beat each other with houses, 'n' tools, 'n' everything you can think of,—so they can't look at each other—it's so awful, so it ain't worth to talk about."[89]

Another novel traced in detail the growth of such neighborhood competition through many years. Toward the end, an elderly schoolteacher who had watched the whole process pointed out that the local farmers were really well off. They had good houses, plenty to eat, sturdy clothes to wear. But still they were dissatisfied, complaining how hard they had to work. "There aren't many who really *toil* for their food either . . . they slave away because they envy others, and those others struggle and strive because they are competing with still others. Envy and class hate is about the last thing I had expected to see here; on the contrary, I dreamed that from these thousands of farm-owners would develop a class which could realize the concept of freedom in a rich life. But things didn't turn out that way."[90] Instead, Americanized immigrant wives flaunted their fine belongings in mutual competition. Leaving a party, one tossed her head when she put on her $8.50 hat. "This was a direct challenge to the others, and Mrs. Overhus busied herself with the lace on her elegant shirtwaist which cost $10 and Mrs. Stenson draped her $11 white silk shawl over her shoulders, while Mrs. Benson drew out her gold watch at $18 and checked its time against the parlor clock."[91]

5. PERSONAL HONOR

Under the stimulus of such competition, the personal honor of many characters was worn away. Story after story showed both newcomers and older settlers succumbing to a variety of temptations and losing thereby the honesty which had never failed back home.

The frontier offered many chances to "help oneself" to property not one's own. A Danish-American hero was often out hunting, and one

211

morning was seen chasing a deer on his pony and bringing it down. Two men fishing in the river shouted to him that that was illegal food; the hunting season had not yet opened. But he asked who had given them special permission to fish with nets. They all laughed. "People didn't take lawfulness so seriously in those days. In their opinion, it was most unlawful to go hungry when there was plenty of game and fish."[92]

Immigrants were also tempted in the early days to take timber not their own.

To steal material for a house was common in those days—at least around here [Wisconsin]. And if it didn't go further than cutting down some of the smaller pines, the owner took it for granted that he was helping the pioneer to that extent, and said nothing. If somebody helped himself to government timber, popular opinion accepted that as perfectly all right. . . . . And so thievery in the woods grew to great proportions, and continued until there wasn't a single decent pine left standing on a government forty, and speculators' forties were laid bare too.

My goodness! It wasn't only big millionaires who stole the hair off the heads of our common government authority in the good old days![93]

Other accounts of the same problem recorded divided opinions in the community on the moral rightness of appropriating timber owned by others. A Norwegian settler who complained about the lack of trees on his new claim was advised to take from Uncle Sam's land; everybody did. Later when a pietistic minister came to the community, he suffered at the discovery that members of his congregation were stealing government property. He called a congregational meeting and charged the culprits with theft. Some had not been sure of their ethics, and now regretted their act; other, living on treeless prairie claims, argued that they had to take timber where they could find it. Some withdrew from church membership over the issue, which was not resolved until no timber worth stealing was left.[94]

The tendency to boast, which the immigrants were shown rapidly picking up from their Yankee environment, often descended to direct untruthfulness. A Danish son had written home that he was moving his wife and son into their own home, but when his old father arrived to live with them the house turned out to be rented. "It was as though everything was completely different in America-letters from what it was in reality."[95]

Many incidents showed characters who told the truth being penalized for their naiveté. One recently arrived Dane received appointment as a railroad mail clerk because the local politician decided it was the Scandinavians' turn to get some patronage. On the appointee's first run an inspector showed up, who was so friendly that the Dane confessed he knew nothing about the work and was not even a citizen. Naturally he was fired in short order. Regretting his own stupidity, the immigrant realized "how *Danish* he was in body and soul, and how this circumstance had cost him many unnecessary twinges of conscience. It was high time he became Americanized!"[96] A Swedish-American greenhorn was warned directly: "If you're too truthful you'll get no job in Chicago. Everybody else tells lies, and we have to do the same to get ahead."[97]

Yet most Scandinavians were pictured stooping to only certain kinds of improbity: swindling, lying, filching what apparently belonged to nobody, shady business practices. Except in a very few instances labeled as exceptional, robbery did not appear, nor murder, nor any serious crime. And some characters did maintain their strict honesty through thick and thin. An old Danish-American farmer had mortgaged the crop of a specific eighty acres on very unfair terms, in desperation for cash. When a hailstorm destroyed just that crop without touching his other eighty, strictly speaking he had every legal right to deliver nothing to the usurer; and so his son argued he should do. But no, the farmer had signed that contract with every intention to pay, and pay he would with the crop on the unharmed eighty, all he had left. "My word when I was a poor rent farmer was never doubted. In those days before all these written contracts were made, men believed my word as if it were written ten times over in ink. That has been a reward to me many times, when I have had few enough rewards to count. Now I am old and near the grave, shall I sell it for five hundred dollars to a lousy banker? The answer is, 'No, by God.' I'll leave my children a name that bears no stain, and I want you to say the same thing when you are as old as I am."[98]

What survived of such probity, however, was represented as being sadly undermined in the older Scandinavian rural communities by political agitators during the agrarian unrest of the 1890s and the First World War. An honest Norwegian-American businessman was on the verge of bankruptcy in the early 1920s because his debtors refused to pay him. "It's as though a new spirit had come into the farming population. Agitators have criss-crossed the state and convinced the farmers that the businessmen in the towns treat them like dogs . . . and that now it's time for the farmers to join together, open their own companies, and let these greedy storekeepers in the towns go to hell."[99] In the nick of time this good character was saved by a loan from a friend; but several other authors made the same complaint about declining honesty in the immigrant group, especially in the second and third generation.

VI. Urban-Rural Ethics

A clear difference in the economic ethics of urban and rural settings appeared throughout the literature.

In long-lasting social groupings, where characters lived many years or all their lives among the same neighbors, they rarely cheated or otherwise misused each other. This was the case in farming settlements, where class differences remained comparatively small and all enjoyed good or suffered bad times together. They might disagree loudly enough on other matters, but most wrongdoing by Old-World standards which the first generation permitted themselves was condoned if not shared by their peers. Exploitation of fellow men took place mainly in the form of overtasking hired help, but the hardworking farmers treated their own families and themselves little better. Only a few villains willing to endure the united disapproval of their neighbors practiced what the authors condemned as business ethics—extorting high interest on loans, foreclosing mortgages, selling shoddy goods at high prices, cheating widows and orphans out of their land. Almost all such improbity stayed within the law; where everyone knew everybody else's income and possessions, ill-gotten gains all too easily betrayed their origin. Therefore what few real misers developed within the group made the money they hoarded by the comparatively honest sweat of their brows. Any transgressions against the rights of others were motivated by the hope of material gain. Crimes of passion remained conspicuously absent from Scandinavian-American literature at all times and places.

In urban settings, the composition of the immigrant group was much more fluid. Even in small towns characters were pictured constantly moving in and out. People who knew each other less well had fewer scruples about getting the better of the other party, at least as long as he remained ignorant of the situation or lacked the means for revenge. Here of course businessmen led the way, but the openness and extent of their exploitation varied according to their enterprise. A storekeeper had to conceal his petty cheating from the customer, who could go to a competitor; a banker or employer could afford to be more open, like the contractor who told all his painters he could afford to keep only one man over the winter—the one who worked hardest.[100] Most immigrant authors assumed that such cynical misuse of others was learned in America, but the few characters who had been businessmen in the Old Country were pictured as little better there. Those who emigrated because they had gone bankrupt only applied their old ways of making money to the greater opportunities of the New World.

One story stated explicitly what many offered evidence to show: that ethical differences were less between the New World and the Old

214

than between town and country. Mor Lisa learned to hate and fear big cities long before she ever left Sweden; one daughter had been "ruined" in Stockholm, a son had been killed in a fight in Gothenburg, and her youngest had eloped to a life of poverty in Chicago. When the old woman came to America, the death of her son-in-law after a sunstroke from overwork on a blistering day confirmed her conviction that the evil of the world was concentrated in big cities.[101] Only rarely did a single author juxtapose such observations from both sides of the Atlantic, but farming people were shown victimized by the holders of money power before migration as well as after in many books. The storekeeper in Norway who sent the sheriff to take a poor man's last cow for his debts was akin to the Dakota merchant who asked Per Hansa what he had at home as security for a charge account. When he had been told, he warned that the immigrant "could keep his wife and youngsters; but the cow he would have to forfeit eventually, if he couldn't raise other means. Business was business!"[103]

Why should there have been so much emphasis on exploitation of the little man in America, when all agreed that he had been much worse off back home? But there he had accepted his position at the bottom of the social scale, or at least recognized that he could escape it only by leaving the whole society. In the New World he expected things to be different. Things were better, to be sure, but the way other people exercised their economic rights, such as taking interest on investment, interfered with what the immigrants conceived as their human rights, like enjoying the fruits of their labor. They had not realized that getting started as independent producers would cost more than land and toil; and farming for cash crops turned out more subject to economic pressures than they remembered from subsistence farming in the Old Country. American individualism, which they had expected would allow them to climb high, often worked against them by imposing too little control on those who were smarter than they in the ways of business. There could be too much freedom in a society whose value orientation seemed to encourage greed.

VII. Authors' Attitudes toward Materialism

Theoretically the social sytem of the New World awarded status and facilities on the basis of the work an individual performed. With this theory the immigrants thoroughly agreed; they had migrated in pursuit of it. But observation of American economics in action convinced most of the authors that such a system stimulated acquisitive drives at the expense of all others. Over and over they pictured how poverty-stricken peasants came to the Promised Land to build a better life, only to be-

215

come so involved in the struggle that they mistook the means for the end. The poetic justice these critics devised to punish such error often revealed that they too had come to think in materialistic terms. In one tale, for instance, a Dane from a poor but honorable family made a respectable fortune as a contractor in America, but devoted all his time to business and neglected his two sons. These grew up scorning everything Danish. They married purebred American wives, who spent the old man's fortune while despising him as a foreigner. The loneliness of his last years, deserted by his family, might strike a reader as punishment enough; but no, he had to die in a poorhouse.[104]

Such unconscious acceptance of materialistic values by the immigrant authors was very common. It dictated the kind of success recorded in countless poor-immigrant-made-good plots: land, comfort, bank accounts. It prescribed life aims in such terms as these from the mouth of a worthy young Norwegian-American: "I want to earn an honest living by my own exertions; I want to live in a nice house, wear nice clothes, and be able to associate with good people. Further than that, I want to make a better world for people to live in, and I think I can do it better as a mechanical engineer than in any other vocation that I might take up."[105]

The "average man" pictured in the literature found such ideals completely reasonable, and may well have resented how preservationist authors constantly scolded him for materialism. A reader could sympathize with the young people at a prairie youth club who packed the house at the first meeting, filled half the chairs at the second, and all stayed away from the third; for the entertainment consisted mainly of a lecture on how dreadful they were. "American youth are empty and flat! They completely lack any ideals or great thoughts! All they are interested in is money, roughhousing, and the latest fashion fad!"[106] A phenomenally popular Norwegian-American scandalmonger probably expressed the feeling of the majority of his readers when he wrote, "We have heard several say . . . that there is much crudeness among our people. Their book learning is small. People have other things to do besides read. But under the apparently crude exterior is often hidden a heart of gold. . . . It may be that we lack spiritual interests—we don't know Latin—but with the labor of our hands and our underdeveloped souls, we have helped build the mightiest nation on earth."[107]

At the same time that immigrant authors of every kind agreed on the dominant materialism of both general American society and their own ethnic group, they also concurred in their portrayal of their homeland as the opposite. Scandinavian peasants were described as ignorant, narrow, uncultured, bound by superstition and tradition, but not as materialistic.

216

What is it like there in Denmark?
—A land where everyone toils for his food,
but no one for gold must fight and feud;
where all take the time both to sing and to play,
and therefore few stumble and fall by the way,
    where a man must plow deep
    but untroubled can sleep
contented with little, his virtue to keep:
See, that's what it's like in Denmark![108]

The same youth-club lecturer who frightened away his audience in the Middle West added another verse to his song when addressing Norwegians on a visit to the Old Country. "Svein talked long about America. He pictured how people there slaved day in and day out, even on Sundays, lived only to grab everything they could get their hands on, forgot all the values of life, plundered their souls. . . . And those who tried to live for something more were spit on." In Norway ancestral fields were growing up to weeds because the children would be off to America. "For they would rather live as soul-enslaved servants of Mammon in America than as spiritual aristrocrats in Norway. 'No,' Svein concluded, 'stay home if you love your fatherland, honor your forefathers and their work, and you will live and die as true and great human beings.' "[109]

Preservationist authors could not accept the implications of such a deterministic view. If their people only mirrored the values of their environment at home or in exile, how could they preserve the first any more than influence the second? Bad as they were, Scandinavian immigrants were almost always credited with being less materialistic than Americans. Surely they could remain so if they preserved the faith of their fathers in their own Lutheran church.

VIII. Influence of the Immigrant Church

All types of writers agreed that this institution expressed and upheld whatever interest the average immigrant had in spiritual matters. Literature, history, the forms of art meant little to him, but he clung to his forefathers' church. The pioneers, whose lives were most dominated by material hardship, were pictured as the most devout of all their group; but was their devotion motivated more by social than by spiritual needs? Some authors at least asked the question. Rølvaag recorded the thoughts of Norwegian pioneers crowded into a hut to hear their first sermon in Dakota. Only a few could climb the ladder of reasoning that the minister raised.

The others realized that he was preaching well, and let it go at that; it gave them a simple satisfaction just to listen . .. And it was so fine and jolly, too, this gathering

217

together; now there would be some excitement in the settlement. One was thinking about the congregation that they would have to organize; another about the location of the new church; still another about the cemetery . . . and to everyone the thought came that men would be needed to manage these activities; well, they would show him that they could govern themselves . . . One woman had it in mind that they would of course start a ladies' aid, now that they had a minister; and that would be great fun, with meetings and cakes and coffee and sewing and all the rest. . . . But those who had not yet been confirmed dreaded the ordeal a little, though at the same time they were glad; at any rate, there would be a change in the daily monotony, and they would of course have some fine new clothes for the confirmation![110]

An old pioneer in a novel published in 1914 expressed prophetic fear that however good the influence of the immigrant church, it would not be strong enough to counteract the materialism he saw rapidly developing among his people. "I'm afraid this spirit will affect the church too. Yes, it will infect the church. For here anybody and everybody shares in making the church."[111] A prohibition novel showed this prophecy fulfilled in the character of a saloonkeeper who was a wealthy pillar of his church and feared no opposition from the other churches either. "They're not dangerous. The ministers are controlled by the members of their congregations—the rich ones, I mean."[112]

The evidence in this novel might have been distorted by the author's anti-saloon purpose, but the story of a Norwegian-American city church published in 1934 offered detailed corroboration. The new minister, son of an aristocratic leader in the synod, had been called to serve a congregation including both old and recent immigrants, second generation as well as first. His chief supporter was a Norwegian banker, who in spite of his business success felt himself snubbed by Yankee society. "So he put himself in the harness and made a great effort in order that the Norwegians might build just as expensive a church as the Americans and Germans. Now he had also secured a swell minister." At first all factions within the large congregation approved of the young pastor. The aristocratic clique liked his "faultless manners, while those who felt themselves left out by the 'swells,' noted with satisfaction that he seemed to treat all alike. Then there was the liberal element, which had joined the church for business reasons or because they wished to support a church—and find support in it. A little religion did no harm, and attending a church was considered respectable; but they did not wish to be hampered in any way by the church. The men visited the saloons and the women the theaters and the young people found their chief diversion in public dances. This element was very strong. Lastly there was a small band of 'elect,' who held their own prayer and testimonial meetings."[113] They liked the new clergyman too because he preached about the love of Jesus Christ and salvation for poor sinners, which they could under-

218

stand. However, the young minister's tendency to agree with everybody, to feel sorry for sinners and try to help instead of punishing them, turned the entire congregation against him group by group. They had well nigh destroyed him as a person when he conveniently died of pneumonia.

In story after story in both urban and rural settings the church life of immigrant communities was described as anything but spiritual. Bitter personal feuds developed between rival leaders within the congregational council or the ladies' aid; gossip and backbiting poisoned the parish air; stinginess kept ministers' salaries almost below the level of bare subsistence. A Dakota grandfather teased his devout wife by reading from *Skandinaven* how ladies' aid societies financed new church buildings by violating all the principles of Christianity, giving banquets, *lutefisk* suppers, and socials in a spirit of petty animosity and cut-throat competition.[114]

The authors often criticized the failure of the church to influence the values of the second generation. Swedish children attending public school studied McGuffey's readers. "From these readers and from the *Youth's Companion* they received their first ultra-parental notions of ethics. Strangely, they did not absorb ethics from the Sunday school, for the teaching there consisted of Bible History and the catechism, which seemed strangely unrelated to everyday life, especially since they were taught in Swedish and had to be learned by rote rather than by sense."[115] In an early novel Rølvaag pictured the second generation only going through the forms of religious faith, drawn to church activities by the fun involved. His devout young heroine felt she was getting less and less out of the young people's meetings at her church. The other youth were so smoothly self-confident! "Worship of God seemed the most facile thing in the world for them. The difficult struggle she had in trying to get nearer to God, so her relationship could be more immediate and childlike—so she could walk by His side every day and put her hand into His at any time—such a struggle none of the others seemed to know anything about. Often she came home from these meetings feeling spiritually enfeebled."[116]

With few exceptions, clergymen were the one element within the immigrant group regularly pictured as nonmaterialistic and self-sacrificing. Most were portrayed sympathetically as leaders who devoted their lives to service, not personal gain. "He had sacrificed himself for his people through a long life. Had ranged over the prairie to bring God's word to all his congregations. He had thought of himself last of all. Poor in goods and gold but rich in love he had been—a man who did his duty as he felt it, quiet, meek, friendly."[117] The clergy were respected for such self-sacrifice, even though members of the congregation often made fun of their impracticality. A Danish pastor's ignorance of farming and inability even to harness a horse were a source of endless amusement to the neighborhood. "That a 'learned man' can be so clumsy, not to say dumb . . . both amazes and amuses us. But we value him just as much for all that; as people say, 'it's not for such things we called him.' "[118]

Respected the clergy were, but not followed as examples. Another prairie farmer resented his minister's harping on the theme of how in the days of the Apostles there were no rich or poor; all shared with each other, and so all should do today.

Of course I don't deny that the man may be right, maybe we *should,* but under present conditions we *don't,* and therefore we have to help ourselves as best we can; but the pastor disapproves of all associations and societies of a "worldly" nature.[119]

None but a few radicals disavowed Christian principles, but some characters did raise the question of how meaningful religion could be to people who lived six days of the week by a philosophy directly opposed to that they joined in praising on Sunday. A son of Danish immigrants could only sneer at a church where the local banker was superintendent of the Sunday school—he who "collected interest from the poor farmers, and when the farmers couldn't pay, he sold their horses and cattle. It was all very legal and very cruel."[120]

In a group threatened with extinction, clearly self-justification was at work in the authors' common assumption that although their fellow immigrants had been corrupted by the American environment, still they retained enough of their previous virtue to make them morally superior to the Yankees. The source of evil influence was always seen as outside the group itself, in their physical if not their social surroundings. It might have been expected that exclusive and isolated colonies could better have preserved their Scandinavian values; but competitive materialism was pictured developing there also, from the temptation of too much prospective wealth or from the terrible suffering of the pioneers.

The constant need to stand guard, the continual lack of security, the endless fight for life and livelihood, had reduced them to bone and marrow, had sucked every drop of blood out of their spiritual life. The wings of their fancy were cut, their thoughts earthbound, their disposition heavy. They never looked beyond the earth their foot trod.[121]

Yet when such parents as these found their children obsessed by material values, they blamed American influence, not their own. No author except Rølvaag considered the possibility that his own group might have contributed to the money-madness which all deplored, in reacting to conditions in America in the same way as other inhabitants.

220

If indeed people in the Old Country were less dominated by materialism, it might have been because emigration removed those most addicted to ambition for goods and gold. All the authors agreed that the vast majority had left their homes in the quest for social betterment, and this was defined largely in tangible terms: food, clothing, houses, cash income, and status as measured by such things. In the fatherland these standards were veiled by a complex of other values operating through relations to family and forebears, home and neighborhood, landscape and tradition. Emigration broke the vital connection of most of these ties with the individual's life, and some of the authors argued that when they had been lost there was little left to occupy the attention of unsophisticated people besides materialism.

First they discarded their love for their parents, then their attachment to all back home they held dear, then the language they had learned from Mother, so love of their childhood faith, of God and their fellow man, then the songs they had learned as children, then their memories and their youthful ideals . . . and when they had uprooted from their hearts and minds everything they had praised before, then there was a great empty space to fill with egotism, selfishness, money-madness and all such.[122]

Scandinavians who valued such emotional ties more than getting ahead, stayed home.[123] Those who sacrificed them to satisfy material needs were the same people who complained of the dearth of spiritual values in America.

The authors recognized that the new environment encouraged the development of certain elements in Scandinavian character which the old one had inhibited. This change they judged was both for better and for worse, but they did not see that what they approved of was inseparably connected with what they condemned. Over and over they proclaimed that the main difference in American life was its opportunities. These they praised, these they had sacrificed so much to seek, yet these they blamed for the corruption of their people. The implication was that if similar openings had existed at home, they would not have led to the same demoralization there. Then, however, it could not have been the opportunities themselves which caused the difficulty, but the social context in which they were embedded, the attitudes which determined how they were used.

Story after story showed that money did not *mean* the same on both sides of the Atlantic. Certainly it was vital in the Old Country too, or so many characters would not have abandoned so much for its sake; but in the small, stable neighborhoods where most of them lived before emigration, wealth was only one attribute of status. Moral rectitude also had a role to play where all were so well acquainted and judged each other by the same system of ethics; but family background and

221

inherited social position were even more important. One of the classics of Norwegian-American literature, H. A. Foss' *The Cotter's Son*, won much of its popularity by its authentic portrayal of this status system. The poor but worthy cotter's son won the love of his landlord's daughter, but marriage was impossible because of the social gulf between them. The boy went off to America to make his fortune, while the landlord ruined his moral standing and status by drinking himself into a quagmire of debt. When his estate was put up for auction, the rich stranger who arrived just in time to outbid all others was of course the cotter's son. His American gold alone did not win him the princess and half the kingdom, however; a large part of his victory was due to his moral superiority to his father-in-law, and he could step into the old man's shoes and assume his abandoned status only by marrying into the family and taking over the ancestral estate. More than mere money was required for such a happily-ever-after in rural Norway.[124]

Available estates and marriageable daughters were strictly limited in number, however, even if one could bring back the gold from America. There was better chance of social advancement in a society which awarded status for individual achievement alone, apart from family history. And how else could performance be measured where people were strangers to each other and lived by different gods, than by the one standard necessary to and valued by all, tangible and objective common currency? Then even hayseed Scandinavians would have an equal chance with all others to win what status they could. Before emigration, no character or poet in all the literature voiced any objection to these aspects of the system he deliberately chose as better than his own.

Wealth as the sole measure of achieved status turned out to have serious drawbacks, however. Those which Scandinavian immigrant authors considered the most important have been recorded here. Their disappointment reflected the inevitable experience of people who move from one kind of social setting to another. While living inside one system, their attitudes and relationships formed by it, they *could* not discover what it would mean to live inside a different social structure. Only after having made the change could they see and feel its full consequences.

The outcome did not mean the same to all Scandinavian immigrants, either. Some got along much better in the new system, stimulated by its individualism and material rewards; some were destroyed in it, trampled by others incited to ruthless greed; most both won and lost in all imaginable degrees and proportions. Many felt the scales so nearly balanced that they could not counsel others whether or not to follow suit. "Thus you can understand that I won't urge you to come to America. No, I won't even *advise* you to. I'll only say that here you

222

don't have to worry about food and clothes; those things come almost by themselves."[125]

Very few authors revealed awareness of other aspects of American culture more in accord with their Old-World value orientation. The voices of native critics of individualism and materialism were almost never to be heard in this immigrant literature. Mention of such writers as Emerson and Mark Twain was so seldom as to remain in each case unique, and was usually made to show an immigrant character's ignorance of the name. A Norwegian visitor was astonished at a second-generation youth: "Good heavens! You an American and haven't even heard of Mark Twain! What in the world do you learn in your schools over here?"[126] No immigrant author considered the possibility that also Americans saw the excesses of economic individualism, and would attempt to curb them in time. Materialism was more difficult to pass laws against, but it too had its native critics of whom most immigrant authors remained unaware. Feeling themselves in American society but not of it, and judging it all to be like what lay immediately at hand, the authors persisted in upholding their value orientation as not only superior but apart, theirs alone because it was Norwegian (or Swedish or Danish, as the case might be). Except in the cause of prohibition, they almost never sought allies under the banner of general Christian or humanistic principles. (A few Socialists remained deviants from their ethnic group in this as in all else.) Transplantation from Scandinavia to the United States changed much else, but not this basic provincialism as long as these authors remained spokesmen for a distinct ethnic group.

Chapter Eight
Change in Morals and Mores

Although most writers felt that change in values from Scandinavian toward American patterns involved degradation and loss, similar modification of morals and mores within the immigrant group often seemed an improvement. Characters found American morality more lenient than their own in some respects but more strict in others. As a rule they resisted the leniency and approved of the greater strictness, which the authors pictured the majority of their group gradually adopting as their own.

Immigrant characters differed sharply in moral attitudes among themselves. Ancient peasant tradition in all three northern nations had fostered customs of hard drinking, dancing, and social games, and comparatively free relations between the sexes before marriage; but the pietistic movements of the late eighteenth and nineteenth centuries introduced strong puritan trends repudiating the earlier tradition, sometimes so strongly as to forbid any kind of worldly merriment. The clash between the two schools of opinion continued within the immigrant group in the New World. At least until the turn of the century the pietistic school was the stronger, and its adherents consistently attacked those aspects of the American environment which encouraged the growth of vices brought along from the Old World.

I. Drinking

The problem of drink overshadowed all others. A number of writers pointed out that the root of the evil lay in the drinking habits of the Old Country. A Danish-American doctor, for example, explained why so many of his countrymen in a prairie town got drunk so often:

It's because they don't know any better. They were poor folks' children back home in Denmark, born in small, crowded huts where it was always nip and tuck with hunger and need, and where the old folk made a festival out of a bottle of Aalborg Aquavit. Then they were bound out to work—for farmers, or on the big estates; and each day was long and cheerless and hard, with work too heavy for their strength.

224

But sometimes in the evening they were sent to the chandler's for a bottle of liquor, which they caroused over in their bunkroom.—Now the same people suddenly become independent, almost rich—crave amusement and pleasure. But most of our farmers can't imagine fun except in connection with beer and liquor.[1]

This recollection of the Old Country during the latter part of the nineteenth century recorded that the ancient Scandinavian custom of drinking heavily but seldom was already changed. As long as liquor was still largely home-distilled on those farms which had barley or potatoes to spare, or was bought with scarce and precious cash, it was too valuable to be wasted on any but the most important fetes. At weddings and funerals, however, at Christmas and midsummer, hospitality required that the host pour with a liberal hand.

Giants in the Earth gave an excellent picture of these ancient drinking customs transplanted to the American frontier. The single bottle of liquor in every sod hut of the tiny settlement was a precious thing, brought forth only as a medicament in the utmost emergencies or in celebration of the most important events. After the first supply trip to the distant town drinks were passed around in jubilation, over the pretended protests of the guests. " 'You shouldn't be handing around costly Christmas treats in the middle of the haying season!' said Tønseten, craftily."[2] When all the settlers gathered to celebrate the thirteenth day of Christmas, a dram or two apiece helped provide holiday gaiety. "Then there was food; there was coffee; there were the pipes; and much friendly chatting went on in Per Hansa's cabin that day." After doing chores they hurried back for the evening.

All felt closely drawn together that night. Their chatting had become singularly intimate and hearty. When the men returned, there was another bottle on the table, not more than half full. None of them had brought it, and none could guess where it had come from.
"Isn't it remarkable," marvelled Tønseten, "that such things can spring up out of the very ground? This is truly the Promised Land! Ah, that is Beret's work, now. I know the bottle!"[3]

The function of such social drinking in private homes survived at least as long as the first generation in some Scandinavian settlements. The last novel of Rølvaag's trilogy described Christmas celebrations in the same community a quarter-century later, when the fun did not begin in earnest until drinks were passed around. "During the evening the merriment ran high; all the men except Peder, and the women with them, sampled Tønseten's Christmas brew."[4]

The opening of saloons in nearby towns introduced a new pattern of drinking which grew up alongside the old one and gradually displaced it. As a character in a prohibition novel complained, "We Norwegian-Americans have brought along from the fatherland a bad custom, a drinking habit, or maybe it should be called a rule of 'treating,' which finds all too good room to grow in our national or innate generosity, especially now that the saloon has sprung up at our very doors."[5] When American conditions made liquor constantly available and provided the ready cash to buy it, what had been a bad habit in the Old World was encouraged to grow into a serious vice in the New.

The saloons were curse of the frontier. They enticed the wary worker so invitingly with music and refreshments, warmth and—intoxication. Mother waited for Father's pay envelope, and perhaps they had planned to take the children shopping this Saturday evening. It grew late and the children fell asleep and Father's supper had been kept hot so long that now it was ruined, now she began to cry and knelt in prayer, her only comfort. And Father, who was so kind and cheerful otherwise, turned so unreasonably contrary and brutal when he finally came home with almost nothing left from what he had toiled a whole week to earn.[6]

Countless stories related the tragedies which gave rise to so much and so passionate prohibition literature: the pioneer father who made the long trip to town to buy the family's winter supplies and after being gone a month returned with nothing, having drunk up every cent; the sensitive intellectual who could find escape from the intolerable hardships of the frontier only by periodically drinking himself "into the shadows"; overworked doctors in a raw mining town who were drunk half the time; factory workers whose only pleasure could be found in the corner saloon, while their families went hungry week after week; lumberjacks and railroad workers who drank up many months' wages on a week's binge. Almost all men who found themselves at odds with America turned to liquor in compensation. Some of them the stories showed finally winning free of the evil temptation, but many destroyed themselves; and the suffering of their families was portrayed graphically in either event.

Yankee neighbors saw hard drinking as one of the most typical characteristics of Swedes in Minnesota. In an American novel, a letter printed in a local newspaper described how the writer's Swedish neighbor went back to his family in Sweden each fall after harvesting his wheat. "My neighbor says that money will go farther over there. He can buy more alcohol for a dollar in Sweden than he can buy for ten dollars here, and everybody knows that a Swede can't enjoy life without plenty of alcohol."[7] Even in their liberal provision of this necessity the Swedes were stingy. They bought spirits raw and diluted them until the cost was very cheap. When they drank so much at home at the same time that they expressed intense hostility to saloons, the Yankees thought them hypocrites.

Of course by no means all members of this immigrant group were pictured as addicted to drink. Women never took more than a sip or two on the most festive occasions. In the whole of the literature not a single feminine character was portrayed even slightly tipsy; on the contrary, most expressed hatred for all kinds of liquor, and even the few old-fashioned peasant wives who took a social nip did so with sly excuses. Clearly the deep-drinking customs of the Old Country belonged only to men. Among these, there were many sterling characters who proclaimed themselves teetotalers, some of whom learned their attitude in pietistic homes, others who adopted it after unfortunate experiences in America. There were also a good number who drank in moderation. At gatherings of Swedish laborers in a large city, one novel reported "unfortunately liquid refreshments flowed as freely here as in Sweden, or maybe even more freely because of more ready money"; but to their credit these working people in general behaved well—did not start fights or loud quarrels.[8] Middle-class farmers continued to enjoy a glass or two with guests in the privacy of their homes, in pure conviviality. Yet prohibition authors argued that temperance in the use of strong drink was impossible, at least for Scandinavians in America. In many a plotted struggle between moderation and abstinence, the former led to drunkenness under the constant temptation of the ubiquitous saloon.

A fair number of prohibition stories by immigrant authors were laid in the Old Country, attacking the Demon Rum in any setting; but the large majority, tracing the calamitous effect of the American saloon on Scandinavian drinking habits, recorded growing prohibitionist zeal within the group. This can be traced in the attitudes of Lutheran ministers. High-Church men, until the 1890s at least, opposed prohibition. They were against drunkenness, of course, but argued for temperance in using all God's gifts. During this period some more pietistic ministers joined and encouraged teetotaler clubs only under considerable opposition from businessmen in their congregations, who believed that saloons attracted shoppers to town. But the moderates lost out. After the turn of the century no Scandinavian immigrant minister could afford to be seen drinking so much as a glass of beer. During a Norwegian-American argument before World War I over whether modern morals were better than those of former times, a young minister said proudly of his colleagues that "people wouldn't stand to see them with a glass of wine or beer in their hands now like in the old days."[9]

A couple of stories referred to conflict within church groups over substituting grape juice for wine in Communion service; the milder drink was always adopted. By 1900 a Swedish-American tale recounted the trials of an editor of Swedetown's oldest newspaper, who had printed off a book of his poems as a premium to subscribers. Buried in pages of traditional morality, one verse advised anyone who wept rather to sip "tears" from the glass's rim, for *these* gave gladness. Aroused readers

227

sent in a flood of protest letters, canceling their subscription in righteous indignation. Typical was Pastor Swan's condemnation of the poem which "without loathing, rather with satisfaction, alludes to the gruesome custom of imbibing."[10] This story was satirical, but it too marked the general trend toward greater puritanism within this ethnic group.

Immigrant journalists sometimes leaned far in the other direction. A considerable minority were portrayed as confirmed drunkards, and a great many were habitual tipplers. As a rule city newspapermen were hard drinkers, while small-town journalists often expressed prohibitionist zeal. Upper-class immigrant characters consistently advocated temperance rather than prohibition, if they expressed any concern over the issue at all; but many a scion of a leading family back home drank himself to ruin in American saloons, along with city-bred workingmen who remained deep drinkers to the last. Both extremes of the social scale were pictured on the whole liberal in regard to drink. It was largely the growing middle class, especially in its rural setting, which developed such thoroughgoing puritanism toward drinking. A miserable newcomer on a prairie farm, plowing in terrible heat for fifty cents a day, only after an inner struggle decided not to run away; for in his despair and loneliness he had drunk too deep one night, and everyone scorned him for that: "—they were respectable folks in that community, and a newcomer who got drunk was reckoned as trash."[11]

II. Dancing and Games

Dancing, social games, and card-playing were viewed with the same dichotomy of attitude, again with growing predominance of the pietistic bias. Pioneers direct from the Old Country, settled in a compact group of friends, could crowd each other's cabins or yards for a rousing evening of folk dances and circle games without a hint of disapproval; and late-arrived city immigrants thronged their Scandinavian Halls to the same end. But in church communities of rural and small-town settings, the literature reflected the rapid growth of puritanism in such matters.

III. Growth and Decline of Puritan Morality

In story after story characters who compared their recollection of earlier days in the Old Country or on the frontier emphasized the change for the better which had taken place in the moral standards of their community. "Where is now the carousing with drink and dancing in private homes on festive occasions such as weddings?"[12] Or an old Norwegian woman, defending so many church activities for young people, recalled how in the old days they had gone to dances every Saturday night and then slept through church on Sunday; she even got engaged on the way home from a dance. "That's the way it went in the old days. And certainly it's not worse to get engaged on the way home from a Christian meeting."[13]

A Danish-American novel laid in a young Nebraska settlement showed one source of pietistic influence from the American environment. During heated discussion throughout the community over a quarrel with some Methodists, one Lutheran goodwife accused the Lutheran men: "You imagine that you have the true doctrine. But you drink and play cards and smoke. Yes, you do, all six of you standing right here. But the Methodists *don't*. They take their Christianity seriously, they do!" The men laughed at her. "What did she mean by *that*? Weren't they as good Christians as any others? If they drank a little over at Ole's, it wasn't as much as they'd been used to in Denmark. If they played cards, it wasn't gambling because they didn't have any money. If they smoked —well, that was one of Methodists' peculiarities, that they counted that a sin."[14]

Another source of puritanism the immigrants carried with them in the Old-Country pietism mentioned earlier. A Norwegian-American novel related how a Haugean minister in the 1870s brought over a strict schoolmaster from Norway to hold religious school a couple of months in each of several neighboring parishes in Minnesota. Children running and shouting on the way home from one of these sessions were overheard by a pious old man, who complained to the schoolmaster. The guilty children were subjected to an inquest and delivered to their parents for punishment. The schoolmaster then instituted a set of strict rules. Boys and girls were henceforth forbidden to play together, and the sin of playing catch with a homemade ball was prohibited. The children held a secret meeting of protest, but concluded that they could do nothing until they were older.[15]

Complaint about the decline in moral behavior of young people was recorded at all periods, but grew progressively stronger toward the turn of the century. Both the second and third generations and newcomers from Europe were accused of levity, worldliness, and positive immorality. It was not rare for even children of ministers and pietistic lay-leaders to go astray, although they usually repented and were recalled to righteousness before the end of the tale. By this time immoral influences were regularly depicted as invading the immigrant communities from the American environment. The eldest son of a pious Norwegian-American minister, for instance, caused his father endless heartache with the godless ideas he had picked up at the public school, where evil-hearted teachers deliberately misled him. A younger son came to the mother in anguish, because his brother had told him card-playing and dancing were not sinful.

I told him that papa had said they were, but he answered that his professor had said the opposite. It's only we Norwegians who insist on such nonsense. His friends at school had also said that Americans aren't so narrowminded. Their minister said the same thing.[16]

Of course this young man went sadly astray in the big city, stealing to cover his gambling losses; but when his long-suffering father saved him once more, he underwent conversion and returned to the way of God.

The time sequence in many of these amateur novels is often difficult to judge, but it would seem that the growth and then partial decline of puritanic pietism within the group followed the curve of churchly enthusiasm accompanying the synodical conflicts discussed earlier. While lines were drawn so sharply between one church and another, individual behavior was shown as an important criterion of demonstrating both one's worthiness to belong to the congregation of one's choice, and the righteousness of that holy community. The false doctrine of rivaling synods was sometimes blamed for misleading people into sin, as one Norwegian-American novel attacked the Norwegian Synod for encouraging its members to drink and dance. When a minister of this stripe got a church organized in a community, the author claimed, "The previously serious, quiet members of Troberg's congregation had now taken another direction under Pastor Babel's 'blessed' church, and holy days were celebrated mostly with dancing and drinking, they even often gathered for a dance and invited people along from church."[17]

Since the social life of small communities centered in church activity, the threat of disapproval from one's nearest associates, or the danger of disgracing the institution most central to one's identity, usually proved enough to keep a family in line. Not until the tension of conflict had relaxed toward the end of the nineteenth century could the multitudinous cross-currents of influence from the American environment again present alternative patterns of behavior as possibilities of moral choice by the younger generation. Leaving the ways of their fathers was almost always portrayed as a sin committed by the young characters in this literature, but the fact that so many did descend to dancing, gambling, and other immoral amusements away from home indicated that the puritanism of their parents was losing its force. "Ma said that dancing was the devil's most dangerous snare for young folks. Yes, so she claimed. But he knew of several people who danced. Charley, for instance. And Charley was a swell guy, in many ways better than himself."[18]

Although moral opposition to drinking, all kinds of dancing, and games of chance remained strongly expressed in this literature from the first to last, a countermovement in support of the more innocent

230

forms of traditional amusements was carried out by Grundtvigian ministers, advocates of "happy Christianity." Characters of this school strongly disapproved of puritanism among their countrymen: "who could have dreamed that anyone would object to such innocent pastimes as games, song, and rifle shooting—things we grew up with in Denmark. . . . I'd like to know if there are many such punctilious pastors over here, for if so we really need to proselytize among the clergy for human values!"[19] Grundtvigian ministers organized old-fashioned circle games and folk dances for young people's meetings in the parsonage, or led group singing of secular songs at private parties. Festivities under such auspices remained on a high moral plane, opening and closing with a prayer or hymn and never descending to drunkenness even if beer was served.

Only people of this school were represented as offering organized opposition to the puritanism of the pietists. Other religious leaders, regardless of their own convictions, had to bow to the stern will of the majority. A young minister from Copenhagen in a Danish prairie congregation was hard put to find an answer when representatives of the young people's club requested the loan of the parish house. They would not divulge what they wanted to use it for, and he had been previously warned that they were planning a dance! He had nothing against dancing personally, but he felt obliged to hold a lecture for the young people. "If you want to have a little party, that's all right. But you know very well there are two things the congregation must keep away from at all costs, and they are—dancing and drink." It turned out that the young people had bought a marble baptismal font which they wanted to install as a surprise, but the minister suffered sleepness nights until he found out.[20]

Some immigrant characters continued their Old-World drinking and dancing customs in America at all periods. Unless they underwent religious conversion, these simply turned their backs on their pietistic countrymen and kept to different ways. They were portrayed disapprovingly by pietistic authors, who usually converted them to the ways of righteousness in the end. As more and more immigrants came from towns and cities, however, and settled in the same, puritan attitudes toward amusements declined as an issue in the literature. At their social halls in Chicago, Minneapolis, and Brooklyn, Scandinavian groups gathered to dance their dances and sing their songs (interspersed with American numbers) without a thought of sin.

IV. Music and Drama

Music was the only art approved by all camps within the Scandinavian group at all periods in the literature. Whenever an author wished to make a hero, or especially a heroine, shine with the light of the muses in popular approval, he endowed the character with the gift of song. Instrumental performers were less common, but they were accepted by all except the most strictly pietistic, who had nothing to say against guitar, piano, or organ accompaniment to songs of devotion. When a rare personality ventured into opera, however, her home community buzzed with unfavorable gossip: "I hear she is on the stage now . . . singing in opera. . . . The theater is the ante-room to hell. . . . I had hoped she might see the error of her ways and come back to the church . . . but now she never will. . . . They never buy return tickets when they start to hell over that road."[21]

Not all shared such horror of the stage. A latitudinarian minority mainly in cities organized amateur drama societies and put on long series of plays. Their serious efforts normally failed to attract much of an audience, but their comedies and farces, taken mainly from the dramatic literature of the home country, often proved successful. As one Norwegian-American confessed, "I'm almost ashamed to admit that when I later saw 'The Buffoon' [a Danish musical comedy] performed by some Danish amateurs in Scandia Hall I got more out of it than out of Ibsen's 'Warriors at Helgeland.' "[22]

What came to be the dominant attitude among the middle-class immigrant groups entrenched in rural and small-town settlements, however, was well illustrated by the experience of an enthusiastic young minister in a factory town. Organizing many new youth activities to draw the second generation to the church, "he soon found that the young Norwegian-Americans living in town had been sadly neglected. There were well-dressed boys and girls out of their teens who had never read a book outside of their school books. Many had a talent for music, however, and declamations were in vogue. He began to practice dialogues with them, and pieces in which several could take part. . . . One thing led to another, and false beards were used when one of the boys was to personate an old man. Instantly the whole congregation was up in arms. The church had become a theatre!" The minister had to apologize and drop the whole activity.[23]

V. Other Arts

Other forms of art were seldom mentioned. Occasionally a social misfit wrote stories or poems, but always as an avocation. Neighbors who found out about such deviation judged the man as a trifle queer. Only a couple of painters appeared in all these books, condemned to sentimental subjects if they were to sell enough pictures to keep from starving. No fellow immigrants bought even these. Of two would-be sculptors, one had long since given up his art and gone to work in a factory;[24] the other, a clumsy symbol of Faustian aspiration, remained a moral outcast.[25] As Rølvaag remarked of a minor character in a short story, "Mr. Erlie Ingolf . . . had probably been meant to be a poet, an actor, or something in that line; but since he came here as a young boy, he had never heard the word art mentioned, and so he became not an artist but a salesman."[26]

Ignorance of practically all aspects of formal art seemed to have bred suspicion of it throughout the immigrant group. A cultured young couple building their home in a prairie community collected their books and pictures and their piano in a hidden room to which the neighbors were never admitted. They felt that their deviance from the materialistic norms of their community was too great to risk public view.[27] All the evidence of the literature thus supported the complaint in many an article and editorial that in cultural contributions to American life, with the possible exceptions of literature and music, Scandinavians came last among ethnic groups.[28]

VI. Sabbath-Keeping

How to keep the sabbath was another moral issue on which the members of this group differed considerably, sometimes within the same family. A Swedish child recalled how her grandmother on the Atlantic crossing once forgot the day and knit a stocking on a Sunday. When her minister son reminded her of what day it was, she turned pale with fright and hastily hid the work. Her son only laughed. "But Grandma she don't laugh, 'cause she is awful sorry she knitted on Sunday. She says it was Sin."[29] Pioneers of all three nationalities, fresh from the strict folkways of settled communities, usually observed the sabbath by dressing in their best, abstaining from all but the most necessary barn work, and holding devotional services in their homes. In the afternoon they might stroll from one hut to another for visiting, but the men restrained their profanity and the women refrained from knitting or mending in honor of the day. No few immigrant children recalled in later life the endless boredom of rural Sundays, when they were forbidden to run or play. One Norwegian mother, who saw sin in all things, destroyed her son's fiddle, frowned when her children laughed, and especially forbade such levity on Sunday, when they had to sit and read dull religious books all day.[30]

This behaviorial pattern was challenged, however, by the exigencies of frontier life. One strict Norwegian minister overheard a church member talk about a neighbor who had been out in the fields that Sunday in an effort to save something from the grasshopper plague. The clergyman demanded the name of the culprit, and ordered the president and dean of the congregation to give him a sharp reprimand under church discipline for his sin. When after long procrastination and repeated orders from the preacher the two officials finally went to see the offender, he defended himself by pointing out how every man in the settlement had done the same. When the two officials reported this unhappy truth back to their minister, he sat in silence a long while before finally rising with the remark that he must be going. "It was the only time anyone in the congregation had ever seen the clergyman at a loss."[31] In the face of common-sense needs, the attitude of zealous pietists toward work on Sunday came to seem a bit ridiculous. A Danish-American tale made fun of a farmer whom a passer-by found madly pumping water for his thirsty stock one baking-hot Monday. What's the matter, was the windmill broken? No, explained the farmer, but there's no wind. There was plenty of wind yesterday; why didn't you fill your watertank then? " 'Yesterday was the Lord's Day, and that day the Bible bids us keep holy,' answers Jens with an unctuous voice and a pious look toward heaven. And now he expounds for Ole the sin in letting a windmill work on Sunday."[32]

Gradually immigrant attitudes changed from piety which refrained from offending an all-seeing God to fear of what the neighbors would say. A newcomer visiting a Swedish-American family in a factory town at the turn of the century, discovered that the two grown daughters were not church members because they did not believe in baptism; but they were shocked when the Sunday guest asked if they could not play the piano or join him in a game of cards—what, let the neighbors know they were breaking the sabbath?[33] In a settled prairie community of Swedes, a strict Lutheran sabbath-keeper in another tale condemned her neighbor for sewing on Sunday morning, and forbade the teacher boarding at her house to iron on the Lord's day. But she herself gave big dinners on the sabbath, since that was the only time her husband was home from work. Once when she discovered at the last minute that she was short three napkins, she drew the window shades before ironing them. After dinner she forbade her daughter to go picking flowers, and snatched the Sunday paper away from her son. But in rare moment of insight that night, sitting alone, she realized she did not keep the sabbath herself as she had been taught to do in the Old Country. She ought to make it family day, and read together with her children to teach them true piety.[34] The moralistic intent of the tale showed the need the author felt to recall readers to preferable Old-World ways of keeping the Lord's day holy.

VII. Secret Societies

A still more important matter on which the God-fearing differed from the more latitudinarian was secret lodges. None had met this issue in the Old Country; the problem developed only in America. Ministers almost unanimously opposed the phenomenon, and the pietistic who followed their lead echoed their views. As one Norwegian-American tale put it, "The pastor did not believe in any kind of insurance. The best insurance was God the Almighty and His Word, and only with great reluctance had the clergyman finally allowed the trustees to insure the church building. All lodges were sinful and had come from freemasonry."[35]

The conflict of this plot was between a Norwegian laborer's faith in God and his fear of leaving his family destitute if he should die. Most of his fellow workers had joined a lodge for the insurance, but he and a pious West-Country man held out—until the latter fell ill and died, and his wife shortly afterwards. While the minister was trying to arrange for the children to be admitted to a Lutheran orphanage, American social workers got a court order giving them control over the children; they were adopted by different families, given strange names, and lost to the Norwegian community. Shaken by this event, Lars joined a lodge and discovered to his surprise that the initiation did not involve horrible oaths. The promise of silence was easy to keep because nothing happened at the meetings worth talking about. He could see nothing wrong in the ceremonies, and was not required to deny his Savior. Nevertheless, for a long time he was afraid he had committed a sin, until he finally found peace in the thought that perhaps God Himself had planted the idea of mutual help in workingmen's hearts. But one winter Lars was fatally injured at logging work. He was brought home to die, and lying in pain he alternated between daytime joy that his family would be provided for, and nighttime fear that insurance was sinful after all. As he breathed his last, he told the minister to burn his policy. The pastor was delighted—this was the victory of God's spirit. But then he realized he would be destroying the only help and hope left to the widow and children, so instead he knelt with them to thank God that Lars had been able to provide for their future.

Several pious characters went through this change of attitude in different stories. Only those outside secret lodges remained their implacable enemies; those who joined were surprised that the ceremonies were not so dreadful after all, and the sickness and life insurance features saved many an immigrant family from going under. The less pietistic joined secret lodges without hesitation for their financial advantages, which came to be of many kinds. In hard times lodges opened soup-kitchens for jobless men of their own national background.[36] Declining pietism or increasing familiarity with secret societies gradually robbed this issue of its significance even for the most churchly. It had dropped out of the literature completely by the time of World War I.

VIII. Premarital Sex

On the subject of premarital sex, the literature contained considerable evidence that the immigrant group in America developed much stricter standards of behavior than had been the rule in the Old Country.

A Swedish-American novel which described at length peasant life in a northern province of Sweden included an account of a three-day wedding celebration, with dancing most of the night. Guests who finally fell asleep on the floor were disturbed toward morning by an uproar from the bridal chamber. The bride had just given birth to a baby! At first this explanation was accounted a joke; the couple had been married only a few hours. But the infant's cries were unmistakable. Word was sent to the minister who had just performed the marriage ceremony to come back and baptize the baby. "This unexpected event changed the program, so that instead of continuing the wedding party . . . the entertainment was concluded with a christening feast and good wishes for the happy birth of a healthy boy. The newly married couple thought themselves fortunate that the baby was not illegitimate." The same author described a church ceremony at which two mothers were "cleansed" after childbirth—one married, the other not. The ritual was the same for both, except that for the first the minister prayed that she might continue to be fruitful, while the second he bade go in peace and sin no more.[37]

This free relation between the sexes before marriage was not promiscuous; it was permitted by peasant mores between engaged or promised couples because economic conditions often delayed their marriage many years. It was usually preferable to be married before children arrived, and unmarried mothers were pictured as feeling shame, especially when the father had gone off to America. But once the mother was married, the matter was forgotten. Having an illegitimate child was considered a temporary handicap, not a lifelong disgrace. Pietists rejected this latitudinarian peasant tradition, however, even in the Old Country. If one of their daughters made such a misstep, her life within the immediate community of believers was ruined forever, and she had no choice but to leave.

The conflict between older tradition and newer puritanism in this matter was not shown transplanted to America like dissension over drink and dancing. Instead the pietistic attitude triumphed almost from the first. No author commented on the possible influence of American morals in this respect, but all who mentioned the matter agreed on the marked difference in premarital sex morality within Scandinavian groups at home and in the New World. When a Danish-American author let a prairie girl go astray, for instance, the terrible gossip ruined not only her own life but that of her entire family—for good.[38] Rølvaag described an incident when a young girl who had given birth to an illegitimate baby and left it to die was forced to stand before the congregation and read aloud a statement of repentance. After the painful scene, a group of young men stood talking outside the church. One commented, "It's not easy to play around with the girls in this country. Back in the Old Country an extra brat or two didn't make so much difference."[39]

In another Norwegian-American novel a newly arrived miss in a prairie city learned that the young people of immigrant families there stood morally above those of the same age back in Norway in several respects. They were not quarrelsome, they did not swear, they usually kept their promises. "She also soon learned that when one of these girls made a misstep, the guilty boy was never the son of a Norwegian immigrant, but someone of another nationality—or a Norwegian newcomer."[40] Summing up the reticence, even hypocrisy about sex in Dakota, a wise old woman tried to teach her motherless granddaughter something of the facts of life:

There are good mothers in this town who are quick with their tongues about the young, but conceived themselves before their marriage vows. . . . I do not mean to frighten you, but who will talk of such things when I am gone? Time runs through my fingers like sand in the sea. I am of the old country, where even the young saw birth and death, and knew the stuff of which our stormy lives are made.[41]

IX. Marriage and Divorce

On one subject all the immigrant authors agreed. They unanimously condemned what they saw as American levity toward the institution of marriage. Civil marriages never occurred in stories with an Old-World setting; the phenomenon was evidently unknown in Scandinavia during the years when most of these authors emigrated. Marriage was considered by the entire group to be a holy sacrament, performable only in church by an ordained man of God, and the two people thus joined could not afterwards be sundered. Norwegians who heard of civil marriages performed by American justices of the peace were suspicious at first. Could such a ceremony really be valid?[42] Even after accepting its legality, many authors criticized the practice. Rølvaag pictured a Norwegian minister maintaining that under normal conditions no lay person might perform this or any other religious ceremony. On the frontier, in the continued absence of any clergyman, it might be excused if the performing official was a regularly elected officer; but, "Such marrying practices as some people have here are sacrilegious and must be discontinued."[43]

An important argument against the civil ceremony was that a relationship entered into so casually could all too easily be broken. Divorce was devil's work to all these authors, pietistic and non-pietistic alike, and all criticized vehemently the comparatively high divorce rate among native Americans. A Swedish-American tale opened with someone asking an immigrant named Anderson why he had never married; fear of picking a lemon was no real excuse, because he could always get a divorce. " 'Ah, I see you are beginning to be Americanized already,' warned Anderson. 'The loose laws governing marriage are the curse of this blessed country. . . . In Sweden, as far as I remember, marriage was always held holy . . . it was considered a heavenly institution, which could not be dissolved on the ground of accidental disagreement or irrational crotchets.' "[44]

Anderson maintained that a good half of his countrymen had been driven morally crazy by the restless nervousness, easy money, and anonymity of big-city life; but the evidence of the entire literature pointed rather to the vast majority maintaining this Old-World view of marriage as sacred. Divorce was extremely rare in the stories, and marriage to a divorced person rarer still. The attitude of small-town Dakota Norwegians was typical. They would rather see a beloved daughter remain an old maid than marry the divorced man she loved. "The Church not only frowned upon divorce, it openly attacked it in theory and practice; and in its theology no divorced person ever escaped the taint."[45]

The immigrant authors constantly complained about the prevalence of divorce in the New World, seeing it as both symptom and cause of the weakening family structure they deplored. Discussion of internal relations of immigrant families appeared frequently in both prose and poetry, for here American patterns were seen in active conflict with those imported from the Old Country.

X. The Family

1. THE EUROPEAN PATTERN

A multitude of stories depicted the structure of the Scandinavian family in both Old- and New-World settings. It was dominated by the father, whose authority over both wife and children in the home country was nearly absolute. He determined the children's discipline, their training and education, their future career, their marriage partner. His power was limited only by the laws of the land and the rules of the Lutheran church. In a considerable number of tales this paternal dominance was shown transferred to America. A meek, obedient wife suffered through a lifetime of her husband's drunkenness, unfaithfulness, stupidity—without a murmur, forgiving all.[46] Or a son who had been left behind to study theology in Norway when his family emigrated hastened after them at his father's order: "As a child I was always accustomed to obey my father's command, and when he told me in his letters to follow here, this had the force of a law to me."[47]

Such behavioral patterns established before emigration were especially apt to persist on the frontier, where family isolation supported paternal dominance. He who was responsible for the physical survival of all had to be able to command their efforts to that end. Only occasionally, when the mother felt the authority of divine writ on her side, did she venture to oppose the father on such matters as holding regular family prayers or making an effort to bring in a minister. The father, as holder of the family purse, had the exclusive right to make the periodical trips to town, even when he repeatedly drank up all the money needed for supplies. As long as he remained the only family member to come in contact with the larger American society, his authority remained unchallenged. Sooner or later, of course, the children began to make their own contacts, most commonly through the public school; but the mother often stayed isolated on the farm, her only social intercourse being with the other farm wives of her church. In such cases the wife remained in lifelong subservience to the husband.

By no means all immigrant wives regretted their inferior position, even when they saw it contrasted with that of Yankee ladies. One Norwegian goodwife was scandalized by the fashionable clothes and idleness of high-class local matrons. "It seems that some of the town businessmen want their wives to leave their babies at home with hired girls and go riding in buggies behind fast trotting horses. Unblushing they sit with idle hands in snug gloves. Never a sock or mitten in their hand, to knit at! And bustles! Isn't that vanity before God?"[48]

Theoretically the children should have been subordinate to both parents, and in a number of stories the mother mediated between a stern father and rebellious young. But often the children grew away from her even faster than from the head of the family, who had some contact with the new society into which they were moving. As one Norwegian-American novelist remarked, "It is one of the tragic phases of immigration that it invariably offers ampler conditions for intellectual growth to man than it does to woman."[49] Other authors considered the

239

word "invariably" too strong, especially in urban settings. These pictured a number of forceful female personalities establishing and maintaining positions of family leadership even while remaining apparently subservient to the male head.[50] It was such a mother, rather than a domineering father, who most often succeeded in inculcating strong filial loyalty to Old-Country traditions in members of the second and third generation.

For the authors agreed that children true to their Scandinavian tradition obeyed the commandment to "Honor thy father and thy mother" much better than American children. An early novel by Rølvaag, for example, told the story of a dutiful daughter who sacrificed first the ambitions of her youth, then her mature desire to serve humanity in social work, and finally her love for a noble-hearted minister in order to devote herself to the care of her crippled, evil-hearted father. He had money enough to hire six nurses, but she obeyed the religious dictum implanted in her by her long-suffering mother and sacrificed her life to caring for him. In the end she was rewarded by his deathbed repentance.[51]

Books in English by second-generation writers recalled such incidents as Norwegian grandparents sending a girl into a November blizzard to fetch milk. "It did not seem the sort of night to send anyone out, let alone an eight-year-old child; but Grandpa was a man—a *Norwegian* man—and they did not set out upon women's errands, as Grandma's patient but determined look seemed to say." Later, taking the train from Dakota to Arizona, "*Bestefar,* being a Norwegian man, had the lower berth. Grandma and I climbed to the upper, where she hoped to keep me from falling out."[52] Or a Norwegian city mother pleaded with a daughter to go to high school instead of taking a job. "It was the first time one of us children had deliberately gone against Mama and Papa, and it was a strange and saddening thing."[53] Many of the emotional problems of such second-generation characters arose from conflict between their deep-rooted family loyalty and their need of breaking away from the influence of foreign-born parents to make their own way in America.

Most authors, however, emphasized that European family structure was modified or destroyed after some time in the United States. Some preferred the greater freedom within the family allowed by American mores. A Swedish immigrant observed that people married earlier and more carelessly in the New World, and divorces were more frequent; but the looser family structure allowed the individual more private rights. Especially the woman had greater equality in marriage. The husband considered it not a shame but a duty to help with housework, such as building fires and washing dishes, while the wife often assisted with family finances either by earning something herself or by doing without a maid.[54]

240

Sometimes a writer attacked the attempt of the immigrant group to maintain their own family ways. A Norwegian Unitarian assailed the Lutheran doctrine of the subservience of women in a short story depicting the futile struggle of an immigrant wife to escape her brutal husband. He beat and abused her, pregnant or not, and the local minister only mildly rebuked him for using physical punishment, while sternly admonishing the woman about her duty to submit to the male. A visitor was so horrified at the treatment the poor wife got that she rushed to her defense, wrote her subversive letters, sent her pamphlets on women's rights and even money to aid her escape. The wife ran away to a brother in Minneapolis, but he was also of the old school and packed her back to her husband. She finally drowned herself and her infant daughter in despair.[55]

2. DEVELOPMENT OF WOMEN'S RIGHTS

This drastic victory of Luther's dogma was exaggerated in the interests of propaganda. In no realistic plot was the woman so helpless. She might well be imprisoned in her marriage by fear of the sin of divorce, but most stories showed immigrant women successfully resisting the dominance of their husbands whenever they desired.

In a typical Swedish-American novel, during the early years when the father spent seed and supply money on drink, the mother said nothing; she was used to such behavior. But toward the end of the book, once when the father was as usual getting drunk in the town saloon, the old wife finally tired of waiting. If he wouldn't drive her home, very well, she'd drive herself. He forbade her to take the horses, but she did anyway; and when he tried to stop her by force, the town doctor happening by warned him that public opinion was against him. A similarly unreasonable husband had been tarred and feathered not long before. Petulantly this one went along with his wife, then, but threatened that he was fed up with America and was going back to Sweden. Go ahead, retorted the old woman. As you are now, your room is preferable to your company. You've lived as you pleased all these years, and I've said nothing, but now things are going to be different.[56]

Even wives with much less to complain about, who had lived content in their subordinate place all the years of isolated farm life, were shown belatedly asserting new rights learned from more urbanized women when the farm couple retired to town. An old husband in a Norwegian-American tale was particularly unhappy after retirement because his wife had joined several women's clubs, which he loathed. "His wife had grown so finicky since she'd joined the W.C.T.U., and gave him all kinds of instructions and commands. He was supposed to say 'Yes, Ma'am' and

241

'I declare' and stop swearing when there were American ladies present. As if a Norwegian could talk English without cussing!"[57] The plot developed the husband's futile attempts to encroach on his wife's area of authority when the local minister foisted an orphaned baby on the childless pair. Step by step she managed to increase her influence until at last the husband agreed to adopt the little tyke; and the reader could see that the man's influence in the family had gone into permanent decline.

In such cases the support of the surrounding society helped the victory of the woman's cause; but where the wife did not assert herself, public opinion could do nothing. This was clearly shown in a Norwegian-American novel where a veritable slave-driver of an immigrant farmer abused his first wife—

Farm women in Norway had never been coddled . . . Ruth was a farmer's wife and would have to do the work of a farmer's wife. Wasting money for unnecessary help was no part of Einar's programme for the future. Dumbly—frightened into wordless acquiescence by the sudden sinister change in her husband—Ruth submitted.[58]

—but was dominated by his second one. She dictated what he should wear, forbade him to drive to town alone except on errands she approved, extorted a generous allowance, forced him to go to church. When he turned on her physically, she beat him off with a hot skillet. The doctor called in to dress his wounds gleefully spread word throughout the neighborhood that Einar had met his match at last.

This difference in the status of womenfolk in America was clearly reflected in the distribution of labor by sex on midwestern farms. The literature regularly showed woman immigrants doing barn and field work on pioneer farms, if anything taking on more and harder tasks during the family's difficult early years. "People didn't pay much attention to what was women's work or men's work. The main thing was to get done what lay at hand."[59] But once this difficult period was over, a gradual change took place in the work of women characters. Field work was the first to be dropped, perhaps because it was the most easily observed by neighbors and passers-by. The authors made no comment on this development, but farm wives who had regularly hurried through housework in the early years to get out into the fields were later pictured only in the kitchen or nursery, or at most weeding a garden. Barn chores continued longer, sometimes for the whole life of an older woman; but the younger wives and growing daughters were soon depicted having no more to do with the stock than feeding the chickens.

Thus many late newcomers who took jobs as hired men on American farms were shocked to discover that they were expected to do women's work—the barn chores. In his first letter home, a typical Norwegian

242

greenhorn reported the unbelievable fact that in this strange country men did all the barnwork. "To think that a *grown man* should sit down and pull at a cow udder! A man as a milkmaid—as a *barn boy!*" But three letters later he confessed that he had turned barn boy too. "Yes, indeed, I have to clean the stalls and do the milking and care for the pigs too. This you certainly don't need to repeat so the young people back home hear about it. They don't know anything about how things are here, and that I *have* to do it."[60]

Immigrants constantly remarked how American daughters and wives were excused from field work even during rush seasons. The sons and husbands got it done, or hired male help. On the other hand, Scandinavians were impressed that Yankee ladies were not above doing their own kitchen and housework. Such differences in sex status struck new arrivals as strange indeed, especially when combined with the American's tendency to treat all women with elaborate courtesy whether they were "ladies" or not. Many an immigrant character expressed his opinion that Yankees went too far.

My conscience hurts when I see how well men many places here treat their women. I think though that they do a little too much for them—bring them everything on a silver platter, as it were. One should of course be good to women, but—they're not made of glass, after all.[61]

A Norwegian-American novel summarized at length the change in the position of immigrant wives in America:

It was of course the woman who should care for both the pigs and the cows. She should be the first up in the morning, make the fire, go out to the barn to feed the animals, milk the cows and let the calves drink; then in to make breakfast and dress the children.

The men weren't used to milking cows in the Old Country; because it was the woman who did all such, and then everybody thought it was only proper that she did it here too.

The wife had also to take part in haying in the summertime. She should stack the hay, help with getting it in . . . and when evening came her program was: to milk, care for the calves and pigs, prepare supper for herself and family, and then get the children to bed. Finally, when it was about eleven o'clock, she was finished with her day's work, if the children didn't screech and scream too much in the night. . . .

But if she had a lot to do, she got paid for it. Usually she got one or two calico dresses a year, a pair of shoes that cost $1.75, and a hat that cost $1.50 every third year.

After the turn of the century, however, when more scientific farming brought higher cash incomes,

The farm wives wore silk dresses now, and in winter fur coats. . . .

Now the men had to milk the cows, feed the pigs, hens and calves, and build the fire in the mornings, chop wood, even carry it in.

Now the wife could stay in a comfortable room, play the piano, have a dress-

243

maker to fit and sew stylish dresses, and instead of a $1.50 hat every third year, nowadays she gets a five-dollar hat—one in the spring and one in the fall.[62]

From this time on criticism of "the new woman" appeared frequently. It might dominate the viewpoint of an author soured on American feminism, or turn up in a list of the drawbacks in New-World life. It was the subject of many a passing remark in a short story, incident in a novel, poem in a periodical or volume of verse. A leading Danish-American pastor-poet devoted three pages of rhyme to "The New Woman. The Complaint of a Despondent Husband," in which the wife of the complainant was pictured as a college graduate who wrote imitations of Ibsen while her husband washed the dishes, and went bicycling while he burned the bread.[63]

Recent arrivals were especially vehement in their declarations that American and Scandinavian-American girls were badly spoiled. Even hired girls flaunted such fine feathers and affected manners after a few months in America that a plain working lad hadn't a chance; and indeed, he who was unwilling to court American style, with buggy rides, compliments, and boxes of chocolate, usually went unwed. Therefore immigrant men often declared that they would have nothing to do with New-World misses. "The American girls were so foolish and so devilish emancipated, and the Norwegian-American ones were about the same—only still worse."[64] To find a decent wife, they would have to import one direct from the Old Country; and many of them did.

Authors remarked constantly on how much "finer" the manners and clothes of womenfolk were in the United States than their husbands'. Clearly many immigrant wives had much less work to do than their counterparts back home, not only because they had been set free from field and barn work but also because their legitimate tasks in housework and child care had grown lighter. The rising status of many families was marked not only by a bigger house and better farm machinery but by the acquisition of household appliances: a pump at the kitchen sink, a washing machine cranked by hand, a gasoline stove.

Birth control learned in the American environment lightened the mother's burden in many smaller families. Fathers sometimes resented this development, as a Norwegian-American businessman, disappointed that his two children had turned out so spoiled, mused over what chance he might have had for one worthwhile child if only there had been more. "But such was not the custom here. This was one of the first things his wife had found out about, how she could keep from having more than two children—he thought bitterly that he could not know how many of his children had been deprived of life unborn. Most of the other families had the children they had brought along from Norway and perhaps one or two more—they learned fast. It was shameful to

244

have many children—no 'fine' family had more than one or two—and it was desirable to be among the 'fine';—and then one could give the children such a better education when one had only one or two."[65]

This development was so rapid only in urban settings, however. Rural families remained large; constant childbearing was frequently mentioned as one of the most grievous trials of frontier mothers, and even well into the twentieth century a Danish farm father in Nebraska was bemused by the statement of his newly married son that he was not going to have children.

"There have been too damn many kids in the Grimsen family as it is."
Peter smoked his pipe in silence. There were many things about the new life in America he didn't understand. This remark by Hans was only one of them. At last he said, "Let's hope for the best."[66]

Occasionally pious arguments were advanced against birth control. A devout Norwegian wife was insulted at a Swedish neighbor's remark about the wet diapers always hanging about her stove. "What did that have to say? That woman had her children too far apart. That was not natural! It is said that some American women know how to make the time long between conceptions, and already Scandinavian women are learning from them. Is that good in the sight of God?"[67] In a Danish-American tale a minister insisted that having "many children . . . is an important part of an ideal home. All sizes."[68]

3. DECLINE OF PARENTAL AUTHORITY

If the immigrant husband's domination over his wife was weakened in America, the literature showed parental authority undermined still more.

One type of parent portrayed sought to preserve the Old-World pattern of strict obedience and never-ending toil by the children. A few stern fathers considered their offspring as cheap labor, drove them early and late, begrudged even the time the law required them to attend school. In a Danish-American tale, an older couple who had come with a grown daughter attempted to keep her completely dependent on them. She was allowed to learn only a little English to work full time (without pay) in her father's store; after all, her only duty was to serve them. A young boarder in the family, however, felt sorry for the girl and told her that her parents had no right to cripple her future life. He gave her a translation job, but when the father heard of it of course he assumed that all the money would come to him. At long last the dutiful daughter revolted and went away to an American school, in order to win her rightful personal independence.[69]

Under such parental tyranny the children in this fiction inevitably rebelled, often by running away. A few were found and returned by the local sheriff, but when they reached the age of 21 the father's legal authority ended, and most of them deserted him for good. Many disappeared successfully into the vast distances and thronging cities of America long before their legal majority. Those who ran away often brought a tyrannous father to terms. A boy fugitive after long wandering found letters from his mother, the first saying the father had reformed and asked the son to return, the last that he had died calling for his boy in vain.[70]

Other harsh fathers were pictured working their children almost beyond endurance for the sake of the whole family. This often occurred during the early years, when the parents had to drive not only themselves but everyone to the breaking-point to meet the next mortgage payment and somehow survive the winter. It was not in the Old-World tradition to spare one's children when one could not spare oneself. Through such experience the children did gain a sense of partaking in and contributing to family welfare during the difficult early years, and no one complained as long as neighbor children were no better off. But Danish boys who were never permitted to go swimming with the sons of Yankee neighbors, or young Swedes who were kept out of school spring and fall to exhaust themselves at the work of grown men, soon grew to resent the demands made on them in contrast to what they saw were the duties of native American children.

What Peter Grimsen wanted for his sons was that they should grow up to be good workers and honest men. What they thought he wanted was that they should work like slaves and never have pleasures like other boys. There were times when they spoke openly of their bitter feelings toward their father.[71]

A Norwegian-American summarized the evidence of many stories: "The old folks understood how to create a farm and a family; but haven't their homes been too rigorous, the drudgery and haste for both adults and children too oppressive? Did they have the time to make their homes attractive?"[72]

The other type of parent appearing most often in the literature had dropped the stern discipline of the Old World to adopt what the authors considered American leniency. Story after story directly contrasted the hard life of parents or grandparents at the same age with the lolling ease of contemporary young people. A Norwegian mother who had emigrated as a child, for instance, recalled how her family had lived in a log cabin for many years; her own childhood had been poverty-stricken but very happy. Her children, on the other hand, were selfish and thoughtless, demanded money and fun as their natural right. Goodhearted and well-meaning as they were, yet they never thought to help her; she worked as hard in her old age as ever.[73]

Many a first-generation author could not resist drawing out a satirical incident to demonstrate how badly spoiled the second generation had become. At a dinner party in a novel devoted to this theme, the guests' children rejoined the adults when the cake plates were passed, to get their share. The hostess gave one little boy a doughnut, as less messy to eat. He was about to set up a howl when his mother hastily traded with him and gave him her cake. He didn't eat doughnuts, she explained proudly to the others, glad that she had been able to effect the exchange before her son threw a tantrum. Then the telephone rang. It was the ten-year-old daughter of one of the guests, who had been left at home. The hostess delivered her message to the girl's mother: " 'She says she wants to know if you're going to stay all day, and it's time for you to come home, 'cause now you've been away long enough, she says.' Mrs. Stenson got up in a hurry and called to Stenson out on the porch that they had to go, for Helen had phoned. Helen was clearly not to be trifled with."

The children, the children!
That was the sole topic of conversation in the parlor—their children and their different accomplishments, or lack of them. What they ate and what they refused to eat. What they took "lessons" in and how much these lessons cost. . . . One grown daughter had to have a clean freshly ironed blouse at least very other day, so there was a lot of washing and ironing in that house. The daughter of another had so much "company" . . . a third guest's daughter was invited to parties with Americans and fine English folk nearly every day. All took "lessons" and all seemed to be ignorant of any kind of housework,—for this was the most unmistakable sign of their gentility and high aspirations.

The guests all agreed with the minister when he talked about how much they must do for their children. The young folks could not be expected to build their own church as their parents had done. Many could not make more money than they needed for their own clothes and for education and amusement. "It was completely unthinkable that modern young people should be expected to do what the immigrant youth had done 25 or 35 years before. It wasn't possible even to draw comparisons; because the former generation had all been humble folk who were used to providing for their own needs and who had nobody to help them, and who could deny themselves many things in both food and clothing which our children can't or won't do without."[74]

XI. Behavioral Patterns in Daily Life

Except on the frontier, doing without was not a behavioral pattern encouraged in America. Back home the lower classes had not aspired to imitate the clothes and food of the "better people", but in the New World where all could be "better," most immigrants strove to adopt

Yankee ways. The resultant changes in clothing, diet, and housing were on the whole accepted gladly as symbols of improved status and standard of living; yet many characters paid a high price for their advancement in uncertainty and shame because of their ignorance of what they were expected to imitate.

1. CLOTHING AND FOOD

Social pressure toward conformity appeared most crudely among children. Unwitting parents sent a boy off to his first day at school with long curls, ruffled blouse, and short pants,[75] or an older lad rejected the hint of his uncle that the other boys would be wearing overalls to the Danish summer school. No, those weren't good enough for the first day, and his new American suit was too good; so this lad wore his Danish knickers and was greeted by raucous laughter, insults, and fights.[76] Even after an immigrant family had spent many years in America, often they had learned too little about such customs to direct an older child moving out into a new situation—like the Danish-American boy who wore new overalls to his first day at the local college, and who suffered the agonies of the damned when he saw no one else was wearing them or had brought a lunch.[77] Immigrant grandchildren were pictured ashamed of mittens or socks a grandmother had knitted for them in Old-Country style.[78]

Change in food customs, although welcomed as a sign of social betterment, sometimes caused emotional problems too. If the immigrant housewife found herself in a congenial community with friends to teach her, and no comment was made on her lapses into the old familiar and her failures in the new untried, she made the transition to American food preparation at her own speed and without special difficulty. But the situation was worse for many who felt the social stigma of being different without means of learning the ways to conform. Typical of these was a mother hurt when her son declined to take a lunch along to a picnic, "for she had divined that the reason was his knowledge that she had nothing to offer but the queer Norwegian food which it would shame him to eat before others. When Johanna got a little older she must go out to service with some fine family in town so she could learn something of American ways, Mariane was thinking silently, but a great fear clutched at her heart that in that way her children would grow away from her."[79]

Nor was it only the criticism of outsiders which members of the immigrant group feared. A Norwegian-American novel opened in the stifling kitchen of Mrs. Lewis Omley, who was rushing about in red-faced sweat trying to get an American-style dinner ready for guests when they came from a church baptism. When another wife had served Norwegian cream porridge and traditional cakes at a confirmation party, "everybody had talked about that such foods weren't used in this country, and one must follow the customs in the place where one lived."[80]

This was the attitude of those who wished to become Americanized as rapidly as possible; but preservationist characters proudly served traditional Old-Country foods at family fetes and social events including both people of their own nationality and outsiders. Thus an old Dane insisted on dark rye bread with jam for Christmas every year. "This fare alone was enough to put his guests into the right mood. Because where can a banished Dane be found who at the sight of a piece of black rye bread doesn't recall countless memories? Of home and childhood. Happy childhood! When this heavy bread was everyday food. But out here in exile it was a delicacy, food fit for a king."[81]

Lutefisk imported from Norway for a big church supper, a homemade cheese brought by a newcomer as a gift, a young city wife carrying traditional "childbed" porridge to a new mother, second- and third-generation characters relishing the pudding and baked goods of Christmas—some food customs were shown surviving indefinitely in certain permissive circumstances. Old-World victuals were fully accepted and openly used as holiday fare (but not for everyday) when immigrant families felt themselves secure in relation to their social environment, either because they had remained within a group of the same national background, or because their neighbors had nothing to say against such harmless variation. One authoress claimed that Norwegian girls serving as maids had taught their American mistresses how to prepare Old-World delicacies in exchange for instruction in the rules and customs of their adopted land. "We have taught our neighbors how to make potato pancakes and waffles, flatbread, yes, *lutefisk* and fruit soup too."[82]

2. HOUSING AND FURNITURE

In construction of their homes, immigrants made little attempt to follow Old-World patterns. On the woodland frontier, occasionally a pioneer built his log cabin dovetailing the corners neatly in the Norwegian fashion;[83] but further west sod huts and board shacks, lacking any prototype in the Old Country, were put up after American models. As soon as they could afford to replace their first shacks, immigrant farmers almost all constructed frame houses exactly like their neighbors'. One old man who wanted to build a copy of his Norwegian home was dissuaded by friends and family, who argued that in America one must do as Americans did.[84] Only a rare exception went to expensive lengths to duplicate his original manor house. A successful immigrant farmer who had been

249

a member of the gentry rebuilt the ancestral home he had left in order to marry a servant girl, every porch and wing exactly as it had been in the Old Country. "This house I have built for you, dear Gunvor. . . . Here we shall live again the good old days—only with the difference that here you are the mistress, not the maid as home in Norway."[85]

In towns and cities, all flats and houses had been built by local contractors, who followed American building principles as a matter of course. Therefore prairie towns with predominantly immigrant populations looked precisely like their Yankee counterparts. A Danish-American author described a South Dakota hamlet as the center of the largest Danish settlement in the area. "But there is nothing whatever typical about Viborg or the other towns to reveal they are Danish. They are built precisely like the other prairie towns out here—" and he described the dull main street with its false-front stores and banks, the side streets with churches and scattered homes. Could not better architecture have been brought in from the Old Country? "We have a good many wealthy men here. But without exception they live in these ugly grey boxes which are called houses here. A genuine Danish brick-and-timber house would be much more beautiful, as well as being a novelty. And all our churches are built according to the same dull model which is found everywhere in the nation. Why not a copy of one of our venerable Danish country churches?"[86]

House furnishings, when mentioned at all, were usually described as typically American. Certainly most immigrants could not afford to bring Old-World furniture with them, even if it had been worth the cost. On the frontier, the crude tables, chairs, and beds which the father of the family built were only as good as his materials and skill made possible; there was never a thought of trying to make this furniture look like what had been left behind. When a family could afford to buy parlor and bedroom sets, naturally selection was made from the standardized American models available.[87] Even the rich were usually limited to "elegant, sturdy furniture as much like that back home as was possible to buy in America."[88] A few exceptions appeared in Norwegian settlements. In a late (1956) novel, Danes who moved into an exclusive Norwegian farming community found that the older inhabitants had "incorporated the Old Country styles in building their homes and decorated them inside in a manner reminiscent of their beloved Norway."[89] Heavy carved furniture and an open fireplace with dried meat hanging in it were described in the house of one elderly couple.

Smaller items of household goods brought from the Old Country were mentioned more often in immigrant homes: copper kettles, wooden baskets, handwoven linens and woolen bedcovers, and above all the heavy wooden chests in which goods had been packed for the long

250

transport. The last were practically omnipresent in frontier homes, where they continued to be used for storage. But as soon as improved economy made possible a better house and store-bought furniture, the few objects brought from the Old Country were normally relegated to basement or attic. Piety toward such as heirlooms was conspicuously lacking in the first and second generations. Most authors who considered the matter criticized this widespread attitude. A Norwegian-American character reacted against discovering an old immigrant chest filled with dirt and planted with flowers beside a prosperous farmhouse:

It seemed to me indefensible to bury this venerable immigrant chest with its strong iron bands and scrolled magnificence. It was a wrong committed against the valley smith who a generation ago had wrought the chest to last an eternity. It was as though one were burying something still too strong to die.[90]

Even when an artistically painted chest had been preserved by its original owner through a long lifetime, it stood unused and forgotten in a dusty cellar when discovered at last by a granddaughter cleaning out the old place.[91]

Exceptions did appear: a city immigrant who furnished his flat with mementos from Sweden; an old farmer who moved a shabby chest, trunk, and baskets brought years before from Norway into his new house over the protests of his children; a childless couple in Wisconsin who had "a beautiful farm, filled with mementos of the Old Country. Lovely pictures, Danish embroidery and pillows, porcelain and silverware from Denmark decorated the rooms."[92] But more typical was the attitude of a wife who had always despised a handmade copper kettle inherited from her husband's grandfather. When she was told that its value as an antique was fifty dollars, her only thought was to sell it at once.[93] One author accused Americans in general of lacking appreciation of heirlooms: "Father's worn Bible, Mother's Hymnal, Grandfather's old chair —off to the rubbish heap with them. What value can such have in a society where everyone lives for the immediate present . . . and where no mementos are preserved and treasured except those that could perhaps be of value in divorce proceedings or a lawsuit."[94]

3. HANDIWORK

Handiwork by immigrant women survived in Old-Country patterns during the lifetime of the first generation, seldom beyond. Pioneer housewives were often depicted knitting thick mittens and socks for the whole family, and sewing their clothing from store-bought materials. Mention of home weaving was rare, and nearly always was limited to the weaving of rugs or blankets. A Norwegian housewife, for instance, earned enough to buy a parlor organ by weaving blankets to sell to her neigh-

251

bors.[95] There was no time for fancywork on pioneer farms, but in later years older women, especially when they had grown daughters at home, were sometimes pictured doing an incredible amount of handiwork. "They wove rugs, pieced and stitched quilts, knitted and crotcheted stockings, shawls, miles of lace and even whole tablecloths." The furniture in this house was decorated with handmade squares of Hardanger embroidery.[96]

After the frontier had passed, reference to knitting and weaving disappeared from the literature, until World War I suddenly created a demand for hand-knitted socks and mittens again. Then more than one immigrant author underlined ironically how a despised and neglected Old-World skill once more came into its own.

Before [the war] the old Norwegian mother or grandmother sat in their corners, they were old-fashioned and superannuated, they were the only ones who knitted, and nobody cared a pin—discarded folks had to have something to do, so they wouldn't venture where they didn't belong. But now grandmother comes out into the light again, she can play with knitting needles, though her eye is dim she can forge ahead where the sharpest miss in gold-rimmed glasses stumbles. And so a gray, untidy old head and a newly waved, young head bow in concord over the difficult stitches, and it's hard work. But mother and grandmother brighten up again, they are included now like everybody else, and a new world can make use of their old, long-scorned skill.[97]

4. HOUSEKEEPING

With their homes, furnishings, and equipment thoroughly American, immigrant housewives usually kept house according to New-World patterns. The literature did not afford much evidence on this matter, perhaps because most of the authors were men; but those who mentioned housekeeping portrayed their heroines persisting in only two Scandinavian customs. A major housecleaning just before Christmas remained an inseparable part of traditional preparations for that major event. Even the farmyard had to be cleaned up so the place looked its best for the holy season.[98] And Scandinavian housewives continued to scrub all the floors of their houses regularly and often. In her sod hut on the Dakota frontier Beret Holm longed for "floors that can be washed on the Sabbath eve."[99] This custom presupposed no rugs, or ones small enough for easy removal, and evidently died out as increasing prosperity enabled immigrants to buy larger factory-made rugs too big to take out for beating; or the practice may have ended when people began to wax their floors around World War I. It was not mentioned in stories laid after this time.

Women authors showed heroines rapidly adopting American housekeeping customs in all other respects. One Norwegian family put teaspoons on the table in a bowl, as a daughter had observed the family doing where she had worked as a maid.[100] Another servant girl adopted the American custom of washing clothes every Monday after she married. At home in Norway, her family had held a big wash only two or three times a year, rinsing out special things as needed in between times; but she saw the advantage of not accumulating such mounds of dirty laundry.[101] A wealth of examples offered convincing evidence that American customs of housekeeping, like cooking, spread into Scandinavian immigrant homes through practices taught girls serving as servants in "better" families. These girls instructed their mothers, and then established Yankee ways as regular usage when they founded their own homes.

5. MANNERS

American table manners and other forms of social intercourse were transmitted to the immigrant group in the same way. A successful Norwegian businessman, whose only daughter was much too "fine" to take any kind of work let alone as servant, complained bitterly over not having enough social contact with Yankees to learn even how to hold a fork in American style.[102] Many characters, however, were able to learn at least the most essential of such customs by beginning their new life as maids or hired men. Young women had a distinct advantage because they so often found employment in "better" town and city families of native stock, and were trained in such customs as part of their work. Newly arrived immigrant men, on the other hand, often took jobs on farms owned by compatriots, whose own Americanization was usually incomplete; and the manners of farm families tended to be simpler as well. Single men with urban employment were universally portrayed as living at boardinghouses, where they were not apt to learn refined table or other manners. Wide and consistent evidence in the literature supports the conclusion that women's advantages in this respect helped increase their power within the immigrant family. In almost every story where the question of manners, clothes, or social customs arose, the woman was the authority whose opinion was accepted without question, if not without grumbling.[103]

Acceptance of American standards in these matters was practically universal. Only in discussion of children's manners did some authors indicate preference for the greater politeness and respect toward their elders taught European boys and girls. A returned immigrant in Kristiania (Oslo), for instance, was pleased by a little flower-girl. "How prettily she curtsied! What if children were taught a little more politeness in America too? It annoyed him to think of the impudence and arrogance which children showed toward adults in the great land of freedom. The fourth commandment was God's word too."[104] Otherwise no writer argued that immigrants should try to continue Old-World customs of social behavior from any level, however much better they would understand and could practice these. Instead the authors consciously or unconsciously set up adoption of American manners as the only possible goal. A Norwegian-American novelist depicted wealthy rural Norwegians entertaining the scions of two rich New England families at a magnificent dinner party. "Both the serving of the repast and the table manners were as refined as if the guests had been dining with one of the old Yankee families in New England itself."[105]

Most authors, however, emphasized rather the friendly informality of American social intercourse. Sometimes a newcomer was able to adopt this immediately, as a young Norwegian seized the opportunity to meet the great Professor Oftedal, casually encountered in a Minneapolis store.

Monson would not be responsible for anything which could have such serious consequences as introducing Jonas to Professor Oftedal; but Jonas was not one who would let such an excellent opportunity to get acquainted slip by him; and bashful or shy he certainly was not. So he went up to the great man and introduced himself. He had already experienced more than once that here in America a person had to blow his own horn.[106]

More timid personality types had greater difficulty, holding back from social contacts when they felt themselves uncertain of how to proceed. Only the threatened failure of a most important child's birthday party drove a shy Danish farm wife to her American neighbors for the first time, to ask for the loan of some equipment. Even then her husband was annoyed, for he did not want to be beholden to anybody. Neither side made any effort to follow up this contact, and the Danish mother remained in lonely isolation.[107]

As a rule, first-generation adult immigrants were pictured practicing American informality of social behavior only within the limits of their own language group. The language barrier and Yankee disdain for dumb foreigners usually inhibited the development of closer personal relations between native and newcomer. In a Minnesota community only a fifteen-year-old Swedish orphan of irrepressible temperament was able to break through the social wall raised by the original inhabitants against his ethnic group. "Far from shrinking from contact with the Yankees, like most Swedes, he ran after them; and the fun poked at him seemed not to hurt his feelings in the least. You had to be pretty prejudiced against his kind not to take a fancy to Sven Opsahl."[108] Within their own group, however, most immigrants adopted informal social forms after the American pattern. An earlier arrived Swede welcomed a newcomer in a narrative poem, "Sit down and eat and make yourself at home. We pay no attention to that ceremonious Swedish nonsense. Help yourself to whatever you want."[109]

6. FRIENDSHIP

On the other hand, many authors criticized acquaintanceships founded in the New World on the ground that they tended to be as shallow as they were easy to strike up. Almost all of the close, life-long friendships appearing in this literature were founded before emigration, or developed between families from the same background who lived all their lives rooted in neighboring soil. Necessary (though not sufficient) conditions of close friendship were that the participants spoke not only the same language but preferably the same dialect, and that they shared similar religious views. Most important of all, however, was that they remained near each other; severance of physical proximity regularly led to the death of the relationship. At a social gathering of Danes in a midwestern city, some of the ladies amused themselves by looking through photograph albums of their host containing "pictures of Danes who at one time or another had lived in the town but who had left for farther west. . . . Soon the general conversation concerned how one was getting along in California, another in Denver, or others in the widespread pioneer colonies of Nebraska. It was strange how many people one had known awhile, had shared the initial unrest of immigration with, had come to like, but now had completely lost sight of."[110]

In cities it was commonplace for an individual who did not himself make the effort to maintain contact with his circle simply to disappear. In a Danish-American tale a young widow whose husband had been killed at his job had to move into the slums, and Danish acquaintances who came too late to offer help could not trace her.[111] Even in small towns the young people endlessly came and went. A Norwegian-American story related how the First Lutheran Church in a little town lost its choir because the membership was so unstable. A first-rate tenor would get a job in town, but when the others had learned to follow his voice, he would accept a better offer elsewhere and move on; or a new teacher would prove an excellent soprano, but would last only that year's appointment. The young people who grew up there would go away to school, or to cities. The choir membership could not be maintained.[112] In rural districts too the rule was out of sight, out of mind. A successful Dane returning from a trip to the Old Country on board ship ran into a former good friend from his early years in a Wisconsin community, who had left the place long before and had never been heard of since.[113]

Even relatives were often depicted losing touch with each other when

255

separated by distance. Elderly parents rarely heard from grown children who had moved away. Many Christmas stories described old people alone on the farm whose children all gathered at one Yuletide for the first time in years. Brothers and sisters seldom met after their parents' death. The young men had taken jobs all over the country, and the young women had followed their husbands moving about for the same reason. Grandparents confused the names of grandchildren they had never seen, and sometimes were not even sure of how many they had. The rush of American life did not encourage letter-writing, and often years passed between visits. Clearly New-World mobility weakened ties of friendship and family which had been much stronger in the Old World.

Thus the authors saw change in the morals and mores of their group in the United States as both good and bad. The liberal-minded commended the greater rights of women and children, and equalitarian ease in social relations; the materialistic gladly accepted bigger and better houses, more food and clothing; the puritanical approved of stricter sex morals and prohibition. But the authors also counted the cost in weakened family solidarity, shallower interpersonal relations, painful ignorance of American ways. "There is so much to remember and so much to forget when one is an immigrant," a Danish-American novelist summed up. "The first days' wonder at everything big and new soon gives way to a feeling of helplessness. A thousand things swirl around him; he is overwhelmed by impressions and experiences; he stands still in admiration and opens his arms to receive it. Later it all grows commonplace without becoming familiar. . . . What is alien begins to irritate."[114] Folkways and mores which were commonplace because one saw them every day, but remained unfamiliar because one continued to see them instead of having internalized them as one's own, served both to mark the first generation as outsiders and to hinder their feeling fully at home. This concomitant of migration, unanticipated but inevitable, was part of the price which Scandinavian immigrants had to pay for their social betterment.

Chapter Nine
The Cost of Success

" 'If I had known, I should never have dared,' is written across the life of every Swedish immigrant,"[1] and echoed by many a Danish and Norwegian one in this literature. Most paid dearly for the social betterment they gained in America, although the kinds of hardship they underwent varied widely. The burdens of those who pioneered were heavier and more numerous than those of all others, and the rest met widely differing fates in rural or urban environments according to the particular phase of American economic development they encountered. Yet within this group of writers spread over four score years, including those who believed the advantages won well worth the cost as well as those who held the opposite, there was remarkable agreement on the types of difficulty which most Scandinavians went through. Many of these difficulties had their own compensations; but in a wide area of emotive matters, as well as unexpectedly great physical hardship, the authors agreed that the immigrants suffered mainly loss, with little or no gain.

I. The "Dog Years"

All writers concurred that practically every immigrant had to suffer through a time of painful adjustment after his arrival regardless of where he went or when. This period they called the "dog years." Sometimes it was pictured as no more than a few months long, but more often it lasted a couple of years or more, occasionally the whole lifetime of a newcomer who met his death among its afflictions.

In general, the "dog years" were defined as continuing as long as an immigrant suffered considerable physical hardship while restricted to the heavy labor assigned the lowest rank of the social scale. Railroad construction and lumbering were most often mentioned as the first jobs of immigrant men, as well as hiring out for farm or (in the case of girls) house work. The individual had little chance for better employment until he had acquired some money and knowledge of American language and ways. For those who went into farming, the "dog years" usually lasted until their crops began to pay well enough to discharge their initial

257

debts and build them a decent house. Danish rental farmers in Nebraska, for instance, agreed that they could just as well forget their first ten years. "It's been twelve [years] now since I came, and it's only in the last two that I have really made anything."[2] Those who arrived in the midst of a depression and could not find work, or who tried their hand at half a dozen kinds of unskilled labor, were accounted as emerging from their period of trial when they finally found a job which offered them the opportunity of advancement—what their initial employment lacked.

He had been a sailor on Lake Michigan and a chauffeur in Detroit, a waiter in Racine and a foundry worker in Kenosha, an oiler of streetcar tracks in Chicago and a hired man on an Iowa farm, a telephone worker in Omaha and a night watchman in Denver . . . he followed the restless crowds of men out of work who wandered from one big city and sawmill and railroad construction job to another. . . . He was well known in city labor bureaus, where he paid two dollars for the chance to do the hardest work for the least pay.[3]

The basis of the "dog years" was thus largely economic.

The main effect of this time of trial, however, was psychological. In a typical Swedish-American tale, a newly arrived innocent was robbed by other Swedes and reduced to many weeks of begging before he found a new friend at a Lutheran church on Christmas Eve. This benefactor comforted him; he should be glad to have suffered such adversity early, "because it always does a young man good to go through hardship during the first time he is here. It's worse for one who makes good in the beginning and has to go through his 'dog years' later, because there aren't many who get by without a longer or shorter time of trial out here."[4] Direct evidence of the beneficial effects of such trials appeared in many stories of spoiled upper-class characters who learned to stand on their own feet in the struggle for survival in America. But indirect evidence was also plentiful that this was the time during which, by being rebuffed and exploited, the immigrants learned that their previously formed expectations toward other people no longer held. The "dog years" performed the function of helping destroy older behavioral patterns so that new ones more appropriate to the different milieu could be formed. As one Norwegian-American character warned a later comer, "There isn't anybody who knows anything when he comes to America. Here everything has to be learned over again from the beginning."[5]

Naturally those who settled in a colony of their own nationality had an easier time of trial. A Danish tramp who turned up in a farming community of fellow immigrants was helped to find all sorts of odd jobs.

There were certainly enough workers to be had, but people wanted to help *him* get started. Others might be more capable, but *he* needed a helping hand. . . . Several let him know that they had once been helped in the same way.[6]

258

This was of course the reason that so many newcomers headed for areas where their predecessors had already set up institutions and patterns of behavior giving preferential treatment to fellow countrymen. Yet even there economic struggle darkened their early years. Beginners almost always had to go into debt to get started, and in hard times there were no jobs for anybody. The effort required to adjust to the situation found on arrival thus varied from one case to another, but exertion was always demanded, and usually proved painful.

II. Pioneer Trials

Most effort both physical and mental was required of the pioneers, whose "dog years" were longest and involved most difficulties. They suffered almost all the trials of other immigrants raised to a higher power, and a few of their own. All newcomers complained of having to work much harder in America than at home, whatever their job; but pioneers, trying to found a complex civilization in a score of years, carried out inhumanly heavy labor with insufficient tools and non-existent help. "It required four men to do the threshing. But they were only two. So two had to do the work of four . . . it fairly took it out of a chap to go on like that from morning to night, with just an hour's rest in the middle of the day."[7]

The price for abuse of their bodies was premature old age. A Danish-American bride arriving at a prairie settlement was greeted with compassion by another farm wife, "a little, thin figure with deep wrinkles under her eyes, who had a strange foggy expression as though she never got enough sleep." When the bride asked who that old woman was, her husband replied, "That wasn't any old woman. She isn't more than 32."[8] The story showed the heroine overtaken by the same fate. Year after year the couple toiled at heavy farm labor. In rush seasons the wife had to work in the fields all day beside caring for the livestock and house. Regularly almost every other year she had a baby. By the time she was thirty she was an old woman, and her husband walked stooped, lifting his knees strangely high as though he were walking in water.

Nor did such overwork cease with the passing of the frontier. An old Dane who came from Europe to end his days with his daughter found her, "who home in Denmark had been a lovely, slim girl, was now fat, stooped, with a grey face and deep wrinkles around her eyes and mouth. As help on the big farm, which Hans Nielsen judged needed at least four hired men and two girls, his son-in-law had only a teen-aged boy. Therefore many things were neglected and much was wasted. The work never ended. There was no pleasant little rest period after meals,

259

and everyone kept busy clear till bedtime."[9] Characters who joined a relative or friend some time after the latter had immigrated invariably commented on how worn and old the earlier arrival looked, how he had lost his fresh complexion in exchange for wrinkles and gold teeth.

The primitive housing of the pioneers caused much hardship in such extremes of weather as they had never known before. The poorest cottage they had left in the Old Country was better shelter than the rough cabins and sod huts which were described as the first houses of many families on the frontier.

There where a person sank exhausted on his bed of straw and pulled his sheepskin over his face to keep off the rain or snow coming through the leaking roof—there where nothing could be done when the ice-cold wind blew in through the grimy door until one's feet grew stiff, while one roasted from the waist up in immense heat from the little stove stuffed full of straw; there where both the first and second child was born . . . where one laid the foundation for all the rheumatism which in old age would bow his back and make life a torment; where the only thing that could keep up one's courage was to see how the farm and therefore prosperity grew from year to year; there where a man sowed the health of his youth in order to harvest freedom from want and the material foundation for his children's future.[10]

Overwork and poor housing contributed to suffering from sickness and death. The drastic change in diet and climate took its toll among the immigrants of all periods, to be sure; digestive disorders were a common plague of the "dog years" everywhere, and sudden death by heat stroke or freezing provided many a twist of plot in both urban and rural settings. Children were lost to diphtheria and typhoid both in city slums and on frontier farms, and mothers perished in childbirth from first to last. Sickness seemed most dreadful in pioneer homes, however, where help was most difficult to come by. As a frontier mother explained to a small daughter about a baby sister just dead, "Birgit was sick from the first. The doctor might have helped her but we could not get him; he lives a long, long way from here and we have no money." The same book recorded smallpox brought later to three neighboring families by an itinerant tinsmith. One of the fathers walked eighteen miles to bring back a newly arrived doctor (civilization was catching up), but he could only vaccinate those who had not yet come down with the disease. The mothers were left to nurse the sick as best they could.[11]

Sometimes the best that could be done was wretched enough. In a Swedish-American tale, a theological student arrived at a frontier congregation to hold Christmas service, and was hurried to a dying mother nearby. He found her lying in a filthy hut with a feeble newborn baby. A half dozen children were huddled under a blanket nearby. Coughing blood onto newspapers spread beside her, the mother told the student that she was dying of tuberculosis. Her only worldly wish was to see once more her son lying sick in the attic. But the youth proved to be so far gone with the same disease that he could not be moved either. All the theologian could do was carry messages between the two of them, and talk a little about the eternal life to come.[12]

Weather as well as distance and poverty also interposed barriers between a sufferer and help on the frontier. In a Danish-American story a wife was brought to bed during a blizzard and had to bear her first child with only her terrified husband to help. Not until four days later was he able to force his way to the nearest neighbors, where the woman only smiled at his story. "Goodness, that's nothing to make a fuss about. It could happen to anybody."[13]

However, few of these characters had been accustomed to professional medical care in the Old Country either, and most of them accepted illness or accident as the will of God. The mother brought out her home remedies, the sufferer either recovered or died, and life went on. Incidence of illness among characters remained in fact quite low. Epidemics which had decimated earlier colonies were described only in historical novels based on secondary sources, and evidently did not recur after the 1870s. Lack of mention of sickness in the great majority of accounts supported the boast of some characters about the sturdy health of Viking blood. The authors were more concerned about mental than physical suffering of newcomers in their efforts to adjust to a new life. Toil they were used to, sickness they took in their stride, but learning to feel at home in an environment so unlike their native one proved to be much more difficult.

Here again the pioneers had the worst of it. Those who found strangers as their new associates suffered less than those who met no human beings at all. The grotesque situation of social beings stripped of all society, preyed especially on the women. Beret Holm in *Giants in the Earth* feared that members of the little settlement would turn into animals so far from human support and restraint.[14] But even she had the company of a few others. Worst of all was the plight of single individuals and families who pushed out ahead of all the rest. A Norwegian-American tale recreated superbly the feelings of a lonely wife whose husband brought her and their two small children to the empty prairie.

. . . it was as though something gave way far down within her when she heard that they had traveled that difficult and dangerous way only to end under an elm tree with swarms of mosquitoes and the desolate solitude as their sole neighbors. They were just as homeless after they had arrived home. And the thought of days, weeks, months, perhaps even years here in this wilderness, where they hardly belonged to human society any more . . . she drew Jon violently to her; for he was the smallest and asked no questions.[15]

At the climax of the story, the two children, watching in vain for the

261

return of their father over the endless plains, grew terrified at the emptiness and rushed sobbing to their mother. Finding small comfort in her,
they had to fight their own fight with the same weapon as she—mute
melancholy.

Many farm wives suffered a special kind of loneliness in their "dog
years" because their men were gone all winter. In a Norwegian-American
novelette an elderly woman recalled how pioneer farmers could not afford
to sit idle during the cold months.

In the early days, all family men, yes bachelors and half-grown youngsters too—for
we came empty-handed—had to leave to find work. . . . In Wisconsin there was
cutting timber, the sawmills, floating the logs out in the spring thaw, rafting lumber
down the Wisconsin and Mississippi. It was heavy work and such a long time away
from home, dangerous too; I was afraid all the time that John, my husband, would
be killed; and then I was homesick, on top of everything else.[16]

The literature recorded no few trials of hunger and cold, of childbirth
and death, while the family head was gone.

III. The Landscape

The landscape of the new home played a part in the emotional reaction
of immigrants to their new setting. Newcomers who were so fortunate
as to find a farm in a countryside not too unlike the homeland escaped
much of the maladjustment felt by all who went out onto the Great
Plains. The reaction of Rølvaag's Beret to the naked desolation of the
Dakota prairie was only one among many accounts of a common experience. The outburst of the hero of a minor amateur novel was typical:

How could people from beautiful, enchanting mountains endure life on this flat
moor without even a decent hill to look at? . . . On this great plain it seemed there
could be nothing great to aspire toward or long for. All poetry and yearning were
as though left out of life, or would be smothered if they appeared.[17]

Yet most books reflected a slow change in attitude toward the prairie
as characters grew accustomed to it. In a Danish-American story, a
recently arrived bride pined in her dark sod hut; the landscape might
not be so different from what she was used to, but she would have
none of it.

Here where they had settled for good, there were no memories, no beauty, nothing
which spoke the language of the heart.

Like the little creek—how ugly it was compared to the sparkling stream by the
mill home in Denmark! And what was there of birdsong? The clumsy bird which
here went by the name of lark couldn't fly higher than the top of a telephone pole
and had only a few poor notes. How could that be compared to the thrilling song
of larks soaring high under heaven above Denmark's moors and fields? . . .

"Here is food for many a poor man who went hungry home in one beautiful
European country or another," was Anton's reply.

But when the young wife's son had grown big enough to toddle outside discovering the wonders of prairie nature, she learned to see with new eyes. "Then she realized that the prairie had many more wildflowers than she had noticed, and its birdsong was more lovely than she had heard before."[18] After the frontier had passed in any one settlement—roads put through, fields fenced in, church spires raised, trees grown up—there was in fact comparatively little unfavorable comment on the physical geography of the new home. Newcomers continued to notice the lack of dominating landmarks among their first impressions, but most of them soon forgot to mention the matter.

Poems and prose passages expressing the recurrent emotion of homesickness almost always expressed longing for the physical objects of the homeland most unlike those of the prairie—mountains, waterfalls, forests, the restless sea. Assuredly people who had grown up in the midst of lovely scenery did miss it on what by contrast seemed a dull and empty plain. A speaker in a Norwegian-American novel admitted that the Middle West had its beauties, but they were poor and few compared to the unique landscape of the northern homeland.[19] But the obvious difference between two types of geography produced unlike effects on those who were or grew to be comparatively contented in their new life and those who did not. How they saw prairie scenery seemed to reflect rather than influence their opinion of America. In homesickness dark forest and soaring peak operated more as symbols of complex feelings involved in the concept of *fatherland* than as objects pined for in their own right. Mountains and lakes were to be found in the New World too. But it was always Norwegian ranges, Swedish lakes, Danish beeches which the homesick and unhappy longed to greet once more; the adjective was clearly more important than the noun. Both such indirect evidence offered by the literature of homesickness, and direct evidence in accounts of immigrants who found beauty in prairie geography too, showed that Scandinavian newcomers proved able to adjust to this drastically different aspect of their new environment more easily than to any other.

IV. Homesickness

Learning to feel at home in the social setting of the new country was much more difficult. The homesickness so abundantly recorded in the literature measured how the immigrants felt toward the segment of American society in which they found themselves, irrespective of geographical location. As a rule homesickness was most acute during the "dog years," when a newcomer found everything strange; but this emotional state often continued or recurred long afterwards, even though in other respects the immigrant seemed to have adjusted satisfactorily to his new environment.

Homesickness was indeed the most prominent and typical feeling expressed throughout all periods of Scandinavian-American literature. One who has read through acres of newspaper verse can safely hazard the guess that at least three-fourths of it dealt exclusively with nostalgia; hardly a volume of collected poems omitted a long section of lyrics on this subject; it was an element—often the strongest and most effectively communicated element—in numerous tales and novels about all kinds of immigrants in every period and place, at every stage of acculturization. More than any other theme, this pervaded the emotional lives of this group in spite of pride in and gratitude for their social betterment.

1. PERSONAL SUFFERING

Unlike personalities developed different types and degrees of homesickness in response to changing situations. It was most intense in its initial stage, which many writers described arising as emigrants crowded the rail of their boat to watch the blue coast of their homeland fade into mist. First then, claimed many poems and tales, did those departing begin to realize the emotional cost of the step they had taken. This initial nostalgia regularly reached its peak during the "dog years," but in many cases subsided like unfavorable reactions to the new landscape when the immigrants became acclimatized.

During his first years in this country, like most newcomers to a strange land he suffered from homesickness and longing for the "Old Country." He wrote many letters, especially to his brother Knut Lovaas, who answered promptly. But as he got better acquainted, and was able to make himself understood in the language of the country, and developed his own affairs to take care of and a good income, he wrote less and less. The last years he lived he often thought of writing or at least answering the letters that came from his brother; but he never did.[20]

Countless verses exhorting immigrants not to forget their dear ones back home, and many tales picturing aged parents waiting for letters from America which never came, support the conclusion that many immigrants ultimately recovered from their initial homesickness.

Another type of nostalgia developed only after years in the New World. This was particularly apt to afflict young people who had emigrated out of wanderlust, or idealists who had turned their backs on a homeland of class hatred and injustice. The Swedish-American poet Jakob Bonggren was an excellent example of the latter. His first book of poems, published in Stockholm in 1882 before his emigration, expressed his strong republican sympathy and criticism of social and economic injustice in a nation still ruled by the well-born.

> Farewell, conceit and falsehood!
> I shall never mourn for you.
> Farewell, you Wall of China
> against the new and true. . . .
> 1 go to quite another land
> where work is not a shame,
> and a free man with honest toil
> can win an honored name.[21]

In his second collection of poems published twenty years later in Rock Island, however, Bonggren had undergone a metamorphosis of attitude. Now he looked back on Sweden with homesickness and longing.

> Wherever I am in the world
> in my faring to and fro,
> to my forefathers' home in the northland
> my thoughts will ever go.
> Footsteps are always heavy
> pressed on a foreign shore.
> I cannot sing, who can hope to see
> my fatherland no more.[22]

In many a tale characters departed in the full flush of lust for adventure and threw themselves into the struggle of their "dog years" without a thought beyond the excitement, only to develop nostalgia for the vanished past much later. Poet after poet described how jauntily he turned his back on his native land to seek his fortune afar, but learned too late the value of the home he had abandoned: "My fatherland I hold far more dear today/Than the day I bade it farewell."[23]

Such individuals seemed able to make initial adjustment to their new environment without much difficulty, only to face emotional problems later. These usually arose from a specific cause touching on deepest feelings: the death of parents in the Old Country, to whom the immigrant had promised to return; conflict with his children, who had gone their own ways; a growing sense of rejection by American society, especially during World War I; old age and the approach of death. The Swedish novelist Vilhelm Moberg caught superbly the typical experience of an old man, who had always been too busy carving his farm from the wilderness to think much of the Old Country, lying in pain waiting for death as he studied a tattered map of Småland and dreamed of his native landscape in a golden haze.[24]

Sometimes nostalgia developed in later years without discernible cause. As one author described the process, one fine day an immigrant felt a twinge like a toothache. It soon went away and was forgotten, but another day it throbbed again, and then again, more painful still. Perhaps months passed of recurrent and deepening melancholy before the malady was recognized as homesickness.[25] A Danish-American poet who seemed to have gone through this experience himself warned young people suffering from America-fever:

> If you are torn by longing, then follow the bent of your heart
> away from want and hardship to a better land apart.
> But don't forget on your journey, wherever you may roam,
> longing for far adventure turns into longing for home![26]

A third type of homesickness, the most common of all, was that felt throughout the entire life of the immigrant, continuing in muted form after the intense suffering of the "dog years", forgotten perhaps for shorter or longer periods, but flaring up regularly. Few could indulge in nostalgia while in full activity, concentrating on the task at hand; but resting on a quiet evening, sitting idle of a Sunday, many a writer felt a tear fall at the thought of his mother and childhood home so far away. One poet recorded his recurrent nostalgia every spring, another at the first snowfall, a third at the sound of Christmas bells. Christmas was the most universal time of sad remembrance, as evinced in countless poems.

> When Christmastime draws near again
> the Swede-American feels melancholy
> remembering his childhood's happy days,
> the joy of Christmas and tree and holly.
> The trees of bygone years were not so fine
> as what he lights today, but they were bright
> with precious memories of joy and love,
> which rise like stars against his sorrowing night.[27]

Such expressions of homesickness in so much of the literature supported the conclusion of many authors that the social betterment won by their characters was bought at the price of lasting unhappiness.

Part of the sadness of those who suffered from nostalgia arose from the fact that no one who had not gone through the same experience could understand it. Many poems addressed to family and countrymen back home tried to communicate something of an emigrant's homesickness, usually in vain.

> O dearest fatherland, in all your beauty
> with somber forests, snow-enmantled peaks . . .
> you do not know how my heart trembles,
> my eye grows wet, my pulsebeat runs away
> at the thought of seeing you once more.
> You cannot surmise this endless longing
> which dwells deep in the heart and grips the soul.
> You cannot understand the son of Svea's need
> to see again your shores, your hills, your lakes.[28]

Another Swedish-American poet described how people he met, when he talked so endlessly of his native land, asked him what drew his heart

266

so irresistibly back to it; what was so wonderful about those particular lakes and shores? He could only answer with another question: "What is the power of love? . . ./One can reason and argue as much as one will,/the bonds of love bind unbroken still."[29]

Neither did the second generation understand this aspect of their parents' emotional life. Many a writer rejoiced that they would be spared this suffering, and saw the only cure for his homesickness in his children's future.

> Well! If this isn't home to us, we'll have to make it so.
> Though the land is strange to me, my boys love it, I know.
> Although the tone of longing from my song ne'er fades away,
> a younger generation will here sing their joy some day![30]

Yet it was a cause of sadness to know that one's dearest memories were alien to one's children. "They had heard of the small mountain settlemet in Norway with the same interest they might have had in an account of Africa or China. The whole was something strange and foreign which was not theirs. Little by little Knut began to understand that he and his children in reality belonged to two different nations. There was a strange chasm between them, and they had struck roots on opposite sides of it."[31] Thus a well-to-do Swedish-American farmer, although proud of the handsome estate he had created in the New World, felt his eye grow dim with

> . . . a tear of longing and of loss,
> which the young generation cannot understand,
> for they cannot conceive of the powerful bond
> which binds my heart to that northern land.[32]

In his first novel Rølvaag inserted a long speech on this aspect of migration, reminding a Norwegian-American audience what it meant to lose their fatherland: more than an incurable hurt to the heart when they cut the emotional bonds tying them to home and kindred; more than lifelong exile when they broke the unconscious spiritual union with their own people and nation; in fact, no one could explain the full meaning of losing one's fatherland. The speaker had a fairly clear idea about it, but he could not define it: "we have lost that which does not permit itself to be expressed in words, we have lost the *unutterable*."[33]

Examination of the content of homesickness, the things which the immigrant felt to be irreparably lost, can however explain something of the matter. Poets drew up list after list:

> Hail ancient Denmark,
> ancestors' earth!
> Heath and sound,
> groves of beech!

267

> Song of larks,
> glistening loam!
> Stream of memories,
> Mother and home![34]

This catalog was largely concrete, though the objects were generalized. In another mood the same poet longed to climb once more the path that led to the door of the cottage where his cradle had stood, to kiss and comfort the grey-haired mother he had left so long ago—or at least pay homage to her grave.[35] Here the deprivation was felt as personal and specific. In many another verse and tale the writer dreamed rather of the peace and calm repose of his childhood home, where he looked on life with happy hope and faith; here he mourned the loss of emotional states produced (retrospect assured him) by a given setting, and to be found nowhere else. But why not? As a Swedish-American poet pointed out, we must all leave the land of our childhood and go out into life, and we long to return only because we have forgotten the sorrow there, remembering alone the joy.[36]

Emigrants had gone through a much more drastic form of departure than the normal from their childhood home. It was not a development but a break. The often reiterated yearning for the fields and home of one's ancestors gave a clue of the sense of family continuity which emigrants from a comparatively stable agricultural culture felt had been their birthright, now lost by their own act.

> There stands an ancient house somewhere,
> which was my home.
> No matter where I go, it will
> remain my home.
>
> My father's father fashioned it
> and ate his bread
> beside its fire, and through its gate
> was borne when dead.
>
> Above the threshold of the door
> my father too,
> when death had closed his weary eyes,
> was carried through.
>
> A century's peace deposited
> its hallowed load
> in grandfather's and father's and
> the clan's abode.
>
> I'll not be carried out when dead
> from that gateway.
> But still I claim and cherish well
> the right to say

> that though I never find firm ground
> to place my foot,
> still somewhere, somewhere far away
> my heart has root.[37]

No one saw clearly this intimate connection between time, place, and family while still in the Old Country. Heartbreak at leaving one's immediate kindred and surroundings was felt to be an individual cross suffered as the means to a greater end. The family's setting had to be abandoned in order to preserve and advance the family itself.

When most of these writers expressed the desire to found a worthy home as the strongest conscious motive for emigration, they did not realize that they were defining the concept of home in terms of the society where they grew up. They expected the home they built in the New World to stand on the same sanctions and embody family solidarity similar to that they had left behind; they assumed that they would exercise authority over and command love and loyalty from their children as their own parents had done.

But the different social structure in America—which was largely what the emigrants went to find—defined both form and content of family life in other ways. In exclusive settlements based largely on subsistence economy, stories sometimes showed Scandinavian groups large enough to maintain their own family patterns for some years; but wherever rival American patterns appeared (ultimately everywhere), these won out. Those immigrants found no cure for their nostalgia who were unable to adapt their desires for what their home should be to what the social environment around them permitted. In their case, it would seem, the Old Country gave them the spiritual means to build a home but not material ones, while America gave them the material means but not the spiritual. Feeling both as necessary, these people could only continue to long for the environment which made possible the home they had once known, making the unconscious step in abstraction found in so much of the literature from the specific abode of one's forefathers to the fatherland in general.

2. ATTITUDES TOWARD THE OLD COUNTRY

Attitudes toward the fatherland were extremely complex. A few immigrants were pictured as nourishing lasting disdain or even hatred for the homeland which had starved them out. More common was condescension toward the little, backward country of one's birth in comparison with the rich opportunities of the New World. First-generation parents often talked about how much worse off they were in the Old Country, so that the children concluded, "It was certainly fortunate that Father and

Mother had had the sense to leave [Norway] so that they could get to be somebody—both they and the children."[38] Admonitions to parents not to disparage the homeland turned up from time to time in immigrant periodicals and editorials. But one could criticize his country and love it too; those who censured the Old Country most strongly often seemed to be trying to justify their having left it, while their hearts continued to yearn for home.

The most widely accepted attitude toward the mother country was that expressed in a Swedish emigrant ballad which enjoyed great popularity around the turn of the century.

> Farewell, O Mother Svea, now I must sail the sea.
> I thank you from my heart because you fostered me.
> Of bread you gave so little, it could not life uphold
> —although to many others you gave wealth manifold.
>
> But still I love you, Sweden, my dearest fatherland,
> and unwillingly must trade you for western prairie sand.
> But bread—that is a problem ahead of all the rest,
> We must like birds take leave of our well-beloved nest.[39]

The majority of immigrants seemed thus able to keep separate the unfavorable aspects of a social and economic system from which they sought to escape and all the rest of a homeland which they continued to love.

In later years, when their motives for emigration had grown dim, some expressed guilt-feelings over having betrayed their native land by leaving it.

> My fatherland, my fatherland,
> there's pain in my breast like fire:
> You gave me life, you gave me soul.
> I betrayed you in faithless ire![40]

However, such guilt was expressed by only a minority of immigrant writers, mainly poets. Old-World authors attributed it to their emigrant characters much more frequently. In a typical European novel, a band of Norwegians gathered in one hut to celebrate their first Christmas in Dakota with a meal and recitations of patriotic poetry by the schoolmaster. "After that there was another silence. This picture of love for one's country had moved them strangely. Ah, *they* had left their native land!"[41]

Yet the fatherland was by no means only a geographical area to these immigrant characters. Most expressed their homesickness as though it were, but this misconception was exploded by those who returned to their native land only to discover that it was no longer theirs. Some came back on visits, once or several times; others intended to settle down again where they were born. Their experience was pictured as the same.

After their first tearful joy at the sight of the dear remembered mountain (or grove or shining water) they found "everything changed from what it had been before. Smaller, narrower, less warmly cordial, less—home-like."[42] The homeland such disillusioned prodigal sons continued to long for was not to be found on any map.

Those authors who advocated the preservation of *danskhed* or *norsk-dom* in exile assumed that some vital elements of the fatherland could be transplanted to another place.

> I have Denmark in my soul
> singing in my blood
> from head to foot, throughout the whole
> although I chose to leave it. . . .
> Denmark is, where Danish folk
> live over all the world![43]

Poet after poet of all three nationalities urged his brothers (for all were sons of the mother country) to preserve their common language and their fathers' heritage, for "We are cut from Denmark,/not from the Danish folk!"[44] This heritage was defined largely in terms of behavioral traits like honesty or piety.

Our longing for home must be transformed into longing for each other, a longing to meet each other in the widest possible spiritual fellowship . . . in order to preserve ourselves and our children as *Danish* Americans, who can stand united on all the spiritual values which we have brought with us over here.[45]

Some authors thus defined the homeland more in terms of the people who inhabited it and the way they lived together than the country itself.

The writers made each his own selection from among these many aspects of the fatherland; some emphasized personal childhood memories, others the general landscape or national traits. Only occasionally did a definition summarize both specific and general and show awareness of the different levels of abstraction involved. Probably the best brief one appeared in Danish-American novel, in which a newcomer to Chicago suffered a flare-up of homesickness after attending a concert of Danish music.

He hardly knew what he was yearning for. It was home and father and mother, of course, the farm and his ordinary surroundings; but it was much, much more. It was the whole parish with its broad hills, it was the forest and the heath and the fjord. It was the whole country with the people and the language, it was the sum of thousands of objects and experiences woven into a wreath with the flowers of memory . . .[46]

Here this author threw considerable light on Rølvaag's "the unutterable." It seemed impossible to verbalize because this concept included every-

271

thing left in a growing person's mind by the thousands of experiences whose regular recurrence in a stable environment taught him to feel at home there because he knew what to expect. Without being aware of it, he had progressively assimilated the assumptions on which local social intercourse was based, so that at each stage of his development he was capable of behaving as he knew he was expected to do.

This sense of remembered security in contrast with their present vulnerability as strangers intensified the immigrants' tendency to look back on childhood as a golden age. Several authors remarked on this proclivity, and a few even maintained that immigrant nostalgia was mostly that.

People talk so much about homesickness and such, but I'm not so sure there's any geography involved at all. The country one left, the name of which is childhood or youth—that nobody can return to. We who go on living in the same place don't notice it the same way as those who leave. People don't understand that it's their own youth or generation they have left behind, and so they confuse it with something geographical—when it's rather something inside us.[47]

Immigrants experienced this longing for lost childhood differently from others. Universally they recalled "the things you want to remember about yesterday, sifted clean of the things you want to forget . . . the little house you were born in, without the leak in the roof and the cold potato and salt that were all you had for supper."[48] Only rarely did a man realize that he was deceiving himself when he talked as though his childhood had been free from sorrow: "that is what is so wonderful about it, that is why I love to lose myself in its memories; but this is strange because at the same time I know very well that my childhood in actuality was anything *but* happy. But I have reached such an age and live at such a distance from the land of my boyhood that no dark shadow can fall over my memories."[49]

Clearly the distance in space as well as time which the immigrants put between themselves and their childhood home modified their attitude toward it. Unhampered by an actuality at hand to hamper their flights of fancy, forgetting the deprivation which had motivated them to leave, they idealized childhood security like a feeble Norwegian-American grandmother, who remembered "when she herself sat on her mother's knee and knew no evil except tears."[50] Under trials of insecurity and rejection as immigrants, they confused the geographical location of their childhood with their memory of being happier there because they were fully accepted, and extended their idea of both to the concept of the *fatherland* in praise and longing.

V. Language

The authors showed language problems to be a paramount cause of immigrant feelings of homesickness and alienation. One and all they portrayed ignorance of English as the greatest single difficulty their characters met. This was the mainspring of their "dog years," and gave rise to mistakes and difficulties without end. The few who learned no English remained at the mercy of Americans all their lives—like a simple-minded Norwegian left in charge of a neighbor's farm, on whom Yankee boys could play a cruel trick because he understood almost nothing of what they said.[51]

Those ignorant of English suffered more than practical difficulties, too. Farm wives, who often had little opportunity to learn the new language, were pictured enduring torments of shame under the contempt of a store clerk with whom they could communicate only by gesture, or hiding in fear from the approach of a traveling salesman. Even when immigrants had passed beyond the helplessness of not being able to talk at all, they often remained unable to express more than the general outline of what they meant, and understood little more of what others said. To avoid such situations, many characters rejected the few opportunities they had for contact with Yankees. In a Danish-American novel, a boy attending a local college in Nebraska faced a problem when the school planned a parents' dinner, with a play in which the boy had an important part. Of course he would like to show his folks how well he was doing, but he did not want to invite them because he was ashamed of their shabby clothes and broken speech. After days of vacillation, he finally asked them half-heartedly. There was a long silence before the father said sadly, "I don't think we can mix very well with Americans. . . . We don't really belong when it comes to such things; even Hans can see that. Now, if it had been in Denmark, Meta, we could have talked with everybody from the preacher and the principal on down. Here we must sit at home while the new life passes us by."[52]

A few characters were pictured as mastering English in areas where they had most relations with Yankees: business and politics. Yet almost all of these too retained their native tongue for their most important social and emotional relationships, with family and friends and God. Many a businessman scrupulously spoke and thought in the language of the republic during his working day, but lapsed with relief into his mother tongue when he came home.

When the conflict over introduction of English into religious services entered the literature, the main objection to the change was from older people who claimed that regardless of their ability to understand the import of the same terms in the new language, they could not *feel* the

273

same toward it. "I can understand a sermon in English as well as I understand a political talk in the language of this country. But the gospel in English cannot touch the most sensitive strings of my heart, and that was why Gunvor and I sat home and read the Bible verse for the day and sang the old hymns in our mother tongue on Sundays instead of going to church" (when Norwegian had been dropped in the regular services).[53]

Mothers especially insisted that their children continue to speak with them in the European dialect, as Beret Holm in Rølvaag's trilogy strove to hold English out of her Dakota home. The youngest son begged to be allowed to learn his religion in English, it was so much plainer! But his mother insisted a Norwegian boy ought to be ashamed to learn his Christian doctrine in a language his own mother could not understand. When later the boy's American teacher told his mother that speaking Norwegian at home had hurt his English and might therefore harm his future, the mother retorted that it was more important for the boy to learn to understand his mother than to "be fine in his talk."[54] However, the fear of such a possible handicap for their children, added to outside social pressure, led many parents to try to speak English at all times, even within the family. Most of the authors strongly condemned this effort, for the English which resulted was usually atrocious. The children corrected their elders constantly, with dire effects on family discipline.

Yet even those adults who went entirely over to the American language in daily life—regardless of how well they spoke it—reverted to their native tongue as they grew old, especially at the approach of death. Then memories of childhood came flooding back. "And with the memories came the language—his mother tongue. . . . The language he had heard and used at his work and also in all other occasions of life, it was no longer sufficient."[55] Ministers especially knew how the thoughts of the dying returned to their source. In a Norwegian-American novel, a Yankee clergyman came to fetch a Norwegian layman to a fellow countryman dying of cancer. Trying to refuse the request, the Norwegian argued that the sick man knew English well.

"Ye-es," said the minister . . . "I've had experience in that direction before. It seems that it's only the native tongue that counts when a poor fellow comes to die His mind is anchored to it in one way or another, and only through it can one get in contact with him. Talk English to him and he drifts away from you. I've tried it."[56]

All the authors were aware of this trial of immigrant experience: inability to use the only language they commanded fully in intercourse with so much of their social environment, sometimes even their own children. But the writers emphasized the emotional loss to their charac-

274

ters; few seemed to understand the wider social significance of language. They did depict speech dividing one group from another and uniting the members of each against outsiders. Characters often expressed annoyance at how Yankees stuck together, and how the unworthy Irish seemed to be admitted at once to membership in the American group because English was their mother tongue too. Some stories recorded how Scandinavians felt ill at ease when they could not follow the conversation of speakers of English, others how Yankees or Irish resented not being able to understand talk in Norwegian or Swedish. A number of writers observed the fact that individuals felt fully at home with and were accepted by only members of their own language group, but no one attempted analysis of the reason: that language bore the freight of assumptions which helped guide how the members of a group felt toward each other. Characters were always delighted when they heard their own tongue spoken in a strange environment because they assumed that the speaker could be trusted to behave as they expected him to, not like the unpredictable Americans. This expectation was often disappointed, but it persisted; and undoubtedly it formed the basis of the preservationist argument that the distinct immigrant group could survive only as long as its language. After listing the virtues which Swedes possessed as their birthright, a Swedish-American argued, "If we lose our language, then in our descendants these good characteristics will disappear, and within a couple of generations we will be assimilated with the Americans, and our Swedish-America will be found only in history books, like the old Swedish colonies on the Delaware."[57]

These authors felt that their special behavioral traits could survive only if members of the transplanted group continued to behave in the same ways as they had back home, and they saw language as both symbolic of and essential to their basic patterns of behavior. Thus a Danish-American insisted that language was the center of all relations between an individual and his environment: "No tragedy is more persistent and real than the sorrow a man must carry in his heart, often unexpressed, all his life long, the tragedy of having left his home country, friends, familiar sights, and that most precious jewel which is the central pivot of human life, the gift of his native dialect."[58]

But in the effort to maintain their native tongue, Scandinavian immigrants faced an insurmountable problem. Small as their group was in relation to the English-speaking population, it was divided into as many linguistic fragments as regional dialects transported across the Atlantic. Author after author pointed to the fact that his people lacked a language common to them all, above all in written form. The gulf between daily life and formal culture was for these people of peasant and working-class origin commensurate with the abyss between their everyday speech

275

and the literary language spoken by ministers, teachers, and other learned men. For most, the mother tongue they clung to was literally that spoken by their mother—a dialect so distinctive that it could survive in recognizable form two, three, or even four generations in America, but not much longer.

Several characters were annoyed when they met a person who had tried to abandon his dialect in favor of the literary language. A Norwegian newcomer was of course very glad to be reunited with his brother in Minnesota, "but I didn't like it that he talked the 'book language.'"[59] Such an attempt to abandon the native dialect was usually considered affectation in people of peasant origin. Yet pastors who came from lowly families felt they should use the "book language" in church. All could read it, but learning to speak it presented no small problem to some theology students. In several accounts of immigrant church services, newcomers noticed that when the preacher read from the Bible, he pronounced the words exactly as written, silent letters and all, or mixed forceful expressions from his dialect into sentences otherwise composed in the literary speach.

Almost all were heir to this dichotomy between the two forms of their native tongue, for only the minority of upper-class immigrants possessed the "book language" as their spoken tongue too. Many authors thought this dichotomy was the major cause of the rapid decline of Scandinavian dialects in the United States. One Norwegian-American deplored that so many dialects had been brought over, when religious training had to be in Dano-Norwegian. The result, he thought, was that most people felt their everyday speech good enough only for common things.[60] Several other writers depicted immigrants who felt that their dialectal speech was a sign of lack of education and low social standing, yet who refrained from speaking the literary language for fear of being accused of snobbery. They did not know it well either. When they were thus reluctant to speak either form of their native tongue, pressure from the American environment proved irresistible; and many who had learned some English were motivated to use it on every possible occasion, even among themselves.

Therefore when cultural leaders exhorted Scandinavian-Americans to preserve their mother tongue, in many cases the appeal fell on deaf ears. What mother tongue? Their vulgar dialect, which the cultural leaders hardly ever condescended to use? Or the "book language," which these peasants had never spoken? As a Swedish-American character pointed out, those who labored to preserve the Swedish literary language among their people in America built on air.

How can anyone require that someone shall preserve what he has never possessed? The emigrant has as little contact with formal Swedish as he has with Strindberg's

276

plays and Lindblad's songs. The emigrant's language is West Gotlandish, Värmländish, Skånsk, Småländish, Dalarnish, and so on. And out here they mix them together and talk all at once. And then after they've been here awhile they begin to mix in a lot of English words, partly because no comparable words exist in their limited provincial dialect and partly because the words mixed in are easier. . . . The development is completely natural and no one should take offense at it.[61]

This character argued that the Swedish language should be taught for its beauty and usefulness like any foreign tongue, to Swedish immigrants also. They had a special relationship to it, but it was certainly not theirs by inheritance.

The style of the prose literature also illustrated the subtle pervasion of the mother tongue by English admixtures. Poetry, tending to use a more formal vocabulary, usually avoided mention of the aspects of everyday life where English loan-words were most common; but ordinary life was almost the exclusive subject matter of this fiction. Here the interpolation of English vocabulary was ubiquitous. The English word was normally spelled with Scandinavian sound-values and declined by the rules of Scandinavian grammar. In Rølvaag's first book, supposedly a collection of letters home by a Norwegian newcomer, the writer mentioned many English terms incorporated into Norwegian-American speech, spelled by sound. For example, his uncle had asked him "at ta denne *svilpeilen* og gaa og *slabbe* den til *pigsa*." Besides translation to Norwegian in the text, the author added footnotes: "1) svilpeilen (= the pail filled with swill). 2) slabbe (= to slop). 3) pigsa (= the pigs)."[62]

The process of "mixingen," as the writers called it, produced distinct new dialects which demarcated those who spoke it from those who stayed in the Old Country. As Rølvaag's newcomer declared, "If uncle came home now and talked such Norwegian as he talks here, you'd think he was speaking English, and it would be impossible to understand everything he said."[63] There were innumerable incidents in the stories showing immigrants mixing English into their original language when they wrote back or returned home, causing incessant misunderstandings among those who had not shared their experience and therefore their language. Occasionally a new arrival or upper-class character protested against the dialect developing in America. "Listen here, you! . . . you'd better break yourself of using that lousy language. . . . This hodgepodge speech is an abomination. It's almost enough to make a gentleman vomit."[64] But the best authors used it without apology, or defended it in a preface or epilogue.

Any excuse for this language is as unnecessary and uncalled for as the apology of the doorkeeper who begged the guests' pardon because it was raining. This language exists. More or less involved, it is used in town and country, by high and low, to a much greater extent than we often wish or will admit. . . . It was Anna Olsson who first made me aware of it, and later showed how important it is in the description of Swedish-American types to let these use in dialogue their own genuine every-day speech, so often unjustly ridiculed.[65]

Contemporary reviewers sometimes objected to the distorted spellings required by approximately phonetic rendition of these special dialects, but much of the desired effect was lost by authors who kept the American spelling of English words they introduced into their Scandinavian text. These could not reproduce the grammatical inflections invariably added from the European tongue, and therefore the English word protruded from its context unnaturally.[66]

Some of the writers recognized that the new dialects reflected new group-formation. Scandinavians in America were unlike either Yankees or their countrymen who stayed home. "When I send out *Landsmænd* from a Danish-American publishing house, it is because these twelve stories and sketches are based on special subjects belonging to America, or contain puns and expressions which only Danish-Americans can be expected to understand."[67]

In spite of countless complaints over the rapid admixture of English vocabulary into the Scandinavian dialects, however, immigrant authors failed to realize that this was the way members of the group actually lost their mother tongue. The fiction writers tended to present their characters with the choice between using English on one hand and Swedish, Norwegian, or Danish on the other, as though the Scandinavian tongue had remained unchanged. "For I can't undestand that because a new language comes in, the old one must go out," Rølvaag's Beret Holm said defiantly to the new Lutheran minister when he proclaimed that Norwegian would have disappeared from Dakota within the next twenty years. Nor was she impressed by his argument that "That's the way it has gone all through history; there is no—absolutely *no*—reason to believe that it could possibly go differently here."[68]

But the books themselves recorded that the immigrants normally learned the new language through corruption of the old one. No more than a handful of characters ever tried to study English as a foreign language, putting together entire sentences at once. All others introduced one or two English words at a time into their European speech. "Many of the Danes who had been in the United States for two or three years would mix Danish and English until it was impossible to tell which language they were trying to speak."[69] A few ultraconservatives like Rølvaag's Beret Holm might maintain their dialects comparatively unmixed, but only because they learned little English and had few contacts with English-speaking people. The majority who learned as much English as possible invariably found themselves losing their mother tongue, first because it was corrupted by introduction of words from the other language, and then

278

because they drifted away from it in using English more and more in daily life. It remained their own form of English, however, mispronounced, ungrammatical, with Norwegian words surviving in unexpected places. Authors and characters alike derived no small amusement from the inability of uneducated people to judge the correctness of the language they tried to speak: like the lady who came into a bookshop in a Norwegian area in Chicago talking what she clearly believed was fine English, but was really at least half Norwegian still.[70]

VI. Formal Culture

Included in the authors' definition of the fatherland were thus family continuity and ties, landscape, folkways, language; but much else was omitted: most aspects of formal culture, for instance—literature, art, history. A few preservationist leaders insisted on the overwhelming importance of such, but the majority of authors made clear that their characters had no contact with or interest in such matters either in the Old Country or in America. Sometimes a storyteller stated this explicitly in sketching the background of children brought up in one of those picturesque cottages back home:

The energetic Swedish culture left them almost untouched; the only form in which it met them was the catechism. Few off there in Hafrekulla knew anything about Sweden's heroic age, there was no time to think about such things. Over their fight for daily bread no battle-scarred banners waved, only ragged clothes hung out to dry; they knew nothing about "Leipsig's plains, Lützen's hills," their own plains were all too stony, and over their hills waved poor quality oats.[71]

Thus a would-be poet in a Danish-American novel maintained that he had more "culture" in his little finger than 95 percent of his countrymen took with them from Denmark.[72] Another Danish-American novelist portrayed settlers in a prairie village bewildered by talk about preservation of their "cultural heritage" in a local dispute over whether to hire a Danish Lutheran or a Yankee schoolteacher. They had no idea of what the *danskhed* advocate was talking about, and guessed that he was trying to further his own private interests behind a smokescreen of meaningless generalities.[73]

The majority of authors pictured the concerns of their characters never rising above their round of daily work except for religion, and occasionally politics. As writer after writer made clear both by example and by complaint, the only "spiritual" interest of most of these immigrants was and remained exclusively in their church. Neither did their religious leaders try to awaken concern for matters of formal culture. On the contrary, the authors felt that many ministers exerted all possible pres-

279

sure in the opposite direction. For instance, a Norwegian-American preacher was pictured criticizing a colleague who had written a funeral psalm. "We have the good old psalms with us and don't need any more; we must uphold our people in their childhood faith . . . There is no market here for so-called *belles-lettres;* there are very few books of that sort which ought to be allowed in the hands of young people."[74] In tales about immigrant clergymen, they were pictured as reading only theological and doctrinaire literature; when an educated Norwegian newcomer at last met a minister with a rich and varied library, he was as surprised as the reader. "He was used to hearing and thinking that the Norwegian-American preachers were strangers to cultural interests outside their own special field."[75]

VII. Folklore and Folk Music

People who lacked contact with formal culture might nevertheless have had a wealth of folklore to bring. Rural districts in Scandinavia remained a treasurehouse of colorful legend and custom throughout most of the period of mass migration. Trolls, elves, and spirits of woods and water, though seldom literally believed in, were still part of the symbolism of daily life; folk dances and traditional games were enjoyed by all but the puritanical; folk tales and music remained living tradition well into the twentieth century. The literature showed comparatively little in these fields surviving transplantation to America.[76]

The influence of pietism within the immigrant group was probably an important factor in turning the attention of many of its members away from such worldly matters. There were several accounts of devout parents in both the Old World and the New destroying the fiddles of their musical sons, who never touched this instrument of Satan again. Tirades against the terrible sin of dancing were common in poetry and prose, and such games as involved chance were often condemned as blasphemy. A Norwegian immigrant father who told his children tales of the Viking gods was chided by his devout wife, who feared the effect of such lusty impiety on the young souls she was striving to teach to walk in the ways of righteousness.[77]

In the field of music, considered least sinful of the folk arts, the literature recorded few folk songs sung in immigrant communities. Only in Danish Grundtvigian homes was there deliberate effort to pass on the tradition of living folk song. In a Wisconsin community, the young people struck up not only traditional songs and country dances but also singing games whenever they came together.[78] In less culturally conscious communities, folk music was seldom mentioned. Rare indeed was an evening of spontaneous entertainment when neighbors took turns at singing remembered folk songs. Occasionally an immigrant father sang over and over "Hor [sic] Herligt er mit Fødeland!" although when his sons joined in they were mouthing words they did not understand; or a grandmother sang Old-Country lullabies to a baby. In one novel where the text of such songs was given, the second-generation mother listening to the grandmother felt "a stab of regret that she had failed to learn and preserve these characteristic old lullabies and much else her mother had brought along from the Old Country. When her cracked voice is heard no more, a great deal will disappear."[79]

When the first generation showed little interest in this aspect of their heritage, the second preserved almost nothing. A lonely newcomer to Dakota complained bitterly about the difference between young people's social activity back home and in the New World.

Almost everything we thought was fun home in Smeviken doesn't exist for these people. Do you remember how we used to gather on the mountain slopes Sunday afternoons and evenings in the summertime and play all kinds of things? Do you remember what fun it was with all the stories and folk tales we told? Do you recall how beautifully the folk songs rang out over the heaths and woods? And then all the feats of strength we tried, and the jokes we played. . . . But there isn't any such life to be found here. No, this is another world, I'd almost said a *dead* world . . . on Sunday evenings in this country a few boys can get together one place or another, but only to tell dirty stories or drink up a keg of beer. . . . If one fellow has gotten a bit ahead he probably has a horse and buggy, so he deserts the others to take some girl out driving. Up to now I haven't seen boys and girls gather for innocent, health-ful, hearty play. All such is too cheap and improper for them, it seems; as if the other should be so much more proper![80]

Young people who were occasionally pictured lifting their voices in song tended toward "My Girl's a Bowery Girl" and "Merrily We Roll Along."[81] When city Swedes at a surprise party called on one of their number to favor them with a few selections, she obliged with "Home Sweet Home," "A Hot Time in the Old Town," and "Beautiful Moon-light." A request for Swedish songs she refused, for such "kärade hon inte för, sa' hon."[82]

Folk music in the form of hymns, however, lived on as a vital tradition as long as the Scandinavian languages. Standard hymn books for adult church members had been brought along with the Bible and family book of sermons, and were soon printed in the New World too. A Norwegian "buggy-priest" arriving at a frontier community in Dakota could direct that all should bring their hymnals to their first service, in full con-fidence that everybody would have one to bring.[83] These books printed only the words of each hymn, for most of the melodies were folk tunes which everyone knew, even the children. Learning hymns was part of their training in Sunday and summer religion school, and they learned them so well that even an irreligious young father could recall any number to sing to his baby.[84] When the surprise-party Swedes decided to join in one Swedish song that absolutely everybody knew, they discovered that it had to be a hymn.[85]

Mention of trolls and other figures of typically Scandinavian folklore was also scarce throughout most of the immigrant literature. The periodicals of the Norwegian-American *bygdelag* organizations provided a significant exception, for they printed many amateur accounts of local legends especially about *hulderfolk* (the "hidden people" of Norwegian mountains and forests).[86] A book of Norwegian folk tales and legends collected in rural settlements of the Middle West was published in 1923.[87] Otherwise only a rare story showed isolated pioneers whiling away an evening with folk tales, or a second-generation adult remembering his mother's account of *hilder* in the Old Country.[88]

Almost all reference to folklore figures placed them in Old-World settings. Evidently these personifications of nature were taken for granted to be so bound by age-old association to specific mountain ranges, waterfalls, skerries, and forests that there could be no question of their coming along to a treeless plain.

These invisible creatures have not been able to settle here in America; so I do not *think* that they exist among us here. . . . As proof, I can say that people do not . . paint crosses with tar or place steel objects over all the doors on the farm, or say magic formulas for everything they do at Christmas time as they did at home. Those things are not done over here.[89]

A very few cases of belief in the emigration of some supernatural beings were clearly exceptions. These concerned not watersprites, *hulderfolk,* and trolls, which belonged to definite localities in the Old Country, but domesticated elves or brownies. A character sketch of an old pioneer recorded his claim to have seen and heard barn brownies several times in the New World, and he was sure they had come along as stowaways.[90]

Rølvaag demonstrated that European folklore could contribute to the immigrant literature. He began *The Boat of Longing,* for instance, with legends about a mystical boat glimpsed off the rocky coast of Norway for many generations. His young hero saw a vision of this boat as a symbol of all greatness and beauty in life, which he emigrated to America in search of—and found instead a job washing floors in saloons.[91] Ancient Norwegian symbols of evil both natural and human proved marvelously adaptable to the Dakota frontier in *Giants in the Earth:* the spirit of the prairie personified as a giant, and the Irish land-stealers like the dumb but dangerous trolls.[92] A few poets also made use of their native folklore in scattered lyrics, but usually the setting of the reference was the Old Country.

Most second-generation characters were shown to be uninterested in such unAmerican topics as folk tales. When a Norwegian newcomer told the sons of his immigrant host about trolls and spirits back home, they had never heard of such foolishness and could see no use in it.[93] Others were mildly interested in folklore as in any other fairy tales, but "the story seemed far away and meaningless."[94] Only a rare imaginative child assimilated some part of the parents' heritage, like the Swedish-American girl in a Michigan mining town who listened spellbound to tales about trolls and a watersprite who sat far out in a Swedish lake and played a violin to a star. These beings—pictured as still in Sweden— were as real to the little girl as the ugly false-fronted streets she walked every day, and more important to her imaginative development. Yet the book made clear that this child was a privileged one. When her father woke her on December 13 with a tray of coffee and cakes, dressed in white in the unique Swedish tradition of St. Lucia, the girl asked if all little kids had a Lucia Day breakfast. Other Swedish playmates she had asked did not even know who Lucia was.

> "They can't know about Lucia and her Day unless their fathers or mothers told them. And everybody doesn't know, to tell."
> I bit into the white cardamon coffee-braid. "Why?"
> "Their people over in Sweden were bönder, maybe, and they had to work very hard, just to live. They had no time to learn about Lucias or their Days."[95]

A mistake in a second-generation novel demonstrated that even when parents made an effort to transmit folklore to their children, the legend could be distorted in the process. In an English-language novel about Danes in Nebraska, a grandfather told his grandson about putting out a bowl of rice for the Troll on Christmas Eve.

> "What's a Troll?" said little Alfred. . . .
> "A Troll is a funny, little, friendly kind of fairy who will watch a lot of things for you, if you have your place nice at Christmas time, and if you are good to all God's creatures."[96]

This confusion of *troll* (a giant) with *nisse* (an elf) illustrated how extenuated was the contact of this author with the language and folklore of his parents. What evidence can be found in the literature thus supports the conclusion that very little of folk tradition survived the removal to America, and most of what did died out with the first generation.[97]

VIII. Old-World Festivals

1. CHRISTMAS

Although nothing in the United States encouraged the preservation of folklore from Scandinavia, the Christianity which both cultures shared provided a possible basis for continuation of Old-World patterns in the celebration of Christmas. American religious freedom guaranteed that any immigrant group might continue to observe such a holy festival as it pleased, and since Yankees celebrated the holiday too, their attitude would not be such a negative influence as with folklore. In this area as in other aspects of church activity, however, initially successful efforts to reestablish European models ultimately failed.

The literature contained no lack of description of how Christmas was celebrated in the Old Country, where it was the climax of the year. Especially the Christmas annuals published much information on the subject, in articles about holiday customs in specific provinces of the Old World as well as stories laid at Christmastime back home. Many tales with New-World settings also contained a wealth of recollection about holiday customs experienced by the characters as children before emigration.[98]

Preparations for the great event usually began a month in advance: brewing Christmas beer and distilling spirits, slaughtering animals fattened to provide spiced meats served only during the holiday season, making special cheeses, preparing dried fish, baking a large assortment of traditional cakes and cookies. Housewives were busy far ahead making clothing, for custom dictated that every member of the family should have at least one new thing to wear for the first time on Christmas Eve. The house was turned upside down for the most thorough cleaning and scouring of the year, and then decorated on the morning of Christmas Eve with foliage and an evergreen tree. In the afternoon the chores were finished as early as possible; the animals were all given an extra measure, a sheaf of grain was hoisted on a pole for the birds, a bowl of rice pudding was left for the elf in the barn. Then the entire family bathed, dressed in their best, and gathered for the reading of the Holy Scripture. Supper varied from one region to another —goose, pork, fish—but usually included rice pudding. After the meal the candles were lit on the tree, and then most accounts pictured the few homemade gifts under its branches distributed by the youngest members of the family as Christmas elves. Always old and young joined hands to dance around the tree as long as breath lasted, singing traditional songs. This was the climax of the climactic day for the children.

Some immigrants remembered the merriment going on until time to leave for midnight mass; in other areas all retired early to be up long before dawn for matins on First Christmas Day; still others walked or drove long distances to special church services at the regular hour. But all attended church, and hearing the Christmas bells ring was often mentioned as the most thrilling memory an immigrant bore throughout his life in exile. The deeply religious significance of this holy day was emphasized in every account.

Christmas Eve was the family's festival, First Christmas Day belonged to the church, but from Second Christmas Day on the festivities were sociable. In some stories the Christmas season continued twenty days, until the thirteenth of January; later tales recorded it as shortened, often to thirteen days but never—even in cities—less than three. The dark afternoons were given to visiting from house to house, eating and drinking heartily of good fare set forth this once a year. Over all the merrymaking hovered a community-wide spirit of shared holiness and mirth which the immigrants remembered as unique. The long festival renewed and reinforced not only bonds of family security but also a joyful relationship to God, while the extensive conviviality bound together all the members of the community.

> Such Christmas joy back home!
> Games, merriment, and fun,
> and all took part, all, every one.[99]

Even those immigrants whose childhood homes suffered the utmost poverty looked back on the Christmas season as so permeated with love and gladness that the remembered glow remained their standard of measuring happiness through all their years.

> Now all the bells are chiming from Denmark's snow-white churches,
> and all the shining parish is tuned to holy joy.
> . . . But I, alas, poor dreamer,
> who sit here in Dakota and dream again of yore,
> I seem to feel the light of Christmas love shine round me,
> and hear my mother beg, "Come home once more!"[100]

Because these immigrants came from a culture with such strong Christmas traditions, most of them suffered worst from homesickness at that time of the year when they had reaffirmed the bonds of home and fatherland. Therefore they strove to reestablish Christmas celebration according to Old-Country patterns in their new surroundings. Farmers succeeded to a considerable extent. From the first winter in a miserable hut, they carried out the ritualistic scouring and scrubbing and served at least the traditional rice pudding if they could afford nothing else.[101] As their finances improved, they slaughtered and baked and brewed more and more in Old-Country style until many a character exclaimed as fellow countrymen gathered from far and near that they might almost be back home. Tale after tale recorded the ceremonious extra rations given the livestock, the sheaf of grain hoisted for the birds, the bathing and donning new clothes for the candlelit joy of Christmas Eve. Poor though they might be, the immigrants delighted to "keep Christmas in our own old-fashioned way in our own home."[102]

Gifts were lacking in the poverty-stricken early years, although one story recorded a settler who in full pride of his newly acquired homestead borrowed horses to drive forty miles to town to buy Christmas presents for the children. "They weren't cotter's children any longer. Father and mother had become farmowners and landholders."[103] On the whole, Scandinavian immigrants disapproved of American emphasis on gifts. One story by a second-generation Norwegian recalled how the heroine's pious mother always frowned on elaborate presents as distracting from the spirit of Christmas.[104] Another story showed a Norwegian mother in Minneapolis sternly forbidding her children to visit store Santa Clauses; it was sinful to identify this figure with Christmas, which celebrated the birth of the Savior.[105]

The deeply religious significance of the festival was constantly emphasized in the literature. Pioneers longed for the clang of church bells ringing Christmas in; never could they feel full joy in the holy season without that sacred sound. But even when church spires rose at last, although each household followed the old customs to the letter, the recurrent ache of homesickness at Christmastime did not disappear. As a Danish-American character complained,

Now it's Christmas again; but you've all surely noticed that it's not the same here as in the Old Country. . . . The heartiness is lacking, which inspires everybody home in our fatherland. There it floats and gleams in the air. Everybody feels it, large and small. Believers and nonbelievers share a feeling of joy and gladness.

Of course we keep Christmas here too. But the holiday feeling is so much weaker here, and doesn't reach as far. There's so much to break the mood. Therefore there is hardly any other time of the year when we are more homesick, when we long more for Denmark, than just at Christmastime.[106]

Although the immigrants succeeded in reestablishing their family and church traditions in celebration of Christmas, they could not impose their patterns on the larger community around them; and they felt the important difference.

Immigrants in town and city settings could preserve much less of their Christmas heritage than rural folk. They were able to carry out very few of the time-hallowed preparatory customs. The slaughtering and brewing disappeared at once, and as a rule only the baking survived. The thorough cleansing of household and persons remained, the celebration of Christmas Eve with distribution of gifts and dancing around the tree; and the religious significance was underscored by traditional visits to church. But the social aspects of the holiday rapidly disappeared. The time of celebration was cut drastically. Many characters complained bitterly over having to work full time or even overtime on Christmas Eve, and then having only one day free.[107] Visiting back and forth among relatives and friends was of course greatly restricted by lack of time.

Even under such handicaps, however, some of the spirit survived. Every first-generation character, however drunken or derelict, felt the pull of remembered joy on Christmas Eve. Numerous tales recorded the turning point of the "dog years" or the finding of a first helpful friend on Christmas Eve, the redemption of a lost soul at a Christmas Eve service, the gathering of a few forlorn countrymen in a boardinghouse to celebrate as best they could the joyous Eve. Even a single man sitting lonely in his cheap room wept to remember the Christmases of his childhood. Taking down his old hymnal, he was moved to pray and then sing a hymn in thanksgiving. Outside his door he heard a whisper in English, "I wonder, if he is crazy!"—but on this holy Eve he had found his God again, and never lost Him more.[108] Thus by couples or handfuls or groups also in cities Scandinavian immigrants sought out each other to celebrate as best they could some few of the customs which in the Old Country had stood for so much warmth and love: of family, of God, and of their fellow men.

In time, however, pervasive influence from the larger society changed many aspects of Christmas celebration, even those under the control of the individual family. No small number of tales and poems expressed the common sentiment of looking back with regret to early Christmases in the "dog years" because then the Old-World spirit had burned so much more brightly. A Norwegian farmer well satisfied with his lot in America—he owned clear a whole section of land and a well-built house, and had given all his children a good education—still complained that "Christmas doesn't mean the same to us as in the first years—it's gotten so American that there's nothing left of it for us. We have the railroad and the town nearby, all modern conveniences in the house, but we don't feel at home, Signe and I."[109]

Ways of observing Christmas in immigrant homes came to cover a wide span. At one end was no celebration at all. A Danish newcomer serving as hired man grew more and more surprised as Christmas approached to observe no preparation in progress. Even the holy Eve was like any other day.

There was no excited whispering among the children of gifts or of Yuletree. The tempting smell of bakestuff, red cabbage, roast goose filled with apples and prunes, and rice cooking on the stove, were absent here. When Henrik at suppertime had come down dressed in his good clothes for a festive evening, the table was set as usual; the daily fare of fried bacon, potatoes and cream gravy graced the flowered oilcloth on the table. Not even a tiny evergreen tree, not a gift or a greeting of "Merry Christmas" from one to another. How could people change so in a few years? Surely they must have celebrated Christmas Eve in their youth home in the Old Country. . . . That evening in his room, he had buried his face in his pillow and cried in sadness and longing.[110]

More typical were a Norwegian grandfather and grandmother still living on their old place, who had preserved many holiday customs and never

287

lost the feeling that this should be a family festival. Finally one year they persuaded all their grown children to return with their families for Christmas. They hoped for a renewal of family unity and love, weakened through long loss of contact. All came, indeed, but the young folks took over the festival completely. No grace was said at the holiday feast, no reading of the Scripture; radio and gramophone blared, the young cousins danced together while their parents played cards and argued baseball and politics. The old people ended up in the kitchen alone, washing dishes.[111]

At the other end of the scale, many families continued to observe their own selection of Old-World customs at least throughout the lifetime of the old folks. In cheery Christmas-annual stories families were united at the holy time to carry out traditions sanctified by years of repetition on a Wisconsin farm, if not in the Old Country. Grandparents spending their first Christmas with a son's family in California managed to create a real Christmas Eve although it was raining outside, and no church bells had "rung Christmas in" at nightfall. Here the reading of Scripture at the dinner table, the lighted tree, *lefse* to eat, and singing of Christmas hymns—even one in Norwegian—made up the exemplary celebration.[112] In other tales dancing around the tree or serving a traditional menu was the ceremonious survival. But nowhere, even at its most ideal, was the picture of a New-World Christmas more than a pale copy with many pieces missing of the shining, shared holiday happiness remembered from back home.

A Danish couple who had kept their traditional Christmas through thirty years pointed out the reason. Since it had been in America all these years, the wife said, perhaps they should call theirs an American Christmas after all. Indeed not, argued the husband, "the Americans don't understand how to celebrate Christmas—that needs a Dane. . . . A Christmas tree can't make Christmas. Our dear fellow citizens lack the power to create true jubilation in the spirit—but we Danes had it, back home, and some of us have been able to preserve it over here— although it hasn't been easy, because many Americans look down on us for it. They think we're overgrown children."[113]

Thus immigrant authors agreed that the Old-World meaning of Christmas was lost in this different environment, whether the process was fast or slow. What had been shared by the whole community in Europe became a private matter in the new land, and after the breakdown of exclusive settlements individual families were incapable of maintaining the full complexity of the tradition. Nowhere were pressures toward Americanization more clearly demonstrated than here, where the immigrants were left apparently free to develop their Old-Country models as they saw fit, where they strove to recreate the celebration in full detail as they had known it before, and yet where different attitudes and practices in the surrounding society destroyed or transformed the intricate pattern including home, church, and neighborhood which typified the deeply meaningful holy days back home.

2. OTHER TRADITIONAL CELEBRATIONS

The other great folk festival of the Scandinavian year, for which there was no counterpart in America, disappeared almost without a ripple from immigrant life. Celebration of midsummer with bonfires, maypoles, and dancing was much older than Christianity in these northern countries, and several accounts of the Old Country pictured various ancient fetes still carried on to observe the longest day of the year. These had never become associated with the church. On the contrary, pietism had long frowned on the pagan sun worship, the superstition of witches abroad, the excesses of drinking and dancing connected with this holiday.

In contrast to innumerable Christmas stories and poems, lack of mention of midsummer celebrations indicated that Scandinavian immigrants did not miss it. As usual, only a Danish Grundtvigian minister wrote a song to be sung "By the Midsummer Blaze," lighted for old memory and new hope,

> to call us with our fathers' tongue
> to great deeds far from Denmark's shore.[114]

A single novel mentioned Swedish-American children dancing around a bedecked maypole in Michigan to celebrate midsummer Swedish style. Yet this book showed that something remained buried in adult hearts too, unconscious and unexpressed until a Swedish folk singer came to give a recital in the wintry mining town. As her last number, she led the audience in a *gångtralla* around the hall.

The neat rows of chairs had been melted into an impatient heap in the middle of the floor. Hats and umbrellas and coats sprawled, disowned and abandoned, all over the heap. Programs lay like magnified snowfall all about.

And around and around and around them, like a snake trying to catch up with its tail and swallow it, marched the Scandinavian Society. Light heads and dark heads, and bushy heads and bald heads. Iron ore and red rust and false-front houses with a saloon in every other one, forgotten. Years gone and miles erased. Marching into Midsummer Day's morning over the hills of home. With blue and yellow flowers in their greying hair.[115]

IX. American Holidays

Though they lost so much of their Christmas, and all of their midsummer festival, these immigrants had the opportunity to acquire American holidays. As a rule, Scandinavian adults were pictured as silent observers

289

at such Fourth of July parades and picnics as they attended. These were not mentioned in exclusive rural settlements, only in mixed and urban ones. and even here with by no means the same frequency as the comparable Norwegian and Danish national holidays. Poems in praise of the adopted land written to commemorate The Fourth of July were very common, but when it came to partaking in exclusively American demonstrations of solidarity and patriotism, the old folks usually stayed home.

The second generation, however, insisted on taking part. Six Danish boys in Nebraska were frantic because their stern father insisted they finish cutting and shocking the grain that always ripened around The Fourth, before they left for town. By the time they got there late in the afternoon most of the events were over, and they were dead tired anyway. But finally the Old-World authority of the father wore thin, and his sons absolutely refused to work on that important day.

It was almost ridiculous how important the Fourth of July had become in the life of the family. In 1912 it was still the most significant, purely American holiday in all the rural communities.

Perhaps this day appeals even more strongly to immigrant children than to native-born Americans. To the children of immigrants it symbolizes the spirit of the country, a spirit they all hunger for, yearn passionately to understand.[116]

One immigrant father in New York City took no interest in local affairs until he saw his own son in brilliant uniform as a drummer-boy marching in a Fourth of July parade. Shouting hurrah then, carried away with love and enthusiasm, the father realized the importance of the boy's American world, and began to take part in it too.[117]

American holidays other than The Fourth almost never appeared in the literature. The sole exception was Thanksgiving, which turned up occasionally in second-generation tales. When adopted, it was celebrated American style, with turkey, pumpkin pie, and all the trimmings, and merely provided the occasion for a family feast. Only once was there mention of Norwegian bread and goat's cheese added to the American menu.[118] Otherwise the birthdays of America's great men, Memorial and Labor Days, even Valentine's Day for the children passed unnoticed in the immigrant communities.

The only typical American fete mentioned often in immigrant stories was the custom of surprise parties. These turned up at housewarmings when the whole neighborhood collected unannounced to welcome a family in its new house, as birthday parties, for celebration of a silver wedding anniversary. The surprise element was not always appreciated. The wife honored at the silver wedding party spent most of the evening regretting that she was wearing an old dress.[119] However, this was a social form limited to the immediate neighborhood or circle of friends, not a holiday belonging to the larger social setting.

All first-generation characters showed plainly that they could not transfer attachment from Old-Country to New-World holidays. Through institutions like churches and patriotic societies they did their best to reestablish their own fetes: the Norwegian and Danish national days, the holy celebration of Easter and Christmas; while a few individuals carried on observance of particular enthusiasms, like a venerable Dane who invited the neighborhood to an old-fashioned harvest festival every year to keep up the ancient Danish custom.[120]

Their own form of Christmas meant more to them, however, than all the rest together, and they found nothing in America to compensate for the partial loss and ultimate transformation of this tradition. This deprivation they felt to be so painful that older immigrants often made a pilgrimage back to the Old Country at Christmas time, to recapture briefly the community spirit there. Once a year at railroad stations all over Sweden the natives began to hear a peculiar brand of Swedish: "All right," "Har du checket trunken?" and "Stoppa din ticket i pocket-boken, så du inte losar den." The children stared with wide and wondering eyes at these strange people in big fur coats, and their parents laughed and said, "Now the Swedish-Americans have come, now Christmas is here."[121]

As the color and festivity of Old-World customs drained away, once the struggle of their "dog years" was over characters began to complain about the dullness of their daily lives. As early as 1879, a small-town doctor in a novel pointed out,

The barren, neutral background of our lives in these western communities . . . makes our poor unpicturesque selves stand out unrelieved in all their native nakedness. It lends no kindly drapery of history or sentiment to round off glaring unplastic angularities and gather the uncouth, colorless details of our existence under a charitable semblance of beauty. Now, in the Old World it is very different; there the rich accessories of life, and its deep, warm historical setting, give even the poorest existence a picturesque or pathetic interest.[122]

Especially the second generation bemoaned how dull life was in their rural communities: "Here there is no spiritual or intellectual life. People have no interests; their thoughts never rise above cattle and pigs and corn."[123]

In cities the complaint was the same. A newcomer invited to girls' homes spent each evening rocking in a rocking chair, looking at photograph albums, and playing "Flinch," which the better people used to pass the time instead of cards. Fun he could hardly call it, but it was better than sitting in his boardinghouse room or hanging around saloons.[124] Even in Chicago, "Life was insipid and tasteless . . . in the Danish colony. People did their work, ate and slept, went to club meetings and parties. And that was all. One always met the same people

291

at every gathering. The same amusements and entertainments attracted the same audience, the same big wheels ruled in all the lodges and clubs, the same names graced the columns of the Danish newspapers. One knew it all by heart. There was no rising and falling rhythm in existence, no growth downward in depth or upward toward the heights; there was no color in life."[125]

Repetition of this complaint through a half-century of the immigrant literature strikingly corroborated Sinclair Lewis's indictment of midwestern life in *Main Street*. The idealistic young wife who was defeated in every effort to introduce culture into Gopher Prairie saw the fate of Scandinavian immigrant traditions there. At a Norwegian Fair at the Lutheran church she had been enchanted by the replica of a Norwegian farm kitchen, where pale women in bright costumes served *rømmegrøt* and *lefse*. She had reveled in the mild foreignness of the exotic novelty.

But she saw these Scandinavian women zealously exchanging their spiced puddings and red jackets for fried pork chops and congealed white blouses, trading ancient Christmas hymns of the fjords for "She's My Jazzland Cutie," being Americanized into uniformity, and in less than a generation losing in the greyness whatever pleasant new customs they might have added to the life of the town. Their sons finished the process. In ready-made clothes and ready-made high-school phrases they sank into propriety, and the sound American customs had absorbed without one trace of pollution another alien invasion.[126]

Chapter Ten
The Divided Heart

I. Problems of a Dual Heritage

The immigrant authors' theories of cultural adjustment were defined and discussed in an earlier chapter (Four); it remains to be considered how they embodied these theories in problems and conflicts in concrete characters' lives. This fiction has preserved much of the complex web of interpersonal relations otherwise lost to history: the individual in continuous reaction to social pressure of past, present, and future.

The attitudes which Scandinavian immigrant characters held toward their European background were shown ranging over a wide spectrum from pride to shame. The most important single factor in determining the individual's viewpoint was the opinions of the people around him. The pressure from native Americans was usually against anything brought from the Old World, but their influence varied in kind and intensity and could be effectively resisted when the immigrant colony was large and compact enough to shield its members from outside stresses. Sometimes even a single personality was strong enough to withstand American pressures. Usually one who showed such self-sufficiency had assimilated a significant portion of the formal culture of his homeland, but occasionally the ultraconservatism of a strong but uneducated character provided the basis for lifelong opposition to American influences.

1. EXTREMES OF REJECTION

A few characters of this type rejected their dual heritage and tried to live by the Old-World part alone. Although they partook in economic activity in the United States, they held themselves apart from other aspects of its life and lived as much as possible within the confines of their own group. Within this minority a handful were pictured maintaining their families in Europe and preserving all their emotive ties there. These either returned each winter with their year's savings or retired there with a hard-earned fortune. One Norwegian gardener who quit a good job to go back home was accused by a fellow immigrant of ingratitude toward the country which had received him; but he pointed out he had given full value in labor for every dollar he got. "The country had use for me and still can use many more, and I gladly give America credit for being a good employer to us all . . . every just and honorable worker will respect and honor a good boss, stand by his side through thick and thin, even die for him if necessary; but little Norway is our mother, and a child's love for his wonderful old mother stands first in his heart."[1]

Others who settled to stay in the Promised Land nevertheless tried to continue to live as Europeans. The prototype of such characters was Rølvaag's Beret Holm. As a middle-aged widow on her Dakota farm, she continued to speak her dialect, held social intercourse only with Norwegian neighbors, went almost nowhere but to church. Rejecting the political and materialistic interests which concerned her fellows, she lived only for her children, her work, and her God. She insisted that her family speak Norwegian, and opposed the new minister bitterly when he advocated English as the language of the future. But gradually the neighborhood, her closest friends, her own children drifted away from her into American interests. Time after time she realized that no one else shared her views. Here a whole race was disappearing without a trace, wandering away from itself, and nobody realized it! When she tried to talk about it, fellow-immigrants only laughed at her; finally she forced herself to stay silent. She came to feel herself a stranger among her own people.[2] Three of her four children left home to escape her, and she had to accept an Irish Catholic daughter-in-law to hold the last son. Her determined strength could resist Americanization for herself, but not for her children.

This total rejection of American culture was attempted by only a small minority in the literature. Many more characters went to the other extreme and disowned the European part of their heritage in an attempt to become wholly American. Only in English-language stories did they sometimes succeed. One Norwegian heroine landing from a river steamer in Minnesota heard her party jeered at as "Greenhorns!" "She was to hear the word often in the next few years, but it never stabbed her as it did some of the newcomers. It acted more as a spur to make greater efforts to become more American." Therefore she refused to remain with relatives in a Norwegian settlement, and after marriage pushed both her husband and her children into American ways as fast as she could discover them. "They were soon well known in the Scandinavian-American group, but Nicholina was not satisfied to stay there. 'We are Americans now," she said, 'we must be with Americans.' She encouraged the children in American contacts."[3] When her sons came home torn and bloody after fights with boys who called them white-headed Swedes, she bound up their wounds and sent them forth to combat again. Needless to say, her family won unbelievably rapid success and acceptance in Minneapolis.

Such accounts of facile assimilation were penned only by second-generation writers, however. No one who had lived through the process himself thus underestimated its difficulties.

2. ATTEMPTS AT RECONCILIATION

The majority of authors opposed both these extremes of rejection as neither feasible nor desirable. They showed all first- and many second-generation characters aware that their dual heritage made them indelibly different from native-born Americans in some respects. These differences were pictured as many or few, essential or trivial, embraced or regretted, all according to the writers' attitude toward the immigrant lot.

Many authors boasted of their double roots. One poet pictured Uncle Sam looking over his shoulder a bit disdainfully at immigrants, the same way people in Sweden looked down their noses at emigrants; but as a hyphenated citizen he was clearly better than any single nationality because "You are ONE, but—I am TWO!"[4] A Danish-American minister admitted that all was not perfect in either the Old World or the New, but both had much to praise and love. Like many another writer he pictured the Danish and American national banners flying side by side on the Fourth of July.

> Which flag is the lovelier
> no one for sure can say;
> both have to deeds of greatness
> waving shown the way . . .
> Danish cross, and stars and stripes,
> both beloved the same,
> remind us where we built our home
> and from whence we came.[5]

Several authors expressed gratitude to the United States for letting them cultivate their memories of the Old Country in peace. A Danish-American poem dated 1895 praised America as beloved in immigrant hearts because "you never demand that we forget or despise our own old mother!" The great, rich nation could only benefit when its adopted citizens honored their forefathers' home.[6] Danish characters from Schleswig especially appreciated their freedom in the New World. All six sons of a Danish family there had emigrated to escape military service under the German Kaiser. The old father would not leave his home to follow them, but after his death the aged mother came to a Danish community in Iowa. Unpacking her Danish flag, she told how they were forbidden to fly it back home; but now she could fly it in Iowa without fear! American guests heard her story with tears in their eyes.

"As long as those who come over here to us from Europe keep such faithful hearts," they said, "our land is in no danger. Those who preserve such love for their people

295

and fatherland, their language and memories, all symbolized in their flag, will also be true to the land they have voluntarily chosen as their home."[7]

II. American Pressures Against the European Heritage

1. INFORMAL SOCIAL SANCTIONS

Very few American characters shared this attitude, however. Usually they exercised all kinds of informal sanctions against anything or anyone not American. Physical outrage against immigrants appeared in a few stories, in the form of fights between ethnic gangs of workingmen or among children; but usually the sanctions of the native group, although involving threats, stopped short of violence. At a Fourth of July picnic a Norwegian boy was so furious at a speech on how America must shut her doors against the immigrant hordes from Europe that he remained seated when the national anthem was played. Someone kicked the back of his chair to force him up, and people nearby laughed at him. One fellow cursed and said, "That's right, give it to those rotten foreigners who think they are just as good as we are.' "[8]

Over and over, in stories from every period and setting, the immigrant authors recorded this dominant attitude among their hosts. A brave Swede who had lost a leg in the Civil War finally found a lonely job as lighthouse keeper on Lake Michigan. All in the rural community hated and slandered him as a "dirty foreigner." In a wild adventure one stormy night he discovered the lamp had been put out, and when he risked his life to relight it, two men lying in wait jumped him. He fell unconscious after fighting them off, and later was accused of neglect of duty. Even after he had finally been cleared and the truth made known, he never was liked in his rural community because he was a "foreigner."[9]

A cultured and successful young Swedish couple in Chicago met the same prejudice. They had settled there determined to associate only with Americans, in order to grow like them as fast as possible. "But our young couple soon had the same experience as all others, that the points of social contact between the native-born and the immigrants are too few and too weak to serve such a purpose." The Swedes discovered that social life in Chicago was superficial and unsatisfactory, lacking any kind of common memory or similar temperament on which to build shared enterprise or atmosphere. "The Swedish-American's inner life is a life of memory in this respect, the native's is a life of hope. When the Swede has toiled through a week in the struggle for his bread, he finds refreshment in meeting on Sunday with his countrymen to reminisce in his own language about how it was back in Sweden . . . whereas the native's thoughts revolve around things as they are here or should be . . . the native-born of nearly every class look down superciliously on all foreigners."[10] Even children of immigrants often adopted this attitude.

The Högden boys were sure of themselves and would not stand to be contradicted, especially by a newcomer; for one who had not been born and brought up in the United States was of course, according to the usual American view, nothing but an ignorant greenhorn. . . . It was like part of their nature, to despise everything which was not American. Even their own parents were less worthy because they had not been born in the States.[11]

The experience of a Norwegian businessman in a small Dakota town epitomized that of the entire immigrant group. "The comparatively few Americans he had known . . . had, he thought, given him all too plainly to understand that they . . . believed themselves to be better people than the immigrants and their American-born children. Yet the children of the immigrants made every effort to be completely American. "If young people of Norwegian background were asked what their nationality was, they replied at once—not without irritation at such a question—that naturally they were Americans. What else could they be? But if a Yankee was asked what these immigrant children were, he always answered without hesitation that they were 'foreigners'—'Norwegians.' Often one heard more or less uneducated Americans use expressions like 'half civilized foreigners' or 'dirty Norwegians' in reference to American-born children of Norwegian immigrants up to the second and third generation. At the same time Americans insisted that it was the inviolable duty of all—also immigrants—to *feel* like Americans, and it was almost a crime to live in America with the awareness that one did not feel thus. While everyone had the duty to be American, in other words, still immigrants did not really have the right to be. It was a duty, but not a right."[12]

Yankees found ridicule the most effective means of imposing their definition of the situation on this ethnic group. In story after story immigrant characters found their names, their ways, their language laughed at in contemptuous derision. Danish boys on their first day at school in Nebraska were teased and then hit by Yankee sons. One Dane returned the blow of a bigger boy and was winning the fight when the others all piled on him. " 'Hit him, Jim,' 'Hit the bastard.' 'He's a damn Dane.' " Then they told the teacher the new boy had started it. Later in the class the teacher asked if anyone knew a poem to recite. No one did. Thinking to save the day, the smallest Danish boy announced he knew one and began to recite it—in Danish. The whole school burst into laughter. After the teacher had quieted them, she told Hans gently that he must not talk in a foreign language. "He had learned his first lesson, and that was that the language he used at home when he spoke

297

to his mother, when he said all the things he liked best to say—the language he loved to speak was something to be laughed at in this Nebraska school. Even his brothers seemed ashamed to think that he did not know better than to recite that poem."[13]

2. THE PUBLIC SCHOOL

The public school was the only institution through which American society exercised direct cultural pressure on the immigrant group at all periods. The authors agreed that this was the most important Americanizing influence in both urban and rural settings, for the imprint it made on the malleable young they carried back into their homes, where it affected their parents.

Yankee pedagogues on every level were pictured as fully aware of the importance of their mission. The head of a teachers' college near Chicago examined a Danish applicant for admission about her patriotism. "Here in America more than in any other country it is essential that all our schools are permeated by a patriotic spirit. The teachers we train must not only be dominated by that spirit . . . but also they should be able to awaken their pupils to realization that on their will rests the future of America, whether it shall become rich and happy as a nation. I won't inquire whether you are Americanized—that word is misused all too often—but whether you have begun to feel and appreciate our national pride and to understand it, understand our history and our unique development. Is this a calling for you, or only a job?"[14]

One American schoolmarm after another was portrayed as inspired in her holy vocation. Miss Clarabelle Mahon, for instance, queen of a one-room country school in Dakota, felt her heart beat faster as she prepared notes for the morrow's lesson in American history; for "the history of her fatherland was the dearest subject she knew—and no place she felt her apostle's call so strongly as out here at Spring Creek, where she had been put in charge of all these immigrant children from many foreign lands . . . Here all that was foreign and heterogeneous must be kneaded together to a single spirit which saw only the greatest; to a single heart which beat in goodness. These foreign children were the clay, she the potter, American history the pattern she must shape and form after. Miss Clarabelle Mahon used the history of her country as a pietist uses Bible stories." Often when the biggest children had their history lesson, she grew so moved and excited that she directed the whole school to listen while she expanded on the text, told about Lincoln's poverty-stricken boyhood or Washington and the hatchet. As the closing ceremony each day she had one of the big pupils recite the Declaration of

Independence or the Gettysburg Address from memory, and then led them all in singing "America."

Now we are finished for today. We have learned much that is good and useful in these few hours, things which should help us to become great men and women. Knowledge is the only weapon we have against ignorance and the old inherited customs brought here from foreign countries. Now we shall end our day by recalling how well off we are, we who have been given citizenship in this blessed home of freedom! . . . Charley Doheny, recite the Declaration of Independence for us . . . all must listen closely to Charley, his pronunciation is so good. It's sad how some of you use our country's language! One would think you came over yesterday![15]

III. Immigrant Reaction to American Pressure

1. OPPOSITION

The struggle between Old- and New-World cultural influences, between first and second generations, between school and home, took clearest form in the matter of language. Another Dakota teacher had written in her best handwriting at the top of the blackboard: "This is an American school; in both work and play we speak only English!"[16] Some of the children still talked Norwegian together on the playground, but many when they came home continued to use the English they had thought in all day, in spite of parental objections.

In book after book parents blamed the public school for luring their children away. The authors often showed the continuous steps of the process in the children's changing language. In a Danish-American home, for instance, the children had all naturally spoken Danish until they started school, for they heard nothing else. But as they grew older they used English more and more, first among themselves but finally even answering in English when addressed in Danish. The mother scolded them time after time, but they made remarks to each other about her in English. Unable to understand what they were saying, she feared the worst. "And she was too poorly educated to be able to assert her maternal influence everywhere against everything alien which was pulling them away. Sometimes she could win them, but other times she drove them further off, and then she could only weep alone."[17]

a. Parental efforts to hold their children

Rølvaag drew with a master's hand the day-by-day struggles between the determination of a strong Norwegian mother to implant her heritage and language in her children and their equally obstinate resistance. The trouble began to grow acute when the youngest started school. As soon as supper was over, the children settled at the kitchen table with their school books and disappeared into a world where the mother could not follow. Sometimes she tried to draw them back with questions: "What were they doing now? What was the lesson about?—no, talk Norwegian now! . . . Either they didn't hear her, or they came with answers which angered her because they were so dumb—they could at least have listened to what she asked! If the youngest two had to explain something, they stammered and fumbled with words, and soon went over to English, but then they could talk well enough." The mother forced them to study a Norwegian ABC book too, but she "saw clearly that hidden powers were taking her children away from her. And strangely enough—they drew the youngest first. Permann and Anna Marie talked English together secretly at every opportunity. Likewise the older boys, when she wasn't working with them. Never anything but English when guests their own age came to the farm. And never did she hear them mention anything that belonged to them and their own kind. . . . Sometimes when she sat and listened to the children, she questioned whether she could really be their mother."[18]

One night the youngest boy read aloud a story from his school book to his sister. She was not interested, remembering it from the year before; so he was stimulated to read with the greatest enthusiasm and feeling. His mother also listened, and when he had finished asked him to come read an article from her Norwegian newspaper for her. The boy came reluctantly after delaying as long as he dared, and then read haltingly, mispronouncing every other word, his voice thick with aversion and tears. The mother finally lost her temper—the wretch *could* read Norwegian—shook him violently and boxed his ears. The older children all showed their disapproval by abruptly leaving the room; one son stopped long enough to say that if this continued, he and the others had better move to the barn. Go ahead! retorted his mother angrily. If things go on this way, we soon won't be able to tell the difference between people and animals![19] Over and over throughout the novel she repeated that it must be against the laws of God and nature for Norwegians to try to talk English. It was as though a sparrow should try to sing like a meadowlark, or a cow grunt like a pig. "The horses grazed in the same pasture as the cows, but they didn't begin to moo for that!"[20]

Other parents who took the opposite course and tried to follow their children into the new life often met with disaster. A Danish mother planned an American-style birthday for her son, so that he could invite American boys from his class whom he never saw outside school. She mastered every catastrophe that arose during the preparations, but after the guests had arrived she lost control. Naturally she gave instructions on how to freeze the ice cream in the only language she knew—Danish.

"Can't your mother talk anything but that foreign language?" said one of the boys to Hans.

Hans blushed feeling the insult that was implied and answered, "Sure she can." "Then why doesn't she?"

"Because she doesn't want to."

"Oh, I bet that's a lie," said another.

"Sure it's a lie," said a third. "My dad says none of these people can talk American, and that they don't want to."

"Who told him so much?" said David now coming into the argument and thoroughly angry. "You tell your dad that he's a damn liar."

"What? My dad a liar? Well, I can tell you something else too, and that is that your dad can't vote. That he ain't even an American. He's just a damn foreigner, that's what he is."

A fist-fight raged until the Danish mother came to stop it. She scolded her sons in Danish, confirming the original accusation. Half the guests left in a huff, and the others as soon as they had downed the mushy ice cream. The failure of the party hurt the mother more than the sons. "She was like the fledgling bird that falls when it tries to fly too soon. For a brief time she had seen herself as emerging from the narrow confines of her purely Danish culture into the new life of America. She had almost made herself believe that she could speak English and through new contacts forget the eternal ache in her heart which drew her back to the Old Country."[21] But because she was never able to learn much English, and Danes in the area were too few to form their own community, she remained in lonely isolation all her life. One by one, she lost all her sons, too, as they left their father's Nebraska farm and struck out on their own, American style.

b. *Renewed interest in the European heritage*

Still other immigrants were so indignant at their rejection by Yankees that they retreated into *norskdom* or *svenskhet*. A young immigrant who regretted the misfortune of his Norwegian birth aspired to rectify it by becoming American as soon as possible. He learned Yankee business ways fast enough, and became a successful banker who practically owned his town; but no native ever invited him home. "Nevertheless Jonas gradually came to meet a good many Yankees in both business and politics, and the better he got to know them, the more his 'Norwegianness' grew. With their stupid and distorted prejudices against immigrants and foreigners and all other nations they involuntarily goaded him into defending the self-evident right of his racial feeling."[22] In the case of the local Norwegian school, for instance, Jonas had first thought it enough with one month of instruction each summer. Then a new minister had allowed confirmation training in English. Jonas soon sent him packing, and put through two months' summer religion school in

301

Norwegian. Later a bill was introduced in the state legislature to limit private and congregational rights in such matters. This never passed, but it aroused much discussion in the immigrant communities; to express his view, Jonas lengthened the summer sessions of the Norwegian church school to three months. In irritation at American exclusiveness, he founded several Norwegian societies and brought many lecturers and concert artists on tour from the homeland to give programs for the local immigrant group.

Several stories and poems also recorded how the experience of being a stranger in a new environment awakened love of the abandoned homeland in many hearts. A Danish boy whose studies had been broken off by hard times hated working in his father's store in a little town on the island of Fyn. In spite of his mother's opposition he accepted the offer of an uncle in Kansas to lend him money for a ticket over. With the uncle's help he settled in a small town of fellow immigrants, who had built a Danish church and a school where he could complete his education. In time he married and became a civic leader, working especially for the preservation of *danskhed*. As his mother wrote, "It is strange, but I think it turned out that you had to move clear to Kansas to learn to love Fyn! You found Fyn in Kansas."[23] In Chicago an old Swede took farewell of a young engineer going home to Sweden. The young man was glad to be going back to his own world, but the older character told how he lived in two. One world was his factory job, dull and mechanical but paying well; the other was his apartment, full of furniture, books and pictures he had imported from Sweden. It looked like back home! He did not ask for sympathy. "Believe me, it was out here I created my two worlds, before I didn't have any."[24]

> America! How did you teach me thus
> to love so deep and true—my fatherland?[25]

2. ACCOMMODATION

Fiction which followed the development of a family or community through many years, however, usually recorded the gradual Americanization of the characters and their progressive acceptance into the native group. "To help the good work along, the Swedes were less and less a peculiar people as the years went by. The old grandfathers and grandmothers never had the heart to give up their accustomed ways. . . . But the younger generation were willing and even eager to fall into step, if for no other reason than it was easier marching that way. . . . In the progress toward conformity the children led the way . . . where the elders had been proud of their nationality, the youngsters were actually ashamed of being Swedes. They wanted to be thought Yankees—to act and look like Yankees was their constant study. . . . The public school was a powerful agency of conciliation, though there was no conscious effort to make it so. The children of the two races worked together at their books and played together at their games and so grew up together, and there was no preserving any permanent barrier between them."[26] A most potent influence working for peace among these neighbors was a growing sense of their common trials. All were farmers, and all suffered alike in the 1880s from the grasshopper plague, the drought, terribly deep snows that one year did not melt until June, and then a killing frost in August. In the lean years of short crops and low prices the Farmers' Alliance grew strong in Minnesota, and in its ranks Swedes and Yankees marched shoulder to shoulder.

a. Americanization of names

The price of acceptance was abandonment of the Old-World heritage. The majority of characters were pictured doing this naturally, almost unconsciously, as soon as they realized that their differentness made them conspicuous. In the matter of their names, for example, stories of every period showed Scandinavians simplifying the spelling and pronunciation or translating the meaning of their names in response to Yankee pressure.

Many immigrants had lacked a permanent surname back home, where in rural districts the custom until the latter part of the nineteenth century remained to identify an individual by adding to his baptismal name his father's appellation (with -son or -datter) and the name of his home. When American conditions required that immigrants take a permanent designation for the family, they had thus several possibilities from which to choose. Some made the decision quite casually. A wealthy Norwegian farmer cleaned up a tramp who had come begging and took him to a neighbor to apply for a job. In order to introduce him, the farmer asked the name of the farm in the Old Country from which the younger man had come. " 'Oh, we didn't have a farm; we were poor.' 'Well, I suppose you use your father's name then?' 'Yes, you can call me Sven Larsen.' "[27] Sometimes characters who Anglicized their names for use in relation to the American environment continued to use their Scandinavian appellations among their countrymen. One comic character went under the Norwegian name of Lars Svingen and the American one of Lewis Johnson at the same time, causing endless confusion.[28]

In this field like many others the behavioral choice made by characters revealed their attitudes toward their double heritage. Those who tried to maintain their Old-World roots insisted on keeping their Scandinavian given and family names, while those who wished to become Americanized as rapidly as possible tended to adopt English names for themselves and their children. Baptizing a baby thus became symbolic of worldly interests as well as Christian faith.

Beret Holm, most conservative of preservationists, took well-founded offense when her first grandson was christened Henry Percival.

"Percival? What was that? What was the meaning of it? It certainly wasn't a human name? Who could it be after?"

"Can't you understand that it's after Dad?" said Peder in irritation. [His father's name had been Per.]

"After Dad? What nonsense! Your brother has at least sense enough not to make fun of the dead. . . . I can't understand what Hans means with putting such a name on a Norwegian boy." . . .

She never spoke the name again. Peder and his sister often went to visit their brother, but Beret stayed home. . . . When they came back, she asked them in detail how everything was over there, and especially about her grandson, but she never mentioned his name.[29]

The name of Holm, which this family had adopted in Dakota,[30] although genuinely Norwegian was simple enough so that the second generation found no cause to change it; but innumerable characters in other stories modified their old or took new family names in response to American pressure. One novelist disclosed in a classroom scene his estimate of the relative number of such assimilationists as against preservationists. A schoolmaster recently arrived from Norway was horrified when he called roll for the first time to discover that only two children still had their good old Norwegian surnames; the other sixteen had acquired what he called "madhouse names."[31] On the other hand, a second-generation teacher who accepted a post in an isolated Norwegian-American town found that the principal was delighted because she knew Norwegian. At last a teacher who could pronounce correctly the children's Old-World names![32]

Many were the trials of immigrant children whose native-born teachers and playmates distorted their Scandinavian names; no Yankee was ever pictured trying to learn one correctly. A Norwegian-American girl hated what she had been baptized: Knutiane. Her teacher could not pronounce either the k before the n or the final e. It came out like "Nutian," which the other children corrupted to "Nutty Ann." The nickname stuck until a new teacher started calling her Nellie.[33] In another novel a Norwegian boy named Ole was rechristened William by the schoolteacher. His parents and grandparents complained, but a Norwegian neighbor who had been in America longer suggested the compromise of keeping both names. " 'Ole' will remind him of his old homeland and 'Willie' will be his new name in the new country."[34] But William was to be his first

304

name; Ole, which Americans could not pronounce correctly, was relegated to second place.

When parents refused to accept this process by which Americans substituted an English given name for the original one, the children often carried out the change themselves after they had grown up. A second-generation son who had left the farm for a city job wrote his father that he had given up his name of Søren "so these American fellows won't have anything to laugh at."[35]

b. *Marriage outside the ethnic group*

The drive of young people to leave their ethnic group and identify themselves with the larger society also appeared in their choice of married partner. In the Old Country the father's will had been law in this matter, and lovers forbidden to marry usually had to emigrate to get their way. Elopement within the country was difficult where banns had to be published three consecutive Sundays before the wedding in the church where it was to take place. In America, however, anybody could take out a marriage license in secret and be married by a justice of the peace at a few minutes' notice. The dowry also lost its importance in a society where money was easily earned and a couple could set up housekeeping on credit. Where the legal, economic, and social structure of the community did not support parental authority, it was reduced to dependence on whatever sense of duty had been instilled in the children; and when this ran counter to their affections, it often failed.

Young characters who came to America without their parents of course felt no conflict of authority. They were free to choose whom they pleased, and the authors often satirized their headlong rush to marry outside their group. Clearly most immigrants considered such a marriage a short-cut to full acceptance by the English-speaking society.

Many writers, however, devised plots which brought a character to grief, in punishment for the desertion of his group. In a typical tale, a poor peasant girl in Sweden found her love for the son of a rich churchwarden returned, but his upper-class father forbade the union. In chagrin the girl emigrated, found an excellent job as chambermaid in the home of a millionaire, and let her sweetheart's letters go unanswered longer each time. When he finally came to Chicago to marry her, she found him beneath her—the greenhorn! She wanted to marry a Yankee, or at least an Irishman. She did, but after spending all her savings the Irish husband deserted her with a baby.[36] In another short story, two Norwegian girls who had been good friends during the early years of their immigrant experience found that "The friendship cooled a bit when Ellen Strand received the honor of becoming Mrs. Howard Jones and was lifted thereby out of the Scandinavian group into the Simon-pure

305

American class, while Julia was stuck in her group after marrying the quiet Norskie Lars Wold."[37] Mrs. Jones managed to keep her husband, but her son turned out badly compared to the model daughter of the Wolds.

Choice of married partner by members of the second generation was a more controversial matter because it involved parental opinions too. In exclusive communities characters escaped this problem like so many others because only young people of the same ethnic background were present to be chosen; but most stories showed Scandinavian-American children developing relationships with Yankee and other immigrant nationalities as they grew up. When older children found their social life and amusement outside the home, parents lost control over their choice of friends, and many a romance budded and bloomed which the older generation found out about too late. A Swedish-American father tried to comfort his wife when their last son declared his intention to marry an Irish Catholic. "If he's bound to have her, then we can't do a thing to it. You see how it is. They do just as they please nowadays, the young ones, anyhow, and don't care at all for what we say in the matter."[38]

Preservationist authors regularly pictured marriage outside of the group as wrong because it involved rejection of both the immigrant parents and their heritage. It destroyed forever the Old-World continuity of the clan. The youngest daughter of elderly Norwegian pioneers married a Yankee boy, whose family had a bad name for sharp business practices.

Only to her husband would Ragnhild admit what this cost her. It wasn't only that Selma slipped out of her life to a degree that no other marriage would have caused; but somehow she also took her brother with her. He was drawn more and more to life outside his own group, and took every opportunity to cultivate the acquaintanceship of the Prices [his sister's in-laws]. Ragnhild Akre's children grew more and more away from her and left behind a void and bereavement for which there was no cure.

Several years after the daughter and her husband had moved away, she brought her two children back to visit their grandparents for the first time. The old people had longed for this event; but the children turned out not to know a word of Norwegian, and made sassy remarks to their mother about how fat the grandmother was, the queer old-fashioned furniture in the house, and so on. After the guests had left, the grandparents agreed that the children were not worth much. "Poor little ones —they belonged to another world. Clever and lively, without a doubt, but—. And the two old people sat and looked at each other."[39]

Assimilationist authors, on the other hand, not only approved of "mixed" marriages but symbolized in them the immigrants' full acceptance into American society. In a second-generation novel in English,

306

a Norwegian son married the daughter of a neighboring Scotch family, to the delight of all the parents. Both grandfathers came to see the first baby when he was born. The Scot asked whether he was a Norwegian or a Scotchman. " 'Pa, he's neither,' replied Helen, 'he's an American.' "[40]

First-generation writers, however, saw that the problem was usually not so easily solved as this. Even with the best will in the world, when immigrants could not communicate with their daughters- or sons-in-law in a language which both commanded, their relationship suffered. In a Danish-American novel, a dying mother and her Americanized children, all married to non-Danes, were brought together by a good character, who recognized the power of the forces which had alienated them. "I can understand that when the language of your homes is English, while that of the old folks is Danish, it makes your relationship difficult. And I can also understand that it's not easy for you to share your lives with your parents when you look on so many important matters from widely different points of view."[41] The children blamed their parents for having brought them to America if they wanted to keep the family Danish. Sadly the old father accepted responsibility for this unforeseen consequence of migration. But the good character, while agreeing that such "mixed" marriages were unavoidable in the New World, argued that they did not necessarily have to sunder hearts. All agreed, and the novel ended with the reunion of the family in the American tradition of personal freedom and individual choice for its members.

All writers recognized that the amalgamation of the melting pot worked most effectively and rapidly through intermarriage. Every such departure from the immigrant group hastened its final dissolution, because the language of such mixed families was always English and the culture American. Only once in all the fiction did a Yankee wife go to the trouble of learning her husband's Norwegian; he already knew English, but the author wanted to contrast her pride in learning a European tongue with the shame of the other Norwegian characters over knowing something they wanted to forget.[42] A third- or fourth-generation descendant might be proud of a Swedish grandmother or a Norwegian great-grandfather, but by then the old folks were dead. For them the marriage of their offspring outside their group was normally pictured as widening the already tragic gulf between generations, except when the first generation aspired to full Americanization themselves. Then they welcomed a "mixed" marriage as public proof of the completion of the process in their children.

c. *Incomplete but tolerable assimilation*

Few first-generation characters ceased to define themselves as different from other Americans to some extent, but the literature showed that many gave up their Old-World ways in natural imitation of the people around them to a point where they achieved tolerable adaptation to their surroundings. Their assimilation was incomplete but passable. The process developed most rapidly and successfully when single immigrant families settled by themselves in town or city settings. "Little by little, the foreignness had disappeared almost entirely from our family life. Only on special occasions did Mama make *lutefisk* or *fladbrod* [sic], and she and Papa seldom spoke Norwegian any more. They had learned to play whist, and went often to neighborhood card parties or to shows."[43] A man and wife who were the only Danes in a little town after thirty years had come to feel at home there.

I also saw clearly how Mama became more and more Americanized in the early years of our marriage. I can remember how my own mother home in Denmark always used to pull off my father's boots when he came home in the evening, but if Mama ever did anything like that for me, she quit long ago. . . . There were so many things which clearly showed me the big difference between my wife here in this country and the women I could remember from my childhood in Denmark.[44]

IV. World War I and 100-Percentism

But then came the war. World War I cast its shadow over this Dane's prairie town too, and its patriotic citizens were convinced that the only thing which could save the country was the total Americanization of the foreign-born. A movement led by the dentist's wife founded an Americanization Committee, which printed leaflets and held meetings in the Odd Fellows Hall. What the Danes found most difficult was the injunction to speak English at home as well as in public. Nobly striving to comply, man and wife sat on the porch every day before dinner each with a book in his lap. Mama read aloud in a pinched, nasal voice that sounded like an ancient phonograph record:

"See de man?" read Mama.
"Yes, I see de man," I answered out of the book.
"Is de man hongri? . . . De supper is reddi aalretti. Der is homemade bread, and from de little garden der is some lettusch. From de fish store der is some pickerel,— and—o, look—der is de sweet and lovely corn syrup!" Here Mama shut her book with a bang and fell into her natural tone of voice as she said in Danish, "So, Peter, now you can come in and eat."

Of course they were forbidden to talk Danish over the telephone. When they forgot a couple of times, the Telephone Office cut them off. So Mama had to be inventive indeed when she called her husband at work. Once she telephoned to ask him to buy a spice at the grocery for a sausage she was making. "I wasn't so thick-headed that I couldn't understand what she meant when she talked about 'rolled sausage,' but what the spice was she needed, I couldn't get. First she said 'allhand,' and then 'tenfingers,' but not until I got home did I realize she meant 'allspice' or 'allehaande.' It was a shame, because she had to make something else out of the meat, and I'm wild about *rundpølse*.'[45]

There were also other foreigners in town—a couple of Bohemian families, an Italian shoemaker, a large Polish family, and an Irishman; but he refused to attend any of the meetings, although he spoke worse English than anybody. The dentist's wife gathered the housewives for instruction on how to keep house in American style. The Danish husband manfully downed all the pie and wheat bread which his wife learned to bake, until his stomach went on strike. Now that the war was over, he could confess they had hoarded rye flour to make their own kind of bread in secret.

He did learn to wear American-style suits, though he felt silly decked out in all the buttons and buckles and outside pockets, and the affectation of a belt instead of suspenders. Bit by bit they exchanged their comfortable old furniture for American: a Persian rug which cost $8, two Japanese vases to stand on the piano. A new wooden bed replaced their iron one, but Mr. Ravn kicked off the foot of it during a Sunday after-dinner nap. The dentist's wife complained that it was a "foreign habit" to rest after a meal, anyway. She turned up at any time of day to see how they were doing, and if their Danish-American newspaper was in sight she glared fit to burn a hole through it. Mr. Ravn told her he had a rich uncle in the Old Country who was very sick, and he was only reading the death notices.

The local Women's Club organized a competition to find which foreign-born citizen was the best language student, and Mama won first prize—a picture of General Pershing. Only she won not in English but in French, which she had learned as a maid in a baron's mansion back home. Inflated by her success, she began to preach about the rights of an American woman. *She* should manage the household finances and give her husband a weekly allowance, which didn't need to be much, either, since the local saloon had closed and smoking was harmful. Concluding that Americanization had gone far enough in his town, Mr. Ravn talked the local Congressman into getting a Washington appointment for that sterling citizen, the town dentist. All his wife's dear foreigners saw her off on the train with flowers and shouts of hurrah; and the Danes could go home to drink a Danish cup of afternoon coffee in peace.

V. The Pain of a Divided Heart

The mild Danish humor of this satire contrasted with Norwegian-American treatment of the patriotic hysteria directed against foreign-born citizens during World War I. Norwegian writers took the matter with utmost seriousness. Some were so outraged by 100-percentism that they still spluttered with righteous indignation in books published six or eight years after the end of the war. Others were deeply saddened by the trials which native American bigotry and persecution brought into immigrant lives, quite apart from the tragedy of those who lost their sons. All realized that the war destroyed a great deal of their double heritage in the worst possible way.

1. THE WAR GENERATION: HYPHENATED AMERICANS

A number of Norwegian-American fictional heroes were pacifists of long standing, and suffered serious moral conflict after President Wilson declared war on Germany. In an argument on the street of a Dakota town one Norwegian farmer defended Senators La Follette and Grönna for daring to vote against America's entry into the war. He had studied the American Declaration of Independence and Constitution long before he emigrated, and agreed with George Washington's warning never to get involved in European wars.

It will cost us many human lives and millions of dollars before we get out of this war. It is the munition makers and great capitalists who are now waving the Stars and Stripes and calling us immigrants hyphenated Americans . . . they have worked up a veritable hysteria for 100-percent Americanism and contempt and suspicion against us who know two or more languages, and were born on the other side of the ocean. . . I have nothing to say in favor of Kaiser Wilhelm . . . but that my only son has been drafted to fight the *German people,* that wounds my very heart.[46]

Haled into court and accused of treason for this public statement, the farmer proved that he had never agitated against the war effort, that he had bought thousands of dollars' worth of Liberty Bonds and given hundreds to the Red Cross. "When I received my citizenship, I gave my oath that I would support the Constitution and the government, and this oath I have kept and will keep as long as I live"—even if the government made a mistake. But he would not retract his opposition to military force used by any nation, and although he disapproved of the German war power, he refused to consider the German people his enemies. This character was found not guilty and set free.

The hero of another novel was not so fortunate. Although born in America, he was so proud of his *norskdom* that he took the unheard-of step of changing the Americanized name his father had given him, Lewis Olson, back to its original Norwegian form of Lars Holte. He also renewed his ties to his father's homeland by marrying a girl recently arrived from there. As the war grew worse in Europe, he watched war hysteria develop among native Americans. The whole town followed the filibuster when Senators LaFollette and Grönna prevented voting on Wilson's war declaration until the Senate adjourned. But a special session was called immediately. The Norwegians and Germans in town supported the minority struggle for peace, while the native Yankees and a few bad Norwegian characters argued for war.

When war was finally declared, the Yankees saw their chance to attack the German and Norwegian groups in the area, whose power in local affairs had grown with their economic success. Condemning the lukewarm patriotism of the immigrants, they tried all kinds of tactics to whip up war enthusiasm. A big ceremony was planned at the raising of a town flagpole, but few decent citizens showed up. The town bullies who were out in force ran wild; in fear of them, a lot of weak people joined the rush to demonstrate their 100-percentism, including a few bad Norwegians. The local Lutheran minister was one of these, and to further his English-language ambitions forced through a congregational resolution that henceforth all services were to be in English. The old people who understood that language poorly were in effect turned out of the church they had built. Shortly afterwards the cars of people returning from a Norwegian Society picnic were attacked by a gang of toughs armed with yellow paint.

Official demands from the government poured in. Committees were set up for a dozen ends, all soliciting contributions, and the draft was organized. The hero Lars had decided he would go when called, but he would not volunteer because all war was unjust. Liberty Bond drives were the worst trial when all were threatened and forced to buy more than they could afford. Those without money had to borrow in order to buy bonds.

Lars, who had minded his lumber business, paid his assessments and contributions, and tried to keep clear of the rest, finally made a misstep one dark night. He happened on a gang of superpatriots engaged in stringing up an effigy of Senator Grönna, and rushed to its defense. Recognized, he was arrested the next day and put on trial for treasonable tendencies. He was so indignant and hurt at the charges that he refused to defend himself, and was condemned to three months in jail. When he came out he felt himself defiled forever, and took the advice which 100-percenters offered in other books too: if he didn't like America, he could leave. With his family he departed for Norway, where his wife's parents had a farm for her to take over. As the ship steamed east, a tornado visited the author's wrath on the wicked town of 100-percent.[47]

Most immigrant heroes, however managed to reconcile pacifism with patriotism by such reasoning as finally satisfied the conscience of a high-minded young Norwegian in Dakota. Suppose that a churl unlawfully attacked peaceful travelers on a public highway time after time; was it not the duty of all to remove him by force? Thus Germany had wrongfully attacked neutral ships on the high seas. America must join other peace-loving nations to stop such lawless activity.[48] By distinguishing between the noble purpose of the true American government and the ignoble 100-percent hysteria of superpatriots, he was able to support the one and oppose the other. He was not drafted because he was a farmer and a father, but he collected money for Liberty Bonds, served on the draft board, reported on the loyalty of the district to higher authorities—for he had refused to join the Farmers' Alliance, which opposed the war. Yet local patriots accused him of being a traitor because his family spoke Norwegian; they even threatened to tar and feather him.

The hero arranged a public hearing to clear himself from this slander, and incidentally to air the author's views on how strong interest in Norwegian culture could be reconciled with true American citizenship. His enemies testified that it must be treason to drink from the muddy wells of European history and literature, but the hero argued that a good citizen must be an honorable man first, and a man improved his self-respect through knowledge of his heritage. Through reading Norwegian history and literature he had gained interest in and insight into English and American history and literature too. In the event of war between Norway and the United States, he would of course fight for America; his first duty was to it. But he would be unhappy to fight against his relatives, as so many had felt in the Civil War. In conclusion he attacked the 100-percentism of the war years as false patriotism. Trying to force Americanization on the immigrants was imitating the archenemy Germany, which had violated human rights in the attempt to Germanize her subject peoples. In this wartime movement invaluable riches had been lost, dark intolerance had crushed the life values of special groups and robbed their people of the heritage which should have been their support and enrichment.[49]

In illustration of this charge, the author devised an incident in which a poison-pen letter was sent to an elderly Norwegian-American minister, who had toiled all his life for peace and the highest values of western culture. The letter accused him of remaining a foreigner in his intellectual life, even studying German theology! He had misused his position of leadership. "For instead of leading an ignorant and tradition-bound foreign group to the sparkling springs of American citizenship, you have worked to preserve old European ways of thought, ideals, folkways and customs—not to mention how you in all your activity had made use of a foreign language and thereby supported your people in their ignorance and kept them away from what could have freed them—the God-given English language. . . . This is treason against the country which has nourished and protected you."[50] The older members of the congregation rallied to their minister's defense, but the young people held their own meeting to pass a resolution against him, and the unhappy old man died of a heart attack while writing his resignation.

Rølvaag refused to blame the young for such an attitude toward their parents' heritage. In an essay published in 1922, he pointed out how the second generation were children of their time.

Again and again they have had impressed on them: all that has grown on American earth is good, but all that can be called *foreign* is at best suspect. Many of our own people have jogged in the tracks of the jingoists.—"Norwegian church service? Why should there be Norwegian church service in America? No, talk English. . . . No full-blooded American can be expected to want to belong to a Norwegian church!". . . The young are extremely sensitive in matters of honor, and much more so in their patriotic honor! It has been—and to some extent still is—a point of honor to be able to prove that nothing *foreign* hangs about one's person. Under such conditions how could anyone expect that young people should show any enthusiasm for their fore-fathers' tongue—that would be to expect the impossible.[51]

Therefore the literature reflected the rush of a suspect group in wartime crisis to prove their patriotism. In most books immigrant sons marched proudly to battle, daughters knitted and made bandages and nursed and collected money, parents took up again farm work too heavy for their years and over-subscribed their assessment in all kinds of drives. But in the midst of their activity and sacrifice the first generation, most of whom had believed themselves good Americans for many years, suffered from renewed condemnation and rejection because of their foreign origin.

In a typical account of this experience, elderly Norwegians saw the body of their only son brought home after an accident in aviation training. He was the first casualty from the town, and the curious streamed to his funeral. Ten times as many came as could crowd into the Lutheran church, so the ceremony was held in the graveyard. Everything was in English, of course; a recent state law forbade any meeting to use a foreign language. A military chaplain preached the graveside funeral, all about patriotism and duty to America in her hour of trial. The sorrow-ing family waited in vain for the solemn words of comfort in the Lutheran burial service, for the symbolic casting of earth when the casket was lowered in silence. Instead the honor guard fired a salute, a bugle blared. As the soldiers marched away and the crowd drove off in cars, the aged mother could not believe that her son had been properly buried. "The minister was not what he should have been, the funeral service was not what it should have been, no quiet, no deep wordless sorrow . . . every-thing was foreign and strange, everything belonged to the great, hard world, yes, the world had taken her son . . . so that this seemed the funeral of a stranger."[52]

The next day the old parents came back alone to repeat in secret what they could remember of the Norwegian-language burial service, hoping that then their sorrow might be lighter to carry. "A new day had dawned . . . and it had no use for them. . . . The church was no longer theirs, the activity they had created . . . was theirs no longer. They go like beggars among all their achievements . . . Homeless, Jens and Lisa Braa-stad return to their expensive home."[53]

2. ROOTLESSNESS AT ALL PERIODS

Such bitter experience during the war brought back to many older characters feelings which long habit and partial assimilation had covered over since their "dog years"—that their fate as immigrants made them strangers in a strange land. This theme appeared at all periods, closely related to homesickness, but flared up with renewed intensity in the winds of 100-percentism.

a. "I have become a stranger upon a foreign shore"

The poets especially remained concerned with how they never came to feel completely at home in America. "In a Strange Land" as a lyric title turned up in book after book of verse throughout the entire time-span of the literature. A Swedish-American poet under this heading in 1899 described himself as a rootless plant carried hither and hither by the waves, a leaf without a branch, a sparrow without a nest. "I have become a stranger/upon a foreign shore."[54] Sixty years later another Swedish-American repeated the theme:

I remember what he said, the steamboat agent who sold my ticket. . . .
How one would forget, forget everything little and narrow back home, forget old friends for new, be sucked into the whirlpool, become citizens of the world.
Citizens of the world! Some of us turn out so, maybe, but most of us—never.
We build our homes, we plant rosevines around the porch and greet our neighbors when they go by, and talk with them sometimes in the evening. With Smith and Jones and Sullivan and Tomasello. Immigrants like us, maybe—from the Emerald Isle, from the sunny South.
Our friends come to visit, to dinner, to coffee, we meet in clubs, in church, at dances. We speak the new land's language, we learn its customs, but deep inside us we carry the feeling of being strangers.
It's not that we live in the pain of longing. It's only that we never come to feel wholly at home.
We become citizens, we vote in elections, we read the morning newspaper about the results, we take part in determining the country's fate, but we remain strangers.
We live in cities with restless life around us. We go to the theatres and see the newest film, we laugh, we are happy, but we always feel like strangers.
We build our homes on the prairie, we plow and are gladdened when the harvests

ripen. We feel that we share in building up, in creating the new land, but we still remain strangers. . . .

And now I know that the steamboat agent who sold my ticket did not tell the truth.[55]

b. *Loss of the old home too*

In a Norwegian-American novel a farmer complained that no one understood him. Although he had chosen to come to America, had become a citizen and sworn loyalty to his new land, had won a large fortune and founded a fine family, had even been elected to public office—still he felt that the root of his being stood in Norway. God had planted it there, and he could thrive only while it stood secure. But he and his wife revisited Norway in 1914, and in that dreadful experience he discovered that he had lost his fatherland. "Father and mother lay in the churchyard, my brother, who had taken over the estate under *odelsrett,* was away holding socialistic lectures; my sister told that he had . . . lost so much money that the estate must soon be sold. . . . A flood of tourists had brought money into the valley, which was badly needed, but which did much harm. The good old ways and customs of both clothing and food had been exchanged for affected imitations of city life, strange to us." He returned to America feeling that the roots of his being had been destroyed, only to find that "here in America since the war started I am regarded as a foreigner or a hyphenated American."[56] In his case like many others, homesickness became homelessness. "They have uprooted themselves from the old earth and cannot take root in the new."[57]

Every character who returned to his homeland after a long absence discovered similar drastic changes.

His heart hammered as he drew near his childhood home . . . he would walk the last distance, he wanted to see the valley as he had seen it when he left and as he had remembered it ever since.

He came over the hilltop under which the whole valley lay spread out, he would see it at once, but—but—He looked again but could not grasp what he saw, he gasped for breath. Could he have taken the wrong road? But no, there he recognized the church, yes, it was the old church. . . . But everything else? Nothing was the way it had been. The fields were gone, and the houses he remembered he could not find, though there were plenty of others; his childhood valley was full of strange buildings.

Even when this Norwegian-American bought a farm and settled down in the valley, it was not what it had been. "Before it had been wide, now it was so narrow he felt he could hardly breathe. . . . He was not in harmony with the local people. He had grown so far away from the few he still knew from his childhood, and the others he could not grow close to. Not even the dearly remembered landscape became his again, he could not find the way back to it, because it was no longer the same

315

landscape. Even the air was different. . . . Now it tasted of dust and gasoline." Asking himself why he had become an outsider in his childhood home, he found the answer. "Because he had left it. If he had stayed there, he would have grown with it. The inevitable changes would have come little by little, and he would have accepted them naturally. . . . That was what had happened over in America, they accepted the new and grew together with it, they grew old together."[58]

Over and over some authors in all periods and of all types repeated that because an immigrant belonged two places, he belonged nowhere. The homesick who returned home found they had become homeless, that they could never settle down either place in peace. For these their dual heritage meant a divided heart which could not grow whole again. A Norwegian novel pictured an immigrant who had gone back to the Old Country seven times and left again, because happiness was always on the opposite side of the sea.

> Come back, and you must leave again; leave, and you long to return. Wherever you are, you will hear the call from your forefathers' landscape, a horn summoning you behind the blue mountains. You have a home over there and a home back here, at bottom you are a stranger both places. Your true refuge is a vision of something far away, and your nature grows like that of the sea, always restless, always in motion.[59]

It must be remembered, however, that on this point as on others the immigrant authors disagreed. Some showed their characters fighting through divided loyalties to a final sense of belonging in America; a few showed characters finally rejecting the United States to return to Europe. But the research for this study has not found a story which followed an immigrant back to his native land for good, to settle down as a contented "returned American".

A recent study of the theme of emigration in Norwegian literature, on the other hand, cites many stories (and some plays and poems) which describe the experience of "returned Americans" as seen by authors who were not emigrants. It concludes:

> In literature which describes the returned Norwegian-American, there are many [characters] who settle down, find peace and happiness, come home in the best sense of the word.
> Many others return to find no peace, remain discontented, feel an inner cleavage which cannot be healed . . . for many the cleft is too great and the inner division lifelong. . . . In the grip of homelessness, the emigrant is a stranger everywhere. . . .
> In 1920 nearly 50,000 returned Norwegian-Americans were living in Norway. This shows at least that it was not unusual that they returned to the Old Country . . . though it does not tell how many went back [to America] again. And never will we get any statistics on the peace of mind they found—or the feeling of homelessness they were never quit.[60]

3. THE SECOND GENERATION

a. *Conflicts of cultural identity*

In some cases where parents succeeded in passing on a portion of their cultural heritage, the children inherited the problem of divided loyalty too. A second-generation teacher complained that because Norwegian was spoken in her home, she had learned it before English. "We also observed customs which had been brought over from Norway. We attended a Norwegian church and we received all our religious instruction in Norwegian. The result has been that all my life I have felt a foreigner in my own country. At least this was true until I went to the university. There one of my instructors helped me to overcome this handicap, and I shall be eternally grateful to her for it."[61] Only after the death of his Swedish father did another second-generation character feel he fully belonged to America. " 'Land where my fathers died'—this phrase, hitherto repeated so automatically . . . broke into his consciousness as he realized for the first time a kinship with this soil. For his father was now a part of American soil."[62]

Other fictional youth of the second generation never recovered from their inner division. A Norwegian boy brought up in the Red River Valley envied a Boston girl he met. Names and places he had only read about were realities to her; she must feel so secure, so completely at home in New England! He aspired to be a teacher, but felt himself unworthy— a person divided against himself because of his double heritage.

I could *learn* American history; learn to teach it too. But not so that it became history which belonged to me. No relative of mine had contributed the smallest deed to it. . . . But Norwegian history I can count even less as mine; for I live and have my work here.

He had thought of trying to become wholly American and letting Norway go, but loyalty to his parents and grandfather prevented this solution. "They are so faithful, content with little, self-sacrificing. Each a complete personality in his own way. Also in relation to them I don't measure up—that split again. . . . When I feel this way, do I have the right to set myself up as a leader for others?"[63]

b. *The immigrant generation gap*

When children resolved or escaped from this inner conflict by identifying themselves wholly as Americans, they often found themselves at variance with their parents, whose ideas of what was right and proper for the young had been formed in another setting. A Norwegian-American teen-ager longed above all else to wear her hair up, but her mother reminded her that when *she* was the same age she always wore a kerchief to hide her braids. "Nobody could expect a farmer's daughter in Minne-

317

sota in the year of our Lord 1883 to go about in a kerchief as though in some remote mountain parish in the Old Country," the girl protested. Later in the same novel, after the young people began coming together regularly for choir practice, the boys wanted buggies of their own and the girls demanded more clothes.

One dress was no longer enough for even a single summer. They had to have something to change off with. The mothers got nowhere, telling how *they* had used their homespun confirmation dress for best until they got their bridal gown. Minnesota was not Norway, and Chickamuck Prairie was not the mountain parish where Father and Mother grew up. The daughters hadn't heard this comparison made for nothing, all the time they were growing up.[64]

Danish-American sons suffered bitterly from their parents' differentness and ignorance of life in America. Once after the whole family had been to town one of the boys could hardly bear his shame over his mother—first because she had insisted on walking up the long hill into town to spare the horse, and then because of her broken English. He forced himself to compliment her on how well she had spoken to the store clerk. "There, he had said it. It was a lie. He had been terribly ashamed of his mother's speech."[65] An older boy wanted desperately to go to school, but he had not been able to finish eighth grade because he had to work on the farm, so he could not attend the local high school. Finally his father scraped up money to send him for one term to a private academy in Fremont.

Had they known more of the ways and opportunities of their own community they could have sent their son to a less expensive school in Weeping Willow itself. There was a small denominational college there, which also gave high-school work and did not require eighth-grade graduation. . . . Although the Grimsons had now lived near Weeping Willow for ten years and were well acquainted, they were wholly unaware of such cultural advantages as it offered. . . . Grimson's boys did not even know that there was a public library in Weeping Willow. It was only a small collection of approximately three hundred books, but that in itself would have been a godsend to Peter's sons.[66]

By the time the third son reached college age, the family had discovered the local college; he could live at home, do his chores morning and evening, and still attend. But in the spring his father wanted him to drop out for full-time farm work. They boy explained that if he quit then he would get no credit for all the work he had done.

"What kind of God damn school is this?" Peter shouted, now no longer able to keep his voice down. "I have paid good money for your education, and now you tell me that they won't give you credit, as you call it, for the time you have gone. Are they cheating us, then, or aren't you telling the truth?"
Hans sighed in despair. How could he make his father understand? This year had revealed to him with deadly clearness how difficult it was to have immigrant parents. . . . He was torn between his deep loyalty to his home and all that it

318

represented on the one hand, and a living enthusiasm for the new life he experienced at school, which seemed so wonderfully American.[67]

Rølvaag pictured superbly incident after incident in the boyhood of Beret Holm's youngest son, when he realized that his mother and he lived in different worlds. As a twelve-year-old, he came home late one evening because he had gone with his Irish friend after school. His mother was carrying out the buckets of slops for the pigs—his chore. "I'll feed the pigs," he said in the broad Northland dialect of the family as he came in.

These were the first Norwegian words he had spoken since he left home early this morning; and the sound of them, the sight of his sister and mother who went here and did their work as they had done all their days—, of the room and everything it held and hid, swept away the whole world he had lived in all day long. This was another world. He had felt the same before, but this evening it seemed so strange that he had to look around.—Was it out there he really belonged or was it here?[68]

Once his mother accompanied him to a political meeting at the school-house. The teacher had sent a special invitation, for Peder was to recite the Gettysburg address. The mother realized as soon as she came into the crowded room that she had made a mistake. No other married women had come. The men grinned at her and whispered together. But Peder could hardly believe that "Mother had come along!—He had to look over to where she sat.—Mother here! The incredible had really happened, that she had stepped out of her own world and followed him into his."[69] By the end of the novel she had gone so far that she gave her permission for him to marry an Irish Catholic; but her daughter-in-law remained a stranger under her roof, and her son and she, though they lived in the same house, met only occasionally at the border of their separate worlds.

This gulf between generations reflected the predicament of the immigrant family in both its internal and external relationships. In America as well as Europe the parents' role was to formulate values, exercise authority over their implementation, and prepare the offspring for entry into the surrounding culture; but these people had learned what they knew about how to fulfill that role in one kind of society, while they had to carry it out in another. All too often immigrant parents maintained their dominance over internal relationships, and thus preserved family loyalty and unity, only to find that the relation of the family unit to the larger environment suffered accordingly. Their children were not properly prepared to move out into the larger society, where they did not feel at home because their personalities had been formed after a different image. Or if the children learned how to be Americans from non-family sources, they no longer fitted into the internal family pattern

319

established by the parents. The literature showed only two ways to solve the problem for the children's best: either the parents also changed in the direction of American requirements, so that harmony between internal and external expectations could be restored; or if they could not effect this change, they resigned from their parental role to the extent of supporting and encouraging the next generation to find its own behavioral models outside the family.

A long discussion of the problem of *danskhed* in successive issues of a Danish-American periodical, with contributions solicited from the leaders of all camps, reached this dual conclusion. All assumed that as parents they must act only for their children's best. "We of the first generation are not unhappy, but our mental balance suffers more or less from the schism in our lives between the old and the new, and what we wish more than all else for the second generation is a harmonious development, a natural spiritual balance, yes, exactly that firm ground underfoot which we feel all too often we lack ourselves."

Let us be honest toward both our cause and our children, and admit that if it is not strong enough to hold them happy and satisfied, then we should give them the right to float free and follow the currents which tug at them. Because our children must first and foremost be brought up to be good American citizens, who speak English without an accent and are equal to the best in that people to which they belong; if we can give them an extra value through Danish language and culture, that is certainly desirable and worth trying, but it is of secondary importance.[70]

Perhaps the natural love of children for parents could hold the second generation within the ranks of Danish-Americans, at least while they were small. But was it right to require this, to hold them back from their natural development as citizens of a country with a great future, when *danskhed* could offer them only memories of the past? No, immigrant parents should rather try to live themselves into their children's world, hoping that their own memories of the beloved Old Country might remain a lullaby in their children's lives, never forgotten but treasured in their hearts.[71]

This theoretical solution often proved impossible in practice. Moving so far into their children's world required modification of adult personality more drastic than most characters could achieve. Therefore the literature showed many parents, resigned to the fact that they could never be fully at home in America, finding consolation in the thought that their children would succeed where they had failed. In these immigrant families the young became of even greater emotional significance than normal, for the second generation not only were the parents' tie to the future but also should justify the struggle and suffering of the immigrant lot.

One Norwegian pioneer who toiled to create a model farm found

320

no contentment in his achievement. "He felt himself a stranger, who belonged somewhere else. . . . Every time he went to work, he looked for the snow-capped peaks of his homeland glittering in the sun, and he saw only the boundless flat prairie." Mountains had been his symbol of ambition and hope, and where he never saw any he felt a gnawing doubt about his call, that all his effort was in vain. But as his son matured, he found some peace of mind "because he felt that he lived again in his son. *He* would claim the heritage. He would achieve what his father could not."[72] A city businessman glowed with pride watching his boys play catch American style.

He saw clearly that his own dream of becoming one of the "better people" could not be realized. It wasn't just a matter of money or clothes. There were several Norwegians who had a lot of money and were well dressed; but they weren't "better people." All had done manual labor like himself. But the children—ah, that was another matter. When he heard the smack of the ball and saw how the boys swung their arms and legs professionally in pitching and catching, it was a sign that their interests were already identical with those of a world from which he was excluded forever but to which the boys would belong.[73]

A Danish farmer, forced to the wall, facing the auction of his farm under a foreclosed mortgage, nevertheless found justification for his wasted life in his sons' future. "Beyond the waters lies all that I have left behind. Your mother and I want you to find a better life than you could have had over there. You will, too. I never fear it, but you must never turn back. Everything lies before you."[74] The American dream had failed in their own lives, but they still believed in it for their children.

A tragic paradox often arose in such cases. To achieve their parents' goal, the second generation had to be fully accepted by American society; but in this process they necessarily moved away from their parents, who were denied such acceptance. The businessman who was so proud of his son's ball-playing joined all his fellows in building a more expensive house than he could afford "for the children's sake. . . . In one way or another they felt as though the children were slipping away from them, or had slipped away. The children were better educated, they had more polished manners, a different language, other interests. Perhaps they had already moved so far from their parents that they didn't have anything to talk to them about except food and clothing. . . . Back of it all lay the fear that they would lose them entirely—that it would become too common and crude for them at home in the end. The bonds were loosened or cut over, and there was so little that could hold them to their home."[75]

Story after story recorded how some parents did lose their children completely. Sometimes they revolted against parental authority, like the family of a wealthy Danish farmer in Iowa. His son had long since

321

disappeared after a quarrel, and the father never mentioned his name; when he forbade his daughter to keep company with a worthless admirer from Copenhagen, she ran away with him and was never heard from again.[76] Sometimes members of the second generation rejected their parents' heritage so strongly that they cut themselves off from the parents too. On a Swedish farm in Minnesota the old folks loved to reminisce about their happy childhood homes across the sea, forgetting the hunger and hardship they had suffered there; but as soon as the children came home from school they fell silent, "for they knew all too well how deplorable the young folks thought it was when the 'old man' served up his poor old stories about how things were home on the croft, and how contemptuously they wrinkled their noses when 'ma' told about the kindness of the landlord's lady." One or another of the children had interrupted them all too often with the question, "Well, if everything was so wonderful there, why didn't you stay in Sweden?"[77] The bright son who went away to school and became a banker grew so far away from his parents through contact with "better" Americans that he did not even write the news when he married his boss's daughter. When a couple of years later he went to visit them, his father shut the door in his face.

Most often, however, the children simply drifted away in the tradition of American mobility. Neither generation rejected the other, but physical distance between them left in loneliness old people whose children were their chief tie to America. A typical Norwegian couple retired to town had enough money from the sale of their farm to live in comfort, but they were unhappy. "The evenings were long and the days too and they slept poorly at night. Somewhere in Canada and on the West Coast there were children they were grandparents to; but they didn't know how many, and weren't certain of their names. It was seldom they heard anything from them and no invitation for a visit ever came. That's the way things go in a big country—the young leave, as they themselves had once left, and now they sat alone just as their own parents had also been left alone long ago."[78]

c. *Successful reconciliation*

By no means all stories pictured relations between the generations as so difficult. Many children remained true to their love for and duty toward their parents, whatever their attitude toward the Old-World heritage. The problem in a Danish-American tale, for instance, was how young lovers separated by a private feud between their Danish fathers could marry without going against their parents' will. The significant touch in the story was the delight of both fathers at the apology the

322

young people made for having spoken slightingly of their elders, in their frustration over not wanting either to give up their love or to go against parental will. "Thanks for that! There are so many young people over here who don't care a jot whether they cross the old folks or not."[79]

Many families also reached a working compromise on the matter of double heritage which left the rest of the relationship between generations in peace. These children conformed to their parents' expectations of maintenance of European patterns in certain areas, in return for being left free to follow American models in all else. A Norwegian religion-school teacher found this situation when he told an older girl his ambition was to teach her generation to be good Norwegians like their parents. "That would take a long time!" she replied. "We're Americans, we are, only we have to be a little Norwegian when we're home and when we're at church."[80] Yet she was interested to hear all he could tell her about Norway, and wanted to visit the country some day.

Those of the second generation who found most value in their dual heritage were the best educated. Sometimes they acquired their learning at a Scandinavian-American school, like a Danish son who reported that there "I learned first to love both my homeland and my fore-fathers' land, both Denmark and America, for both have produced so many great men whom we can be proud of and whom we should strive to imitate."[81] In other cases well-educated parents, usually from upper-class homes in Europe, transmitted their love of the literature, music, and history of the Old Country to children grateful for the privilege of sharing in such wealth. Still other second-generation characters gained a liberal education through private study on their own. A young Dakota farmer and his wife enjoyed the music of both Norway and the United States, drew strength from Emerson, Lincoln, Tennyson on one hand and Bjørnson, Ibsen, Garborg on the other. The husband wrote poems on "Mit hjem" in Norwegian and "The Home of Nations" in English; but any conflict of loyalty he resolved overwhelmingly in favor of his own homeland, not his father's. In his independence of thought and wealth of culture, he was presented as an ideal Norwegian-American.[82]

Such members of a small intellectual elite met their European background not only at second hand, through their parents' memories, but also directly, in the same books which formed the basis of formal culture in the Old Country. Therefore they had to command the language. In all cases where second-generation characters found such deep and genuine meaning in their dual heritage, they were bilingual.

For others who had lost this key, their Old-World background still held some emotional significance. When they felt secure as Americans many found varying degrees of interest and pleasure in such vestiges of their European inheritance as they cared to cultivate. Some discovered

323

that they felt strangely at home on their first visit to that foreign country where their ancestors had lived, like an American-born poet on a visit to his parents' homeland, Norway:

> Strange to have come so far
> And found a land not strange, a race
> Not alien, but familiar
> And intimate, and precious, and my own.
> Surely I must have known
> This gaunt and granite place
> Of wild green rivers, blue ice, and luminous night
> Since birth, and claim it now of my own right
> As heritage.[83]

4. THE ELDERLY

Especially those who maintained a close relationship with an immigrant grandparent preserved some genuine feeling for an Old Country they had never seen. In a number of such cases the family elders carried out some measure of their function to provide ties with the past, although others were almost completely cut off from their children's children by physical distance or language difficulties. Both patterns of relationship were recorded at all periods; the main difference was not in time but in setting. Closer family ties in the Old-World tradition tended to survive in rural communities of exclusive settlement. In these even immigrants brought over in their old age to live their last years in American comfort were sometimes pictured happy and at home. More often, however, such elderly newcomers pined after transplantation, and not a few tales described old people who died in the luxurious homes of their children from sheer homesickness. Renewal of their closest family ties could not compensate for destruction of the entire web of relationships with the immediate social environment in the Old Country.

Not many old people came with the waves of immigration, which were typically made up of young adults; but in the few cases where grandparents were pictured in pioneer communities, they were looked up to and deferred to as honored patriarchs. Those who came young and grew old in their adopted country, on the other hand, were seldom accorded such respect. One Norwegian grandfather sat ignored at the dinner table of his wealthy farmer son. Conversation ran on the poor food in the Old Country, but since it was in English the old man could not take part. "He feels so oddly strange, the ostracized old pioneer, where he sits abandoned by his own people. His son speaks an unknown language in an alien land, and as he thinks of the bygone past his eyes fill with tears."[84]

Most grandparents in the literature, however, were not so wretched as this. Especially grandmothers were pictured developing warm relationships with those of their children's children with whom they could maintain extended contact. One widow who went to live with a grown son found not only kindness and comfort but consolation in the three children of the family. They knew no Norwegian, and her English was poor, but they managed to communicate. She tried to remedy their surprising ignorance of religious matters, and proved the saving angel who nursed the little girl when she fell sick.[85]

The best treatment given to the family elders, however, was in the American tradition, and Americans did not greatly respect age and the past. Old people were seldom needed. The tradition which it was their responsibility to preserve back home could not be handed on in America because it had no function there. One grandmother could not scour and bake for Christmas in her daughter-in-law's house because everything was always neat and shining, and most of the food was bought prepared.[86] Another grandmother applied for admission to the local old-people's home because she felt herself in the way. Only when refused entry was she reconciled to coming home again. At least she could knit and darn, and who would tell Norwegian stories if she didn't? Only one granddaughter listened, but one was better than none.[87] The author did not raise the question of how many grandchildren might have been in the circle around her if the family had stayed in the Old Country.

VI. The Final Balance-Sheet of Loss and Gain

Were the benefits gained through migration to America really worth their cost? After long deliberation, some authors answered yes, others no; but all agreed that the price exacted for social betterment was higher than any had anticipated.

Few if any of those who left home and fatherland to join the ranks of the pioneers suspected all the conditions and consequences that this step involved.

The goal was worthy and enticing. One's own home, economic independence, political and religious freedom . . . but the costs were great and the requirements exacting.

Home, fatherland, relatives and friends, not to mention language and nationality, all must gradually be sacrificed to reach the goal, a sacrifice so great that the immigrant could seldom even conceive it all at once.[88]

The direct physical suffering and toil which the literature recorded most authors accounted a reasonable price for what was won. This had been expected, although many agreed that "Truly America was not the 'promised land' which I dreamt about back home; but here I was my own master, and though I often had to work much harder than at home, my work was well paid."[89] People borne up by hope for a better future could outdo themselves in accomplishing the impossible, which created that future after all. But a few characters asked whether they might not have won a better life at home too, if they had invested such prodigious effort there.

A Norwegian newcomer who admired tremendously all that his countrymen had achieved in America felt at the same time how much both homeland and immigrant had lost. "Here the emigrated Norway had taken part in creating Uncle Sam's national wealth while the bogs and moors back home were still waiting for willing hands. . . . But the immigrants' loss was greater. Contentment, harmony, and joy of life in their home surroundings were lost forever. Those who returned to the Old Country after making their fortune could tell about that. . . . But if they had stayed home and been willing to work the way they are forced to work here in America, nobody would have to go hungry in Norway either."[90] Swedish factory workers too "could not escape the thought that if they had expended back home the same intensive, strenuous, and assiduous work, if they had learned the same economy and prudence that bitter necessity had taught them in America, they would certainly have prospered better there."[91]

In a long-established prairie settlement, elderly Norwegian farmers remembered how poor and backward was the land they had left. Their modern American houses and machinery proved how much they had bettered their lot by migration. But one day a newcomer turned up as a hired man—a rare occurrence, for most of the few who still came from that part of the world now stayed in eastern cities. The old settlers gathered around him and listened amazed to what he had to tell about great changes in the Old Country. Electric lights glittering far up the mountainsides, engineering feats like putting a waterfall in a few huge pipes, big machines on the little farms. "A new day had dawned there too, they realized, and harvest machinery and separators buzzed back home just like out here on the prairie. Memories of childhood and youth flooded back. Maybe it was wrong to have left Father and Mother. Maybe they could have drained the bog if they had stayed home."[92]

The literature showed that the two main factors determining immigrant attitudes toward their experience were the degree of social betterment they won and the adaptability of their temperament. Those from the poorest classes in the homeland as a rule were happiest in their new homes. As several authors recognized, the difference between old and new in such lives was the greatest, and all to the good.

Most Swedes in the States come from the poor landless peasant class. They have toiled in the fields for wretched pay. . . . They have never had any rights or any chance to escape from their common depressed milieu. . . . For them America is the promised land with honey and manna, with freedom and independence. Their highest ideals are soon fulfilled.[93]

Indeed they had emotional problems in struggling to be accepted, but they had felt themselves rejected in Old-World society too.

Most important to the emotional reaction of transplantation was difference in personality types. Rølvaag's Per Hansa was the pioneer incarnate:

> That summer Per Hansa was transported, was carried farther and farther away on the wings of a wondrous fairy tale—a romance in which he was both prince and king, the sole possessor of countless treasures. . . .
> These days he was never at rest, except when fatigue had overcome him and sleep had taken him away from toil and care . . . he found his tasks too interesting to be a burden; nothing tired him, out here. Ever more beautiful grew the tale; ever more dazzlingly shone the sunlight over the fairy castle.[94]

But his wife Beret lost her mind under the trials of frontier life. By the end of the novel her husband realized why. As he told a visiting minister, "She has never felt at home here in America. There are some people, I know now, who never should emigrate, because, you see, they can't take pleasure in that which is to come—they simply can't see it!" Later the unhappy man confessed to his best friend that his family tragedy was his own fault. "I should not have coaxed and persuaded her to come with me out here. . . . You remember how it was in Nordland: We had boats that we sailed to Lofoten in, big crafts that could stand all kinds of rough weather, if properly handled; and then there were the small boats that we used for home fishing; the last were just as fine and just as good for their own purposes as the other kind for theirs, but you couldn't exchange them. . . . For you and me, life out here is nothing; but there may be others so constructed that they don't fit into this life at all; and yet they are finer and better souls than either one of us."[95]

Other authors of all three nationalities created many characters of both these types; but the majority of personalities fell between them. If not able to live so completely in the future, at least they were not bound so immovably to the past. Their lives made up the body of Scandinavian immigrant experience, recorded by this literature in endless variations of loss and gain.

> There is a spiritual struggle between the Old and the New Worlds over every human being who comes here at our age—we *cannot* throw away everything that we bring along from Denmark. . . . Neither can we become full-blooded Americans; we simply *cannot* assimilate what is foreign to us so that it becomes our own flesh and blood—we cannot suckle twice at our mother's breast either physically or spiritually.[96]

Yet this was precisely the heart of the difficulty, that immigrants had to undergo socialization two times. To American society the "greenhorns" were grown-up children, unpredictable and potentially dangerous because they lacked knowledge about the expectations of the new environment, and understanding of how to respond to them. They had to be taught a second time how to behave as social beings before they could be accepted as members of the host society.

Discovery of the need to undergo this Americanization was a shock to Scandinavian immigrants, who had expected to be accepted immediately on the sole basis of the work they could perform. The pain they felt in the process measured the unexpected dissimilarity between adopted land and homeland, in spite of a common basis in western civilization. Persistent feelings of homesickness and rootlessness betrayed that their first socialization as Scandinavians obstructed their second socialization as Americans, producing such an effect as Rølvaag described in his first novel. A speaker at a gathering of Norwegian-Americans compared his emigrated countrymen to a music box from which a tinker tried to remove its only tune, a waltz, and put in a hymn. When wound up, the altered box played the strangest music ever heard, a hymn in waltz time, with notes and bars of both kinds of music all mixed up together. "Thus it is with us foreign-born citizens in this country: we are neither the one nor the other, but both at once."[97]

Because they were unlike anyone else, Rølvaag held, the immigrants had become strangers. "We are strangers to the people we left behind, and we are strangers to the people we came to. We gave up the fatherland which was our heritage of a thousand years, and we of the first generation can never find another. . . . We have ceased to be a harmonious part of a larger whole; we have become something by ourselves, uprooted, without organic relationship either here or there." There were writers enough who agreed with him, but even he had to modify this tragic view when addressing his fellow immigrants directly: "It is hard to live one's life among a foreign people, people with completely different values from ours. It is hard to feel oneself a stranger among strangers. That you've never felt, you say? No, out here in a big Norwegian settlement, where everything is much like what you were used to from the Old Country, it's not to be expected that you would."[98]

Not only in the big settlements but everywhere, even in large cities, even in single homes, many immigrants created their own subculture which was completely cut off neither from the people they had left behind nor from the people they had come to. Together with those of similar background and experience they formed their own in-group, which provided protection for them in their exposed position as marginal men. This group was large and permanent enough to create a wide variety of distinctive institutions, from which its members could sally forth into fields and relationships dominated by American patterns, and into which they could retreat when the strain of encountering conflicting values in the larger society became too severe. Change was the keynote of group, institutional, and individual life alike, for from each sortie the participants returned a little different, bringing their mutation back with them to work upon each other and all.

This was perhaps the widest meaning of the divided heart of a group in transit, as carrying all its swirling eddies and conflicting currents it moved massively away from European toward American models. The literature itself demonstrated in its rise, flowering, and decline that the hybrid culture which produced it grew out of the needs of human beings in transition, and died only when the long-lasting crisis of adjustment had ended in effective assimilation of a foreign part with the native whole. Yet the very success of the process, now practically completed, has tended to obscure its difficulties. Historians have unanimously considered such north-European Protestants as the most rapidly and easily Americanized of all immigrant groups, after the British. Scandinavian-American literature presents considerable evidence that even for them the immigrant experience lasted longer and cost more than has generally been recognized.

Seven brothers and sisters shared my early years, and we lived on top of each other. If they had written of those days, each account would have been different, and each one true. We saw the same events at different heights, at different levels of mood and hunger—one suppressing an incident as too much to bear, another building it large around him, each reflecting one world according to the temper of his day, his age, the chance heat of his blood. Recalling it differently as we were bound to do, what was it, in fact, we saw? Which one among us has the truth of it now? And which one shall be the judge? The truth is, of course, that there is no pure truth, only the moody accounts of witnesses.

Laurie Lee, "The Idea Was to Live Over Again Both the Good and the Bad," an article on the motivation to write autobiography in *The New York Times Book Review* for 30 August 1964, p. 6.

Chapter Eleven
Afterword

This study has a history of its own. It started over a quarter-century ago as a private interest surviving from my childhood, which I hoped could be developed into a doctoral dissertation. Further than that I had no thought to go.

But American society has changed so fast in recent years! Among other things, the current "ethnic revival" may lend this modest study more importance now than it had before. In its original version, completed in 1962, I did not use the word *ethnic,* only *immigrant, national,* or *cultural*; now I find I have peppered the revised text with that newly popular term. Rølvaag's "cultural pluralism" seemed defeated and dying when he died in 1931, but at present it appears to be not only revived but swimming in the mainstream of current events. Only recently did I first meet the term *culture shock,* defined as "the effect that immersion in a strange culture has on the unprepared visitor. . . . It is what happens when the familiar psychological cues that help an individual to function in society are suddenly withdrawn and replaced by new ones that are strange and incomprehensible."[1] This is of course what I had described in detail as the initial stage of the immigrant experience, but there I have chosen to use the name of this increasingly important concept in a slightly different form (cultur*al* shock) as a reminder that immigrants were not visitors.

From the beginning I thought vaguely of the immigrant as a prototype of modern man, uprooted from a stable past and moving in bewilderment toward an unpredictable future. Revising my study after a decade of youth revolt and widening generation gap, I have become even more convinced that he was so. In fact, I think immigrant experience was in many ways quite close to what Alvin Toffler calls "future shock":

> Take an individual out of his own culture and set him down suddenly in an environment sharply different from his own, with a different set of cues to react to—different conceptions of time, space, work, love, religion, sex, and everything else—then cut him off from any hope of retreat to a more familiar social landscape, and the dislocation he suffers is doubly severe. Moreover, if this new culture is itself in constant turmoil, and if—worse yet—its values are incessantly changing, the sense of disorientation will be still further intensified.[2]

331

However, the Scandinavian immigrant's experience was not fully so disorienting as this. Granted that both the culture he had left and the one to which he came were rapidly changing, that in migrating he leapt ahead from an earlier and more stable to a later and more disorganized stage of development; still *his* form of cultural shock was partially cushioned by the support of his ethnic group. Clearly in a nation receiving so many and such different strangers over so long a period, the formation of such ethnic groups was both a psychological and a sociological necessity, equally important for the uprooted individual and the larger society to which he came.

In my speculative moments, I wonder if the current ethnic revival may become one antidote for future shock. Ascribed-group membership, acquired at birth, does have the advantage of relative permanence in an unstable cultural situation, provided that it remains meaningful to the individual concerned. There's the rub, of course—the meaning. What did, and does, membership in an ethnic group *mean*? Many more specialized studies are needed of all American immigrant groups, not only straight histories of who settled where and what they accomplished—the objective facts of ethnic group formation—but also attempts to tell their inside story, what it was like to be that kind of immigrant, rather than (for instance) a Scandinavian one. The first kind of history has been and is being written, more of it in recent years. But we also need many studies of the second kind before comparative analysis of the immigrant traditions can proceed very far. Are there whole rooms of German-American literature, Polish-American, Czech-American, Irish-American (and all the others) waiting in historical libraries for scholarly analysis? Indeed much remains to be done before we can begin to generalize in confidence about the meaning of *the* American immigrant experience, and what it can teach about the psychological and sociological problems of modern man.

What was it like to be an immigrant? On the basis of the evidence presented here, we must conclude that it was both painful and difficult, more so than most histories have admitted. Yet this study is no more than part of an answer to that general question. It considers only one kind of immigrant, from a strictly circumscribed point of view. Limited as it is to fiction and poetry as source material, this study can in fact answer only one of the evaluative questions I asked at the beginning: Would a picture of Scandinavian immigrant life be coherent? Would it be complete? Would it be valid? Certainly it would be an "inside story," but would it be true?

I think it is coherent; that criterion can be judged on the basis of internal evidence alone. But the other criteria cannot; *they* can be assessed only by comparison with other sources. *I* think I know the answers to my

332

questions, but only because I have checked the entire study, subject by subject, against other evidence. Readers who wish to do the same are referred to the following general histories dealing with Scandinavian immigrant life:

Theodore C. Blegen, *Norwegian Migration to America* (Northfield, Minn., 1931, 1940), 2 vol.

ed. Karl Hildebrand, Axel Fredenholm et al., *Svenskarna i Amerika* (Stockholm, 1924-26), 2 vol.

George M. Stephenson, *The Religious Aspects of Swedish Immigration* (Minneapolis, 1932)

Helge Nelson, *The Swedes and the Swedish Settlements in North America* (Lund, Sweden, 1943), 2 vol.

ed. J. Iverne Dowie and Ernest M. Espelie, *The Swedish Immigrant Community in Transition* (Rock Island, Ill., 1963)

Sture Lindmark, *Swedish America, 1914-1932* (Uppsala, 1971)

Thomas P. Christensen, *Dansk amerikansk historie* (Cedar Falls, Iowa, 1927)

Johannes Knudsen and Enok Mortensen, *The Danish-American Immigrant* (Des Moines, Iowa, 1950)

Georg Strandvold, *Danes Who Helped Build America* (New York, 1960)

Paul C. Nyholm, *The Americanization of the Danish Lutheran Churches in America* (Copenhagen, 1963).

There are also numerous and invaluable specialized studies published in both book and periodical form, especially by the Norwegian-American Historical Association (Northfield, Minn.) and the Swedish Pioneer Historical Society (Chicago). The wealth of historical material being collected and studied for these two national groups is prodigious; Danish-Americans, on the other hand, lacking a historical society, are doing much less. In Europe, the Swedes have taken the lead with a uniquely thorough and detailed series of projects dealing with their emigrant history, including some aspects of its branches in the United States.[3]

Checked against much of this historical material, my picture of Scandinavian immigrant life is incomplete. I have pointed out some specific gaps in footnotes, but there are others. Of course imaginative literature is worthless as source material for establishing objective facts; I have rather sought in it attitudes toward and reactions to what is called fact. Precisely here some pieces of the picture are missing. They may exist in literary items I have not yet found, particularly in the periodical literature; but even if so, they can hardly be typical. Typically, these Scandinavian-American authors have ignored the considerable achievements in art, music, and science by some members of their ethnic group; typically, they have failed to record knowledge of American literature and culture among their intellectual elite; typically, they have omitted reference to both first- and second-generation individuals who became outstanding successes in various fields of American life—businessmen, political leaders, all kinds of professionals and intellectuals. For the story of such as these we must turn to other source material. Of course such accomplishments were achieved in the host society, outside the boundaries of the ethnic group; yet immigrants clearly felt that such attainments reflected glory on the entire nationality, they became part of group self-definition, and therefore one would expect them more fully reflected in the realistic accounts of imaginative literature. But Scandinavian-American fiction and poetry have rather described and expressed the lives of average people, and of the failures who otherwise have lived and died leaving little trace to history. This limitation is the strength of this source material, its unique contribution to historical studies; but it precludes completeness.

Then there is the question of validity. Granted that, checked against other evidence, my portrait of Scandinavian immigrant life is generally valid—as far as it goes. When it is not complete, can it be true?

In 1962-3 I sent copies of my original manuscript to a number of both first- and second-generation Scandinavian-Americans asking for criticism and comment. Those of the first generation reported that for them it rang true. However, since these were authors on whose writings (among others') I had based the study, their testimony only bore witness that I had succeeded in constructing a picture in accord with the evidence I had chosen; it was no judgment of the validity of that evidence itself.

From second-generation American scholars (themselves to be classed as "successes") I got a different reaction. They thought the picture of Scandinavian immigrant life here presented too dark, too tragic. They could not remember their parents expressing such lasting homesickness, such rootlessness, such never feeling at home; nor had they felt such a painful generation gap between themselves and their parents. On the contrary, their parents' foreign heritage had strongly influenced their life work. Several of them questioned my choice of source material. Might it not be, they reasoned, that people of a certain sensitivity turn to self-expression in fiction and poetry to sublimate feelings of unhappiness and inadequacy? Might not limitation of source material to imaginative literature therefore automatically select the testimony of those personality types least adapted to immigrant life—the sensitive, the introvert, the tender-hearted and thin-skinned—who would feel it as most painful? The resultant picture would then, of course, be disproportionately dark.

To test this hypothesis I devised another experiment, the evidence of which I hope to report on later since it is too comprehensive to include here. I turned to Scandinavian-American autobiographies and reminiscences, which are even more numerous than works of fiction and poetry. This genre, like the novel, provides the interpretation I have always wanted, the perspective, the looking back in judgment over a long-term process. I reasoned that more robust personality types who had made good as immigrants, who felt they had achieved success worth recording, would at least be as apt to write autobiographies as sensitive types would tend toward fiction and poetry. In this more conventional source material I have found in general the same picture of immigrant experience as in imaginative literature: the same pain of cultural shock, the same trials of being rejected, the same sense of not belonging fully, the same divided heart. I found also the same dichotomy of first-generation attitudes as in the other literature toward this common core of experience. Some felt it as a challenge through which they won to a richer and happier life as hyphenated Americans than they could have had back home; some felt permanently scarred or even crippled by their experience; most fell somewhere in between. Second-generation autobiographies, like fiction and poetry, recorded special problems of identity and loyalty in formative years; however, these problems were normally overcome as adults.

Both autobiographies, which I consider interpretative literature, and fiction and poetry, which I have called imaginative, written by members of this ethnic group, have as their central theme the cultural shock of the Scandinavian immigrant experience. Of course this theme seldom appears in either Scandinavian or American literature because writers of these nationalities did not share the experience; in the few cases where they did treat it, they wrote as observers, not participants. (Think of the contrast between Rølvaag and Willa Cather in their treatment of this theme.) The only other source of information on this topic available to history are journals and letters. Keeping journals was not a Scandinavian tradition, and these immigrants left comparatively few of them, most devoted to recording weather, crops, and prices. "America-letters," on the other hand, have been preserved in vast numbers. Some few of these contain the same kind of generalizing judgment and interpretative insight as autobiographies and fiction, though many others are more like lyrics in expressing only opinions or observations in a passing mood. A long series of letters put together can, of course, be the equivalent of an autobiography or an epistolary novel. But most letters are only fragments of a personal record, and (as contemporaries knew) the "America-letters" of Scandinavian immigrants were often unreliable because they expressed the boasts of wishful thinking fully as much as actual opinions or observations of fact. Historians have too often failed to recognize that *all* these genres of source material are "only the moody accounts of witnesses." History should make use of them all.

I have singled out imaginative literature to be the basis of this study as an experiment, which I hope has demonstrated its value as historical source material. Such a source requires that techniques of literary history and criticism be added to historical analysis, but this extra effort can add elements of great value to the writing of history. Here I think this method has opened records preserved in Scandinavian-American fiction and poetry to show how a complex social and psychological process of assimilation actually took place, how an ethnic group was absorbed into a larger society through the individual experiences of its members. We have seen that this process took place in three stages: first, initial rejection by the host society of individuals with unsuitable identity; second, retreat by these into their own reference group, which, by gradually changing its own patterns of behavior from a mixture of Scandinavian and American models toward exclusively American ones, modified the identity of its members so that, third, they could be accepted as individuals by the host society; and as they left the transitional group it gradually dissolved. I consider this the historical side of my study, a generalized account of what happened to large numbers of people in a pattern which also describes the experience of many other groups, and is still being followed today.

The literary side of my study is something else, not general but particular: concrete detail and varied color, personal moods, some of the confused complexity of individual human lives, what it *felt like* to be this kind of immigrant at that time and place. From these "moody accounts of witnesses" I have tried to tell the inside story of people like my grandmother in a vanished time.

Notes

Scholarly notes indicated by note numbers, will be found in this section at the end of the book. Footnotes deemed to be of interest to the general reader will be placed at the bottom of the relevant page.

CHAPTER ONE

1 Vernon Parrington, "Introduction" to text edition of Rølvaag's *Giants in the Earth,* copyright 1929 by Harper and Brothers. Reprinted in *Main Currents in American Thought* (New York, 1930), Vol. 3, p. 387.
2 Vol. II, *The American Transition* (Northfield, Minn., 1940), p. vii.
3 Konni Zilliacus, author of several traveler's accounts as well as many short stories about immigrant life in United States, served as an editor of *Svenska Tribunen* in Chicago for about five years. He left America permanently in 1894.
4 "The inability of even educated Americans to keep straight the geographies and achievements of the various Scandinavian nations [Norway, Sweden, and Denmark] has long been the exasperation of these peoples, but it is of course founded in the undeniable anthropological and cultural similarity of the Northern nations when compared with other groups." Einar Haugen, "Swedes and Norwegians in the United States," *Norsk geografisk tidsskrift,* Vol. XI, No. 5-6 (1947), p. 189. Professor Haugen also points out that the "indefinable but real differences" in personality traits between the three nationalities, along with their divergences in speech, cultural background, and Old-World political loyalities, were gradually dissipated in America, so that they became even more homologous there.
5 Copies of the manuscript, entitled *Double Heritage,* a thesis presented to the Committee on Higher Degrees in the History of American Civilization at Harvard University, were deposited at Widener Library in 1963. Other copies may be found at the Minnesota Historical Society Library in St. Paul, and the Emigrant Archives of the University of Oslo Library in Norway.
6 Laurence M. Larson, *The Changing West* (Northfield, Minn., 1937), p. 64.
7 M. Sørensen, *Trækfugle* (Copenhagen, 1903), n.p. Quotations from books with titles in a Scandinavian language have been translated by the present writer.
8 Editorial entitled "Unwritten Chapters" in the English-language periodical *Scandinavia,* Vol. I, No. 2 (Feb. 1924), pp. 84-5. (Italics added.)

CHAPTER TWO

1 *Omkring fædrearven* (Northfield, Minn., 1922), p. 60.
2 See Part 3 of the bibliography at the end of this volume.
3 This bibliography has been compiled by Thor M. Andersen, and will be published in the near future by the American Institute of the University of Oslo. Other bibliographies are Giovanni Bach, *The History of the Scandinavian Literatures* (New York, 1938), pp. 74-84, 144-58, 221-30; Enok Mortensen, *Danish-American Life and Letters* (Des Moines, 1945); C. G. Wallenius, "Svensk-Amerikanarnas litteratur," *Yearbook* of the Swedish Historical Society of America, Vol. II (1908), pp. 5-12; O. Fritiof Anders, *The Cultural Heritage of the Swedish Immigrant; Selected References* (Rock Island, 1956), pp. 113-32.
4 Danish and Norwegian, in written form, were then practically identical. For an account of *Nordlyset,* see Clarence A. Clausen and Andreas Elviken, eds., *A Chronicle of Old Muskego: The Diary of Søren Bache* (Northfield, Minn., 1951),

337

pp. 217-18, and Arlow William Andersen, *The Immigrant Takes His Stand: The Norwegian-American Press and Public Affairs 1847-1872* (Northfield, Minn., 1953), pp. 11-16.

For a discussion of *Skandinavia*, see Theodore C. Blegen, *Norwegian Migration to America: The American Transition* (Northfield, 1940), pp. 287, 288; A. N. Rygg, *Norwegians in New York* (Brooklyn [1941?]), p. 10; "The Danish-American Press," in Enok Mortensen and Johannes Knudsen, *The Danish-American Immigrant*, (Des Moines, Iowa, 1950), 55. 35-37.

5 *Ved arnen* was published in La Crosse, Wisconsin, September 1, 1866, through December 15, 1870, as an independent magazine. In 1884 its publisher, B. Anundsen, began issuing it as a regular section of *Decorah-posten*. See Anundsen, "Hvordan 'posten' blev til" (How 'The Post' Began), in *Decorah-posten*, September 5, 1924.

6 An early periodical was *Billed-magazin: Et ugeblad til nyttig og belærende underholdning* (Illustrated Magazine: A Weekly Paper for Useful and Instructive Entertainment), published at Madison, Wisconsin, by Svein Nilsson, 1868-70. An exception to the normally short careers of these periodicals was *For gammel og ung: Et kristelig familieblad* (For Old and Young: A Christian Family Paper), published at Wittenberg, Wisconsin, 1881-1955. A full account of Norwegian-American periodicals and of some that were Danish-American is Johannes B. Wist, "Pressen efter borgerkrigen" (The Press after the Civil War), in *Norsk-amerikanernes festskrift 1914* (Decorah, 1914), pp. 181-203, Wist mentions, p. 160, the interesting case of a woman's magazine published in Cedar Rapids, Iowa, in duplicate editions—one in Dano-Norwegian and one in Swedish, the titles being *Kvinden og hjemmet* and *Kvinnan och hemmet* (The Woman and the Home). Descriptions of a number of Swedish-American magazines appear in a pamphlet by Gustaf N. Swan entitled *Swedish-American Literary Periodicals* (Rock Island, 1936), and in Chap. 9, "Newspapers, Periodicals, and Annuals," of Anders' *The Cultural Heritage of the Swedish Immigrant*.

7 In December, 1909, *Valkyrian* was combined with the youth's magazine *Ungdomsvännen* (The Friend of Youth—Rock Island, Illinois, 1895-1918).

8 See Blegen, *Norwegian Migration: American Transition*, pp. 582-584; Einar Haugen, *The Norwegian Langauge in America: The Bilingual Community*, (Philadelphia, 1953), Vol. I, pp. 181-86.

9 There were of course other types of publications than those mentioned here. Because newspapers and magazines for this ethnic public were much alike in both contents and frequency of publication, statistical studies often do not separate them. A recent account of the Norwegian-American press claims a total of about 800 publications of all types for this national group alone between the 1840s and the present. Of these about one-third were connected with some church organization. The approximately 575 secular publications can be classified by content as follows: news, 225; ethnic organizations, 70; literature, 25; prohibition, 20; humor, 15; music, 10; industry, 5; agriculture, 5; insurance, 5; politics, 5; education, 5. Clearly the last six types of publication would not be a market for fiction or poetry, while the others would to a greater or lesser extent. Newspaper article by Olaf Holmer Spetland, "Den norsk-amerikanske presse," *Aftenposten* (Oslo) for 24 Nov. 1971, p. 4 (morning edition).

10 "Hardly more than a couple of volumes of collected poems have been put out by publishing companies; the rest were published and paid for by the authors themselves. Not one achieved more than one edition and in the vast majority of cases 'the poet' let the matter rest with one book—probably couldn't afford any more." Waldemar Ager, "Norsk-amerikansk skjønlitteratur" (Norwegian-American Belles-Lettres) in Wist, *Festskrift*, pp. 305-6.

11 Accurate figures on Scandinavian-Aemrican titles are not available. Enok Mortensen's *Danish-American Life and Letters* includes about 90 books of fiction and 40 of poetry, besides other types of literature. O. Fritiof Anders' bibliography of "Religious and Secular Literature" in *The Cultural Heritage of the Swedish Immigrant* includes about 150 titles of fiction and 175 of poetry. Thor M. Andersen's bibliography of Norwegian-born authors in the United States before 1930,

338

to be published shortly by the Universitetsforlaget, Oslo, will run to two volumes. This will, however, include all types of writing and publication, not merely belles-lettres. Files compiled by the present author contain nearly a thousand separate titles of fiction and poetry for the three Scandinavian groups combined, excluding periodical material.

12 Written in English, *Gunnar* appeared as a serial in the *Atlantic Monthly* in 1873 and in book form in Boston the following year.

13 Reine's book was printed by *Fædrelandet og emigranten* (The Fatherland and Emigrant—La Crosse). Dan's *Taarer og smil* appeared in Skanderborg, Denmark, in 1868, his *Alperoser* in Copenhagen in 1871. Borchsenius' book was published in Madison, Wisconsin. The Øresund of his title is the narrow sound lying between Denmark's easternmost island and Sweden.

14 Typical titles are *Chicago anarkisterne* (The Chicago Anarchists—1888); *Præstehistorier: Skildringer af nordmændenes aandsliv i Nordamerika* (Stories of Ministers: Descriptions of the Spiritual Life of the Norwegians in North America—1893); *Den nye Minnesota-biblen: fortsættelse af Wisconsin-biblen* (The New Minnesota Bible: A Continuation of the Wisconsin Bible—1901); *Falk og jødinden: Fortælling fra Norge og Amerika* (Falk and the Jewess: A Tale from Norway and America—1901); *Paul O. Stensland og hans hjælpere: eller Milliontyverne i Chicago* (Paul O. Stensland and His Assistants: or, The Million-Dollar Thieves in Chicago—1907); *Paven i Madison: eller, Rasmus Kvelves merkværdige liv og hændelser* (The Pope in Madison: or, Rasmus Kvelves' Remarkable Life and Doings—1908). Waldemar Ager calls Stenholt "the only Norwegian-American author who has been able to live by the pen, although the living was wretched enough." *Festskrift*, p. 296.

15 Ager, in *Festskrift*, p. 294.

16 The scholarly reader is reminded that source material for biographical information in this chapter is identified in the footnotes of my article, "'The Scandinavian Immigrant Writer in America," *Norwegian-American Studies* (Northfield, Minn., 1962), Vol. 21, pp. 31 ff., and in Chap. Two of my manuscript doctoral dissertation "Double Heritage" (1963) on file in Widener Library of Harvard University, and in Universitetsbiblioteket (the University Library) of Oslo, Norway. A recent biography should be added to this source material: Emory Lindquist, *An Immigrant's Tow Worlds: A Biography of Hjalmar Edgren* (Rock Island, 1972).

17 This essay, entitled "Skjønlitterære sysler blandt norsk-amerikanerne" (Literary Efforts among Norwegian-Americans), was read before the Symra Society of Decorah, Februar 17, 1939, and published in part in *Decorah-posten*, February 24, March 3, March 10, 1939.

18 See Per E. Seyersted, "Hjalmar Hjorth Boyesen: Outer Success, Inner Failure," *Americana Norvegica; Norwegian Contribution to American Studies,* eds. Sigmund Skard and Henry H. Wasser, Vol. I (Philadelphia, 1966), p. 212.

19 Kristofer Janson was considered to important an author by his contemporaries in Norway that he was awarded a writer's pension by the Norwegian parliament in 1876. He resigned it when he emigrated in 1881 to accept an appointment as a Unitarian minister in Minneapolis. As a champion of liberal ideas in theology and women's rights, he attacked the dogma of the Norwegian-American Lutheran clergy. See, for example, his collections of short stories: *Præriens saga* (Chicago, 1885), *Nordmænd i Amerika* (Copenhagen, 1887), and *Fra begge sider havet* (Christiania, 1890). He returned to Norway in 1893 because of the scandal connected with his divorce. See Per Sveino, "Kristofer Janson and His American Experience," *Americana Norvegica*, Vol. III (Oslo, 1971), pp. 88-104.

20 See Haugen, *Norwegian Language*, Vol. 1, Chapter 8. It should be mentioned that the term *nynorsk* (called "New Norse" by Professor Haugen) postdates the controversy discussed here. The word did not become official until 1929, although it had been widely used earlier.

21 Anna Olsson's earliest tales in both Swedish-American dialect and literary Swedish appeared in *Från solsiden* (Rock Island, Illinois, 1903). Her own childhood story, *En prärieunges funderingar* (Musings of a Prairie Child), came out

in Rock Island in 1917 and in Stockholm in 1919, the second furnished with a glossary of Americanized terms. She translated it as *I'm Scairt: Childhood Days on the Prairie* (Rock Island, 1927).

22 The tales in English were called *Returning Home* (Minneapolis, 1920), and the novel, *Byen paa berget* (The City on the Hill—Minneapolis, 1925).

23 Wist, in *Festskrift*, pp. 161-64.

24 Liljencrantz's titles include two juveniles and the following: *The Thrall of Leif the Lucky* (Chicago, 1902), *The Ward of King Canute* (Chicago, 1903), *Randvar, the Songsmith* (New York, 1906), *A Viking's Love and Other Tales of the North* (Chicago, 1911). See George Leroy White, *Scandinavian Themes in American Fiction* (Philadelphia, 1937), pp. 25-30.

25 *Elling* was highly recommended by William James, Corstvet's professor at Harvard. See Albert O. Barton, "Alexander Corstvet and Anthony M. Rud," in *Norwegian-American Studies and Records* (1931), Vol. VI, p. 146.

CHAPTER THREE

1 Personal experience and secondary sources form the main basis of the following description of Scandinavian society. The author has lived twenty years in Norway, with frequent visits to the other two countries. The best summaries of nineteenth- and early twentieth-century social history may be Ingrid Semmingsen, *Veien mot vest*, Vol. I (Oslo, 1942), pp. 216-262, and Vol. II (Oslo, 1950), pp. 42-85, 181-239; Eli F. Heckscher, *Svenskt arbete och liv* (Stockholm, 1957), Chaps. V and VI; Hans Jensen, "Landbelovgivning og ejendomsforhold," in K. J. Kristensen, ed., *Det danske landbrug* (Copenhagen, 1944), pp. 7-36. Perhaps the most detailed American study of this subject is Florence E. Janson, *The Background of Swedish Immigration* (Chicago, 1931). In addition to such historical material, the author has found countless supporting and illustrative details in both Scandinavian and Scandinavian-American literature. Rich and full descriptions of nineteenth-century rural life are given by novelists who never emigrated, especially the Norwegian Johan Bojer in *The Emigrants* (New York, 1925, and the Swedish Vilhelm Moberg, *The Emigrants* (New York, 1951).

2 Norwegian novelists, on the contrary, frequently portrayed emigrant agents as villains who lured ignorant peasants to America merely to sell them their tickets (at a commission). See the study of the theme of emigration in Norwegian literature by Jørund Mannsåker, *Emigrasjon og dikting* (Oslo, 1971) pp. 38-42.

3 Kristian Østergaard, *Danby folk* (Cedar Falls, Iowa, n.d.), pp. 97-101.

4 J. A. Erikson, "Det forjættede land," *Ved arnen*, Vol. 64, Nr. 18 (9 Nov. 1937), pp. 25-6.

5 For example, Ole E. Rølvaag, *The Boat of Longing* (New York, 1933), pp. 49-59. Emigrant guidebooks and advertising pamphlets of land companies, etc., almost never appeared in this literature. Main sources of knowledge about the U.S.A. were shown to be letters and oral accounts by earlier emigrants. Compare Mannsåker, *Emigrasjon og dikting*, pp. 42-53, who found that Norwegian authors who never left home more often portrayed notions about America being spread by the printed word.

6 Kristian Østergaard, *Anton Arden og møllerens Johanne* (Armstrong, Ia., 1897), p. 12.

7 Johannes K. Moen, *Knut Langaas* (Minneapolis, 1926), p. 43.

8 Simon Johnson, *Stier på ny jord* (MS, 1952), p. 109.

9 M. Sørensen, "Smeden i Viborg," *Misteltenen* for 1916, p. 9.

10 Waldemar Ager, "Norsk-amerikansk skjønlitteratur," in Johannes B. Wist, ed., *Norsk-amerikanernes festskrift* (Decorah, Iowa, 1914), p. 293.

11 Ole A. Buslett, *Paa veien til Golden Gate* (n.p., n.d.), p. 6.

12 Edward Schuch, *Emigranterne* (Chicago, 1917), p. 12.

13 Ole A. Buslett, *Fra min ungdoms nabolag* (Eau Claire, Wisc., 1918), pp. 4-5. This account was clearly based on the author's childhood memory of the trip. The story was told from the viewpoint of the oldest son (the position of the

writer in his own family) and the voyage was dated in 1868, the year his family emigrated.

14 See for example Knut Brodin, ed., *Emigrantvisor och andra visor* (Stockholm, 1938), "Vi sålde våra hemman," pp. 8-9, and "Utvandrarens visa," pp. 28-9.

15 Magnus Elmblad, "Petter Jönsingens resa till Amerika," first published in a Swedish-American newspaper in 1872, reprinted in Elmblad's *Samlede dikter* (Chicago, 1878), pp. 125-7. In other reprints the hero was called Jönsson. See E. Gustav Johnson, "Swedish Emigrant Ballad," a comment and a translation, in *Scandinavian Studies,* Vol. XX, No. 4 (Nov. 1948), pp. 193-201.

16 Hans A. Foss, *Husmannsgutten* (Oslo, 1936), p. 59.

17 Peter A. Lindberg, *Adam: en berättelse* (Chicago, 1899), p. 82.

18 J. A. Erikson, "Gunhild og Jörgen," *Ved arnen,* Vol. 69, Nr. 54 (25 March 1943), p. 1.

19 Laura R. Bratager, *Digte og smaafortællinger* (Minneapolis, 1914), p. 14.

20 Vilhelm Berger, *Ungdomskärlek* (Worcester, Mass., 1908), p. 8.

21 Knut Brodin, ed., *Emigrantvisor och andra visor* (Stockholm, 1938), p. 13. In this translation of immigrant verse, as in all to follow, I have observed the Scandinavian practice of beginning lines of poetry with a lower-case letter except when a capital is required by grammar. Non-capitalization, violating the English verse convention, is thus a reminder to the reader that the original langauge was not English. While I have given more attention to sense than sound in each translation, I have made an effort to reproduce something of the level of artistry. Most of my efforts are doggerel because most of the originals were.

22 M. Hartvig, "Undervejs, lynskud fra en dansk emigrants overfart til Amerika," *De Forenede Staters danske almanak* for 1914, p. 123. For example, "Jebel," "En svensk students äfventyr i Amerika," *Valkyrian,* Vol. VI, Nr. 1 (Jan. 1902), pp. 37-40.

23 Lindberg, *Adam,* p. 101.

24 Jon Norstog, *Svein; forteljing* (Minot, N. Dak., 1909), pp. 11-12.

25 Brodin, *Emigrantvisor,* p. 9.

26 J. A. Erikson, "Det forjættede land," Nr. 21, pp. 4-6.

27 Lindberg, *Adam,* p. 101.

28 A. Erikson, "Det forjættede land," Nr. 21, pp. 6-8.

29 Kristian Østergaard, *Blokhuset* (Copenhagen, 1892), pp. 151-2.

30 Frederick J. Blichfeldt, *Aalborg akvavit og andre amerikanske fortællinger,* (Copenhagen, 1904), p. 55.

31 Lindberg, *Adam,* p. 102.

32 "A," *Danske emigranter,* (Esbjerg, Denmark, 1890), pp. 33-6. This is a European, not an immigrant novel.

33 Norstog, *Svein,* pp. 16-17.

34 Østergaard, *Anton Arden og møllerens Johanne,* p. 28.

35 Erikson, "Det forjættede land," No. 22, p. 1.

36 "A," *Danske emigranter,* p. 54-7.

37 Hartvig, "Undervejs," pp. 124-5.

38 Rølvaag, *The Boat of Longing,* pp. 283-7.

39 Carl Hansen, *Præriens børn* (Cedar Rapids, Iowa, 1896-7), p. 10.

40 Hjalmar H. Boyesen, "En farlig dyd, fortælling fra immigrantlivet," *Husbibliothek,* Vol. 19, Nr. 1 (Jan. 1892), p. 11.

41 "A," *Danske emigranter,* p. 81.

42 J. Valdemar Borchsenius, *Ved Øresund og Mississippi* (Chicago, 1884), p. 10.

43 Boyesen, "En farlig dyd," p. 11.

44 Borchsenius, *Ved Øresund og Mississippi,* pp. 9-10.

45 Norstog, *Svein,* pp. 24-7.

46 All the characters in Vilhelm Berger's collection of short stories, *Emigrant-öden* (New York, 1904), stayed in the East—in Brooklyn, Pennsylvania, New England mill towns. None were farmers, and none went west.

47 "Jebel," "En svensk students äfventyr i Amerika," *Valkyrian,* Vol. VI, Nr. 2, (Dec., 1902), p. 93.

48 Oscar L. Strömberg, *Där prärien blommar* (Uppsala, 1933), p. 9.

49 "Aage," *Jens; fortælling* (Chicago, 1889), p. 32.
50 Buslett, *Fra min ungdoms nabolag,* p. 6.
51 Eriksen, "Det forjættede land," No. 22, p. 2.
52 Moen, *Knut Langaas,* p. 18.
53 Erikson, "Det forjættede land," Nr. 22, p. 4.
54 Blichfeldt, *Aalborg akvavit,* p. 56.
55 Erikson, "Det forjættede land," Nr. 22, p. 5.
56 Hans P. Gravengaard, *Christmas Again!* (Boston, 1936), pp. 12-13.
57 Henning Berger, "86 Clark Street," *Valkyrian,* Vol. XIII, Nr. 7 (July 1909) pp. 377-80.
58 Vilhelm Berger, *Ungdomskärlek,* p. 21.
59. Hans A. Foss, *Den amerikanske saloon* (Grand Forks, Dak., 1889), p. 27
60 Hansen, *Præriens børn,* p. 16.
61 *Ibid.,* pp. 32-4.
62 Rølvaag, *Amerika-breve* (Minneapolis, 1912), p. 11.
63 Waldemar Ager, *Gamlelandets sønner* (Oslo, 1926), p. 34.
64 Hjalmar H. Boyesen, *Falconberg* (New York, 1879), p. 23.
65 Adam Dan, *Prærierosen* (Chicago and Minneapolis, 1892), p. 9.
66 Ager, *Gamlelandets sønner,* p. 17.
67 Enok Mortensen, *Saaledes blev jeg hjemløs* (Holbæk, Denmark, 1934), p. 197.

CHAPTER FOUR

1 Elmer T. Peterson, *Trumpets West* (New York, 1934), p. 38. The wife of this Swedish immigrant was a Yankee, so here Old- and New-World skills were ranked as equal. Note that in a story laid 70 years before publication the author's testimony must be at second hand.
2 Ole E. Rølvaag, *Giants in the Earth* (New York, 1929), pp. 195-6, 214, 319.
3 Peter A. Lindberg, *Adam; en berättelse* (Chicago, 1899), p. 80.
4 Rølvaag, *Giants in the Earth,* p. 312.
5 Carl Hansen, *Præriens børn* (Cedar Rapids, Iowa, 1896-7), p. 15.
6 Einar Lund, "Solveig Murphy," *Ved arnen,* Vol. 58, Nr. 25 (5 Jan. 1932), pp. 11-12.
7 Sigurd J. Simonsen, *The Clodhopper* (New York, 1940), p. 21. The story opened in 1888, so this evidence is probably second-hand.
8 L. M. Bothum, *En historie fro nybyggerlivet* (Dalton, Minn., 1915). References to this topic are scattered throughout the book.
9 Simon Johnson, *From Fjord to Prairie* (Minneapolis, 1916), pp. 45-6.
10 Waldemar Ager, *Gamlelandets sønner* (Oslo, 1926), p. 161.
11 Rølvaag, *Giants in the Earth,* p. 129.
12 Bothum, *En historie fra nybyggerlivet,* p. 82.
13 Rølvaag, *Giants in the Earth,* pp. 159-64.
14 Kristian Østergaard, *Danby folk* (Cedar Rapids, Iowa, n.d.), pp. 33-4.
15 Anthony Rud, *The Second Generation* (New York, 1923), p. 183.
16 Lars Hellenes, *I onkel Sams land* (Kragerø, Norway, 1934), pp. 90-1.
17 Bernt Askevold, *Trang vei* (Fergus Falls, Minn., 1899), p. 33.
18 Sophus K. Winther, *Take All to Nebraska* (New York, 1936), p. 26.
19 Julius B. Baumann, "Matti Savo, et billede fra skogslivet," *Jul i vesterheimen* for 1920, n.p.
20 Enok Mortensen, *Jeg vælger et land* (Cedar Falls, Iowa, 1936), p. 63.
21 In a Norwegian-American tale, an elderly second-generation scholar taught girls of the third generation that "They were created in the image of a European nation, they were the product of its culture and development. . . . The long development of which they were the children in their heart of hearts, even though they now lived in another country—that concerned them greatly." Simon Johnson, *Fire fortællinger* (Minneapolis, 1919), pp. 42-3.
22 In his book on Norwegian heritage, *Omkring fædrearven* (Northfield, Minn., 1922), Ole E. Rølvaag maintained that no immigrant group in the United

States besides the Norwegian had created a literature in its own language (pp 57-60). This outstanding cultural leader of his group was completely ignorant of the considerable literature published before that date by both Danes and Swedes.

23 Frederik L. Grundtvig, *Kirke og folk* (Cedar Falls, Iowa, 1909), pp. 108-9. The original was poetically superior to this translation only in its metre and rhyme scheme.
24 Enok Mortensen, *Saaledes blev jeg hjemløs* (Holbæk, Denmark, 1934), p. 57.
25 Kristian Østergaard, *Blokhuset* (Copenhagen, 1892), p. 128.
26 Johan Person, *I Svensk-Amerika* (Worcester, Mass., 1900), short story "Lyckoriddarne" (The Knights of Fortune).
27 E. M. Favrholdt, *Emigranter*, Vol. I (Copenhagen, 1930), p. 65.
28 Waldemar Ager, *I Sit Alone* (New York, 1931), pp. 55-6.
29 Grundtvig, *Kirke og folk*, p. 109.
30 Johannes B. Wist, *Nykommerbilleder* (Decorah, Iowa, 1920), p. 10.
31 Hellesnes, *I onkel Sams land*, p. 17.
32 Ager, *Gamlelandets sønner*, p. 246.
33 Anna Olsson, *Från solsiden* (Rock Island, Ill., 1903), p. 159.
34 Rølvaag, *Giants in the Earth*, p. 281.
35 Sigmund Rein, "Udvandreren," *Ved arnen*, Vol. 68, Nr. 44 (5 May 1942), p. 16.
36 Simon Johnson, "En idyl fra nybyggertiden," *Jul i vesterheimen* for 1934, n.p.
37 Carl Hansen, *Præriefolk* (Copenhagen, 1907), pp. 9, 41.
38 P. C. Danielson, *Læg og lærd* (Minneapolis, 1920), pp. 10-11.
39 Hansen, *Præriens børn*, pp. 67-8.
40 Ramsey Benson, *Hill Country* (New York, 1928).
41 Ager, *Gamlelandets sønner*, p. 167.
42 Oliver A. Linder, *I västerland* (Rock Island, Ill., 1914), p. 89.
43 Hans A. Foss, *Den amerikanske saloon* (Grand Forks, Dak., 1889), pp. 25-6.
44 For example, Einar Lund, "Solveig Murphy," *Ved arnen*, Vol. 58, Nr. 25 (5 Jan. 1932), p. 15.
45 Rølvaag's *Omkring fædrearven* was certainly the most extended and detailed discussion of this topic, especially pp. 7-108; a typical shorter article was Iver Iversen, "Den norske selvbevisthet (Norwegian Selfconsciousness), in Peter T. Reite, ed., *Fra det ameriaknske-Normandi* (Moorhead, Minn., 1912), pp. 37-42. A good Swedish-American article was Vilhelm Berger, "Några svenska karaktärdrags amerikanisering" (The Americanization of Some Swedish Characteristic, *Valkyrian*, Vol. XII, Nr. 2 (Feb. 1908), pp. 114-21.
46 For example, H. E. Mose, "En lille nisse rejste," (A Little Elf Departed), *Julegranen* for 1950, n.p.; an unsigned editorial, "Vor dansk-amerikanske ungdoms fremtid" (The Future of Our Danish-American Youth), in the newspaper *Danskeren* for 21 Nov. 1905, p. 2.
47 A few articles analyzed general Scandinavian characteristics in English-language publications, such as N. C. Fredriksen, "From Home," *Scandinavia*, Vol. II, Nr. 3 (March 1885), pp. 65-8.
48 Vilhelm Berger, *Emigrant-öden* (New York, 1904), p. 116.
49 Rølvaag, *Omkring fædrearven*, p. 21.
50 Ole E. Rølvaag, *Fortællinger og skildringer* (Minneapolis, 1937), pp.52-60.
51 Albert Housland, *Stavangergutten* (Minneapolis, 1917), pp. 68-9.
52 J. A. Erikson, "Det forjættede land," *Ved arnen*, Vol. 64, Nr. 26 (4 Jan. 1938), p. 15.
53 Waldemar Ager, in an introduction to Rølvaag, *Fortællinger og skildringer*, p. 14.
54 Mary W. Williams, "Scandinavian Qualities and American Ideals," *Jul i vesterheimen* for 1921, n.p.
55 For instance, Rølvaag, *Omkring fædrearven*, pp. 89-93.
56 For example, in M. Falk Gjertsen, *Harald Hegg; billeder fra prærien* (Minneapolis, 1914), p. 18.
57 Mauritz Stolpe, *Samlade dikter* (Rock Island, Ill., 1940), p. 69.
58 Rølvaag, *Omkring fædrearven*, pp. 96-7.

59 Waldemar Ager, "Den anden side," *Kvartalskrift,* Vol. III, No. 2 (Apr. 1907), p. 10. Cf. Ørnulv Ødegaard, *Emigration and Insanity; a Study of Mental Disease among the Norwegianborn* [sic] *Population of Minnesota* (Copenhagen, 1932). "In the first place our results show that the rate of insanity among the Norwegianborn [sic] of Minnesota is higher than in Norway. . . . The reason for this seems to be the physical and mental strain of immigrant life rather than constitutional psychopathic tendencies . . ." (p. 192).
60 Ager, *Gamlelandets sønner,* p. 157.
61 Hjalmar H. Boyesen, *Falconberg* (New York, 1879), pp. 215-6.
62 *Ibid.,* p. 94.
63 Berger, "Några svenska karaktärsdrags amerikanisering," especially p. 19.
64 Rølvaag, *Omkring fædrearven,* pp. 83-9.
65 Norwegian joy was expressed for example by Erik A. Travaas, *Hjemve* (Minneapolis, 1925), in "Mit fædreland" (My Fatherland), pp. 20-1; Swedish disgust found typical expression in "Ludvig," "Tacksägelse" (Thanksgiving), *Valkyrian,* Vol. IX, Nr. 11 (Nov. 1905), p. 556.
66 Antonette Tovsen, "Fortidlig ude," *Ved arnen,* Vol. 50, Nr. 21 (18 Dec. 1923), p. 8.
67 C. P. Kjærbye, "Modersmaalet (The Mother Tongue), *De Forenede Staters danske almanak* for 1914, p. 178.
68 Henry G. Leach, "Danskere, jeg har kendt" (Danes I Have Known), *Julegranen* for 1950, n.p.
69 H. E. Mose, "En lille nisse rejste," n.p. Contributing self-importance to Danish character at the same time as calling it unjustified surely supports rather than contradicts other generalizations about Danish modesty. On the other hand, followers of the "happy Christianity" of Bishop N. F. S. Grundtvig must be excepter from the statement about Danes in America being the least nationalistic of the three groups. This articulate minority sought to preserve not only its joyous Lutheranism but also the song and dance, legend and story of ancient folk tradition in the homeland. Danish-American Grundtvigians were as nationalistic as Norwegian-American preservationists, though not so belligerent. Norwegian cultural nationalism was of course also strongly influenced by Grundtvigianism. See Gudrun Hovde Gvåle, *O. E. Rølvaag, nordmann og amerikaner* (Oslo, 1962), pp. 19 ff.
70 Otto Crælius, "På familjepic-nic," *Kurre-kalender* for 1900, pp. 59-60.
71 M. Sørensen, *Hinsides Atlanten* (Copenhagen, 1906), p. 152.
72 E. F. Madsen, *Fra de stille skove* (Minneapolis, 1896), p. 23.
73 C. F. Peterson, "Hafvets hittebarn," *Valkyrian,* Vol. VIII, No. 10 (Oct. 1904), p. 526.
74 Østergaard, *Danby folk,* pp. 94-5.
75 Gustav N. Malm, *Härute* (Lindsborg, Kan., 1919), p. 108.
76 Enok Mortensen, "The Whole Community," *Yule* for 1947, p. 46.
77 Enok Mortensen, *Jeg vælger et land,* p. 82.
78 Berger, "Några svenska karaktärsdrags amerikanisering," p. 121.
79 P. M. Magnussen, "Ett folk med många språk" (One People with Many Languages), in the newspaper *Svenska journalen* for 8 Sept. 1895, p. 4.
80 Arthur Landfors, *Från smältugnan* (Stockholm, 1932), pp. 132-3. My translation by no means does justice to the poetic beauty of the original.
81 For example, the families of Choate Burgass and Karl Kaas in Ole A. Buslett, *Benediktus og Jacobus* (Eau Claire, Wisc., 1920).
82 Oluf C. Molbech, *Over havet* (Copenhagen, 1904), pp. 20-1, 29-30.
83 Ole E. Rølvaag, *Their Fathers' God* (New York, 1931). The mother's warning was expressed in the preceding volume, *Peder Seier* (Oslo, 1951), p. 85.
84 Vilhelm Berger, "Klockeklang" (Bell Chime), *Valkyrian,* Vol. IX, Nr. 3 (March 1905), pp. 186-8.
85 Rølvaag, *Their Fathers' God,* p. 210.
86 Lund, "Solveig Murphy," *Ved arnen,* Nr. 20 to 29.
87 Swedish-language book and periodical publication culminated somewhat earlier, between the turn of the century and World War I his without a similar upswing

344

in the 1920s, according to tables and graphs compiled by Nils Hasselmo. See his article, "Det svenske språket i America" (The Swedish Language in America) in *Språk i Norden 1971*, (Årskrift for språknemndene i Norden), pp. 129-32.
88 Vilhelm Berger, "Lyckopenningen," *Valkyrian*, Vol. IX, Nr. 6 (June 1905), pp. 286-7.
89 Oliver A. Linder, "Svenskhetens bevarande" (The Preservation of Swedishness), in the newspaper *Svensk-amerikaneren* for 25 Nov. 1926.
90 Peterson, *Trumpets West*, pp. 18, 23.
91 E. M. Favrholdt, *Emigranter*, Vol. II (Copenhagen, 1931), p. 151.
92 Aron Bergström, *Från ljus genom skuggor til ljus* (Rock Island, Ill., 1925), pp. 255, 227.
93 Signe Ankarfelt, "Hvarför vi sjunga" (Why We Sing), *Valkyrian*, Vol. IV, Nr. 9 (Sept. 1900), p. 449. There is metre and rhyme in the original, but its poetic imagery is no better than in this translation.
94 Mortensen, *Saaledes blev jeg hjemløs*, pp. 118-9.
95 *Ibid.*, p. 244.
96 Mortensen, *Jeg vælger et land*, p. 9.
97 *Ibid.*, p. 39.
98 *Ibid.*, p. 92.
99 *Ibid.*, p. 93.
100 *Ibid.*, p. 117.
101 *Ibid.*, p. 171.
102 Quoted by "Don Andro," "Allt för sin kärleks skull," *Valkyrian*, Vol. IV, Nr. 3 (March 1900), p. 157.

CHAPTER FIVE

1 Waldemar Ager, "Norsk-amerikansk skjønlitteratur," in Johannes B. Wist, ed., *Norsk-amerikanernes festskrift* (Decorah, Ia., 1914), p. 292.
2 Simon Johnson, *Fallitten paa Braastad* (Minneapolis, 1922), pp. 8-10.
3 Einar Lund, "Solveig Murphy," *Ved arnen*, Vol. 58, Nr. 25 (5 Jan. 1932), p. 12.
4 Carl Hansen, *Landsmænd* (Cedar Falls, Iowa, 1908), short story "Gamle Hans Nielsens sidste jul" (Old Hans Nielsen's Last Christmas).
5 Carl W. Andeer, *Augustana-folk; andra samling* (Rock Island, Ill., 1914), pp. 33-4.
6 Vilhelm Berger, *Hundår och lyckodagar* (New York, 1905), p. 6.
7 Frederick J. Blichfeldt, *Aalborg akvavit og andre amerikanske fortællinger* (Copenhagen, 1904), p. 62.
8 For example, in George T. Rygh, *Morgenrødens vinger* (Minneapolis, 1909).
9 Gustaf Wicklund, *Gnistor från rimsmedjan* (Minneapolis, 1906), p. 47.
10 J. A. Erikson, "Det forjættede land," *Ved arnen*, Vol. 64, Nr. 22 (7 Dec. 1937), pp. 2, 4.
11 Hansen, *Landsmænd*, short story "Kalkunen" (The Turkey).
12 Ulrikka F. Bruun, *Ragna* (Chicago, 1884), pp. 31. 90.
13 Kristian Østergaard, *Dalboerne* (Copenhagen, 1913), pp. 9-10.
14. Peter A. Lindberg, *Adam; en berättelse* (Chicago, 1899), p. 113.
15 Hjalmar H. Boysen, *Falconberg* (New York, 1879), p. 213.
16 James A. Peterson, *Hjalmar, or The Immigrant's Son* (Minneapolis, 1922), p. 65.
17 "Peter Ravne," "Fra Ravnekrogen," *Misteltenen* for 1919, p. 23.
18 Oluf C. Molbech, *Over havet* (Copenhagen, 1904), p. 16.
19 Frederikke Johansen, *Foraar* (Askov, Minn., 1932), p. 55.
20 Eilert Storm, *Alene i urskogen* (Chicago, 1907), pp. 28-9.
21 Skulda Banér, *Latchstring Out* (Cambridge, Mass., 1944), pp. 17, 20, 25.
22 Lund, "Solveig Murphy," Nr. 21, p. 4.
23 Waldemar Ager, *Christ Before Pilate* (Minneapolis, 1924), p. 84.
24 Johan Bojer, *The Emigrants* (New York, 1925), pp. 23-4. Note that this is a native Norwegian author, not an immigrant.

25 M. Sørensen, *Hinsides Atlanten* (Copenhagen, 1906), p. 63.
26 Simon Johnson, *From Fjord to Prairie* (Minneapolis, 1916), p. 273.
27 Carl Hansen, *Præriens børn* (Minneapolis, 1895), p. 65.
28 August Faber, ed., *Til minde om pastor Peter Eriksen* (Clinton, Iowa, n.d.), p. 49.
29 E. M. Favrholdt, *Emigranter*, Vol. III (Copenhagen, 1934), p. 105.
30 Oliver A. Linder, *I västerland* (Rock Island, Ill., 1914), pp. 41-2.
31 Hansen, *Præriens børn*, p. 9.
32 Hansen, *Landsmænd*, p. 9.
33 Sørensen, *Hinsides Atlanten*, pp. 31, 52.
34 Drude K. Janson, *En saloonkeepers datter* (Minneapolis and Chicago, 1889), p. 47.
35 Hansen, *Landsmænd*, p. 79.
36 Vilhelm Berger, *Emigrant-öden* (New York, 1904), p. 110.
37 Simon Johnson, *Fire fortællinger* (Minneapolis, 1917), p. 17.
38 Hans A. Foss, *Valborg* (Decorah, Ia., 1927), p. 34.
39 John Dahle, "Norskdom," *Vor tid,* Vol. I, Nr. 1 (May 1904), p. 50.
40 In a novel opening in Norway, a father and mother argued about how much they should give the minister when he confirmed their son. The father said they should give ten crowns, while the mother pointed out how wealthy the minister was anyway, with his fixed salary of 6,000 crowns a year; as laborers they got only between 800 and 900. Albert Housland, *Stavangergutten* (Minneapolis, 1917), pp. 44-5.
41 Erikson, "Det forjættede land," Nr. 18, p. 3.
42 Simon Johnson, *Stier på ny jord* (MS, 1952), p. 105.
43 Boyesen, *Falconberg,* p. 99.
44 Margarethe E. Shank, *The Coffee Train* (New York, 1954), pp. 20-1.
45 Rygh, *Morgenrødens vinger,* p. 36.
46 Nils N. Rønning, *The Boy from Telemark* (Minneapolis, 1933), p. 79.
47 Adam Dan, *Prærierosen* (Minneapolis and Chicago, 1892), p. 39.
48 Lars Hellesnes, *I onkel Sams land* (Kragerø, Norway, 1934), p. 122.
49 M. Falk Gjertsen, *Harald Hegg; Bilder fra prærien* (Minneapolis, 1914), p. 4.
50 Ager, *Christ Before Pilate,* p. 21.
51 Gjertsen, *Harald Hegg,* p. 4.
52 Favrholdt, *Emigranter,* Vol. III, p. 100.
53 For instance, L. M. Bothum, *En historie fra nybyggerlivet* (Dalton, Minn., 1915), especially the summarizing statement pp. 82-3.
54 Hellesnes, *I onkel Sams land,* p. 26.
55 Johnson, *Fallitten paa Braastad,* especially p. 35.
56 Johannes B. Wist, *Jonasville* (Decorah, Iowa, 1922), Chap. IV.
57 Kristian Østergaard, *Et købmandshus* (Hetland, S. Dak., 1909), p. 12.
58 For example, Carl M. Norman-Hansen, *Chicago-noveller* (Copenhagen, 1893) pp. 52-5.
59 For instance. Enok Mortensen, *Saaledes blev jeg hjemløs* (Holbæk, Denmark, 1934), pp. 13-5.
60 Waldemar Ager, *Paa veien til smeltepotten* (Eau Claire, Wisc., 1917), pp. 72-3, 149.
61 For instance, Elmer T. Peterson, *Trumpets West* (New York, 1934), p. 28.
62 J. J. Skordalsvold, "Stor-Jo hørte Kristina Nilsson," *Jul i vesterheimen* for 1923, n.p.
63 Person, *I svensk-amerika,* short story "Främlingslegionan (The Foreign Legion).
64 Wist, *Jonasville,* pp. 115-7.
65 Molbech, *Over havet,* p. 17.
66 Enok Mortensen, *Jeg vælger et land* (Cedar Falls, Iowa, 1936), p. 126.
67 Hansen, *Landsmænd,* pp. 134-5.
68 "Jebel," "En svensk students äfventyr i Amerika," *Valkyrian,* Vol. VI, Nr. 5 (May 1902), p. 251.
69 Molbech, *Over havet,* p. 224.
70 Hellesnes, *I onkel Sams land,* pp. 20-1.

71 Hansen, *Landsmænd*, pp. 60-1.
72 Lindberg, *Adam; en berättelse*, p. 10.
73 C. F. Peterson, "Det svenske samvetet i den amerikanske politiken" (The Swedish Conscience in American Politics), *Valkyrian*, Vol. III, No. 2 (Feb. 1899), p. 65.
74 Dahle, "Norskdom," p. 52.
75 Bojer, *The Emigrants*, p. 151.
76 Emil F. Madsen, *Fra de stille skove* (Minneapolis, 1896), pp. 113-4.
77 Oluf C. Molbech, *Den gule by* (Copenhagen, 1905), p. 43.
78 Hans A. Foss, *Den amerikanske saloon* (Grand Forks, Dak., 1889), p. 34.
79 Jim Roeberg, *Blandt norske farmere* (Minneapolis, 1905), pp. 29-30.
80 Anders Ahlin, "En grönkölings romans," *Valkyrian*, Vol. XI, Nr. 1 (Jan. 1907), p. 41.
81 Nils N. Rønning, *Lars Lee, the Boy from Norway* (Minneapolis, 1928), p. 87.
82 Sophus K. Winther, *Take All to Nebraska* (New York, 1936), p. 48.
83 Sigurd J. Simonsen, *The Clodhopper* (New York, 1940), p. 83.
84 Dan, *Prærierosen*, p. 37.
85 Anna Olsson, *Från Solsiden* (Rock Island, Ill., 1903), p. 126.
86 Lund, "Solveig Murphy," Nr. 21, pp. 7-8.
87 E. M. Favrholdt, *Emigranter*, Vol. I (Copenhagen, 1930), short story "En gammel præst" (An Old Minister).
88 Dan, *Prærierosen*, p. 43.
89 Olsson, *På solsiden*, p. 137.
90 Herman E. Jørgensen, "Bare en bare er middels," *Jul i vesterheimen* for 1930, n.p.

CHAPTER SIX

1 M. Sørensen, *Hinsides Atlanten* (Copenhagen, 1906), pp. 44-5.
2 Nicolai S. Hassel, "Alf Brage, eller skolelæreren i Minnesota," *For Hjemmet*, Vol. V, Nr. 1 (15 Jan. 1874) to Nr. 12 (30 June 1874).
3 *Ibid.*, Nr. 3, p. 33.
4 For instance, Hjalmar H. Boysen, *Falconberg* (Boston, 1879), p. 37.
5 Kristian Østergaard, *Nybyggere* (Copenhagen, 1891), pp. 178 ff., and Frederikke Johansen, *Foraar* (Askov, Minn., 1932), pp. 46 ff.
6 Østergaard, *Nybyggere*, pp. 166-73.
7 Borghild Dahl, *Homecoming* (New York, 1953), pp. 120 ff. The story was laid a generation earlier.
8 Carl Hansen, *Landsmænd* (Cedar Falls, Iowa, 1908), p. 61.
9 Simon Johnson, *Fire fortællinger* (Minneapolis, 1919), pp. 72-4, 152, 163.
10 O. C. Rolfsen, "Ufred," *Ved arnen*, Vol. 69, Nr. 29 (24 Jan. 1939), p. 5.
11 Dorthea Dahl, *Byen paa berget* (Minneapolis, 1925), p. 116.
12 For example, Olaf Guldseth, "Da en 'mayflower' bar trøstebud til presten," in *Jul i vesterheimen* for 1916, n.p.
13 J. A. Erikson, "Det forjættede land," *Ved arnen*, Vol. 64, Nr. 35 (8 March 1938), p. 4.
14 For instance, Waldemar Ager, *Paa veien til smeltepotten* (Eau Claire, Wisc., 1917), p. 18.
15 Kristian Anker, *Helene* (Blair, Nebr., 1928), p. 50. The date was not specified for this incident in a Danish community in Nebraska, but mention of automobiles owned by many farmers in the area indicates a date in the early 1920s.
16 Peer O. Strømme, *Hvorledes Halvor blev prest* (Grand Forks, N. Dak., 1910), pp. 193 ff.
17 D. Dahl, *Byen paa berget*, pp. 37-8.
18 For instance, Olaus Rinde, *Forandringer paa Stone Hill* (Minneapolis, 1934), pp. 93-4.
19 Ole E. Rølvaag, *Amerika-breve*, (Minneapolis, 1912), pp. 110, 133.
20 Johansen, *Foraar*, p. 71.
21 Rølvaag, *Amerika-breve*, p. 136.

22 P. H. Pearson, *Prairie Vikings* (East Orange, N. J., 1927), p. 49.
23 *Ibid.*, p. 55.
24 August Faber, ed., *Til minde om pastor Peter Eriksen* (Clinton, Iowa, n.d.), pp. 52-6.
25 Erik Hetle, "Kem sin son er du?" *Jul i vesterheimen* for 1940, n.p. The unnamed college in the story was of course St. Olaf, the author-professor Ole E. Rølvaag.
26 Anna Hallander, "Sångfuglar" (Songbirds), *Valkyrian*, Vol. X, Nr. 7 (July 1906), p. 329.
27 G. A. Skugrud, *En banebryder* (n.p., 1889), p. 38.
28 Dahl, *Byen paa berget*, pp. 57-8.
29 Carl Hansen, *Præriefolk* (Copenhagen, 1907), p. 125.
30 Waldemar Ager, *I Sit Alone* (New York, 1931), p. 116.
31 E. F. Madsen, *Fra de stille skove* (Minneapolis, 1896), pp. 93-6.
32 Johannes B. Wist, *Jonasville* (Decorah, Iowa, 1922), Chapter IV.
33 Vilhelm Berger, "När Kalle Ekstedt skrev ihjel Svenska Posten," *Valkyrian*, Vol. VIII, Nr. 7 (July 1904), p. 357.
34 Enok Mortensen, *Jeg vælger et land* (Cedar Falls, Iowa, 1936), p. 72.
35 Dansk-amerikanske forfattere, *Fortællinger og digte* (Minneapolis and Chicago, 1906), short story by Carl Hansen, "En spekulant" (A Speculator).
36 Waldemar Ager, *Paa veien til smeltepotten*, pp. 106-7.
37 Enok Mortensen, *Saaledes blev jeg hjemløs* (Holbæk, Denmark, 1934), pp. 102-3.
38 Kristian Baun, *Blodets baand* (Copenhagen, 1938), p. 204.
39 C. P. Kjærbye, "Modersmaalet" (The Mother Tongue), *De Forende Staters danske almanak* for 1914, p. 179.
40 Johan Bojer, *Vår egen stamme* (Oslo, 1950), p. 232.
41 Hjalmar H. Boyesen, *Falconberg* (New York, 1879), p. 119.
42 Wist, *Jonasville*, pp. 180-1, 228, 244-5.
43 Kristian Østergaard, *Anton Arden og møllerens Johanne* (Armstrong, Iowa, 1897), p. 93.
44 Hjalmar H. Boyesen, "Et sønderknust hjerte," *Husbibliothek*, Vol. 19, Nr. 9 (Sept. 1892), p. 386.
45 Hansen, *Præriefolk*, pp. 9-10, 41.
46 Ager, *I Sit Alone*, p. 57.
47 Lars Hellesnes, *I onkel Sams land* (Kragerø, Norway, 1934), p. 158.
48 Ole A. Buslett, *Sagastolen; Fortælling fra det norske Nord-Amerika* (Chicago, 1908), p. 11.
49 Waldemar Ager, *Hverdagsfolk* (Eau Claire, Wisc., 1908), p. 10.
50 Peer Strømme, *Den vonde i vold* (Grand Forks, N. Dak., 1910), p. 75. This book purports to be written by one Halfdan Moe, and Strømme claimed only to have edited the manuscript. There is evidence, however, that Strømme chose to conceal his authorship because of the controversial and outspoken nature of his material.
51 "Jebel," "En svensk students äfventyr i Amerika," *Valkyrian*, Vol. VI, Nr. 5 (May 1902), pp. 253-4.
52 Berger, "När Kalle Ekstedt skrev ihjel Svenska Posten," pp. 357-60.
53 Baun, *Blodets baand*, pp. 80 ff.
54 Bojer, *Vår egen stamme*, p. 232.
55 Ole E. Rølvaag, *Giants in the Earth* (New York, 1929), pp. 362-9 *passim*.
56 Ager, *Paa veien til smeltepotten*, p. 154. Compare Sture Lindmark, "Citizenship," in *Swedish America, 1914-1932* (Uppsala, 1971), pp. 41-9.
57 Kristian Østergaard, *Dalboerne* (Copenhagen, 1913), p. 116.
58 For instance, Johannes B Wist, *Nykommerbilder* (Decorah, Iowa, 1920), pp. 64 ff.
59 For instance, Edward Sundell, *Lycklige dagar* (New York, 1894), pp. 177-8.
60 Ramsey Benson, *Hill Country* (New York, 1928), p. 142.
61 D. Dahl, *Byen paa berget*, p. 69.
62 D. Dahl, *Returning Home*, p. 63.
63 Sigurd J. Simonsen, *The Brush Coyotes* (New York, 1943), p. 126.

64 Gustaf Wicklund, *Gnistor från rimsmedjan* (Minneapolis, 1906), pp. 60-1.
65 Østergaard, *Anton Arden og møllerens Johanne*, p. 161.
66 M. Falk Gjertsen, *Harald Hegg; billeder fra prærien* (Minneapolis, 1914), p. 139.
67 Waldemar Ager, "Norsk-amerikansk skjønliteratur," in Johannes B. Wist, ed., *Norsk-amerikanernes festskrift* (Decorah, Iowa, 1914), p. 292.
68 Johannes K. Moen, *Knut Langaas* (Minneapolis, 1926), pp. 79 ff.
69 Ole E. Rølvaag, *Their Fathers' God* (New York, 1931), p. 294.
70 Johnson, *Fire fortællinger*, pp. 156-7.
71 Simon Johnson, *Frihetens hjem* (Minneapolis, 1925), p. 213.
72 Mortensen, *Jeg vælger et land*, p. 112.
73 Hans A. Foss, *Den amerikanske saloon* (Grand Forks, Dak., 1889), pp. 264-99 *passim.*
74 Wist, *Jonasville*, Chapters XIX-XXIV.
75 Ole A. Buslett, *Benediktus og Jacobus* (Eau Claire, Wisc., 1920).
76 Hansen, *Prærietolk*, p. 128.
77 *Ibid.*, p. 125.
78 Peter A. Lindberg, *Adam; en berättelse* (Chicago, 1899), pp. 51-2.
79 Nils N. Rønning, *Lars Lee, the Boy from Norway* (Minneapolis, 1928), p. 13.
80 K. B. Birkeland, *Han kommer* (Minneapolis, 1895), p. 138.
81 Anna M. Carlson, *The Heritage of the Bluestem* (Kansas City, Mo., 1930), pp. 41-2.
82 Johnson, *Fire fortællinger*, p. 71.
83 Bojer, *Vår egen stamme*, pp. 169, 173.
84 Kristian Østergaard, *Danby folk* (Cedar Falls, Iowa, n.d.), pp. 136-7.
85 Ole E. Rølvaag, *Fortællinger og skildringer* (Minneapolis, 1937), pp. 84-99.
86 "Jebel," "En svensk students äfventyr i Amerika," Nr. 12, p. 640.
87 Bernt B. Haugan, *Et besøk hos presten* (Faribault, Minn., 1895), p. 17.
88 Gustav Malm, *Härute* (Lindsborg, Kan., 1919), p. 108.
89 Vilhelm Berger, *Hvardags-händelser* (Boston, 1903), p. 93.
90 Kristian Østergaard, *Et købmandshus* (Hetland, S. Dak., 1909), p. 146.
91 Bojer, *Vår egen stamme*, p. 167.
92 J. A. Erikson, "Større end det største," *Ved arnen*, Vol. 65, Nr. 31 (7 Feb. 1939), p. 8.
93 Waldemar Ager, *Gamlelandets sønner* (Oslo, 1926), p. 103.
94 E. M. Favrholdt, *Emigranter*, Vol. III (Copenhagen, 1934), p. 102.
95 *Ibid.*, p. 100.
96 D. Dahl, *Byen paa berget*, p. 21.
97 Ole Shefveland, *Marit Gjeldaker* (West Union, Iowa, 1924), p. 144.
98 Hellesnes, *I onkel Sams land*, p. 38.
99 Jens Ingversen, *Kaldskapellanen* (Copenhagen, 1926), p. 131.
100 "Don Andro," "Allt för sin kärleks skull," *Valkyrian*, Vol. IV, Nr. 3 (March 1900), pp. 150-7.
101 For a sociological analysis of Norwegian-American church controversy, with historical background, see Nicholas Tavuchis, *Pastors and Immigrants; The Role of a Religious Elite in the Absorption of Norwegian Immigrants* (Studies in Social Life VIII, The Hague, 1963).
102 Edward Schuch, *Emigranterna* (Chicago, 1917), pp. 8-11.
103 Anon., *Kamp og sejr* (n.p., n.d.), pp. 28-9.
104 For example, L. M. Bothum, *En historie fra nybyggerlivet* (Dalton, Minn., 1915), p. 68.
105 Shefveland, *Marit Gjeldaker*, p. 153.
106 Nils N. Rønning, *The Boy from Telemark* (Minneapolis, 1933), pp. 70-1.
107 Birkeland, *Han kommer*, pp. 125 ff.
108 L. M. Bothum, *En historie fra nybyggerlivet* (Dalton, Minn., 1915), pp. 42-106 *passim.*
109 Favrholdt, *Emigranter*, Vol. III, p. 114.
110 Berger, *Hvardags-händelser*, p. 83.
111 Kristofer Janson, *Præriens saga* (Chicago, 1885), short story "En bygdekonge"

(A Parish King). It should be noted that this author was himself a Unitarian minister, who returned to Norway.
112 Buslett, *Benediktus og Jacobus*, p. 55.
113 The incident referred to occurred in Johannes B. Wist, *Hjemmet paa prærien* (Decorah, Iowa, 1929), pp. 196-203, and is mentioned again in the sequel, *Jonasville*, pp. 19-20.
114 Hassel, "Alf Brage," Nr. 6, p. 85.
115 Adam Dan, *Prærierosen* (Chicago and Minneapolis, 1892), especially pp. 92-3.
116 Madsen, *Fra de stille skove*.
117 Waldemar Ager, *Fortællinger og skisser* (Eau Claire, Wisc., 1913), p. 5.
118 Anon., "I ferien," *Vor tid*, Vol. II, Nr. 2 (Feb. 1906), pp. 722-37.
119 Hellesnes, *I onkel Sams land*, p. 39.
120 Marcus Thrane, *Den gamle Wisconsin Biblen* (Chicago, 1938), p. 15.
121 D. Dahl, *Byen paa berget*, pp. 136-8.
122 Hellesnes, *In onkel Sams land*, pp. 40-1.
123 Nils N. Rønning, *Bare for moro* (Minneapolis, 1913) pp. 12-13.
124 Wist, *Hjemmet paa prærien*, pp. 68-9.
125 Dan, *Prærierosen*, pp. 10, 28.
126 Carlson, *The Heritage of the Bluenstem*, p. 44.
127 Erikson, "Større end det største," Nr. 32, p. 5. The quotation immediately following is *ibid.*, p. 2.
128 P. Smith, Jr., "Studentenes juletræfest m.m.," *Norsk-amerikansk julebog* for 1921, p. 42.
129 Carl Hansen, *Præriens børn* (Minneapolis, 1895), p. 55.
130 Erikson, "Større end det største," Nr. 38, p. 2.
131 Schuch, *Emigranterna*, p. 159.
132 Østergaard, *Nybyggere*, p. 117 ff.
133 Østergaard, *Dalboerne*, p. 199.
134 Anna Olsson, *Bilder från jubelfesten* (Rock Island, Ill., 1912), p. 42.
135 Carl W. Andeer, *Augustana-folk* (Rock Island, Ill., 1911), p. 64.
136 Shefveland, *Marit Gjeldaker*, p. 141.
137 Hassel, "Alf Brage," Nr. 6, p. 85.
138 Frederik L. Grundtvig, *Kirke og folk* (Cedar Falls, Iowa, 1909) pp. 173-4.
139 Ager, *Fortællinger og skisser*, p. 14.
140 Waldemar Ager, "Et drømmebilde" (A Dream-Picture), in Peter T. Reite, ed., *Fra det Amerikanske-Normandi* (Moorhead, Minn., 1912), p. 29.
141 "Jebel," "En svensk students äfventyr i Amerika," Nr. 5, p. 254.

CHAPTER SEVEN

1 Gustaf Wiman, *Dikter och sånger* (Waltham, Mass., 1913), p. 67.
2 Carl Hansen, *Præriens børn* (Minneapolis, 1895), pp. 26, 28.
3 Wiman, *Dikter och sånger*, p. 94.
4 For instance, Dorthea Dahl, *Byen paa berget* (Minneapolis, 1925), in which the comparison of a happy family to a city on a hill is expanded on p. 255.
5 Waldemar Ager, *Paa veien til smeltepotten*, (Eau Claire, Wisc., 1917), pp. 194-5.
6 Alexander Marlowe, "No Room," *Christmas Chimes* for 1928, p. 23.
7 Aron Bergström, *Från ljus genom skuggor til ljus* (Rock Island, Ill., 1925), p. 84.
8 Magnus Elmblad, *Samlade arbeten*, Vol. II (Minneapolis, 1890), p. 47.
9 Ole E. Rølvaag, *Pure Gold* (New York, 1930).
10 Simon Johnson, *From Fjord to Prairie* (Minneapolis, 1916), pp. 309-10. His other novel with the same theme is *Stier på ny jord* (MS, 1952).
11 Ole E. Rølvaag, *Giants in the Earth* (New York, 1929), p. 202.
12 *Ibid.*, pp. 154-5.
13 Kristian Østergaard, *Nybyggere* (Copenhagen, 1891), p. 130.
14 Kristian Baun, *Blodets baand* (Copenhagen, 1938), short story "Livets forlis" (The Shipwreck of a Life).

15 Hjalmar H. Boyesen, "En farlig dyd," *Husbibliothek*, Vol. 19, Nr. 1 (Jan. 1892) to Nr. 3 (March 1892).
16. Anders Ahlin, "En gröngölings romans," *Valkyrian*, Vol. XI, Nr. 1 (Jan. 1907), pp. 50-1.
17 Hans A. Foss, *Den amerikanske saloon* (Grand Forks, Dak., 1889), pp. 101-11.
18 C. F. Peterson, "Hafvets hittebarn," *Valkyrian*, Vol. VIII, Nr. 2 (Feb. 1904), p. 88.
19 Adam Dan, *Maleren* (Minneapolis, 1901), p. 34.
20 Matthea Thorseth, *Cradled in Thunder* (Seattle, 1946), pp. 11-15.
21 Laura R. Bratager, *Over hav og land* (Minneapolis, 1925), pp. 43-4.
22 For instance, Holder C. Nielsen, "Den bedste julegave," *Julegranen* for 1950, n.p.
23 M. Sørensen, *Trækfugle* (Copenhagen, 1903), pp. 16-17
24 Johannes B. Wist, *Nykommerbilder* (Decorah, 1920), p. 77.
25 The two novels by Johannes B. Wist about Jonas Olsen in Dakota are *Hjemmet paa prærien* (Decorah, 1921), and *Jonasville* (Decorah, 1922).
26 Samuel M. Hill, *Uggletoner i vargetider* (Portland, Oreg., n.d.), p. 25.
27 Ager, *Paa veien til smeltepotten*, p. 55.
28 M. Sørensen, *Hinsides Atlanten* (Copenhagen, 1906), p. 47.
29 J. A. Erikson, "Gunhild og Jørgen," *Ved arnen*, Vol. 69, Nr. 58 (22 April 1943), pp. 14-15.
30 Enok Mortensen, *Saaledes blev jeg hjemløs* (Holbæk, Denmark, 1934), pp. 186, 219.
31 Eilert Storm, *Alene i urskogen* (Chicago, 1907), p. 290.
32 Bergström, *Från ljus genom skuggor till ljus*, p. 76.
33 Ernst Lindblom, *På försök, fem svensk-amerikanske dikter* (Chicago, 1888), pp. 9-10, 12-14.
34 Ture Nerman, in a foreword to a volume of poems by Arthur Landfors, *Från smältugnen* (Stockholm, 1932). The claim is borne out by evidence in Martin S. Allwood, ed., *America-svensk lyrik genom 100 år* (distributed by Bonniers, New York, 1949). See especially the section "Besvikelse" (Betrayal), pp. 62-7, and "Politiken" (Politics), pp. 82-92.
35 A recent revival of Swedish interest in Joe Hill has been marked by the publication of two books about him and a collection of his songs: Ture Nerman, *Joe Hill, arbetssångaren: mördare eller martyr?* (Joe Hill, Labor Singer: Murderer or Martyr?—Stockholm, 1968); Ingvar Söderström, *Joe Hill, diktare och agitator* (Joe Hill, Poet and Agitator—Oskarshamn, 1970); Enn Kokk, *Joe Hills sånger* (The Songs of Joe Hill—Lund, 1969). An earlier study was Barrie Stavis, *The Man Who Never Died* (New York, 1954), translated to Swedish in 1955.
    A Swedish film based on Joe Hill's life was shown internationally in 1971.
36 Jon Norstog, *Glitretind* (Minot, N.D., 1909), p. 33.
37 Hansen, *Præriens børn*, pp. 33, 38.
38 Johan Enander, "Farmaren" (The Farmer) in the newspaper *Svenska journalen-tribunen* for 5 Sept. 1894, p. 2.
39 Wist, *Nykommerbilder*, pp. 147-50.
40 Enok Mortensen, *Jeg vælger et land* (Cedar Falls, Iowa, 1936), pp. 167 ff.
41 Enok Mortensen, *Mit folk* (Askov, Minn., 1932), short story "En knusende pæn begravelse" (A Terribly Nice Funeral).
42 Peterson, "Hafvets hittebarn," Nr. 4, p. 218.
43 *Ibid.*, p. 221.
44 Bergström, *Från ljus genom skuggor till ljus*, p. 80.
45 Sophus K. Winther, *Mortgage Your Heart* (New York, 1937), pp. 116-7.
46 Emil L. Mengshoel, *Mené tekél* (Minneapolis, 1919), pp. 4-6.
47 George T. Rygh, *Morgenrødens vinger* (Minneapolis, 1909).
48 Norman Matson, *Day of Fortune* (New York, 1928), pp. 63-6.
49 Thorseth, *Cradled in Thunder*, especially pp. 231-43.
50 A rare exception was the violent revenge taken by an anarchist in Mengshoel, *Mené tekél*, p. 415. He blew up the church during the wedding ceremony of his beloved to a wicked capitalist, evidently destroying both her and himself

351

along with the evil rich.
51 Sophus K. Winther, *Take All to Nebraska* (New York, 1936), pp. 99-100.
52 Sophus K. Winther, *This Passion Never Dies* (New York, 1938), pp. 194-6.
53 Albert Houeland, *Stavangergutten* (Minneapolis, 1917), especially pp. 72-4.
54 Hans A. Foss, *Valborg* (Decorah, 1927), pp. 14, 41.
55 Simon Johnson, *Fire fortællinger* (Minneapolis, 1917), pp. 74 ff.
56 "Aage", *Jens* (Chicago, 1889), p. 32.
57 Sørensen, *Trækfugle*, pp. 35-6.
58 Storm, *Alene i urskogen*, pp. 17-20. The first edition of this book was published in Kristiania (Oslo) in 1899.
59 "A. K. A.," "Då man gick som kogubbe øfver Atlanten," *Valkyrian*, Vol. IX, Nr. 11 (Nov. 1905), pp. 569-73.
60 Mortensen, *Mit folk*, short story "Firkløveren" (The Four-Leaf Clover).
61 Wilhelm Reslow, "I främmande land" (In a Foreign Land), *Valkyrian*, Vol. X, Nr. 1 (Jan. 1906), p. 60.
62 L. M. Bothum, *En historie fra nybyggerlivet* (Dalton, Minn., 1915), pp. 102-4.
63 Signe Solheim, "Paa andre veie," *Ved arnen*, Vol. 68, Nr. 40 (7 Apr. 1942), p. 5.
64 Foss, *Valborg*, p. 102.
65 Ager, *Paa veien til smeltepotten*, p. 34.
66 M. Sørensen, "Smeden i Viborg," *Misteltenen* for 1916, Vol. IV, p. 13.
67 Rølvaag, *Giants in the Earth*, p. 111.
68 Solheim, "Paa andre veie," Nr. 41, p. 13.
69 Martha Ostenso, *O River, Remember!* (London, n.d.), pp. 70-1.
70 Lars Hellesnes, *I onkel Sams land* (Kragerø, Norway, 1934), pp. 18, 102.
71 Kristian Østergaard, *Danby folk* (Cedar Falls, Iowa, n.d.), p. 54.
72 Hellesnes, *I onkel Sams land*, pp. 95-6.
73 Waldemar Ager, "Den anden side" (The Other Side), *Kvartalskrift*, Vol. III, Nr. 2 (Apr. 1907), p. 7.
74 A sense of the nobility felt to be inherent in primogeniture and *odelsrett* was well expressed in Bertram Jensenius, "Adel i odel," *Norden*, Vol. I, Nr. 2 (Jan. 1929), pp. 13-14.
75 Rølvaag, *Their Fathers' God*, p. 253.
76 Winther, *This Passion Never Dies*, pp. 38-9.
77 Johannes Knudsen, "En krise," in *Dansk nytaar* for 1960, pp. 47-52.
78 Sigmund Rein, "Udvandreren," *Ved arnen*, Vol. 68, Nr. 44 (5 May 1942), p. 14.
79 Anton Kvist, *Sange fra veien* (Chicago, 1948), p. 13.
80 Waldemar Ager, 'Hvorledes ægteparet fik nattero," *Jul i vesterheimen* for 1915, n.p.
81 Winther, *This Passion Never Dies*, p. 37.
82 Sørensen, *Trækfugle*, p. 42.
83 Johnson, *Fire fortællinger*, pp. 108-11 *passim*.
84 Ole A. Buslett, "Og de solgte ut," *Jul i vesterheimen* for 1913, n.p.
85 Johnson, *Fire fortællinger*, pp. 108-9.
86 Rølvaag, *Their Fathers' God*, p. 148.
87 Johnson, *Fire fortællinger*, p. 109.
88 Carl Hansen, *Præriefolk* (Copenhagen, 1907), p. 89.
89 Johnson, *From Fjord to Prairie*, p. 307. The distorted spelling in the original has been somewhat normalized.
90 Johnson, *Fire fortællinger*, p. 157.
91 Ager, *Paa veien til smeltepotten*, p. 29. This scene is of course highly satirical.
92 Kristian Østergaard, *Dalboerne* (Copenhagen, 1913), p. 37.
93 Ole A. Buslett, *Fra min ungdoms nabolag* (Eau Claire, Wisc., 1918), pp. 40-1.
94 Bothum, *En historie fra nybyggerlivet*, pp. 11, 54-6.
95 Mortensen, *Mit folk*, p. 97.
96 Oluf C. Molbech, *Over havet* (Copenhagen, 1904), pp. 106-21.
97 Peter A. Lindberg, *Adam; en berättelse* (Chicago, 1899), p. 131.
98 Winther, *This Passion Never Dies*, p. 181.
99 Foss, *Valborg*, p. 165.

100 Ager, *Paa veien til smeltepotten,* p. 34.
101 C. M. Norman-Hansen, *Chicago-noveller; ny samling* (Copenhagen, 1893), short story "Den store by" (The Big City).
102 Bojer, *The Emigrants,* p. 48.
103 Rølvaag, *Giants in the Earth,* p. 177.
104 Baun, *Blodets baand,* short story "Jens Hwol."
105 James A. Peterson, *Hjalmar, or The Immigrant's* Son (Minneapolis, 1922), p. 168.
106 Jan Norstog, *Ørnerud* (Grand Forks, N.D., 1907), pp. 42-3.
107 Lars A. Stenbolt, *Præste-historier* (Minneapolis, 1893), pp. 103-4.
108 Adam Dan, *Sommerløv* (Cedar Falls, Iowa, 1903), p. 56.
109 Norstog, *Ørnerud,* p. 115.
110 Rølvaag, *Giants in the Earth,* p. 375.
111 Johnson, *From Fjord to Prairie,* p. 311.
112 A. H. Mason, *I ørneskyggen* (Eau Claire, Wisc., 1907), p. 33.
113 Waldemar Ager, *Christ Before Pilate* (Minneapolis, 1934), pp. 63, 46.
114 Margarethe E. Shank, *The Coffee Train* (New York, 1954), p. 16.
115 Elmer T. Peterson, *Trumpets West* (New York, 1934), p. 28.
116 Ole E. Rølvaag, *Paa glemte veie* (Minneapolis, 1914), p. 142.
117 Einar Lund, "Solveig Murphy," *Ved arnen,* Vol. 58, Nr. 21 (8 Dec. 1931), p. 5.
118 Adam Dan, *Vaarbud* (Minneapolis and Chicago, 1902), p. 35.
119 Hansen, *Præriens børn,* p. 67.
120 Winther, *This Passion Never Dies,* p. 32.
121 Sørensen, *Hinsides Atlanten,* p. 16.
122 Ager, *Paa veien til smeltepotten,* p. 269.
123 For example, Kristofer Janson, *Fra begge sider havet* (Kristiania, 1890), p. 17. Norwegian fiction contained many more incidents of prospective immigrants who changed their minds and stayed home than Norwegian-American fiction did. See Jørund Mannsåker, *Emigrasjon og dikting* (Oslo, 1971), pp. 132-4.
124 H. A. Foss, *Husmannsgutten* (Oslo, 1936), 12th ed. This story was first published in 1884.
125 Ole E. Rølvaag, *Amerika-breve* (Minneapolis, 1912), p. 174.
126 Rølvaag, *Their Fathers' God,* p. 157.

CHAPTER EIGHT

1 Carl Hansen, *Præriefolk* (Copenhagen, 1907), p. 92.
2 Ole E. Rølvaag, *Giants in the Earth* (New York, 1929), p. 89.
3 *Ibid.,* p. 254.
4 Ole E. Rølvaag, *Their Fathers' God* (New York, 1931), p. 204.
5 Hans A. Foss, *Den amerikanske saloon* (Grand Forks, Dak., 1889), p. 173.
6 Laura R. Bratager, *Over hav og land* (Minneapolis, 1925), p. 35.
7 Ramsey Benson, *Hill Country* (New York, 1928), p. 72.
8 "Jebel", "En svensk students äfventyr i Amerika," *Valkyrian,* Vol. VI, Nr. 11 (Nov. 1902), p. 572.
9 Ole Shefveland, *Marit Gjeldaker* (West Union, Iowa, 1924), p. 127.
10 Ernst Skarstedt, "Alt bättre och bättre, humoresk ur det svensk-amerikanska tidningsmannslifvet," *Prärieblomman kalender* for 1900, p. 88.
11 Hans Rønnevik, "En vise," *Jul i vesterheimen* for 1931, n.p.
12 Shefveland, *Marit Gjeldaker,* p. 127.
13 Peter C. Danielson, *Læg og lærd* (Minneapolis, 1920), p. 23.
14 Kristian Østergaard, *Dalboerne* (Copenhagen, 1913), p. 73.
15 L. M. Bothum, *En historie fra nybyggerlivet* (Dalton, Minn., 1915), pp. 68-71.
16 Shefveland, *Marit Gjeldaker,* p. 92.
17 Foss, *Livet i vesterheimen* (Kristiania, 1896), p. 138.
18 Ole E. Rølvaag, *Peder Seier* (Oslo, 1951), p. 152.
19 E. F. Madsen, *Fra de stille skove* (Minneapolis, 1896), p. 103.
20 J. Christian Bay, "Det bankede . . ." *Julegranen* for 1910, n.p.

23 - The Divided Heart

21 Anna M. Carlson, *The Heritage of the Bluestem* (Kansas City, Mo., 1930), p. 183.
22 Waldemar Ager, *I Sit Alone* (New York, 1931), p. 175. For a full discussion of typical immigrant drama, see Henriette C. K. Naeseth, *The Swedish Theatre of Chicago 1868-1950* (Rock Island, Ill., 1951), especially Chapter IV.
23 Waldemar Ager, *Christ Before Pilate* (Minneapolis, 1924), p. 89.
24 Enok Mortensen, *Saaledes blev jeg hjemløs* (Holbæk, Denmark, 1934), p. 59.
25 Jon Norstog, *Exodus* (Watson City, N. Dak., 1928-31). The fruitless soul-searchings of the sculptor hero, Sigbjørn Djuve, extend through three volumes.
26 Ole E. Rølvaag, *Fortællinger og skildringer* (Minneapolis, 1937), p. 118.
27 Simon Johnson, *Frihetens hjem* (Minneapolis, 1925), pp. 72 ff.
28 For example, Mary W. Williams, "Scandinavian Qualities and American Ideals," *Jul i vesterheimen* for 1921, n.p.
29 Anna Olsson, *I'm Scairt; Childhood Days on the Prairie* (Rock Island, Ill., 1927), p. 66.
30 Martha Stoles, "Syv og halvfems," *Jul i vesterheimen* for 1926, n.p.
31 Kristine Haugen, "Da Lars Berg skulde under kirketukt," *Norden*, Vol. I, Nr. 11 (Oct. 1929), p. 8.
32 M. Sørensen, *Trækfugle* (Copenhagen, 1903), p. 21.
33 Axel Tode, "I främande land," *Valkyrian*, Vol. IV, Nr. 12 (Dec. 1900), p. 609.
34 Anna Olsson, *Bilder från jubelfesten* (Rock Island, 1912), short story "Söndagsfirande" (Keeping the Sabbath).
35 Waldemar Ager, *Fortællinger og skisser* (Eau Claire, Wisc., 1913), p. 15.
36 For example, the kitchen opened by Svenska Föreningarnes Nationalförbund in Chicago in the 1890s, mentioned in Vilhelm Berger, *Ungdomskärlek* (Worcester, Mass., 1908), pp. 40-1.
37 Peter A. Lindberg, *Adam; en berättelse* (Chicago, 1899), pp. 65, 56.
38 Hansen, *Præriefolk*, p. 67.
39 Rølvaag, *Peder Seier*, p. 27.
40 Waldemar Ager, *Paa veien til smeltepotten* (Eau Claire, Wisc., 1917), p. 160.
41 Margarethe E. Shank, *The Coffee Train* (New York, 1954), p. 238.
42 Hans A. Foss, *Allehaande* (Minneapolis, 1907), p. 33.
43 Rølvaag, *Giants in the Earth*, p. 369.
44 Anders Ahlin, "En gröngölings romans," *Valkyrian*, Vol. II, Nr. 1 (Jan. 1907), p. 40.
45 Shank, *The Coffee Train*, p. 22.
46 For example, Aagot Raaen, *Grass of the Earth* (Northfield, Minn., 1950).
47 Foss, *Livet i vesterheimen*, p. 47.
48 Matthea Thorseth, *Cradled in Thunder* (Seattle, 1946), p. 35.
49 Hjalmar H. Boyesen, *Falconberg* (New York, 1879), p. 120.
50 For example, the title character in Kathryn Forbes, *Mama's Bank Account* (Sydney, Australia, 1950). The book was originally published in New York in 1943.
51 Ole E. Rølvaag, *Paa glemte veie* (Minneapolis, 1914).
52 Shank, *The Coffee Train*, pp. 20, 83.
53 Forbes, *Mama's Bank Account*, p. 130.
54 "Jebel," "En svensk students äfventyr i Amerika," Nr. 6, p. 352.
55 Kristofer Janson, *Præriens saga*, short story "Kvinden skal være manden underdanig" (Women, Submit to Your Husbands!). The exaggeration in the plot was typical of this author, who also after his return to Norway remained the implacable enemy of the Lutheran State Church.
56 Leonard Strömberg, *Där prärien blommar* (Uppsala, 1933), p. 236.
57 Waldemar Ager, "Hvorledes ægteparret fik nattero," *Jul i vesterheimen* for 1915, n.p.
58 Anthony Rud, *The Second Generation* (New York, 1923), p. 137.
59 Kristian Østergaard, *Danby folk* (Cedar Falls, Iowa, n.d.), p. 11.
60 Ole E. Rølvaag, *Amerika-breve* (Minneapolis, 1912), pp. 12-13, 42-3.
61 *Ibid.*, p. 47.
62 Bothum, *En historie fra nybyggerlivet*, pp. 104-5.

63 Adam Dan, *Sommerløv* (Cedar Falls, Iowa, 1903), pp. 206-8.
64 Bertram Jensenius, "Adel i odel," *Norden,* Vol. I, Nr. 2 (Jan. 1929), p. 14.
65 Ager, *Paa veien til smeltepotten,* p. 201.
66 Sophus K. Winther, *This Passion Never Dies* (New York, 1938), p. 76.
67 Thorseth, *Cradled in Thunder,* p. 35.
68 Ethan Mengers, "The Return of the Angels," *Christmas Chimes* for 1928, p. 91.
69 J. Christian Bay, "Hvor tvende verdener mødes," *Ved arnen,* Vol. 27, Nr. 9 (23 Oct. 1900), pp. 129-35.
70 C. K. Malmin, "Hitchhiking," *Jul i vesterheimen* for 1939, n.p.
71 Sophus K. Winther, *Mortgage Your Heart* (New York, 1937), p. 28.
72 Ole A. Buslett, *Sagastolen* (Chicago, 1908), p. 42.
73 Waldemar Ager, "Bare mor," *Jul i vesterheimen* for 1928, n.p.
74 Ager, *Paa veien til smeltepotten,* pp. 22-9 passim.
75 Sophus K. Winther, *Take All to Nebraska* (New York, 1936), p. 46.
76 Hans P. Gravengaard, *Christmas Again!* (Boston, 1936), p. 56.
77 Winther, *Mortgage Your Heart,* p. 150.
78 For example, Vilhelm Berger, *Hvardags-händelser* (Boston, 1903), short story "Mormor" (Grandmother).
79 Dorthea Dahl, "The Holy Day," *Jul i vesterheimen* for 1922, n.p.
80 Ager, *Paa veien til smeltepotten,* p. 6.
81 M. Sørensen, *Hinsides Atlanten* (Copenhagen, 1906), p. 105.
82 Bratager, *Over hav og land,* p. 42.
83 James A. Peterson, *Hjalmar, or The Immigrant's Son* (Minneapolis, 1922), p. 32.
84 James A. Peterson, *Solstad, The Old and the New* (Minneapolis, 1923), pp. 324-6.
85 Foss, *Valborg,* p. 78.
86 M. Sørensen, "Smeden i Viborg," *Misteltenen* for 1916, p. 12.
87 Victor Berger, *Svensk-amerikanska meditationer* (Rock Island, 1916), p. 120.
88 Foss, *Valborg,* p. 78.
89 Agnes Ringsborg, *Sunshine Beyond Shadows* (Blair, Neb., 1959), p. 84. The original edition of this novel was published in Danish in 1956.
90 Waldemar Ager, *Udvalgte fortællinger* (Minneapolis, 1918), p. 106.
91 Shank, *The Coffee Train,* p. 281.
92 Ebba T. Launsby, "Farmer Greisdals julebørn," *Dansk nytaar* for 1960, p. 53.
93 Dorthea Dahl, "Kopper-kjelen," *Norden,* Vol. II, Nr. 8 (Dec. 1930), pp. 18-19.
94 Ager, *Fortællinger og skisser,* pp. 41-2.
95 Thorseth, *Cradled in Thunder,* pp. 266, 268, 293-4.
96 Borghild Dahl, *Karen* (New York, 1947), pp. 232, 234.
97 Johnson, *Frihetens hjem,* p. 217.
98 Winther, *This Passion Never Dies,* pp. 121-2.
99 Rølvaag, *Giants in the Earth,* p. 312.
100 Dorthea Dahl, *Byen paa berget* (Minneapolis, 1925), p. 14.
101 B. Dahl, *Karen,* pp. 90, 121.
102 Johannes B. Wist, *Jonasville* (Decorah, Iowa, 1922), p. 117.
103 For instance, Jim Roeberg, *Blandt norske farmere* (Minneapolis, 1905), p. 24.
104 George T. Rygh, *Morgenrødens vinger* (Minneapolis, 1909), pp. 103-4.
105 Foss, *Valborg,* p. 107.
106 Johannes B. Wist, *Nykommerbilleder* (Decorah, Iowa, 1920), pp. 48-9.
107 Winther, *Take All to Nebraska,* pp. 251-5.
108 Benson, *Hill Country,* p. 54.
109 Gustaf Wiman, *Dikter och sånger* (Waltham, Mass., 1913), p. 74.
110 Kristian Østergaard, *Et købmandshus* (Hetland, S. Dak., 1909), pp. 113-4.
111 Rasmus Andersen, *Den forældreløse Margrethe* (n.p., 1907), p. 50.
112 Dorthea Dahl, *Returning Home* (Minneapolis, 1920), short story "The Choir in Hancock."
113 "A," *Danske emigranter* (Esbjerg, Denmark, 1890), pp. 39-40.
114 Mortensen, *Saaledes blev jeg hjemløs,* p. 66.

CHAPTER NINE

1 From the introduction by Ernst F. Philblad to the reprint of a short story by Gustaf N. Malm, "Peace and Good Will" (n.p., n.d.), originally printed in *The American Scandinavian Review*, Vol. IV, Nr. 1 (Jan.-Feb. 1916), pp. 9-16.
2 Sophus K. Winther, *Mortgage Your Heart* (New York, 1937), p. 71.
3 Carl Hansen, "Det brækkede ben," *De Forenede Staters danske almanak* for 1914, p. 171.
4 Magnus Hallenborg, "När nöden är som störst," *Valkyrian*, Vol. XIII, Nr. 12 (Dec. 1909), p. 635.
5 Knut B. Birkeland, *Han kommer* (Minneapolis, 1895), p. 175.
6 Kristian Østergaard, *Danby folk* (Cedar Falls, Iowa, n.d.), p. 22.
7 Johan Bojer, *The Emigrants*, (New York, 1925), p. 225.
8 Carl Hansen, *Præriens børn* (Cedar Rapids, Iowa, 1896-7), p. 35.
9 Carl Hansen, *Landsmænd* (Cedar Falls, 1908), p. 53.
10 Kristofer Janson, *Præriens saga* (Chicago, 1885), p. 7.
11 Aagot Raaen, *Grass of the Earth* (Northfield, Minn., 1950), pp. 17, 35-6.
12 K. G. Wilhelm Dahl, *Hedens barn* (Malmö, Sweden, 1913), short story "Jul på heden" (Christmas on the Prairie).
13 Hansen, *Præriens børn*, p. 23.
14 O. E. Rølvaag, *Giants in the Earth* (New York, 1929), for example p. 155.
15 Simon Johnson, "En forpostfegtning," *Jul i vesterheimen* for 1916, n.p.
16 Ole A. Buslett, *Veien til Golden Gate* (n.p., n.d.), pp. 6-7.
17 Iver Bernhard, "Nyveien til Fevatn," *Ved arnen*, Vol. 59, Nr. 32 (21 Feb. 1933), p. 4.
18 Kristian Østergaard, *Anton Arden og møllerens Johanne* (Armstrong, Iowa, 1897), pp. 208, 210.
19 Ole E. Rølvaag, *Amerika-breve* (Minneapolis, 1912), p. 167.
20 Palma Pederson, "Det rette valg," *Ved arnen*, Vol. 61, Nr. 32 (19 Feb. 1935), p. 6.
21 Jacob Bonggren, *Förstlingar; en samling dikter* (Stockholm, 1882), p. 217.
22 Jacob Bonggren, *Sånger och sagor* (Rock Island, Ill., 1902), p. 41.
23 Edward Anderson, *Dagsländor* (Chicago, n.d.), p. 28.
24 Vilhelm Moberg, last chapter entitled "Epilogue" in *Siste brev hjem* (Last Letter Home—Oslo, 1959).
25 From an introduction by Karin Michaëlis to Joost Dahlerup, *Vi udvandrere* (Copenhagen, 1924), p. 8.
26 Anton Kvist, *Lurerne kalder* (Copenhagen, 1927), p. 19. The original is much better poetry than this translation shows.
27 Gustav Wicklund, *Gnistor från rimsmedjan* (Minneapolis, 1906), p. 18.
28 Fredrik A. Bloom, *Hvita svanor* (Chicago, 1916), p. 11.
29 Edward Anderson, *Dagsländor*, p. 29.
30 Kristian Østergaard, *Sange fra prärien* (Copenhagen, 1912), p. 86.
31 Kristian Prestgard, "The Tragedy of the Immigrant," *Scandinavia*, Vol. I, Nr. 5 (May 1924), pp. 43-4.
32 "Ludvig," "En svensk-amerikaner," *Valkyrian*, Vol. X, Nr. 12, (Dec. 1906), p. 614.
33 Rølvaag, *Amerika-breve*, p. 173.
34 Kvist, *Lurerne kalder*, p. 15.
35 Anton Kvist, *Fred og fejde* (Chicago, 1917), p. 21.
36 Oskar A. Fliesburg, *Vildrosor och tistlar* (Minneapolis, 1899), p. 117.
37 Arthur Landfors, *Träd som bara grönska* (Stockholm, 1962), pp. 16-17. The original is much superior poetically to this translation.
38 Simon Johnson, *Fire fortællinger* (Minneapolis, 1919), p. 8.
39 Knut Brodin, ed. & compl., *Emigrantvisor och andre visor* (Stockholm, 1938), p. 13. A Norwegian version of the same ballad was also very popular, reprinted as "Farvel du Moder Norge" (Farewell, Mother Norway), in Theodore Blegen and Martin Ruud, *Norwegian Emigrant Songs and Ballads* (Minneapolis, 1936).

pp. 341-3. This translation, like the others in this chapter, has been made by the present writer.

40 Jon Norstog, "Mitt fedraland," *Dølen,* Vol. I, Nr. 1 (1903), p. 13.
41 Bojer, *The Emigrants,* p. 161. For a discussion of Norwegian authors' portrayal of guilt feelings in emigrant characters, see Jørund Mannsåker, *Emigrasjon og dikting* (Oslo, 1971), pp. 141-2.
42 Dahlerup, *Vi udvandrere,* p. 8.
43 Adam Dan, *Sommerløv* (Cedar Falls, Iowa, 1903), p. 71.
44 August L. Bang, *Livet i vold* (Cedar Falls, Iowa, 1938), p. 65.
45 Østergaard, *Danby folk,* p. 95.
46 Enok Mortensen, *Saaledes blev jeg hjemløs* (Holbæk, Denmark, 1934), p. 82.
47 Waldemar Ager, "Sjel til salgs," *Jul i vesterheimen* for 1935, n.p.
48 Skulda Banér, *Latchstring Out* (Cambridge, Mass., 1944), p. 130.
49 Dahlerup, *Vi udvandrere,* p. 30.
50 Simon Johnson, *Frihetens hjem* (Minneapolis, 1925), p. 273.
51 Simon Johnson, *From Fjord to Prairie* (Minneapolis, 1916), pp. 240-8.
52 Winther, *Mortgage Your Heart,* p. 173.
53 Hans A. Foss, *Valborg* (Oslo, 1928), p. 147.
54 Ole E. Rølvaag, *Peder Seier* (Oslo, 1951), pp. 28-9.
55 Julius Baumann, "Den sidste akt," *Jul i vesterheimen* for 1922, n.p.
56 Ager, *I Sit Alone,* p. 303.
57 Vilhelm Berger, "Några ord i vår språkfråga" (Some Words on Our Language Question), *Valkyrian,* Vol. VIII, Nr. 3 (March 1904), p. 134.
58 Winther, *Mortgage Your Heart,* p. 189.
59 Nils N. Rønning, *Bare for moro* (Minneapolis, 1913), p. 7.
60 Nils N. Rønning, "Når et folk mister sitt morsmål" (When a People Loses Its Mother Tongue), *Jul i vesterheimen* for 1943, p. 36.
61 Gustaf N. Malm, *Härute* (Lindsborg, Kan., 1919), pp. 28-9.
62 Rølvaag, *Amerika-breve,* p. 34.
63 *Ibid.*
64 Johannes B. Wist, *Nykommerbilleder* (Decorah, Iowa, 1920), p. 64.
65 Malm, *Härute,* p. 122. For a linguist's discussion of this problem, see Nils Hasselmo, "Language in Exile," in J. Iverne Davie and Ernest M. Espelie (eds.), *The Swedish Immigrant Community in Transition* (Rock Island, 1963), pp. 121-46.
66 "Saa kom Depressionen, men vi suffered ikke, for Klaus solgte on time, eller ogsaa traded han for Majs, Oats, Køer, og even goats." Agnes Ringsborg, "Et eventyr uden lige," *Dansk nytaar* for 1960, p. 59.
67 Hansen, *Landsmænd,* p. 7.
68 Rølvaag, *Peder Seier,* p. 163.
69 Sigurd J. Simonsen, *The Clodhopper* (New York, 1940), p. 24. The classic linguistic study of immigrant language is Einar Haugen, *The Norwegian Language in America* (Philadelphia and Oslo, 1953), 2 vol. Reprinted in 1970. For an account of research on Swedish-American dialects, see Nils Hasselmo, "Det svenska språket i Amerika," *Språk i Norden 1971* (Årsskrift for språknemndene i Norden), pp. 125-62. The article includes a full bibliography.
70 Ingemar Bru, "Dagbogsoptegnelser," in Halvor Hanson, ed., *Norsk-amerikansk julebog* (Chicago, 1921), p. 67.
71 Vilhelm Berger, *Emigrant-öden* (New York, 1904), pp. 76-7. The line cited refers to Sweden's period of expansion under Charles XII, battles in the fertile plains of Germany during the Thirty Years' War.
72 Enok Mortensen, *Jeg vælger et land* (Cedar Falls, 1936), p. 77.
73 Kristian Østergaard, *Nybyggere* (Copenhagen, 1891), p. 172.
74 Ole A. Buslett, introduction to story "Fram!" *Busletts,* Nr. 2 (April 1922), p. 8.
75 Lars Hellesnes, *I onkel Sams land* (Kragerø, Norway, 1934), p. 120.
76 Other sources, however, indicate more survivals of this type than the literature does. For instance, a series of ten radio programs were broadcast over the Norwegian National Radio between 28 Dec. 1961 and 9 May 1962, consisting

of tape recordings of traditional folk music both instrumental and vocal collected among Norwegian-Americans in 1961. Some of the performers were first generation, many second, a few third. The program director, Rolf Myklebust, found choral and folk-dance groups still functioning in larger cities of the Middle West.

77 Thorseth, *Cradled in Thunder*, pp. 135-6.
78 Johansen, *Foraar*, pp. 64, 114.
79 Johnson, *Frihetens hjem*, pp. 174-5.
80 Rølvaag, *Amerika-breve*, pp. 78-9.
81 Ager, *Udvalgte fortællinger*, pp. 108, 112.
82 These "she didn't care for, she said." ("Kärade" for "cared" is a typical example of an English word inflected and spelled in Swedish.) Otto Cralius, "På surprise-party," *Kurre-kalender* for 1899, p. 45.
83 Rølvaag, *Giants in the Earth*, p. 367.
84 Ole E. Rølvaag, *Their Fathers' God* (New York, 1931), p. 200.
85 Cralius, "På surpriseparty," p. 48.
86 For a discussion of the types of tales and mention of many specific ones printed in *bygdelag* magazines, see Ella V. Rølvaag, "Norwegian Folk Narrative in America," *Norwegian-American Historical Association Studies and Records*, Vol. XII (1941), pp. 33-59.
87 Thor Helgeson, ed. and compl., *Folkesagn og folketro, fortalt af de første nybyggere paa Indilandet* (Eau Claire, Wisc., 1923).
88 Rølvaag, *Their Fathers' God*, pp. 234-5. *Hilder*, or magical mirages seen especially at sea, should not be confused with *hulder*.
89 E. N. Remme, "Jul blandt nybyggerne," *Samband*, Nr. 80 (Dec. 1914), p. 73, cited by E. Rølvaag, "Norwegian Folk Narrative in America," p. 37.
90 Knut Teigen, *Ligt og uligt* (Minneapolis, 1907), p. 61. A Norwegian author, Bojer in *The Emigrants*, pictured a cotter's wife happily accepting her immigrant lot after catching a glimpse of the family brownie in their sod barn. "Fancy his coming with them all this way! Well, after this everything was sure to come right" (p. 106).
91 Ole E. Rølvaag, *The Boat of Longing* (New York, 1933).
92 Rølvaag, *Giants in the Earth*, for example, pp. 116-7, 125, 330-1, 349.
93 J. A. Erikson, "Det forjættede land," *Ved arnen*, Vol. 64, Nr. 23 (14 Dec. 1937), p. 1.
94 Norman Matson, *Day of Fortune* (New York, 1928), p. 39.
95 Banér, *Latchstring Out*, pp. 125-6. In Sweden, however, the custom is for girls to wake their parents with a tray on St. Lucia's Day, not the other way around.
96 Sophus K. Winther, *This Passion Never Dies* (New York, 1938), p. 122.
97 No mention has been made of the sole figure of American legend to come out of Scandinavian immigration to the Middle West, Febold Feboldson, because none of these immigrant writers was aware of him. Although defined as Swedish, he seems to have been a purely American creation in the image of Paul Bunyan. See Paul R. Beath, *Febold Feboldson; Tall Tales from the Great Plains* (Lincoln, Nebr., 1948). Paul Bunyan himself might have had a Norwegian grandfather in the folk-tale figure of Mumle Gåsegg; both were outsize figures of exaggerated strength and incredible deeds. For the Norwegian tale, see P. Chr. Asbjørnsen og Jørgen Moe, *Samlede Eventyr*, Vol. I (Oslo, 1953), pp. 108-20.
98 See the extended description of a Norwegian rural Christmas in A. B. Pedersen, *Mor Hansen* (Rothsay, Minn., 1900), pp. 178 ff., which has served as the basis of the following generalized passage.
99 Jon Norstog, *Glitretind* (Minot, N. Dak., 1909), p. 39.
100 Bang, *Livet i vold*, pp. 135-6.
101 In a story laid in the north woods of the United States, a Norwegian living alone was too poor to buy more than rice and raisins for his Christmas supper. Unexpectedly he received $10 by mail, which he promptly spent on gifts for his few neighbors. When he got home again, he laughed to discover that he had left only his original rice and raisins. No wonder he had gone bankrupt! But when the rice pudding stood steaming on his table, it alone made his Christ-

mas Eve. Anna D. Fuhr, "Severine and Company," *Jul i vesterheimen* for 1935, n.p.

102 Carl Hansen, "Rasmus's Jul" (Rasmus' Christmas), *Smaablomster fra vor lille have*, Vol. I, Nr. 10 (Dec. 1901), p. 18.

103 O. P. Vangsnes, "Jeg glemmer aldrig den første jul," *Jul i vesterheimen* for 1914, n.p. This tale, laid in the 1870s, implied changing Christmas customs in the Old Country. Evidently giving gifts had been adopted by wealthy people in Norway, but the lower classes had not yet followed suit.

104 Dorthea Dahl, "The Story That Was Never Written," *Jul i vesterheimen* for 1920, n.p.

105 Borghild Dahl, *Homecoming* (New York, 1931), p. 40.

106 M. Sørensen, "Jul i skoven, fortælling fra Wisconsin," *Julegranen* for 1906, n.p.

107 One Swedish boss, understanding well how homesickness for the Old Country was always worst at Christmas, tried to give his immigrant employees two or three days off for the holidays. "Jebel," "En svensk students äfventyr i America," Nr. 11, p. 572.

108 J. Christian Bay, "Juleaften," *Smaablomster fra vor lille have*, Nr. 10 (Dec. 1901), p. 9.

109 Hans A. Foss, "Nybyggerens jul," *Norsk-amerikaneren*, Vol. I, Nr. 2 (Oct.-Dec. 1916), p. 86.

110 Agnes Ringsborg, *Sunshine beyond Shadows* (Blair, Neb., 1959), p. 48.

111 Waldemar Ager, *Skyldfolk og andre* (Eau Claire, Wisc., 1938), short story "Juledrømmen som brast" (The Christmas Dream Which Burst).

112 Mona Aanrud, "Glade jul," *Jul i vesterheimen* for 1948, pp. 28-32.

113 "Peter Ravn," "Fra ravnekrogen," *Misteltenen* for 1922, pp. 23-4.

114 F. L. Grundtvig, ed., *Sangbog for the danske folk i Amerika* (Aarhus, Denmark, 1910), "Ved St. Hans-blusset," p. 139.

115 Banér, *Latchstring out*, pp. 150-1. Blue and yellow are the colors of the Swedish flag.

116 Winther, *Mortgage Your Heart*, p. 188.

117 Dahlerup, *Vi udvandrere*, pp. 102-8.

118 Matson, *Day of Fortune*, p. 117.

119 D. Dahl, *Byen paa berget*, pp. 229-33.

120 M. Sørensen, *Hinsides Atlanten* (Copenhagen, 1906), p. 105.

121 Vilhelm Berger, *Hundår och lyckodagar* (New York, 1905), p. 41. Until 1971 The Norwegian-American Line ran an annual Christmas boat to bring Norwegian-Americans back to the Old Country just in time for Christmas. Charter flights are still carrying on the tradition.

122 Hjalmar H. Boyesen, *Falconberg* (New York, 1879), p. 118.

123 Sørensen, *Hinsides Atlanten*, p. 72.

124 Ager, *Paa veien til smeltepotten*, p. 57.

125 Mortensen, *Saaledes blev jeg hjemløs*, p. 182.

126 Sinclair Lewis, *Main Street* (New York, c. 1943), pp. 265-6.

CHAPTER TEN

1 Ruth L. Fjeldsaa, "Guld og glans," *Ved arnen*, Vol. 51, Nr. 15 (4 Nov. 1924), p. 9.

2 Ole E. Rølvaag, *Peder Seier* (Oslo, 1951), pp. 142, 160, 164.

3 Frances Sterrett, *Years of Achievement* (Philadelphia, 1932), pp. 67, 132-3.

4 Johan G. R. Banér, *Barr* (Chicago, 1926), p. 26.

5 Adam Dan, *Sommerløv* (Cedar Falls, Iowa, 1903), pp. 248-9.

6 *Ibid.*, p. 282.

7 Adam Dan, *Solglimt* (Minneapolis, 1899), p. 38.

8 Dorthea Dahl, "The Holy Day," *Jul i vesterheimen* for 1922, n.p.

9 Johan A. Enander, *Valda skrifter* (Chicago, 1892), short story "Fyrvaktaren" (The Lighthouse-keeper).

10 C. F. Peterson, "Hafvets hittebarn," *Valkyrian*, Vol. VIII, Nr. 6 (June 1904), p. 332.

11 J. A. Erikson, "Det forjættede land," *Ved arnen*, Vol. 64, Nr. 22 (7 Dec. 1937), p. 8.
12 Johannes B. Wist, *Jonasville* (Decorah, Iowa, 1922), pp. 113-4.
13 Sophus K. Winther, *Take All to Nebraska* (New York, 1936), pp. 53, 66.
14 J. Christian Bay, "Hvor tvende verdener mødes," *Ved arnen*, Vol. 27, Nr. 9 (23 Oct 1900), p. 134.
15 Rølvaag, *Peder Seier*, pp. 65, 66-7.
16 *Ibid.*, p. 114.
17 Kristian Østergaard, *Nybyggere* (Copenhagen, 1891), p. 183.
18 Rølvaag, *Peder Seier*, pp. 141-3.
19 *Ibid.*, pp. 143-4.
20 *Ibid.*, p. 160.
21 Winther, *Take All to Nebraska*, pp. 269-75 passim.
22 Wist, *Jonasville*, p. 117.
23 Holger O. Nielsen, "Fra Fyn til Kansas," *Julegranen* for 1949, n.p.
24 Henning Berger, *Där ute* (Stockholm, 1901), short story "Bomans två världar" (Boman's Two Worlds).
25 O. C. Molbeck, "Amerika," in the newspaper *Dannevirke* for 11 March 1891, p. 5.
26 Ramsey Benson, *Hill Country* (New York, 1928), pp. 161-2.
27 Hans A. Foss, *Valborg* (Oslo, 1928), p. 89.
28 Hans A. Foss, *Livet i vesterheimen* (Kristiania, 1896), pp. 52 ff.
29 Rølvaag, *Peder Seier*, pp. 189-90.
30 Ole E. Rølvaag, *Giants in the Earth* (New York, 1929), pp. 284-7.
31 Jon Norstog, *Ørnerud* (Grand Forks, N.Dak., 1907), p. 28.
32 Borghild Dahl, *Homecoming* (New York, 1953), p. 128.
33 Dorthea Dahl, *Byen paa berget* (Minneapolis, 1925), p. 16.
34 James A. Peterson, *Hjalmar, or The Immigrant's Son* (Minneapolis, 1922), p. 49.
35 Hans A. Foss, *Den amerikanske saloon* (Grand Forks, N.Dak., 1889), p. 70. See the detailed and documented discussion of name-changing in Einar Haugen, *The Norwegian Language in America*, Vol. I, (Philadelphia and Oslo, 1953), Chap. IX.
36 Otto Crælius, "Like barn leka bäst," *Prærieblomman kalender* for 1902, pp. 58-63. See the statistical study of Swedish immigrant intermarriage in Sture Lindmark, *Swedish America, 1914-1932*, (Uppsala, 1971), pp. 50-63 and in Ulf Beijbom, *Swedes in Chicago: A Demographic and Social Study of the 1846-1880 Immigration* (Uppsala, Sweden, 1971), pp. 136-43.
37 Signe Solheim, "Den rette," *Jul i vesterheimen* for 1941, n.p.
38 Gustaf N. Malm, "Peace and Good Will," *The American-Scandinavian Review*, Vol. IV, Nr. 1 (Jan.-Feb. 1916), p. 11.
39 Simon Johnson, "Jon og Ragnhild," *Jul i vesterheimen* for 1935, n.p.
40 Peterson, *Hjalmar*, p. 273.
41 Kristian Østergaard, *Dalboerne* (Copenhagen, 1913), p. 199.
42 Waldemar Ager, *Paa veien til smeltepotten* (Eau Claire, Wisc., 1917), pp. 16-17.
43 Kathryn Forbes, *Mama's Bank Account* (Sydney, Australia, 1950), p. 134.
44 "Peter Ravn," "Fra Ravnkrogen," *Misteltenen* for 1919, p. 23. Compare a recent study of the progressive acclimatization of Swedish-Americans from Carl-Erik Måwe, *Värmlänningar i Nordamerika: Sociologiska studier i en anpassningsprocess* (Värmlennings in North America: Sociological Studies in a Process of Adjustment—Säffle, Sweden, 1971), Chap. VII.
45 *Ibid.*, pp. 23-4.
46 Foss, *Valborg*, pp. 140-1.
47 Hans Rønnevik, *100 procent* (Carlisle, Minn., 1926).
48 Simon Johnson, *Frihetens hjem* (Minneapolis, 1925), pp. 208-9.
49 *Ibid.*, p. 359.
50 *Ibid.*, p. 225.
51 Ole E. Rølvaag, *Omkring fædrearven* (Northfield, Minn., 1922), p. 68.
52 Johnson, *Frihetens hjem*, pp. 256-7.

53 *Ibid.*, p. 264. Research for this study did not discover any Swedish-American fiction on this theme, but this national group suffered fully as much from 100-percentism. See Chapter VI, "World War I," in Lindmark, *Swedish America, 1914–1932*, pp. 64-136.
54 Jakob Bonggren, *Sånger och sagor* (Rock Island, Ill., 1902), p. 42.
55 Arthur Landfors, *Träd som bara grönska* (Stockholm, 1962), pp. 13-15.
56 Foss, *Valborg*, p. 146.
57 Waldemar Ager, "Den anden side" (The Other Side), *Kvartalskrift*, Vol. III, Nr. 2 (Apr. 1907), p. 8.
58 Sigmun Rein, "Udvandreren," *Ved arnen*, Vol. 68, Nr. 44 (5 May 1942), pp. 14-15.
59 Johan Bojer, *Vår egen stamme* (Oslo, 1950), p. 280.
60 Jørund Mannsåker, *Emigrasjon og dikting* (Oslo, 1971), pp. 272-3. Compare a sociological study of a group of returned Swedish emigrants in Måwe, *Värmlänningar i Nordamerika*, Chap. V.
61 B. Dahl, *Homecoming*, p. 163.
62 Elmer T. Peterson, *Trumpets West* (New York, 1934), p. 298.
63 Simon Johnson, *Stier på ny jord* (MS, 1952), pp. 342-3.
64 D. Dahl, *Byen paa berget*, pp. 15-16, 59.
65 Winther, *Take All to Nebraska*, p. 262.
66 Sophus K. Winther, *Mortgage Your Heart* (New York, 1937), pp. 109-10.
67 *Ibid.*, p. 171.
68 Rølvaag, *Peder Seier*, p. 80.
69 *Ibid.*, p. 90.
70 "Per Ørn," "Den anden generation" (The Second Generation), *Uglen*, Vol. I, No. 11 (Oct. 1909), pp. 161-2.
71 *Ibid.*, Nr. 12, pp. 180-1.
72 A. H. Mason, *I ørneskyggen* (Eau Claire, Wisc., 1907), pp. 90-1.
73 Ager, *Paa veien til smeltepotten*, p. 35.
74 Sophus K. Winther, *This Passion Never Dies* (New York, 1938), p. 233.
75 Ager, *Paa veien til smeltepotten*, pp. 166-7.
76 Adam Dan, *Vaarbud* (Minneapolis, 1902), short story "Farmer Jens Jakobsen (Brudstykke af en historie fra Iowa)", (An Unfinished Story from Iowa).
77 M. Hallenborg, "Du skall hedra din fader och din moder," *Valkyrian*, Vol. XIII, Nr. 9 (Sept. 1909), p. 477.
78 Simon Johnson, "Jon og Ragnhild," n.p.
79 Dan, *Vaarbud*, p. 62.
80 Lars Hellesnes, *I onkel Sams land* (Kragerø, Norway, 1934), p. 144.
81 Thorvald Knudsen, "Georg," *Julegranen* for 1902, n.p.
82 Johnson, *Frihetens hjem*, pp. 268-9, 323, 360.
83 Ted Olson, *Hawk's Way* (New York, 1941), p. 41.
84 Peter T. Reite, ed., *Fra det amerikanske-Normandi* (Moorhead, Minn., 1919), p. 35.
85 Dorthea Dahl, *Returning Home* (Minneapolis, 1920), short story "The Grandmother."
86 Dorthea Dahl, "Julekvad," *Norden*, Vol. III, Nr. 7 (Dec. 1931), pp. 3-5.
87 Waldemar Ager, *Udvalgte fortællinger* (Minneapolis, 1918), short story "Løst fra alt" (Released from Everything).
88 Gustaf N. Malm, *Charli Johnson* (Chicago, 1909), p. 5.
89 Anon., "Gamla och nya hem" (Old and New Homes), *Vega*, Vol. I, Nr. 2 (June 1889), p. 65.
90 Hellesnes, *I onkel Sams land*, pp. 118-9, 136, 143.
91 Aron Bergström, *Från ljus genom skuggar till ljus* (Rock Island, Ill., 1925), p. 80.
92 Einar Lund, "Solveig Murphy," *Ved arnen*, Vol. 58, Nr. 24 (29 Dec. 1931), pp. 13-14.
93 Axel V. Grafström, *Skånska baron* (Stockholm, 1915), p. 26.
94 Rølvaag, *Giants in the Earth*, p. 110.
95 *Ibid.*, pp. 385, 416.

96 O. C. Molbech, *Over havet* (Copenhagen, 1904), pp. 9-10.
97 Ole E. Rølvaag, *Amerika-breve* (Minneapolis, 1912), p. 173.
98 *Ibid.*, pp. 169-71.

CHAPTER ELEVEN

1 Alvin Toffler, *Future Shock* (London, 1970), p. 19.
2 *Ibid.*, p. 20.
3 Swedish research projects in emigrant history are being carried out on three main levels. Down at the grass roots, amateur local historians and history study circles are collecting and/or copying source material from private families and local authorities which deals with thousands of individual emigrants. This material is being catalogued and preserved at the Emigrant Archive (Emigrant-institutet) in Växsjö in southern Sweden.

  This institution is also carrying out its own own systematic collection on microfilm of many kinds of emigrant records: for instance, all discoverable references to emigration in Swedish newspapers; police, church, tax and other records bearing on the emigrant movement; microfilming all known Swedish immigrant church records and newspaper files everywhere in the world.

  The third level of emigration research is going on at Swedish universities, where group projects by graduate students of history and sociology are making detailed studies of emigration at selected periods in various localities. Independent specialized scholarly studies are also beginning to appear, such as Ulf Beijbom, *Swedes in Chicago: A Demographic and Social Study of the 1846-1880 Immigration* (Uppsala, Sweden, 1971), published jointly by Scandinavian University Books and the Chicago Historical Society; and Carl-Erik Måwe, *Värmlänningar i Nordamerika* (Sociological Studies of a Process of Adjustment with Special Reference to the Emigration from Östmark-Säffle, Sweden, 1971).

A Selected Bibliography

I. SCANDINAVIAN-AMERICAN LITERATURE

1. Norwegian-American

Aanrud, Mona. "Glade jul" (Merry Christmas). *Jul i vesterheimen* for 1948, pp. 28-32.
Ager, Waldemar. *Afholdssmuler fra boghylden* (Prohibition Trifles from the Book-shelf). Eau Claire, Wis., 1901.
   When You are Tired of Playing. Eau Claire, 1907.
      Published in Norwegian as *Fortællinger for Øyvind.* Eau Claire, 1906.
   I strømmen (In the Main Stream). Eau Claire, 1908. 2nd ed.
   Hverdagsfolk (Ordinary People). Eau Claire, 1908.
   Paa drikkeondets konto (Charged Against the Demon Rum). Eau Claire, 1909. 4th ed.
   Blade af en dagbog (Pages from a Diary). Eau Claire, 1909.
Fortællinger og skisser (Stories and Sketches). Eau Claire, 1913.
   Paa veien til smeltepotten (On the Way to the Melting Pot). Eau Claire, 1917.
   Udvalgte fortællinger (Selected Short Stories). Minneapolis, 1918.
Ny samling fortællinger og skisser (New Collection of Stories and Sketches). Eau Claire, 1921.
   Det vældige navn (The Mighty Name). Eau Claire, 1923.
   Christ Before Pilate. Minneapolis, 1924.
      Published in Norwegian as *Kristus for Pilatus.* Eau Claire, 1910.
   Gamlelandets Sønner (Sons of the Old Country). Oslo, 1926.
   Under forvandlingens tegn. (Metamorphosis). Eau Claire, 1930.
I Sit Alone. New York, 1931.
      Published in Norwegian as *Hundeøine.* Oslo, 1929.
   Skyldfolk og andre (Relatives and Other People). Eau Claire, 1938.
   "Da sneen gik bort" (When the Snow Disappeared). *Kvartalskrift,* Vol. III, Nr. 1 (Jan. 1907), pp. 4-7.
   "Hvorledes ægteparret fik nattero" (How the Old Folks Found Repose). *Jul i vesterheimen* for 1915, n.p.
   "Da graagaasen trak mot syd" (When the Wild Goose Flew South). *Jul i vester-heimen* for 1917, n.p.
   "Bare mor" (Just Mother). *Jul i vesterheimen* for 1928, n.p.
   "Et nutidseventyr" (A Modern Adventure). *Jul i vesterheimen* for 1929, n.p.
   "Sjel til salgs" (Soul for Sale). *Jul i vesterheimen* for 1935, n.p.
Anon. "I ferien" (During Vacation). *Vor tid,* Vol. II, Nr. 2 (Feb. 1906), pp. 722-37, to Nr. 4 (Apr. 1906), pp. 825-37.
Askevold, Bernt. *Trang vei* (The Straight and Narrow Path). Fergus Falls, Minn., 1899.
   "Julefortælling" (Christmas Story). *Jul i vesterheimen* for 1912, n.p.
Asslagsson, Olai. *Langt, langt derute* (Far, Far Away). Kristiania (Oslo) 1919.
   De øde vidder (The Empty Prairies). Kristiania, 1921.

Bakke, Thorvald. *Crystal and Crown.* Minneapolis, 1900.
   Et tomt hus (An Empty House). Thorsby, Ala., 1927.

Bangsberg, John. *Louise Enerby; fortælling fra folkelivet* (Louise Enerby: A Story of Everyday Life). Minneapolis, 1929.
Bauman, Julius B. *Digte* (Poems). Eau Claire, Wis., 1909.
    Fra vidderne; nye digte (From the Prairies: New Poems). Minneapolis, 1915.
    Samlede digte (Collected Poems). Minneapolis, 1924.
    "Julefortælling" (Christmas Story). *Jul i vesterheimen* for 1913, n.p.
    "Matti Savo; et billede fra skogslivet" (Matti Savo: A Tale of Life in the Woods). *Jul i vesterheimen* for 1920, n.p.
    "Den sidste akt" (The Last Act). *Jul i vesterheimen* for 1922, n.p.
Beck, Richard. *A Sheaf of Verse*. Grand Forks, N. Dak., and Winnipeg, Canada, 1966.
Benson, John. *Ved gry og kveld* (At Dawn and Evening). Chicago, 1889.
Bernhart, Iver. "Nyveien til Fevatn" (The New Road to Fevatn). *Ved arnen,* Vol. 59, Nr. 31 (14 Feb. 1933) pp. 1-8, to Nr. 33 (28 Feb. 1933), pp. 1-8.
Birkeland, Knut Bergeson, *Han kommer* (He Is Coming). Minneapolis, 1895.
    Farlige mænd (Dangerous Men). Minneapolis, 1896.
Blegen, Theodore, C., and Ruud, Martin B., eds. & trs. *Norwegian Emigrant Songs and Ballads*. Minneapolis, 1936.
Bothum, L. M. *En historie fra nybyggerlivet* (A Story of Pioneer Life). Dalton, Minn., 1915.
Boyesen, Hjalmar Hjorth. *Tales from Two Hemispheres*. Boston, 1877.
    Falconberg. New York, 1879.
    Ilke on the Hilltop and Other Stories. New York, 1881.
    Idyls of Norway and Other Poems. New York, 1882.
    The Modern Vikings. New York, 1887.
    "En farlig dyd" (A Dangerous Virtue). *Husbibliothek,* Vol. 19, Nr. 1 (Jan 1892), pp. 10-12, to Nr. 3 (March 1892), pp. 102-7.
    "Et sønderknust hjerte" (A Broken Heart). *Husbibliothek,* Vol. 19, Nr. 9 (Sept. 1892), pp. 385-6.
Bratager, Laura Ringdal. *Digte og smaafortællinger* (Poems and Sketches). Minneapolis, 1914. 2nd ed.
    Over hav og land (Over Land and Sea). Minneapolis, 1925.
Bru, Ingemar. "Dagbogsoptegnelser" (Diary Entries).*Norsk-amerikansk julebog.* Chicago, 1921, pp. 65-77.
Bruflodt, Christian Olson. *Den største undergang; sanddrue sange* (The Greatest Destruction: True Songs). Stoughton, Wis., c. 1915.
Bruun, Ulrikka Feldtman. *Lykkens nøgle* (The Key to Fortune). Chicago, 1880.
    Fiendens faldgruber (The Enemy's Pitfalls). Chicago, 1884.
    Sange, dikte, og rim (Songs, Poems, and Rhymes). Chicago, c. 1920.
Buslett, Ole Amundson. *Fram!* (Forward!). Chicago, 1882.
    Leiligheds digte (Occasional Poems). Chicago, 1882.
    Øistein og Nora; digt (Øistein and Nora: A Poem). Madison, Wis., 1884.
    Rolf Hagen; fortælling (Rolf Hagen: A Story). La Crosse, Wis., 1893.
    Torstein i nybygden (Torstein on the Frontier). Fergus Falls, Minn., 1897.
    Sagastolen; fortælling fra det norske Nord-Amerika (The Story Corner: A Tale from Norwegian North America). Chicago, 1908.
    I parnassets lund (In the Grove of Parnassus). Northland, Wis., 1911.
    Glans-om-sol, og hans folks historie (Radiant-Sun and the Story of His People). Northland, 1912.
    Fra min ungdoms nabolag (About Neighbors of My Youth). Eau Claire, Wis., 1918.
    Benediktus og Jacobus. Eau Claire, 1920.
    Veien til Golden Gate (The Road to the Golden Gate). N.p., n.d.
    "Julebrev" (Christmas Letter). *Kvartalskrift,* Vol. I, Nr. 4 (Oct. 1905), pp. 7-13.
    "Og de solgte ut" (And they Sold Out). *Jul i vesterheimen* for 1913, n.p.
    "Butt og bøle" (Food and Lodging). *Jul i vesterheimen* for 1915, n.p.

Dahl, Borghild M. *Karen*. New York, 1947.
    Homecoming. New York, 1953.

Stowaway to America. New York, 1959.
A Minnetonka Summer. New York, 1960.
Under This Roof. New York, 1961.
This Precious Year. New York, 1964.
Dahl, Dorthea. *Fra hverdagslivet* (From Everyday Life). Minneapolis, 1915.
Returning Home. Minneapolis, 1920.
Byen paa berget (The City on the Hill). Minneapolis, 1925.
"Sangkoret i Hancock" (The Choir in Hancock). *Jul i vesterheimen* for 1917, n.p.
"The Story That Was Never Written." *Jul i vesterheimen* for 1920, n.p.
"The Holy Day." *Jul i vesterheimen* for 1922, n.p.
"The Beckoning Distance." *Jul i vesterheimen* for 1926, n.p.
"Rooted." *Jul i vesterheimen* for 1929, n.p.
"Groveir" (Growing Weather). *Jul i vesterheimen* for 1934, n.p.
"Jul hjemme" (Christmas at Home). *Jul i vesterheimen* for 1935, n.p.
"Kopper-kjelen" (The Copper Kettle). *Norden,* Vol. II, Nr. 8 (Dec. 1930), pp.
   18-19, 27-8, 31.
"Julekvad" (Christmas Carol). *Norden,* Vol. III, Nr. 7 (Dec. 1931), pp. 3-5.
Dalager, Kristofer. *Jordens skjød* (The Lap of Earth). Lake Park, Minn., 1925.
Danielson, Peter C. *Læg og lærd* (Town and Gown). Minneapolis, 1920.
d'Aulaire, Ingri and Edgar Parin. *Nils.* New York, 1948.
Duefjeld, Nils Nilsen. *I storm og stille* (In Storms and Stillness). Brooklyn, 1940.

Erikson, J. A. *Det forjættede land* (The Promised Land). Decorah, Iowa, c. 1938.
   Also printed in *Ved arnen,* Vol. 64, Nr. 18 (9 Nov. 1937), pp. 1-8, to Nr. 35
   (8 March 1938), pp. 1-8.
"Større end det største" (Greater than the Greatest). *Ved arnen,* Vol. 65, Nr. 32
   (14 Feb. 1939), pp. 1-8, to Nr. 47 (30 May 1939), pp. 1-7.
"Den trofaste Jon" (Faithful Jon). *Ved arnen,* Vol. 66, Nr. 34 (27 Feb. 1940),
   pp. 1-8, to Nr. 38 (26 March 1940), pp. 1-10.
"Gunhild og Jørgen." *Ved arnen,* Vol. 69, Nr. 54 (25 March 1943), pp. 1-8, to
   Nr. 61 (13 May 1943), pp. 9-12.
"Det er forskjel paa Henning og Haakon" (There's a Difference between Peter
   and Paul). *Ved arnen,* Vol. 71, Nr. 16 (21 Dec. 1944), pp. 2-6.
"Præriedronningen" (The Prairie Queen). *Ved arnen,* Vol. 71, Nr. 24 (15 Feb.
   1945), pp. 1-8, to Nr. 38 (24 May 1945), pp. 1-6.
"Et forlis" (A Shipwreck). *Ved arnen,* Vol. 72, Nr. 11 (15 Nov. 1945), pp. 1-8,
   to Nr. 20 (17 Jan. 1946), pp. 1-14.

Fjeldsaa, Ruth L. "Guld og glans" (Gold and Glitter). *Ved arnen,* Vol. 51, Nr. 14
   (24 Oct. 1924), pp. 1-9, to Nr. 20 (9 Dec. 1924), pp. 1-4.
"Stækkede vinger" (Broken Wings). *Ved arnen,* Vol. 53, Nr. 34 (15 March
   1927), pp. 1-7, to Nr. 41 (3 May 1927), pp. 1-7.
"Hans ungdoms borg" (The Fortress of His Youth). *Ved arnen,* Vol. 60, Nr. 20
   (28 Nov. 1933), pp. 1-8, to Nr. 21 (5 Dec. 1933), pp. 9-16.
"Julens rene toner" (The Pure Tones of Christmas). *Jul i vesterheimen* for
   1938, n.p.
Forbes, Kathryn. *Mama's Bank Account.* New York, 1943.
Foss, Hans Anderson. *Den amerikanske saloon* (The American Saloon). Grand
   Forks, Dak., 1889.
Livet i vesterheimen (Life in the Western Home). Kristiania (Oslo), 1896. 3rd ed.
Allehaande (Allspice). Minneapolis, 1907.
Valborg. Decorah, Iowa, c. 1927.
Husmannsgutten (The Cotter's Son). Oslo, 1936. 12th ed. Published in English
   as *The Cotter's Son.* Alexandria, Minn., 1963.
"Nybyggerens jul" (The Pioneer's Christmas). *Norsk-amerikaneren,* Vol. I, Nr. 2
   (Oct.-Dec. 1916), pp. 85-6.
Fuhr, Anna Dahl. "Da juleklokkene kimte" (When the Christmas Bells Chimed).
   Jul i vesterheimen for 1922, n.p.

"Stemninger" (Moods). *Jul i vesterheimen* for 1923, n.p.
"Maakene" (The Seagulls). *Jul i vesterheimen* for 1930, n.p.
"Severine and Company". *Jul i vesterheimen* for 1935, n.p.

Gamble, Lillian M. *Mor's New Land.* New York, 1951.
Gjertsen, M. Falk. *Harald Hegg; billeder fra prærien* (Harald Hegg: Sketches from the Prairie). Minneapolis, 1914.
Grundysen, Tellef. *Fra begge sider af havet* (From Both Sides of the Ocean). Chicago, 1877.
Guldseth, Olaf. "Da en 'mayflower' bar trøstebud til presten" (When a Mayflower Brought Comfort to the Minister). *Jul i vesterheimen* for 1916, n.p.
Gunheim, Olav. *Dikt, draum og rim* (Poems, Dreams, and Rhymes). Santa Rosa, Calif., 1963.

Hammerfors, Lise B. *Lille humør* (Little "Good Spirits"). Minneapolis, c. 1916.
Markblomster (Wild Flowers). Minneapolis, c. 1917.
Solglimt (Ray of Sunshine). Minneapolis, 1920.
Hanson, Haldor Johan, ed., *Norsk-amerikansk julebog.* Chicago, 1921.
Harildstad, J. A. *Bondegutten Hastad under asylbehandling i den nye verden* (Farmer-boy Hastad under Treatment in a Mental Hospital in the New World). Minneapolis, 1919.
Hassel, Nicolai Severin. "Alf Brage, eller skolelæreren i Minnesota" (Alf Brage, or the Schoolteacher in Minnesota). *For hjemmet,* Vol. V, Nr. 2 (31 Jan. 1874), pp. 17-22, to Nr. 11 (15 June 1874), pp. 161-5.
"Rædselsdagene; et norsk billede fra indianerkrigen i Minnesota" (Days of Terror; A Norwegian Story of the Indian War in Minnesota). *For hjemmet,* Vol. V, Nr. 13 (15 July 1874), pp. 193-9, to Nr. 19 (15 Oct. 1874), pp. 289-94.
Juletanker og julefortællinger (Christmas Thoughts and Christmas Tales). Decorah, Iowa, 1897.
Haugan, Bernt B. *Et besøk hos presten* (A Visit to the Minister). Faribault, Minn., 1895.
Haugen, Kristine. "Da Lars Berg skulle under kirketukt" (Lars Berg's Church Discipline). *Norden,* Vol. I, Nr. 11 (Oct. 1929), p. 8.
Heir, Martin. "Da Tore Gundersen Speilberg kom til Amerika" (When Tore Gundersen Speilberg Came to America). *Vor tid,* Vol. II, Nr. 5 (May 1906), pp. 883-95.
Helgeson, Thor, ed., *Folkesagn og folketro, fortalt af de første nybyggere paa Indilandet* (Folk Sayings and Beliefs of Norwegian Pioneers in the Land of Indians). Eau Claire, Wis., 1923.
Hellesnes, Lars. *I onkel Sams land* (In Uncle Sam's Country). Kragerø, Norway, 1934.
Hetle, Erik. "Kem sin son er du?" (Whose Son Are You?) *Jul i vesterheimen* for 1940, n.p.
Hilsen, Einar. *Strengelek; dikt og sange.* (Strumming; Poems and Songs). Fargo, N. Dak., 1915.
Holand, Hjalmar Rued. *Old Peninsula Days.* Ephraim, Wis., c. 1925.
Holberg, Ruth Langland. *Tansy for Short.* New York, 1952.
Houeland, Albert. *Stavangergutten* (The Boy from Stavanger). Minneapolis, 1917.

Ingvoldstad, Orlando. *Rimes for Rusty.* Pasadena, Calif., 1964.

Janson, Drude Krog. *En saloonkeepers datter* (A Saloonkeeper's Daughter). Minneapolis and Chicago, 1889.
Tore; fortælling fra prærien (Tore: A Story from the Prairie). Kristiania (Oslo), 1894.
Jensenius, Bertram. "Adel i odel" (The Nobility in Alodium). *Norden,* Vol. I, Nr. 2 (Jan. 1929), pp. 13-14.
Jørgensen, Herman E. "Bare en bare er middels" (If One Is Only Average). *Jul i vesterheimen* for 1930, n.p.

Johnson, Simon. *Et geni* (A Genius). Eau Claire, Wis., 1907.
Lonea. Eau Claire, 1909.
From Fjord to Prairie. Minneapolis, 1916. Published in Norwegian as *I et nyt rige*. Minneapolis, 1914.
Fire fortællinger (Four Stories). Minneapolis, 1917.
Fallitten paa Braastad (The Bankruptcy at Braastad). Minneapolis, 1922.
Frihetens hjem (Freedom's Home). Minneapolis, 1925.
Stier på ny jord (Paths on New Earth). MS deposited in University of Oslo Library, 1952.
"Blaa øine" (Blue Eyes). *Jul i vesterheimen* for 1914, n.p.
"En forpostfegtning" (A Pioneer Outpost). *Jul i vesterheimen* for 1916, n.p.
"Jims sidste dag" (Jim's Last Day). *Jul i vesterheimen* for 1918, n.p.
"Den graa prest" (The Grey Minister). *Jul i vesterheimen* for 1919, n.p.
"Naar livet bærer slør" (When Life Wears a Veil). *Jul i vesterheimen* for 1921, n.p.
"Borgere" (Citizens). *Jul i vesterheimen* for 1924, n.p.
"Det vaakende øie" (The Watching Eye). *Jul i vesterheimen* for 1926, n.p.
"Havfuglen" (The Sea Bird). *Jul i vesterheimen* for 1928, n.p.
"En idyl fra nybyggertiden" (An Idyll from Pioneer Days). *Jul i vesterheimen* for 1934, n.p.
"Jon og Ragnhild." *Jul i vesterheimen* for 1935, n.p.
"Paul Olson sitt land" (Paul Olson's Land). *Jul i vesterheimen* for 1940, n.p.
"I utferdens spor" (On the Emigration Trail). *Jul i vesterheimen* for 1948, pp. 8-12.
Jones, Thelma. *Skinny Angel*. New York, 1946.

Lima, Ludvig, ed. *Norsk-amerikanske digte i udvalg* (A Selection of Norwegian-American Poems). Minneapolis, 1903.
Lock, Otto. *Syndens sold* (The Wages of Sin). Eau Claire, Wis., 1909.
Der var engang; digte (Once Upon a Time: Poems). Patterson, Calif., c. 1913.
De svundne dage (Bygone Days). N.p., 1914.
I bunden stil; en samling digte (In Traditional Meters: A Collection of Poems). (Patterson, Calif., 1920).
Lund, Einar. "Solveig Murphy." *Ved arnen,* Vol. 58, Nr. 20 (1 Dec. 1931), pp. 1-8, to Nr. 29 (2 Feb. 1932), pp. 1-11.
"Solstrålen i nybygget" (The Sunbeam of the Settlement). *Jul i vesterheimen* for 1945, pp. 25-9.
Lund, L. H. *Vesterlandiana og andre historier* (Westerlandiana and Other Stories). Chicago, n.d.
Lunde, Fridthjof. *Døgnfluen* (Mayflies). Eau Claire, Wis., 1908.

Malmin, C. K. "Hitchhiking". *Jul i vesterheimen for* 1939, n.p.
Mason, A. H. *I ørneskyggen* (In the Eagle's Shadow). Eau Claire, Wis., 1907.
"Grundskaden" (The Basic Injury). *Kvartalskrift,* Vol. III, Nr. 2 (Apr. 1907), pp. 13-19.
"Hyrekaren kvæder" (The Hired Hand Sings). *Kvartalskrift,* Vol. V, Nr. 1 (Jan. 1909), pp. 9-11.
Matson, Norman. *Day of Fortune*. New York, 1928.
Meelberg, Theo. O. *Kristelige sange* (Christian Songs). Fargo, N. Dak., 1917.
Melby, Gustav. *Vildblomsten; en samling vers* (The Wild Flower: A Collection of Verses). Seattle, 1892.
The Seamless Robe, and Other Poems. Boston, 1914.
The Lost Chimes, and Other Poems. Boston, 1918.
Twilight: A Collection of Verse. Minneapolis, 1921.
Blue Haze and Other Poems. Minneapolis, 1925.
Light and Shade. St. Paul, 1931.
Mengshoel, Emil Lauritz. *Øen Salvavida; et samfundsbillede* (The Isle of Salvavida: A Portrayal of Society). Girard, Kan., 1904.
Mené Tekél; norsk-amerikansk arbeiderfortælling fra slutten af det 19. aar-

hundrede (Mené Tekél: A Norwegian-American Workers' Story from the End of the 19th Century). Minneapolis, 1919.

Moen, Johannes Knudson. *Knut Langaas; et kapitel fra emigranternes, pioneerernes, og prærieens saga* (Knut Langaas: A Chapter from the Saga of the Emigrants, the Pioneers, and the Prairie). Minneapolis, 1926.

Moen, Robert Ashton. *The Sailing of Leif the Lucky and Other Poems.* New York, 1965.

Morgan, Nina Hermanna. *Prairie Star.* New York, 1955.

Mortensen, John. *Nogle blade* (Some Pages). Eau Claire, Wis., 1914.

Nordberg, Carl Edin. *Presten som ikke kunde brukes, og andre skisser* (The Minister Who Couldn't Be Used, and Other Sketches). Minneapolis, 1922.
Indremissionspresten i storbyen (The Inner Mission Minister in the Big City). Minneapolis, 1923.
Nykommeren som blev diakon (The Newcomer Who Became Deacon). Minneapolis, 1924.

Norstog, Jon. *Yggdrasil.* Kristiania (Oslo), 1902.
Haakon Sollid; fortælling. (Haakon Sollid: A Story). Minot, N. Dak., 1906.
Ørnerud; fortælling. Grand Forks, N. Dak., 1907.
Glitretind. Minot, 1909.
Svein; forteljing. Minot, 1909.
Frå audni (Out of Desolation). Watson City, N. Dak., 1923.
Livshorpa (The Harp of Life). Watson City, 1927.
Exodus. Watson City, Vol. I, 1928; Vol. II, 1930; Vol. III, 1931.
Når elvane møtest (When the Rivers Meet). Bergen, Norway, 1934.
Havet (The Ocean). Watson City, c. 1938.
"Fyrsten" (The Duke). *Jul i vesterheimen* for 1918, n.p.
"Mundharpen" (The Mouthharp). *Jul i vesterheimen* for 1924, n.p.

Nygaard, Norman Eugene. *They Sought a Country.* New York, 1950.

Odden, Halvor Gunnarson. *Bygaks, samlede langs med veien* (Barley Ears Gathered Along the Way). Decorah, Iowa, n.d.

Odland, Martin Wendell. *The New Canaan.* Minneapolis, 1933.

Ødegaard, Oscar Olson. *Fra visergutt til millionær* (From Errand Boy to Millionaire). Fargo, N. Dak., 1917.
Fortællinger og digte (Stories and Poems). Wyndmere, N. Dak., 1924.
Kjærlighed og lenger (Love and Chains). Wyndmere, 1930. 2nd ed.

Olson, Eleonora and Ethel. *Yust for Fun: Norwegian-American Dialect Monologues.* Minneapolis, 1925.

Olson, Ted. *A Stranger and Afraid.* New Haven, Conn., 1928.
Hawk's Way. New York, 1941.

Ostenso, Martha. *Wild Geese.* New York, 1925.
The Dark Dawn. New York, 1926.
The Mad Carews. New York, 1927.
The Young May Moon. New York, 1929.
The Waters Under the Earth. New York, 1930.
There's Always Another Year. New York, 1933.
The White Reef. New York, 1934.
O River, Remember! New York, 1943.

Oyen, Henry. *Gaston Olaf.* New York, 1917.
Twisted Trails. New York, 1921.
Tarrant of Tin Spout. New York, 1922.

Pedersen, A. B. *Mor Hansen; et romantisk billede fra livet* (Mother Hansen: A Romantic Tale from Real Life). Rothsay, Minn., 1900.

Pederson, Palma. *Syrener, digte* (Lilacs: Poems). La Crosse, Wis., 1911.
Under ansvarets svøbe (Under the Lash of Responsibility). Eau Claire, 1923.
Ragna. Eau Claire, 1924.
Genier (Geniuses). Eau Claire, 1925.

"Det rette valg" (The Right Choice). *Ved arnen,* Vol. 61, Nr. 32 (19 Feb. 1935), pp. 1-8, to Nr. 35 (12 March 1935), pp. 7-14.
Peterson, James A. *Hjalmar, or The Immigrant's Son.* Minneapolis, 1922.
Solstad, The Old and the New. Minneapolis, 1923.
Peyton, Karen. *The World So Fair.* Philadelphia, 1963.
Love Song. Philadelphia, 1964.

Quam, Erik Tobias. "Aasmund Kvalstads ottiende fødselsdag" (Aasmund Kvalstad's Eightieth Birthday). *Vor tid,* Vol. I, Nr. 7 (Apr. 1905), pp. 349-53.

Raaen, Aagot. *Grass of the Earth.* Northfield, Minn., 1950.
Rein, Sigmun. "Udvandreren" (The Emigrant). *Ved arnen,* Vol. 68, Nr. 44 (5 May 1942), pp. 14-16.
Reine, Rasmus O. *En liten samling af psalmer og religiøse digte* (A Little Collection of Psalms and Religious Poems). La Crosse, Wis., 1871.
Reite, Peter Thoresen, ed. *Fra det amerikanske-normandi* (From the American Normandy). Moorhead, Minn., 1912.
Rinde, Olaus. *Forandringer paa Stone Hill* (Changes at Stone Hill). Minneapolis, 1934.
Ristad, Ditlef Georgson. *Fra det nye normandie* (From the New Normandy). Edgerton, Wis., 1922.
Kvad (Songs). Minneapolis, c. 1930.
Roeberg, Jim. *Blandt norske farmere; skitser fra prærien* (Among Norwegian Farmers: Sketches from the Prairie). Minneapolis, 1905.
Rølvaag, Ole Edvart. *Amerika-breve, fra P. A. Smevik til hans far og bror i Norge* (Letters from America, from P. A. Smevik to His Father and Brother in Norway). Published under the pseudonym of Paal Mørck. Minneapolis, 1912. Published in English as *The Third Life of Per Smevik.* Minneapolis, 1971.
Paa glemte veie (On Forgotten Paths). Minneapolis, 1914.
Omkring fædrearven (Concerning Our Heritage). Northfield, Minn., 1922. Essays.
Giants in the Earth. New York, 1929. 2nd ed. Published in Norwegian as *I de dage* (In Those Days), Oslo, 1924, and *Riket grundlægges* (The Founding of the Kingdom), Oslo, 1925.
Peder Victorious. New York 1929. Published in Norwegian as *Peder Seier,* Oslo, 1928.
Pure Gold. New York, 1930. Published in Norwegian as *To tullinger* (Two Fools). Minneapolis, 1920.
Their Father's God. New York, 1931. Published in Norwegian as *Den signede dag* (The Blessed Day). Oslo, 1931.
The Boat of Longing. New York, 1933. Published in Norwegian as *Længelsens baat.* Minneapolis, 1921.
Fortællinger og skildringer (Stories and Tales). Minneapolis, c. 1937.
Rønnevik, Hans. *100 procent.* Carlisle, Minn., 1926.
"En vise" (A Ballad). *Jul i vesterheimen* for 1931, n.p.
Rønning, Nils Nilsen. *Bare for moro* (Just for Fun). Minneapolis, 1913.
Lars Lee, The Boy from Norway. Minneapolis, 1928. Published in Norwegian as *Gutten fra Norge.* Minneapolis, 1924.
The Boy from Telemark. Minneapolis, 1933.
"Naar døren aapnes" (When the Door Is Opened). *Jul i vesterheimen* for 1918, n.p.
"Der stod kvinder bak os" (There Were Women Behind Us). *Jul i vesterheimen* for 1922, n.p.
Rolfsen, O. C. "Ufred" (Conflict). *Ved arnen,* Vol. 65, Nr. 29 (24 Jan. 1939), pp. 1-8, to Nr. 30 (31 Jan. 1939), pp. 1-8.
Rud, Anthony M. *The Second Generation.* New York, 1923.
Rudie, K. K. *Sol og skygge* (Sun and Shadow). Minneapolis, 1903.
Rygh, George Alfred Taylor. *Morgenrødens vinger* (The Wings of Dawn). Minneapolis, 1909.
"Lady Alice." *Jul i vesterheimen* for 1911, n.p.

369

"The Flight of Years." *Jul i vesterheimen* for 1925, n.p.
"And So, No More." *Jul i vesterheimen* for 1926, n.p.
"The Two Sisters." *Jul i vesterheimen* for 1927, n.p.
"A Home-Coming." *Jul i vesterheimen* for 1929, n.p.
"The Dominie." *Jul i vesterheimen* for 1930, n.p.

Sætre, Allan. *Farmerkonen Marit Kjølseths erfaringer i Chicago* (The Chicago Experiences of Marit Kjølseth, Farmer's Wife). Chicago, 1918. 24th ed.

Selnes, Johan. *Lyng; digte og fortællinger* (Heather: Poems and Stories). Kristiania (Oslo), c. 1912.
Vaarsol; digte og fortællinger (Spring Sun: Poems and Stories). Kristiania, c. 1914.
Bølgeslag (Wash of Waves). Kristiania, 1915.
Vestlandstoner; digte og fortællinger (Western Echoes: Poems and Stories). Minneapolis, 1919. 3rd ed.
"Vi lovet at komme —" (We Promised to Come—). *Jul i vesterheimen* for 1915, n.p.
"Ole Petter og norsk-amerikanerinden" (Ole Petter and the Norwegian-American Lady). *Jul i vesterheimen* for 1917, n.p.

Sether, Gulbrand. *Sønnen paa Hofstad* (The Son at Hofstad), Chicago, 1917.

Severson, Sever H. *Dei møttes ve Utica* (They Met at Utica). Stoughton, Wis., 1892.

Shank, Margarethe Erdahl. *The Coffee Train*. New York, 1954. 2nd ed. 1968.
Call Back the Years. Minneapolis, 1966.

Shefveland, Ole. *Pastor Gram*. Minneapolis, 1899.
Marit Gjeldaker. West Union, Iowa, 1924.

Simonsen, Finn Rein. "Den gamle blikkenslager" (The Old Tinker). *Jul i vesterheimen* for 1926, n.p.

Skordalsvold, Johannes J. "Stor-Jo hørte Kristina Nilsson" (Big Jo Heard Kristina Nilsson). *Jul i vesterheimen* for 1923, n.p.

Skugrud, G. A. *En banebryter* (A Pioneer). N.p., 1889.

Smedsrud, Peder. *I ensomme stunder* (In Lonely Hours). Hillsboro, N. Dak., 1899.

Smith, P., Jr. "Studentens juletræfest m.m." (The Student's Christmas Party, etc.). *Norsk-amerikansk julebog* for 1921, pp. 39-54.

Sneve, Ole Svendsen. *Sange og digte tilegnet afholdsagens venner* (Songs and Poems Dedicated to Friends of Prohibition). Eau Claire, Wis., 1896.
Samlede sange og digte (Collected Songs and Poems). Silvana, Wash., 1912.

Solheim, Signe. "Paa andre veie" (On Other Paths). *Ved arnen*, Vol. 68, Nr. 40 (7 Apr. 1942), pp. 1-7, to Nr. 43 (28 Apr. 1942), pp. 9-16.
"Den rette" (The Right One). *Jul i vesterheimen* for 1941, n.p.
"Ardis." *Jul i vesterheimen* for 1943, n.p.

Stenholt, Lars A. *Fra trælle til folk* (From Bondsmen to Human Beings). Minneapolis, 1889.
Præste-historier; skildringer af nordmændenes landsliv i Nordamerika (Stories About Ministers: Tales of Norwegian Lives in North America). Minneapolis, 1893.
Paven i Madison; eller Rasmus Kvelves merkværdige liv og hændelser (The Pope in Madison: or, Rasmus Kvelve's Remarkable Life and Doings). St. Paul, 1908.

Sterrett, Frances Roberta. *Years of Achievement*. Philadelphia, 1932.

Storm, Eilert. *Alene i urskogen* (Alone in the Primeval Forest). Chicago, 1907. 2nd ed.

Straus, Leonore Thomas. *The Tender Stone*. New York, 1964.

Strømme, Peer Olsen. *Hvorledes Halvor blev prest* (How Halvor Became a Minister). Decorah, Iowa, 1893. Published in English as *Halvor: A Story of Pioneer Youth*. Decorah, 1960.
Den vonde ivold (In the Power of Evil). Grand Forks, N. Dak., 1910.
Unge Helgesen (Young Helgesen). Grand Forks, 1911.
Digte (Poems). Minneapolis, 1920.

Teigen, Knut Martin Olson. *Ligt og Uligt* (This and That). Minneapolis, 1899.
Vesterlandske digte (West Country Poems). Minneapolis, 1905.
Blandt vestens vikinger (Among the Vikings of the West). Minneapolis, 1907.

Thorseth, Matthea. *Cradled in Thunder.* Seattle, 1946.
Thrane, Marcus. *Den gamle Wisconsin bibelen* (The Old Wisconsin Bible). Chicago, 1938. 6th ed.
Tovsen, Antonette. "Blaaveis" (Anemones). *Ved arnen.* Vol. 47, Nr. 18 (30 Nov. 1920), pp. 1-10, to Nr. 19 (7 Dec. 1920), pp. 1-10.
"Fortidlig ude" (Too Early). *Ved arnen,* Vol. 50, Nr. 21 (18 Dec. 1923), pp. 6-10.
"Naar strengene brister" (When the Strings Break). *Ved arnen,* Vol. 51, Nr. 35 (24 March 1925), pp. 1-8, to Nr. 42 (12 May 1925), pp. 1-8.
"Rebekka." *Ved arnen,* Vol. 56, Nr. 16 (5 Nov. 1929), pp. 1-8, to Nr. 27 (21 Jan. 1930), pp. 1-7.
"Markens trælle" (Slave of the Earth). *Ved arnen,* Vol. 61, Nr. 12 (2 Oct. 1934), pp. 1-8, to Nr. 14 (16 Oct. 1934), pp. 9-16.
"Toner" (Echoes). *Ved arnen,* Vol. 62, Nr. 35 (10 March 1936), pp. 1-8, to Nr. 47 (2 June 1936), pp. 1-12.
"Dybe hjulspor" (Deep Wheel Tracks). *Ved arnen,* Vol. 69, Nr. 29 (21 Jan. 1943), pp. 1-8, to Nr. 57 (15 Apr. 1943), pp. 1-7.
"Det siste forsøk" (The Last Attempt). *Jul i vesterheimen* for 1935, n.p.
"Hvite seil" (White Sails). *Jul i vesterheimen* for 1936, n.p.
"Da kronprinsparet kom" (When the Crown Prince and Princess Came). *Jul i vesterheimen* for 1941, n.p.
Travaas, Erik Arnesen. *Hjemve; norske digte og fortællinger* (Nostalgia: Norwegian Poems and Stories). Minneapolis, 1925.

Vangsnes, O. P. "Jeg glemmer aldrig den første jul" (I'll Never Forget That First Christmas). *Jul i vesterheimen* for 1914, n.p.

Wergeland, Agnes M. *Amerika og andre digte* (American and Other Poems). Decorah, Iowa, c. 1912.
Efterladte digte (Posthumous Poems). Minneapolis, c. 1914.
Wist, Johannes B. *Nykommerbilleder* (Newcomer Scenes). Decorah, Iowa, 1920.
Hjemmet paa prærien (The Home on the Prairie). Decorah, 1921.
Jonasville. Decorah, 1922.
Reisen til Rochester (The Trip to Rochester). Minneapolis, 1922.

Xan, Erna Oleson. *Home for Good.* New York, 1952.

2. Swedish-American

"A. K. A." "Då man gick som kogubbe öfver Atlanten" (Crossing the Atlantic on a Cattle Boat). *Valkyrian,* Vol. IX, Nr. 11 (Nov. 1905), pp. 569-76.
Ahlin, Anders. "En gröngölings romans" (A Greenhorn's Romance). *Valkyrian,* Vol. XI, Nr. 1 (Jan. 1907), pp. 40-54.
"Hämnden" (The Revenge). *Valkyrian,* Vol. XI, Nr. 2 (Feb. 1907), pp. 77-81.
Albrecht, Esther A. *Riders of the North Star.* New York, 1970.
Allwood, Martin S., ed. *Amerika-svensk lyrik genom 100 år* (Swedish-American Poetry Through 100 Years). Distributed by Bonniers, New York, 1949.
Andeer, Carl. *I brytningstid* (In Changing Times). Rock Island, Ill., 1904.
Augustana-folk. Rock Island, 1911.
Augustana-folk; andra samling (Second Collection). Rock Island, 1914.
Anderson, Axel. *Gnistor; dikter* (Sparks: Poems). Rockford, Ill., n.d.
Anderson, Edward. *Dagsländor;* dikter (Dragonflies). Chicago, n.d.

Banér, Johan Gustaf Runesköld. *Barr.* Chicago, 1926.
Banér, Skulda V. *Latchstring Out.* Cambridge, Mass., 1944.
First Parting. New York, 1960.
Bengtson, Berndt; Erikson, Gustaf; Hill, S. M.; and Lönnquist, C. A. *Fyrväplingen; valda stycken* (The Four-Leaf Clover). N.p., c. 1912.

Berger, Victor. *Svensk-amerikanska meditationer* (Swedish-American Meditations). Rock Island, 1916.

Berger, Vilhelm. *Rätt och slätt* (Pure and Simple). Boston, 1902.

Hvardags-händelser (Everyday Experiences). Boston, 1903.

Emigrant-öden (Emigrant Fates). New York, 1904.

Hundår och lyckodagar ("Dog Years" and Happy Days). New York, 1905.

Ungdomskärlek (Puppy Love). Worcester, Mass., 1908.

Pytt i panna (Hash). Worcester, 1912.

"Klockeklang" (Bell Chime). *Valkyrian*, Vol. IX, Nr. 3 (March 1905), pp. 186-8.

"Lyckopenningen" (The Lucky Coin). *Valkyrian*, Vol. IX, Nr. 6 (June 1905), pp. 286-7.

Bergqvist, Olle. *Sune Vegult*. Stockholm, 1908.

Bergström, Aron. *Från ljus genom skuggor till ljus* (From Light Through Shadows to Light). Rock Island, Ill., 1925.

Björk, Hjalmar. *Stigens rosor* (Roses Along the Path). Kungsbacka, Sweden, 1973.

Bjorn, Thyra Ferré. *Papa's Wife*. New York, 1955.

Papa's Daughter. New York, c. 1956.

Mama's Way. New York, c. 1959.

Bloom, Fredrik A. *Vågskvalp; dikter och sånger* (Wash of Waves: Poems and Songs). Omaha, Nebr., 1898.

Hvita svanor; blandade dikter (White Swans: Miscellaneous Poems). Chicago, 1916.

"När Kalle Ekstedt skrev ihjel Svenska Posten" (When Kalle Ekstedt Wrote The Swedish Post to Death). *Valkyrian*, Vol. VIII, Nr. 7 (July 1904), pp. 357-60.

Bonggren, Jakob. *Förstlingar; en samling dikter* (Beginnings: A Collection of Poems). Stockholm, 1882.

Sånger och sagor (Songs and Stories). Rock Island, Ill., 1902.

Brieskorn, Roland, ed. *Toner från svensk-Amerika* (Echoes from Swedish-America). Vänersborg, Sweden, 1931.

Brodin, Knut, ed. *Emigrantvisor och andra visor* (Emigrant Ballads and Other Ballads). Stockholm, 1938.

Budd, Lillian. *April Snow*. New York, 1951.

Land of Strangers. New York, 1953.

April Harvest. New York, 1959.

Carlson, Anna M. *The Heritage of the Bluestem*. Kansas City, Mo., 1930.

Carlsson, K. Alex. *I öst- och västerled* (Eastward and Westward). Chicago, 1946.

Cederblad, Herman. *Vågspel; dikter* (Wave Music: Poems). N.p., c. 1922.

Cælius, Otto. "På surpriseparty" (At a Surprise Party). *Kurre-kalender* for 1899, pp.

"Et bröllop, som ej blev af" (A Wedding Called Off). *Kurre-kalender* for 1901, pp. 179-88.

"Lika barn leka bäst" (Birds of a Feather). *Prärieblomman kalender* for 1902, pp. 58-63.

"I 'Little Hell'" (In "Little Hell"). *Kurre-kalender* for 1903, pp. 123-9.

Dahl, K. C. Wilhelm. *Hedens barn* (Children of the Prairie). Malmö, Sweden, 1913.

"Don Andro." "Allt för sin kärleks skull" (All for Love). *Valkyrian*, Vol. IV, Nr. 3 March 1900), pp. 150-7.

Edgren, August Hjalmar. *Dikter i original och öfversättning* (Original Poems and Translations). Lund, Sweden, 1884.

Blåklint; ny diktsamling (Blue Cliffs: New Collected Poems). Stockholm, 1894.

Brustna återljud; dikter (Broken Echoes: Poems). Stockholm, 1904.

Elmblad, Magnus. *En svensk sång om den stora branden i Chicago af Anders Nilsson, arbetskarl* (A Swedish Poem about the Great Fire in Chicago, by Anders Nilsson, Laborer). Chicago, 1872.

Samlade dikter (Collected Poems). Chicago, 1878.

Gunnar och Anna, eller nybyggarne (Gunnar and Anna, or The Pioneers). Chicago, c. 1880.
Samlade dikter (Collected Poems). Stockholm, 1889.
Enander, Johan Alfred. *Valda skrifter* (Selected Writings). Chicago, c. 1892.
Engstrand, Stuart David. *They Sought for Paradise*. New York, 1939.
Erickson, Phoebe. *Black Penny*. New York, 1951.
Erikson, Hulda. *Vildblommor från den stora ängen* (Wild Flowers from the Great Meadow). Chicago, 1913.

Fliesburg, Oskar Alfred. *Cristoforo Colon*. St. Paul, Minn., 1893.
Vildrosor och tistlar (Wild Roses and Thistles). Minneapolis, 1899.
Fredenholm, Axel. *Purpur och hemspunnet; dikter och sånger* (Purple and Homespun: Poems). Seattle, 1909.
Dikter (Poems). New Britain, Conn., 1918.
Toner och tankar (Rhymes and Reflections). Worcester, Mass., n.d.

Grafström, Axel V. *Skånska baron* (The Baron from Skåna). Stockholm, c. 1915.

Hallenborg, Magnus. "For stjernebaneret" (For the Stars and Stripes), *Valkyrian,* Vol. IX, Nr. 5 (May 1905), pp. 224-6.
"Den förlorade sonen" (The Prodigal Son). *Valkyrian,* Vol. XI, Nr. 12 (Dec. 1907), pp. 598-600.
"Du skall hedra din fader och din moder" (Honor Thy Father and Thy Mother). *Valkyrian,* Vol. XIII, Nr. 9 (Sept. 1909), pp. 477-81.
"När nöden är som störst" (When the Need Is Greatest). *Valkyrian,* Vol. XIII, Nr. 12 (Dec. 1909), pp. 632-6.
Hamilton, Joseph C. *Bror Erik; en bild ur Chicagolifvet* (Brother Erik: A Tale of Life in Chicago). Chicago, 1932.
Hellberg, Karl: *Västanfläkt; dikter* (Western Breeze: Poems). N.p., c. 1926.
Hill, Joe. *Joe Hills sånger*. Enn Kokk, ed. Lund, Sweden, 1969.
Hill, Samuel Magnus. *Uggletoner i vargatider.* (Owl Hoots in Wolf Times). Portland, Oreg., c. 1910.
Holmes, Ludvig. *Dikter* (Poems). Rock Island, Ill., c. 1896.
Nya dikter (New Poems). Rock Island, 1904.
Hult, Gottfrid Emanuel. *Reveries and Other Poems*. New York, 1909.
Outbound. Boston, 1920.

Ingvall, Aron. *Till vänskapen* (To Friendship). Brooklyn, 1919.
"Stångjernshammaren" (The Sledgehammer). *Valkyrian,* Vol. V, Nr. 8 (Aug. 1901), pp. 407-8.
"Själsadel" (Nobility of Soul). *Valkyrian,* Vol. XII, Nr. 3 (March 1908), pp. 137-41.

"Jebel." "En svensk students äfventyr i Amerika" (A Swedish Student's Adventures in America). *Valkyrian,* Vol. VI, Nr. 1 (Jan. 1902), pp. 37-40, to Nr. 12 (Dec. 1902), pp. 640-3.
"En segervinnare i lifvets strid" (A Victor in the Strife of Life). *Valkyrian,* Vol. XII, Nr. 5 (Apr. 1908), pp. 174-80.
"Kamp och seger" (Battle and Victory). *Valkyrian,* Vol. XII, Nr. 8 (Aug. 1908), pp. 387-91.
Johanson, Albert. *Ängsblommor; lyriska dikter* (Meadow Flowers: Lyric Poems). Minneapolis, n.d.
Jchansson, Albert Edward. *In Strictest Measure: 50 Sonnets.* Boston, 1944.
Judson, Clara Ingram. *They Came from Sweden*. Boston, 1942.

Landén, L. H. *Röster ur djupet; dikter* (Voices from the Depths: Poems). Oakland, Calif., 1919.
I frihetens land (In the Land of Freedom). Chicago, n.d.

Landfors, Arthur. *Från smältugnen* (From the Melting Pot). Stockholm, 1932.
Träd som bara grönska (Trees That Never Bear). Stockholm, 1962.
Larsson, Olaf Gottfred. *Samlade dikter* (Collected Poems). Rockford, Ill., c. 1918.
Lindberg, Peter August. *Adam; en berättelse* (Adam: A Narrative). Chicago, 1899.
Lindblom, Ernst. *På forsök, fem svensk-amerikanska dikter* (On Trial: Five Swedish-American Poems). Chicago, 1888.
Linder, Oliver Anderson. *Glada grin, vers och prosa* (Merry Grins: Verse and Prose). Chicago, c. 1890.
I västerland (In the Western Land). Rock Island, Ill., 1914.
Lönnquist, Carl Adolph. *Dikter af Teofilus* (Poems by Teofilus). Rock Island, Ill., 1907.
Sundet vid Åreskär och andra dikter (The Sound by Åreskär and Other Poems). Malmö, Sweden, 1913.
Vildros, ett nytt knippe (Wild Roses, A New Handful). Rock Island, 1916.
The Christ: Sonnets. N.p., 1935.
Lundeberg, Axel. *John Johnsons hemkomst från Amerika* (John Johnson's Return from America). Chicago, c. 1907.

Malm, Gustav. *Charli Johnson.* Chicago, 1909.
Härute. (Out Here). Lindsborg, Kan., 1919.
"Peace and Good Will." *The American-Scandinavian Review,* Vol. IV, Nr. 1 (Jan.-Feb. 1916), pp. 9-16.
Malmquist, Marie Valborg. *"Färgödlan" tillägnad mitt hemland Sverige* ("The Colored Lizard"—Dedicated to My Homeland, Sweden). Jemtland, Me., 1919.
Forest Echoes. Brockton, Mass., 1920.
Kristina. N.p., c. 1926.
Modig, Andrew. *Purpurstänk på aftonsky* (Purple Rims on Evening Clouds). Beresford, S. Dak., 1911.

Norman, Carl Gustaf. *Emigrantens sånger.* (The Emigrant's Songs). Chicago, 1914.
Nyvall, David. *Vers och saga* (Verse and Story). Minneapolis, 1890.
Skogsdrillar; lyriska dikter (Wood Lyrics). Chicago, c. 1901.

Österholm, Albin Nicolaus. *Valda dikter* (Selected Poems). Chicago, 1904.
Olofson, A. *I gryningstid; dikter* (At Dawn: Poems). Worcester, Mass., 1905.
Olson, Ernst Wilhelm. *Valda dikter* (Selected Poems). Rock Island, Ill., 1947.
Olsson, Anna. *Från solsiden* (From the Sunny Side). Rock Island, 1903.
Bilder från jubelfesten (Pictures from the Jubilee). Rock Island, 1912.
Ellens julfest med flera berättelser för de små (Ellen's Christmas Party and Other Tales for Children). Stockholm, 1912.
På Heidelberget med flera berättelser (On Heidelberg Mountain and Other Narratives). Rock Island, 1914.
I'm Scairt: Childhood Days on the Prairie. Rock Island, 1927. Published in Swedish as *En prärieunges funderinger.* Rock Island, 1917.
Två små gossar och deras äfventyr (Two Small Boys and Their Adventures). Rock Island, n.d.

Pearson, Peter Henry. *Prairie Vikings.* East Orange, N.J., 1927.
Person, Johan. *I svensk-Amerika* (In Swedish America). Worcester, Mass., 1900.
Svensk-amerikanska studier (Swedish-American Studies). Rock Island, Ill., 1912.
"Oskar och hans folk" (Oscar and His People). *Valkyrian,* Vol. III, Nr. 3 (March 1899), pp. 138-43.
"Ett minne af en murfvel" (A Reminiscence of a Journalist). *Valkyrian,* Vol. IV, Nr. 12 (Dec. 1900), pp. 629-33.
"Den sista dollarn" (The Last Dollar). *Valkyrian,* Vol. V, Nr. 3 (March 1901), pp. 136-8.
"De första spadtagen" (Breaking New Ground). *Prärieblomman kalender* for 1902, pp. 12-19.

374

Peterson, C. F. "Hafvets hittebarn" (The Ocean Foundling). *Valkyrian*, Vol. VIII, Nr. 1 (Jan. 1904), pp. 21-9, to Nr. 12 (Dec. 1904), pp. 661-6.
Peterson, Elmer T. *Trumpets West*. New York, 1934.
Peterson, Frederick. *Poems and Swedish Translations*. Buffalo, N.Y., 1883.
In the Shade of Yggdrasil. New York, 1893.
Peterson, Frithiof Jeremias. *Ismael Hagarson*. Chicago, 1915.
Under nattvakten (During the Night Watch). Chicago, n.d.
Peterson, Gustaf A. *Minnen och känslor* (Memories and Moods). Egg Harbor City, N.J., 1934.

Schuch, Edward. *Tvenne familjer* (Two Families). Rock Island, Ill., 1914.
Emigranterna (The Emigrants). Chicago, 1917.
Skarstedt, Ernst Teofil. *Under vestliga skyar* (Under Western Skies). Tacoma, Wash., 1907.
"Alt bättre och bättre, humoresk ur det svensk-amerikanska tidningsmannslifvet" (Better and Better, A Humorous Tale of Swedish-American Journalism). *Prärieblomman kalender* for 1900, pp. 87-95.
Stenbock, Harald. *Segelvind i morgonväkt* (Favorable Wind in the Morning Watch). Dayton, Iowa, 1911.
Stenwall, Ruth Rohne. *Ax plockade på lifvets åker* (Ears of Grain Garnered in Life's Meadows). New Britain, Conn., 1908.
Stolpe, Mauritz. *Samlade dikter* (Collected Poems). Rock Island, Ill., 1940.
Strömberg, Oscar Leonard. *Ett dystert arf* (A Dark Heritage). Minneapolis, 1898.
Unge röster; dikter (Young Voices: Poems). Chicago, 1907.
Smed Johan (Johan the Blacksmith). Chicago, 1911.
Där prärien blommar (Where the Prairie Blooms). Uppsala, Sweden, 1933.
Dygd och brott (Virtue and Sin). Chicago, n.d.
Stromberg, Ella. *Vilda blommor; blandade dikter* (Wild Flowers: Miscellaneous Poems). Stillwater, Minn., 1928.
Stromberg, Helga Sofia. *Through Windows of Love*. New York, 1940.
Drömda världar (Worlds of Dream). Minneapolis, 1943.
Från solljusa stränder (From Sunny Shores). Minneapolis, n.d.
Sundell, Edward. *Lyckliga dagar* (Happy Days). New York, 1894.
"Emigrantens berättelser" (The Emigrant's Narrative). *Valkyrian*, Vol. I, Nr. 1 (Jan. 1897), pp. 38-41, to Nr. 2 (Feb. 1897), pp. 40-2.
"Vi måste ju dö" (We All Must Die). *Valkyrian*, Vol. I, Nr. 9 (Sept. 1897), pp. 39-40.
"Julfröid" (Christmas Joy). *Valkyrian*, Vol. I, Nr. 12 (Dec. 1897), pp. 42-6.
"Fantasier" (Fantasies). *Valkyrian*, Vol. IV, Nr. 4 (Apr. 1900), pp. 190-1.
'Vignetter" (Vignettes). *Valkyrian*, Vol. VI, Nr. 2 (Feb. 1902), pp. 97-8, to Nr. 3 (March 1902), pp. 140-1.
"Programmet" (The Program). *Valkyrian*, Vol. VII, Nr. 2 (Feb. 1903), pp. 69-71.
"För snöd vinnings skull" (For the Sake of Minimal Gain). *Valkyrian*, Vol. X, Nr. 1 (Jan. 1906), pp. 21-2.
Sundelöf, Wilhelm. *Dikter* (Poems). Boston, c. 1913.

Thune, Oscar. *I skymningen; några rimförsök* (In the Gloaming: Some Attempts At Rhyme). Bridgeport, Conn., 1923.
Tode, Axel. "I främande land" (In a Foreign Land). *Valkyrian*, Vol. IV, Nr. 12 (Dec. 1900), pp. 607-11.
Turngren, Ellen. *Listen, My Heart*. New York, 1956.
Shadows into Mist. New York, 1958.
Hearts Are the Fields. New York, 1961.

Valley, Astrid. *Marching Bonnet*. New York, 1948.

Wœrner, Ninian. *I höst- och vinterkväll* (In Fall and Winter Evenings). Minneapolis, 1895.
Pennstreck (Pen Strokes). Minneapolis, 1896.

Wermelin, Alfred. *Dikter*. (Poems). Chicago, 1889.
 En blick på lifvet (A Look at Life). Marinette, Wis., 1898.
 Ljus och skuggor (Light and Shadows). Marinette, 1900.
Wicklund, Gustaf. *Gnistor från rimsmedjan* (Sparks from the Rhymesmith). Minneapolis, 1906.
Wiman, Gustaf. *Dikter och sånger* (Poems and Songs). Waltham, Mass., 1913.
Wright, Robert L. *Swedish Emigrant Ballads*. Lincoln, Nebr., 1965.

3. Danish-American

"Aage". *Jens; fortælling* (Jens: A Story). Chicago, 1889.
Anderson, Henry. *Milepæle* (Milestone). Joliet, Ill., 1938.
Anderson, Rasmus. *Bispegaarden i Oklaho og præstehuset i Utah* (The Bishop's Seat in Oklaho and the Parsonage in Utah). Neenah, Wis., 1897.
 Den forældreløse Margrethe (Margrethe the Orphan). Cedar Falls, Iowa, 1902. Jørgen. Brooklyn, N.Y., 1906.
Ander, Kr. *Helene*. Blair, Nebr., 1928.
Anon. *Kamp og sejr* (Battle and Victory). N.p., n.d.

Bang, August L. *Digte og viser* (Poems and Ballads). Copenhagen, 1912.
 Livet i vold (In the Throes of life). Cedar Falls, Iowa, 1938.
Baun, Kristian. *Blodets baand* (The Bonds of Blood). Copenhagen, 1938.
Bay, J. Christian. *Fortællinger og digte* (Stories and Poems). Chicago, 1906.
 Mod og mands hjerte (Courage and Man's Heart). Copenhagen, 1955.
 "Hvor tvende verdener mødes" (Where Two World's Meet). *Ved arnen*, Vol. 27, Nr. 9 (23 Oct. 1900), pp. 129-35.
 "Juleaften" (Christmas Eve). *Smaablomster fra vor lille have*, Nr. 10 (Dec. 1901).
 "Det bankede —!" (Someone Knocked—!). *Julegranen* for 1910, n.p.
 "Bes'far vinder slaget" (Grandpa Wins the Battle). *Dansk nytaar* for 1960, pp. 26-35.
Borchsenius, J. Valdemar. *Ved Øresund og Mississippi*. Chicago, 1884.

Christensen, C. L. *Stormen* (The Storm). Ann Arbor, Mich., n.d.
 Sagn (Legends). Brooklyn, N.Y., 1922.
 Havneløbet (The Port). Brooklyn, 1924.
 Fart (Passage). Brooklyn, 1931.
 Livets Høst (The Autumn of Life). Brooklyn, 1931.
Christensen, Carlo. *Æventyret kaldte* (Adventure Called). New York, 1932.
Christensen, Nathaniel Peter. *Thomas*. New York, 1959.

Dahlerup, Joost. *For vind og vove* (Adrift). Copenhagen, 1908.
 Vi udvandrere (We Emigrants). Copenhagen, 1924.
Dan, Adam. *Taarer og smil* (Tears and Smiles). Skanderborg, Denmark, 1868.
 Alperoser (Alpine Roses). Copenhagen, 1871.
 Sejrende kræfter (Victorious Powers). Cedar Falls, Iowa, 1882.
 Prærierosen (The Prairie Rose). Minneapolis and Chicago, 1892.
 Solglimt (Glimpse of Sun). Minneapolis and Chicago, 1899.
 Maleren (The Painter). Minneapolis and Chicago, 1901.
 Vaarbud (Message of Spring). Minneapolis and Chicago, 1902.
 Sommerløv (Summer Leaves). Cedar Falls, 1903.
Dansk-amerikanske Forfattere. *Fortællinger og digt* (Stories and Poems). Minneapolis and Chicago, 1906.
Dickerson, Inga H. *Trina*. New York, 1956.

Erickson, Howard. *Son of Earth*. New York, 1935.
Eriksen, Peter. *Til minde om pastor Peter Eriksen* (To the Memory of Pastor Peter Eriksen). Clinton, Iowa, n.d.
Eskesen, Eckhardt V. *Mod lyset* (Towards the Light). Copenhagen, 1904.

Favrholdt, E. M. *Emigranter* (Emigrants). Copenhagen, Vol. I, 1930; Vol. II, 1931, Vol. III, 1934.

Gravengaard, Hans Peter. *Christmas Again!* Boston, 1926.
Grundtvig, Frederik Lange. *Kirke og folk* (Church and People). Cedar Falls, Iowa, 1909.
  ed., *Sangbog for det danske folk i Amerika* (Songbook for the Danish People in America). Aarhus, Denmark, 1910.
Hannibal, Peter M. *Thrice a Pioneer*. Blair, Nebr., 1901.
  Protect Our Schools: A Story with a Ring to It. Dannebrog, Nebr., 1901.
  Uncle Sam's Cabin. Dannebrog, c. 1910.
Hansen, Carl. *Præriens børn* (Children of the Prairie). Cedar Falls, Iowa, 1896-7. 2nd ed.
  Præriefolk (Prairie People). Copenhagen, 1907.
  Landsmænd (Fellow Countrymen). Cedar Falls, 1908.
  Dansk jul i Amerika (Danish Christmas in America). Copenhagen, 1909.
  Nisqually. Copenhagen, 1912.
  Fra prærien (From the Prairie). Cedar Falls, 1918.
  "Rasmus's jul" (Rasmus's Christmas). *Smaablomster fra vor lille have,* Nr. 10 (Dec. 1901).
  "Det brækkede ben" (The Broken Leg). *De Forenede Staters danske almanak* for 1914, pp. 171-5.
  "Hvidegaards Danmarkstur" (Hvidegaards's Trip to Denmark). *De Forenede Staters danske almanak* for 1915, pp. 145-52.
Hartvig, M. "Undervejs, lynskud fra en dansk emigrants overfart til Amerika" (Under Way, Glimpses of a Danish Emigrant's Voyage to America). *De Forenede Staters danske almanak* for 1914, pp. 123-5.

Ingversen, Jens. *Kaldskapellanen* (The Resident Curate). Copenhagen, 1926.

Jensen, Martin. *Firkløveret* (The Four-Leaf Clover). Blair, Nebr., 1936.
Johansen, Frederikke. *Fredelund* (Peaceful Grove). Askov, Minn., 1930.
  Foraar (Spring). Askov, 1932.

Kirkegaard, Ivar. *Halvkloden rundt* (Half the Globe Around). Racine, Wis., 1905.
  Danske dage (Danish Days). Copenhagen, 1906.
Knudsen, Johannes. "Et barn er født" (A Child Is Born). *Julegranen* for 1947, n.p.
  "Julebefordring" (Christmas Transport). *Dansk nytaar* for 1957, pp. 22-6.
  "En krise" (A Crisis). *Dansk nytaar* for 1960, pp. 47-52.
Knudsen, Thorvald. "Georg". *Julegranen* for 1902, n.p.
Kristensen, Evald R. *Smaafortællinger* (Sketches). Omaha, 1924. 3rd ed.
Kvist, Anton. *Fyr og flamme* (Enthusiasm). Chicago, 1910.
  Fred og fejde (Peace and Controversy). Chicago, 1917.
  Danske strenge (Danish Chords). Chicago, 1925.
  Lurerne kalder (The Lurs Are Calling). Copenhagen, 1927.
  Sange fra vejen (Songs Along the Way). Chicago, 1948.

Launsby, Ebba Trampe. "Peter Olsen fro Wisconsin." *Dansk nytaar* for 1957, pp. 27-32.
  "Julestormen" (The Christmas Storm). *Dansk nytaar* for 1958, pp. 20-4.
  "Farmer Greisdals julebørn" (Farmer Greisdal's Christmas Children). *Dansk nytaar* for 1960, pp. 53-7.
Lunn, J. C. *Vigtige sandheder* (Important Truths). Harlan, Iowa, 1903.

Madsen, Emil Ferdinand. *Fra de stille skove* (From the Silent Woods). Minneapolis, 1896.
  Havet (The Sea). Clinton, Iowa, 1900.

377

Savmøllens svanesang (The Sawmill's Swansong). Clinton, 1900.
Vore fædres kirke; jubilæumskantate (Our Father's Church: Anniversary Cantata). Clinton, 1901.
Fastelavnbollerne fra Clinton (The Hot Cross Buns from Clinton). Clinton, 1902.
"En lænket ørn" (A Chained Eagle). *Julegranen* for 1898, n.p.
Marlowe, Alexander. *The Unthrown Stone*. Boston, 1918.
"Guardian Angels on Broadway". *Christmas Chimes* for 1922, pp. 18-33.
"No Room." *Christmas Chimes* for 1928, pp. 22-36.
Mengers, Ethan. 'The Return of the Angels." *Christmas Chimes* for 1928, pp. 89-101.
Moe, Meta. *Inntil tredie og fjerde led* (Unto the Third and Fourth Generation). Copenhagen, 1937.
Fru Lena Bang. Copenhagen, 1939.
Molbech, Oluf Christian. *Over havet* (Across the Sea). Copenhagen, 1904.
Den gule by (The Yellow City). Copenhagen, 1905.
Kampen om prærien (The Fight over the Prairie). Copenhagen, 1915.
Mortensen, Enok. *Mit folk* (My People). Askov, Minn., 1932.
Saaledes blev jeg hjemløs (Thus I Became Homeless). Holbæk, Denmark, 1934.
Jeg vælger et land (I Choose a Country). Cedar Falls, Iowa, 1936.
"The Whole Community." *Jule* for 1947, pp. 38-46.
"De fattiges rige jul" (The Rich Christmas of the Poor). *Julegranen* for 1950, n.p.
"Al god troskab" (Fidelity). *Dansk nytaar* for 1957, pp. 12-8.
"Vandrer uden tornyster" (Wanderer without a Knapsack). *Dansk nytaar* for 1960, pp. 36-41.

Nielsen, Emanuel. *Toner fra det fjerne* (Distant Echoes). Copenhagen, 1938.
Dawn in Denmark. Milwaukee, Wis., 1944. Published in Danish as *Denmark til ære*. Chicago, 1944.
The Valiant People. Chicago, 1945.
The Heart Has Many Doors. Iowa, 1958.
The Eagle and the Man. Boston, 1962.
Nielsen, Holger O. "Fra Fyn til Kansas" (From Fyn to Kansas). *Julegranen* for 1949, n.p.
"Den bedste julegave" (The Best Christmas Gift). *Julegranen* for 1950, n.p.
"Nikotin". "Thi solen skinner over retfærdige og uretfærdige" (Because the Sun Shines on the Righteous and the Unrighteous). *Uglen*, Vol. II, Nr. 7 (June 1910), pp. 145-7.
"Skibbrud" (Shipwreck). *Uglen*, Vol. II, Nr. 8 (July 1910), pp. 169-70.

Østergaard, Kristian. *Fra skov og prærie* (From Forest and Prairie). Ashland, Mich., 1883.
Vesterlide (Westward). Odense, Denmark, 1889.
Nybyggere (Pioneers). Copenhagen, 1891.
Blokhuset (The Blockhouse). Copenhagen, 1892.
Anton Arden og møllerens Johanne (Anton Arden and The Miller's Johanne). Armstrong, Iowa, 1897.
Et købmandshus (A Merchant's House). Hetland, S. Dak., 1909.
Sange fra prærien (Songs from the Prairie). Copenhagen, 1912.
Dalboerne (The Valley Dwellers). Copenhagen, 1913.
Hedens børn (Children of the Prairie). Copenhagen, 1922.
Danby folk (Danby People). Cedar Falls, Iowa, n.d.
"Mindets engel" (The Angel of Remembrance). *Julegranen* for 1896, n.p.
"Doctor Herning." *Jul i vesterheimen* for 1917, n.p.

Petersen, Christiane. *Adelheid og bazaren i Beatrice* (Adelheid and the Bazaar in Beatrice). Blair, Nebr., 1912.
Peterson, P. M. *En emigrant; hans kamp og seier* (An Emigrant's Struggle and Victory). N.p., c. 1904.
"Ravn, Peter." "Fra ravnekrogen" (From the Raven's Nest). *Misteltenen* for 1919, pp. 23-4.

"Fra ravnekrogen." *Misteltenen* for 1921, pp. 16-17.
"Fra ravnekrogen." *Misteltenen* for 1922, pp. 22-4.
Ringsborg, Agnes. *Fortællinger fra hverdagslivet* (Stories from Everyday Life). Blair, Nebr., 1955.
Sunshine Beyond Shadows. Blair, 1959. Published in Danish as *Gaa væk, skygge, lad solen skinne.* Blair, 1956.
"Et eventyr uden lige" (A Unique Adventure). *Dansk nytaar* for 1960, pp. 58-61.
Schack, Thor. *Normannernes sidste gæstebud, samt andre digte* (The Norsemen's Last Banquet and Other Poems). Chicago, 1925.
Simonsen, Sigurd Jay. *The Clodhopper.* New York, 1940.
The Brush Coyotes. New York, 1943.
The Mongrels. New York, 1946.
Sørensen, M. *Trækfugle* (Birds of Passage). Copenhagen, 1903.
Udvandrerfolk (The Emigrant People). Copenhagen 1904.
Hinsides Atlanten (On the Other Side of the Atlantic). Copenhagen, 1906.
"Jul i skoven" (Christmas in the Woods). *Julegranen* for 1906, n.p.
"Naboer, skitse fra en dansk koloni" (Neighbors: Sketch from a Danish Colony). *Misteltenen* for 1914, pp. 11-14.
"Smeden i Viborg" (The Blacksmith in Viborg). *Misteltenen* for 1916, pp. 12-14.
Stauning, A. K. *Plain Poems for Plain People.* Tyler, Minn., 1926.
Stoles, Martha. "Syv og halvfems" (Ninety-seven). *Jul i vesterheimen* for 1926, n.p.
Svenningsen, S. C. *Digte* (Poems). N.p., 1901.

Thorgaard, Jens. *Fjernt fra Danmark* (Far from Denmark). Tyler, Minn., 1925.

Volk, John. *Sange og dikte* (Songs and Poems). New York, 1938.

Winther, Sophus Keith. *Take All to Nebraska.* New York, 1936.
Mortgage Your Heart. New York, 1937.
This Passion Never Dies. New York, 1938.

II. OTHER LITERATURE ON SCANDINAVIAN-AMERICAN THEMES

1. Scandinavian

a. Fiction

"A." *Danske emigranter; eller liv og forhold i Nordamerika* (Danish Emigrants, or Life and Conditions in North America). Esbjerg, Denmark, 1890.
Angered-Strandberg, Hilma. *På prärien* (On the Prairie). Stockholm, 1898.
Från det nya och gamla landet (From the New and the Old Country). Stockholm, 1899.
Den nya världen (The New World). Stockholm, c. 1917.

Berger, Henning. *Där ute* (Out There). Stockholm, 1901.
"Rösten som kallede" (The Voice Which Called). *Valkyrian*, Vol. XIII, Nr. 2 (Feb. 1909), pp. 85-8.
"86 Clark Street." *Valkyrian*, Vol. XIII, Nr. 7 (July 1909), pp. 377-80.
"Bill Johnsons lycka" (Bill Johnson's Luck). *Valkyrian*, Vol. XIII, Nr. 9 (Sept. 1909), pp. 482-4.
Blichfeldt, Frederick J. *Aalborg akvavit og andre amerikanske fortællinger* (Aalborg Aquavit and Other American Stories). Copenhagen 1904.
Bojer, Johan. *The Emigrants.* New York, 1925. Published in Norwegian as *Vår egen stamme.* Oslo, 1924.

Hogstad, Øyvind. *Nyt land* (New Land). Kristiania (Oslo), 1917.
I nybyggerland (In Pioneer Country). Kristiania, 1919.

Janson, Kristofer. *Præriens saga* (Saga of the Prairie). Chicago, 1885.
Vildrose (Wild Rose). Minneapolis and Chicago, 1887.
Nordmænd i Amerika (Norwegians in America). Copenhagen, 1887.
Bag gardinet (Behind the Curtain). Minneapolis, 1889.
Fra begge sider havet (From Both Sides of the Ocean). Kristiania, 1890.
Sara. Kristiania, 1891.
Du er kjød av mit kjød (You are Flesh of My Flesh). Kristiania, 1895.
Digte (Poems). Kristiania and Copenhagen, 1911.

Moberg, Vilhelm. *The Emigrants.* New York, 1951.
Invandrarna (The Immigrants). Stockholm, 1952.
Nybyggarna (The Pioneers). Stockholm, 1956.
Sista brevet til Sverige (The Last Letter to Sweden). Stockholm, 1959.

Norman-Hansen, Carl Martin. *Chicago-noveller* (Chicago Short Stories). Copenhagen, 1892.
Chicago-noveller; ny samling (New Collection). Copenhagen, 1893.

Zilliacus, Konni. *Utvandrarehistorier* (Emigrant Stories). Helsinki, 1892.
Nya utvandrarehistorier (New Emigrant Stories). Helsinki, 1897.
"Hvitt ljus" (White Light). *Valkyrian,* Vol. IV, Nr. 2 (Feb. 1900), pp. 97-101, to Nr. 3 (March 1900), pp. 143-9.
"På prärien" (On the Prairie). *Valkyrian,* Vol. V, Nr. 8 (Aug. 1901), pp. 426-30.
"Elias Möykkäs Amerikafärd" (Elias Möykkä's Voyage to America). *Valkyrian,* Vol. XI, Nr. 2 (Feb. 1907), pp. 102-8.

b. Literary History

Lagerroth, Erland and Ulla-Britta. *Perspektiv på utvandrarromanen; dokument och studier* (Perspective on Vilhelm Moberg's Emigrant Novels: Documents and Studies). Uddevalla, Sweden, 1971.

Mannsåker, Jørund. *Emigrasjon og dikting; utvandringa til Nord-Amerika i norsk skjønnlitteratur* (Emigration and Literature: Emigration to North America in Norwegian Belles-Lettres). Oslo, 1971.

2. American

Benson, Ramsey. *Hill Country.* New York, 1928.
Blake, Eleanor. *Seedtime and Harvest.* New York, 1936.

Cannon, Cornelia James. *Red Rust.* New York, 1928.
Cather, Willa. *O Pioneers!* New York, 1913.
The Song of the Lark. New York, 1915.

Garland, Hamlin. *Main-Travelled Roads.* New York, 1891. Short story, "Among the Corn Rows."

Lewis, Sinclair. *Main Street.* New York, 1920.

III. SCANDINAVIAN-AMERICAN LITERARY HISTORY

1. Norwegian-American

Ager, Waldemar. "Norsk-amerikansk skjønlitteratur" (Norwegian-American Belles-Lettres), in Johannes B. Wist, ed., *Norsk-amerikanernes festskrift,* pp. 291-306. Decorah, Iowa, 1914.

Beck, Richard. "Norwegian-American Literature," in Giovanni Bach, *The History of the Scandinavian Literatures*, pp. 74-84. New York, 1938.
Blegen, Theodore. "Frontiers of Culture," i *Norwegian Migration to America*, Vol. II, *The American Transition*, pp. 585-96. Northfield, Minn., 1940.

Evans, Eyvind J. "Norsk-amerikanske lyrikere: kjente og mindre kjente" (Norwegian-American Poets: Well-known and Less-known). Series of weekly articles in *Minnesota Posten* (Minneapolis) beginning in October, 1969.

Haugen, Einar. "Diktende trang" (The Urge to Write), in *Norsk i Amerika* (Norwegian in America), pp. 98-116. Oslo, 1939.
Hoidahl, Aagot D. "Norwegian-American Fiction since 1880." Norwegian-American Historical Association *Studies and Records*, Vol. V (1930), pp. 61-83.

Johnson, Simon. "Skjønlitterære sysler blandt norsk-amerikanerne" (Literary Doings among the Norwegian-Americans). *Decorah-Posten* (Decorah, Iowa), for 24 Feb., 3 March, 10 March 1939.
Josephsen, Einar. "An Outline of Norwegian-American Literature." *Scandinavia*, Vol. I, Nr. 4 (Apr. 1924), pp. 50-5.

Kildal, Arne. "Utflytterfolkets poesi" (The Emigrant People's Poetry). *Samtiden* (Oslo), Vol. 60, Nr. 6 (1951), pp. 397-410.

Olson, Julius E. "Literature and the Press," i Harry Sundby-Hansen, *Norwegian Immigrant Contributions to America's Making*, pp. 125-38. New York, 1921.

Thorson, Gerald H. "First Sagas in a New World: A Study of the Beginnings of Norwegian-American Literature." Norwegian-American Historical Association *Studies and Records*, Vol. XVII (1952), pp. 108-29.

2. Swedish-American
Alexis, Joseph E. *La littérature suédoise d'Amérique*. Paris, 1930.
Allwood, Martin S. "One Hundred Years of Swedish Poetry in America." *American Swedish Handbook*, Vol. III (Rock Island, Ill., 1948), pp. 131-9.
Amerika-svensk lyrik genom 100 år (Swedish-American Poetry Through 100 Years).
"Innledning" (Introduction), pp. vii-xxx, and "Biografiska notiser" (Biographical Information), pp. 145-66. Distributed by Bonniers, New York, 1949.

Benson, Adolph B. "Swedish-American Literature," i Giovanni Bach, *The History of the Scandinavian Literatures*, pp. 144-58. New York, 1938.
Bonggren, Jakob. "Svensk-amerikansk litteratur." *Prärieblomman kalender* for 1902 (Rock Island), pp. 67-76.
"Swedish-American Literature," in Erik Westman, ed., *The Swedish Element in America*, Vol. II, pp. 313-23. Chicago, 1931.

Linder, Oliver A. "Writers of Swedish Life in America." *The Scandinavian-American Review*, Vol. VI, Nr. 3 (May-June 1918), pp. 154-8.
Svenskarna i Amerika, Vol. II, pp. 193-213. Stockholm, 1926.

Skarstedt, Ernst. *Svensk-amerikanske poeter i ord og bild* (Swedish-American Poets in Words and Pictures). Minneapolis, 1890.
Pennfäktare; svensk-amerikanske författare och tidningsmän (Knights of the Pen: Swedish-American Authors and Newspapermen). Stockholm, 1930. 2nd ed.
Swan, Gustaf N. "Svensk-amerikanska författare" (Swedish-American Authors). A series of 15 articles on individual authors in *Ungdomsvännen*, Vol. IX, Nr. 11 (Nov. 1904) to Vol. XII, Nr. 8 (August 1907).

"An Introduction to Swedish-American Literature." *Augustana Historical Society Publications,* Vol. VI (1936), pp. 11-32.

3. Danish-American

Christiansen, Thomas P. "Dansk-amerikansk litteratur," in *Dansk-amerikansk historie,* pp. 158-67. Cedar Falls, Iowa, 1927.

Mortensen, Enok. "Danish-American Literature," in Johannes Knutsen and Enok Mortensen, *The Danish-American Immigrant,* pp. 25-34. Des Moines, Iowa, 1950.

Strandvold, Georg. "Danish-American Literature," in Giovanni Bach, *The History of the Scandinavian Literatures,* pp. 221-30. New York, 1938.

4. Scandinavian-American

Skårdal, Dorothy Burton. "The Scandinavian Immigrant Writer in America." *Norwegian-American Studies,* Vol. 21 (1962), pp. 14-53.

For bibliographies of Scandinavian-American literature, see Footnote 3 in Chapter II.

Index of Scandinavian Immigrant Authors*

* Refeernces to notes at the end of the book are in italics, with the chapter number in roman numerals.

Dahl, K. G. Wilhelm: *IX 12.*
Dahle, Johan: **V *39.***
Dahlerup, Joost: *IX 117.* (*IX 25;* See also Michaelis, K.: *IX 42, 49.*)
Dan, Adam: 27, 36, 39. *II 13. III 65. V 47, 84, 88. VI 115, 125. VII 19, 108, 118. VIII 63. IX 43. X 5, 6, 7, 76, 79.*

Edgren, A. Hjalmar: 39. *II 16.*
Elmblad, Magnus: 37, 38, 51, 62. *III 15. VII 8.*
Enander, Johan A.: *VII 38. X 9.*
Engstrand, Stuart David: **48.**
Erikson, J. A.: *III 4, 18, 26, 28, 35, 51, 53, 56. IV 52. V 10, 41. VI 13, 92, 127, 130. VII 29. IX 93. X 11.*

Fahrholdt, E. M.: *IV 27, 91. V 29, 52, 87. VI 94, 95, 109.*
Fjeldsaa, Ruth: 30. *X 1.*
Fliesburg, Oskar A.: *IX 36.*
Forbes, Kathryn (pseud.): *VIII 50, 53. X 43.*
Foss, Hans A.: 30, 34, 222. *III 16, 59. IV 43. V 38, 78. VI 73. VII 17, 54, 64, **99**, 124. VIII 5, 17, 42, 47, 85, 88, 105. IX 53, 109. X 27, 28, 35, 46, 56.*
Fredriksen, N. C.: *IV 47.*
Fuhr, Anna D. *IX 101.*

Gamble, Lillian M.: 49.
Gjertsen, M. Falk: *IV 56. V 49, 51. VI 66.*
Grafström, Axel V.: *X 93.*
Gravengaard, Hans P.: *III 56. VIII 76.*
Grundtvig, Frederik L.: *IV 29. VI 23, 138. IX 114.*
Grundysen, Tellef: 23-4, 35, 40.
Guldseth, Olaf: *VI 12.*

Hallander, Anna: *VI 26.*
Hallenborg, Magnus: *IX 4. X 77.*
Hansen, Carl: 27. *III 39, 60, 61. IV 39. V 4, 5, 11, 27, 31, 32, 35, 67, 71. VI 8, 29, 35, 45, 76, 77, 129. VII 2, 37, 88, 119. VIII 1, 38. IX 3, 8, 9, 13, 67, 102.*
Harildstad, J. A.: 42.
Hartvig, M.: *III 22, 37.*
Hassel, Nicolai S.: 32. *VI 2, 3, 114, 137.*
Haugan, Bernt B.: *VI 87.*
Haugen, Kristine: *VIII 31.*
Helgeson, Thor: *IX 87.*
Hellesnes, Lars: *IV 16, 31. V 48, 54, 70. VI 47, 98, 119, 122. VII 70, 72. IX 75. X 80, 90.*
Hetle, Erik: *VI 25.*
Hill, Joe: 196. *VII 35.*
Housland, Albert: *IV 51.* **V 40. VII 53.**

Ingversen, Jens: *VI 99.*
Iversen, Iver: *IV 45.*

Janson, Drude K.: *V 34.*
Janson, Kristofer: 42, 51. *II 19. VI 111. VIII 55. IX 10, 34, 35.*
Jensenius, Bertram: *VII 74. VIII 64.*
Jørgensen, Herman E.: *V 90.*
Johansen, Frederikke: *V 19. VI 20. IX 78.*
Johansson, Albert Edward: 50.
Johnson, Simon: 27, 40, 52. 163. 164. *III 8. IV 9, 21, 36. V 2, 26, 37, 52, 55. VI 9, 70, 82. VII 10, 55, 83, 85, 87, 88, 90. VIII 27, 97. IX 15, 38, 50, 51, 79. X 39, 48, 50, 52, 53, 63, 78, 82.*

384

Knudsen, Thorvald: *X 81.*
Kvist, Anton: 40. *VII 79. IX 26.*

Landfors, Arthur: 19. *IV 80. VII 34. IX 37. X 55.*
Larsson, Gösta: 47.
Launsby, Ebba T. *VIII 92.*
Leach, Henry G.: *IV 68.*
Liljencrantz, Ottilia Adelina: 48. *II 24.*
Lindberg, Peter A.: *III 17, 23, 27, 31. IV 3. V 14. VI 78. VII 97. VIII 37.*
Lindblom, Ernst: *VII 33.*
Linder, Oliver A.: *IV 42, 89. V 30.*
Lund, Einar: *IV 6, 44, 86. V 3, 22, 86. VII 117. X 92.*

Madsen, Emil: *IV 72. V 76. VI 31, 116. VIII 19.*
Magnussen, P. M.: *IV 79.*
Malm, Gustav N. *IV 75. VI 88. IX 1, 61, 65. X 38, 88.*
Malmin, C. K.: *VIII 70.*
Marlowe, Alexander: *VII 6.*
Mason, A. H.: *VII 112. X 62.*
Matson, Norman: 48. *VII 48. IX 94, 118.*
Mengers, Ethan: *VIII 68.*
Mengshoel, Emil L.: 42. *VII 46, 50.*
Moen, Johannes K. *III 7, 52. VI 68.*
Molbech, Oluf C.: *IV 82. V 18, 65, 69, 77. VII 96. X 25, 96.*
Morris, Edita: 47.
Mortensen, Enok: *II 3, 4. III 67. VI 20, 24, 76, 77. IV 94, 95, 96, 97, 98, 99, 100, 101. VI 34, 37, 72. VII 30, 40, 41, 60, 95. VIII 24, 114. IX 46, 72, 125.*
Mose, H. E.: *IV 46, 69.*

Nielsen, Emanuel: 40.
Nielsen, Holder C.: *VII 22.*
Nielsen, Holger O.: *X 23.*
Norstog, Jon: 34, 44-5. *III 24, 33, 45. VII 36, 106, 109. VIII 25. IX 40, 99. X 31.*

Østergaard, Kristian: 27. *III 3, 6, 29, 34. IV 14, 25, 74. V 13, 57. VI 5, 6, 43, 57, 65, 84, 99, 132, 133. VII 13, 71, 92. VIII 14, 59, 110. IX 6, 18, 29, 45, 73. X 17, 41.*
Olson, Ted: *X 83.*
Olsson, Anna: 27, 46, 52. *II 21. IV 33. V 85, 89. VI 134. VIII 29, 34.*
Ostenso, Martha: 48-9. *VII 69.*
Oyen, Henry: 47.

Pearson, P. H.: *VI 22, 23.*
Pedersen, A. B.: *IX 98.*
Pedersen, Palma: *IX 20.*
Person, Johan: 27. *IV 26. V 63.*
Peterson, Elmer T.: *IV 1. V 61. VII 115. X 62.*
Peterson, James A.: 48. *V 16. VII 105. VIII 83, 84. X 34, 40.*
Peyton, Karen: 49.
Prestgard, Kristian: *IX 31.*

Raaen, Aagot: *VIII 46. IX 11.*
Rein, Sigmund: 36. *IV 35. VII 78. X 58.*
Reine, Rasmus O.: 36. *II 13.*
Reite, Peter T.: *IV 45. X 84.*
Remme, N. E.: *IX 89.*
Reslow, Wilhelm: *VII 61.*
Riis, Jacob A.: 46, 115.
Rinde, Olaus: *VI 18.*

385

General Index*

Agriculture, methods in, 83, 203-4; implements, 83; differences Europe-America, 83, 85; tradition of land ownership, 206-8; moral worth of rural life, 208-9.
Algren, Nelson, American author, 47, 51.
"America fever," 59.
America, opportunities in, 59, 61, 115; immigrant attitudes toward, 107-11, 293-5; freer class structure in, 100, 120-1, 124, 126, 134-6; classes in, 133-4, 135-6; economic and social betterment in, 119-24, 129, 138; *See also* American culture, American institutions, Americanization, Climate, Cultural conflict, Economic life, Geography.
American culture, tools, 84-5; work patterns, 86, 259; tempo, 86, 259; models of behavior, 111, 124-7, 130, 132, 134-5, 183, 253, 254, 320; individualism and self-reliance, 138, 143, 185-6, 215, 307; attitudes toward Scandinavian immigrants, 96-7, 254, 296-8; materialism, 163-4, 189-90, 193, 195, 210, 211, 215-6, 223; moral corruption, 183, 191-4, 206, 238. *See also* America, American institutions, Cultural conflict.
American institutions, church, 151, 169, 170-1, 172; family, 240, 246; women's rights, 239, 240, 242-5; divorce, 237-8; the press, 155; social organizations, 153, 235; schools, 140, 144, 146, 148-9, 151, 229, 298-9. *See also* Fraternal lodges, Holidays, Newspapers, Periodicals, Politics.
American-Scandinavian Foundation, 105.
Americanization, definition, 21, 112; development toward, 86-7, 294, 302-3, 307, 308; completion of, 118, 185, 291-2, 329; pressures toward, 87, 117-8, 296-9, 302-3, 312, 313; in churches, 169-71; of names, 136, 303-5, 310; marriage outside ethnic group, 305-7; language as measure of, 98, 274, 278-9, 299; customs as measure of, 125, 287-9, 292; immigrant attitudes toward, 112-7, 293-4, 320. *See also* Assimilationists, Cultural conflict, Nationality, Preservationists.
Anders, O. Fritiof, American scholar, *II 3, 6, 11.*
Anderson, Arlow William, American scholar, *II 4.*
Anderson, Rasmus B., American professor, 35.
Anderson, Thor M., Norwegian scholar, *II 3, 11.*
Anundsen, B., Norwegian-American publisher, 30, *II 5.*
Architecture, houses, 78, 249-50; churches, 168.
Archives of Scandinavian-American history, in Scandinavia, 11-12, 27; in America 11, 17, 27.
Art, 232-3, 334.
Assimilationists, defined, 87; ideal of cultural pluralism, 107, 331; goals, 108, 109, 112-3, 306-7; victory of, 117-8. *See also* Americanization, Nationality, Preservationists.
Augsburg Seminary, 140, 148.
Augustana College (Rock Island, Illinois), 27, 46, 150.

Bach, Giovanni, American scholar, *II 3.*
Ballads, immigrant, *see* Folk music.
Barton, Albert O., American scholar, *II 25.*
Beath, Paul R., American scholar, *IX 97.*

* References to notes at the end of the book are in italics, with the chapter number in roman numerals.

Beijbom, Ulf, Swedish scholar, *X 36.*
Benson, Ramsay, American author, *IV 40, VI 60, VIII 7, 108, X 26.*
Berger, Henning, Swedish author, *III 57, X 24.*
Bethany College, (Kansas) 149, 150.
Bjørnson, Bjørnstjerne, Norwegian author, 30, 323.
Blegen, Theodore, American scholar, 15, 333, *I 2, II 4, 8, IX 39.*
Blichfeldt, Frederick J., Danish author, *III 30, 54, V 7.*
Boat of Longing, The, novel by O. E. Rølvaag, 282, *III 5, 38, IX 91.*
Bojer Johan, Norwegian author, 155, *III 1, V 24, 75, VI 40, 54, 83, 91, 102, IX 7, 41, 90, X 59.*
Brodin, Knut, scholar, *III 14, 21, 25. IX 39.*
Brooklyn (New York), 49, 231.
Brotherhood societies, *see* Fraternal lodges.
Bygdekultur (dispersed rural settlement), 54-7. *See also* Scandinavia, social history
Bygdelag (Norwegian-American lodges), 33, *II 8, 34, 44.*

California, 203, 255, 288.
Capps, Finis Herbert, American scholar, 19n.
Castle Garden (New York City), 69, 71.
Cather, Willa, American author, 335.
Catholic, 182, 168, 306. *See also* Irish.
Chicago (Illinois), 27, 35, 37, 39, 40, 69, 74, 75, 76, 78, 79, 86, 89, 90, 114, 133,
    153, 158, 173, 179, 197, 199, 202, 203, 206, 213, 231, 271, 279, 291, 296, 302,
    305, 333; place of publication, 23, 33, 47.
Children. *See* Scandinavian-American Institutions, position of children, generation
    gap.
Children's books about Scandinavian immigration, 49-50.
Christensen, Thomas P., scholar, 333.
Christmas, *see* Holidays.
Churches, *see* Religion, American institutions, Scandinavian institutions.
Civil War, 296, 312; Scandinavian regiments in, 93, 104.
Clausen, Clarence, American scholar, *II 4.*
Climate, in America, 72, 83, 104.
Colleges and universities, 38-9, 61, 104, 139-41, 149-51. *See also* college names.
Corstvet, Alexander, American author, 48.
Cultural conflict, 84-5, 98, 143; in behavioral models, 86, 87-8, 125, 129, 131, 143,
    146, 153, 170, 181, 207, 209-10, 213, 234, 236-7, 238, 240, 246, 252-3, 259-60, 269,
    288-9, 296-7, 303-4, 308, 318; in education, 146, 148; in religion, 169-70, 233-4.
    See also Immigrant experience.
Cultural shock, 20, 23, 25, 331, 332.
Customs, *see* Scandinavian culture, Scandinavian-American culture.

Dakota, 15, 40, 47, 76, 77, 78, 82, 83, 93, 95, 119, 131, 133, 138, 146, 152, 160, 163,
    164, 180, 193, 204, 215, 217, 237, 240, 262, 270, 274, 278, 281, 282, 285, 294,
    297, 298, 299, 304, 310, 312, 323.
Dana College (Blair, Nebraska), 11, 150.
Dania, Danish-American lodge, 105.
Decorah (Iowa), Nordic Festival in, 19; Norwegian cultural center, 19, 27, 33;
    publication in, 29, 32, 33.
Denmark, 16, 53, 54, 58, 66, 106, 109, 115, 116, 117, 128, 173, 224, 259, 262, 279,
    308, 323; national character, general, 97-101, specific, 102-3. *See also* Scandinavia.
Des Moines (Iowa), 27; place of publication, 33.
Det norske selskab i Amerika, Norwegian-American cultural society, 33, 46, 105.
Dialects, *see* Language.
Dickens, Charles, English author, 30.
Disease and sickness, on frontier, 260-1; mental, 100.
"Dog years." 96, 194, 205, 257-9, 260, 262, 263, 264, 265, 266, 287, 291, 314.
Dowie, J. Iverne, American scholar, 333, *IX 65.*
Drinking customs, *see* Scandinavian culture, Temperance movement.

Economic life, as pressure toward Americanization, 87; better pay and living standards in America, 119-24; business ethics, 189-91, 192-4, 214-5; banks, 191, 200; trusts, 201; depressions, 197, 200, 202-3; declining economic opportunity, 201-3; exploitation of workers, 194-5, 198-200, 214, 215; social protest, 195-201. *See also* Agriculture, Work.
Education, *see* American institutions, Scandinavian-American institutions, Colleges.
Eielsen, Elling, Norwegian-American church leader, 174, 175.
Ellis Island (New York), 69, 70.
Elviken, Andreas, American scholar, *II 4.*
Emerson, Ralph W., American author, 223, 323.
Emigration, motives for, 56, 57-61; preparation for, 63-4, 81-2. *See also* Immigrants, Scandinavian culture, Travel.
England, stage on Atlantic voyage, 66.
English language, *see* Language.
Espelie, Ernest M., scholar, 333, *IX 65.*
Ethnic group, definition, 17; identity, 41, 295, 312, 332; formation, 79, 88-107, 184, 301-2, 328-9; settlements, 104, 306, 324; importance of church to, 181-2, 184; societies, *see* Fraternal lodges. *See also* Nationality, consciousness of.
Europe, see Scandinavia.

Faber, August.[1], *V 28*[2], *VI 24.*
Farrell, James T., American author, 51.
Finland, 16, 41.
Folk dance, 228, 231, 280.
Folklore, 280, 280-3, *IX 86, 87, 88, 89, 90;* Febold Feboldson, *IX 97;* Asbjørnsen and Moe, *IX 97. See also* Scandinavian-American culture, folklore.
Folk music, 280-2, *III 14, IX 39, 76;* ballads, 62, 270; hymns, 231-2.
Food, *see* Scandinavian-American culture, food.
Fourth of July, *see* Holidays.
France, Anatole, French author, 30.
Fraternal lodges, 33, 79, 105, 153-5, 235-6, 302. *See also* Bygdelag, Dania, Det norske selskab i Amerika, Symra, Scandinavian-American culture, cultural societies.
Fredenholm, Axel, scholar, 333.
Frontier, *see* Pioneers and pioneering.

Garborg, Arne, Norwegian author, 323.
Generation gap, *see* Immigrants, second generation, and Scandinavian-American institutions, generation gap.
Geography, American, 75, 77-8, 262-3; prairie, 82, 262; compared with Scandinavian, 75, 77-8, 262-3, 321.
Germans and Germany, 84, 86, 100, 148, 218, 295, 310, 311, 312, 332.
Giants in the Earth, novel by O. E. Rølvaag, 11, 30, 82, 84, 93, 100, 189, 204, 225, 261, 282; *I de dage,* 30; *Riget grundlægges,* 30.
Grand View College (Des Moines, Iowa), 27, 33, 250.
Grey, Zane, American writer, 30.
Grundtvig, N. F. S., Danish religious leader, 145, 149, 174, 178, *IV 69.*
Gvåle, Gudrun Hovde, Norwegian scholar, *IV 69.*

Hamsun, Knut, Norwegian author, 51.
Handlin, Oscar, American historian, 7, 11, 12.
Hasselmo, Nils, American scholar, *IV 87, IX 65, 69.*
Hauge, Hans Nielsen, Norwegian religious leader, 174.
Haugen, Einar, American linguist, *I 4, II 8, 20, IX 69, X 35.*
Heckscher, Eli F., Swedish scholar, *III 1.*
Hervin, O. S., Norwegian-American journalist, 34.
Hildebrand, Karl, scholar, 333.
Historical associations, libraries, 27, 33; publications, 47; Norwegian-American, 33-4, 333; Swedish Pioneer Historical Society, 333; Augustana Historical Society, 394.
Holidays, Christmas, 56, 122, 169, 225, 252, 283-9, 291; Easter, 169, 291; mid-

summer, 13, 56, 289; Seventeenth of May, 102, 153; Seventh of June, 102, 106, 152; Fourth of July, 104, 290, 296; Thanksgiving, 290.
Homesickness, 23, 24, 42, 54, 115-6, 263-9, 270, 271, 285, 314, 324, 328, 334.
Housekeeping, *see* Scandinavian-American culture, customs and folkways.

Ibsen, Henrik, Norwegian playwright, 323.
Iceland, 16, 42.
Identity, and culture, 20; change as immigrants, 24, 327-9; immigrant group, 41, 88-105, 184, 334; importance of church to, 183-4.
Illinois, 11, 35, 39, 46, 47, 119, 201.
Immigrant experience, Scandinavian, 14, 15, 23, 256, 328-9; consciousness of differentness, 72, 123, 126, 315; language problems, 72, 88, 90, 273-9, 234-5; attitudes toward homeland, 65-6, 269-72, 279; group formation, 88-107, 184, 301-2; comparisons between Scandinavia and America, 75, 76, 77, 78, 120-7, 237, 269; mobility, 210, 255-6; rootlessness, 114-7, 256, 313-6, 320-1, 328. *See also* Cultural conflict, Homesickness, Scandinavian-American culture and institutions.
Immigrants, Scandinavian, motives of, 58-61; characteristics of, 61; exploitation of, 71, 75-6; involuntary immigrants, 61; definition as strangers, 72, 96-7, 123, 328-9; distribution in America, 18, 73, 78-9; upper-class, 61; returned to Scandinavia, 202, 270-1, 293-4, 311, 315, 316; second generation, 297, 317-24. *See also* Personality.
Iowa, 27, 31, 34, 77, 78, 82, 136, 178, 201, 295, 321.
Irish, 24, 68, 75, 84, 97, 100, 106, 110, 112, 134, 161, 162, 199, 204, 275, 294, 305, 306, 309, 319. *See also* Catholic.

Janson, Florence E., American scholar, *III 1.*
Janson, Kristofer, Norwegian and Norwegian-American author, *see* Author Index.
Jeg vælger et land, novel by Enok Mortensen, 114, 115-7.
Jensen, Hans, Danish scholar, *III 1.*
Jews, 68, 110.
Johnson, E. Gustav, American scholar, *III 15.*
Journalism and jounalists, training, 129; difficult finances, 158, 191; drinking, 158, 228. *See also* Newspapers.

Kansas, 78, 110, 149, 167, 302.
Kierkegaard, Søren, Danish church leader, 174.
Kjærbye, C. P., Danish-American, *IV 67, VI 39.*
Knudsen, Johannes, Danish-American scholar, 333, *IV 4, 8, VII 77.*
Kokk, Enn, Swedish scholar, *VII 35.*
Kristensen, K. J., Danish scholar, *III 1.*

LaFollette, Senator, 310, 311.
Language, dialects, 44, 45, 90, 92-3, 275-7, 319; orthography, 45; controversy in Norway, 44-5, 276, *II 20;* bond of, 88-91; as measure of assimilation, 98, 300-1; corruption by English, 43, 158, 277-9; transition to English, 116, 147-8, 274, 299, 313; attempts to preserve, 90-1, 275, 300; forms of address in, 124-5.
Larson, Laurence M., American scholar, *I 6.*
Law and lawyers, 191-2, 197.
Lewis, Sinclair, American author, 292.
Lie, Jonas, Norwegian author, 30.
Lincoln, Abraham, 323.
Lindmark, Sture, Swedish scholar, 19n, 333, *VI 56, X 36, 53.*
Lindquist, Emory, American scholar, *II 16.*
Literature, Scandinavian-American, as historical source material, 21-3, 25-6, 52, 293, 336; realism in, 23-4; defined, 27, 36, 47-8, 50-2; borderline cases, 48, 51; history of, 27, *II 2, 36;* bibliographies, 27, *II 3;* markets for, 28-36; authors all amateurs, 23, 38, 40; reading public, 37-8; poetry, 28-9, 37, 195-6; low critical standards, 34-5, 43; social criticism in, 42, 195-6, 197-201; themes in, 37, 42; in English, 46-8.
Luther College (Decorah, Iowa), 27, 148, 150.

Magazines, *see* Periodicals.
Mannsåker, Dagfinn, Norwegian historian, 12.
Mannsåker, Jørund, Norwegian scholar, *III 2, 5, VII 123, IX 41, X 60*.
Masonic lodges, 133, 154, 235-6.
Måwe, Carl-Erik, Swedish scholar, *X 44, 60*.
Middle West, 35, 42, 47, 60, 82, 113, 203, 217, *IX 76*, historical collections in, 17, 27; Scandinavian immigrants in, 18, 73; land available in, 24; frontier, 82.
Milwaukee (Wisconsin), 74, 78.
Minneapolis (Minnesota), 35, 133, 134, 180, 199, 231, 241, 254, 294; place of publication, 32, 33, 34, 37, 42, 47, 48.
Minnesota, 11, 23, 27, 33, 34, 77, 78, 81, 160, 161, 174, 175, 177, 201, 226, 229, 254, 294, 318, 322.
Moberg, Vilhelm, Swedish author, 155, 265, *III 1, IV 24*.
Money, inflation of in America, 76-7; different meaning of in America, 76-7, 221-2.
Mortensen, Enok, Danish-American minister and scholar, 333, *II 3, 4. See also* Author Index.

Naeseth, Henriette C. K., American scholar, *VIII 22*.
National character, 21, 97-103, 191, 288, 310.
Nationality, consciousness of, 41, 65-6, 68, 71, 88-91, 94-5.
Nebraska, 11, 12, 13, 14, 15, 31, 75, 77, 140, 160, 229, 245, 255, 282, 283, 298, 301.
Nelson, Helge, scholar, 333.
Nerman, Ture, Swedish scholar, *VII 35*.
New York City, 28, 33, 47, 48, 49, 50, 68, 69-71, 73, 74, 156, 182, 201.
Newspapers, Scandinavian-American, number of, 19n, 104; markets for literature, 28-30; functions of, 155-7; in fiction, 95, 101, 152, 155-9, 191, 226, 227; *Danne-virke, X 25; Danskeren, IV 46; Decorah-posten*, 29, 30, *II 17; Emigranten*, 29; *Fædrelandet og Emigranten, II 13; Nordisk Tidende*, 19n.; *Nordlyset*, 28, *II 4; Nordstjärnen, 33; Skandinaven*, 29, 35, 157; *Skandinavia*, 28, *II 4; Svenska jour-nalen (-tribunen), IV 79. VII 38; Svensk-amerikaneren, IV 89*.
Nilsson, Svein, Norwegian-American publisher, *II 6*.
Nordic, defined, 16.
Norman-Hansen, Carl M., Danish author, *V 58, VII 101*.
Norsk-amerikanernes festskrift, ed. Johannes B. Wist, *II 6, 10, 14, 15, III 10, V 1, V1 67*.
North Park College (Chicago), 27.
Northfield (Minnesota), 27, 333.
Norway, 16, 54, 55, 56, 120, 129, 140, 173, 174, 205, 215, 217, 239, 267, 282, 294, 315, 317, 323, 324, 326; national character, general, 97-101, specific, 102; language conflict in, 44-5, 276. *See also* Scandinavia.
Norwegian Research Council for Science and the Humanities, 12.
Nyholm, Paul C., scholar, 333.

Ødegaard, Ørnulv, Norwegian scholar, *IV 59*.
Oftelie, Torkel, Norwegian-American editor, 34.
Omaha (Nebraska), 13, 14, 190, 198.

Parrington, Vernon, American scholar, 15.
Periodicals, Scandinavian-America, 17, 19n, 30-4; almanacs, 31, Christmas annuals, 31; literary magazines, 32-3; humor magazines, 34; *American Scandinavian Review, IX 1, X 38; American Swedish Monthly, 47; Billed-magazin, II 6; Børne-blad*, 31; *Busletts*, 34, *IX 74; Christmas*, 32; *Christmas Chimes, VII 6, VIII 68;* Dagen, 38; *Dansk almanak*, 31; *Dansk nytaar*, 31, *VII 77, VIII 92, IX 66; De Forenede Staters danske almanak, III 22, 37, IV 67, VI 39, IX 3; Dølen 34, IX 40; For gammel og ung, II 6; For hjemmet, 32, VI 2, 3, 114; Hemmets vän*, 33; *Hus-bibliothek, III 40, 43, VI 44, VII 15; Jul i vesterheimen, 32, IV 19, 36, 54, V 62, 90, VI 12, 25, VII 80, 84, VIII 11, 28, 30, 57, IX 15, 47, 55, 101, 103, 104, 112, X 8, 37, 39; Julegranen*, 31, *IV 46, 68, 69, VII 22, VIII 20, IX 106, X 23, 81; Kirketidende*, 30; *Kurre-kalender, IV 70, IX 82, 85; Kvartalskrift, 33, IV 59,*

VII 73, X 57; Kvinden og hjemmet, II 6; Maanedstidende 30; *Misteltenen, V 17, VII 66, VIII 86, IX 113, X 44, 45; Norden, 33, VII 74, VIII 31, 64, 93, X 86; Nordlandslaget,* 34; *Norsk-amerikansk julebog, VI 128, IX 70; Norsk-amerikaneren, IX 109; Northland Magazine,* 47; *Norwegian-American Studies and Records, II 16, 25, IX 86; Prärieblomman kalender, 35, VIII 10, X 36; Samband, IX 89; Scandinavia, 47, I 8, IV 47, IX 31; Smaablomster fra vor lille have, 33, IX 102, 108; Smuler,* 34; *Spøg og alvor,* 34; *Spøgefuglen,* 34; *Symra,* 33; *Telesoga,* 34; *Uglen, X 70, 71; Ungdomsvännen, II 7; Valkyrian, 32-3, II 7, III 47, IV 45, 63, 65, 73, 78, 84, 88, 93, 102, V 68, 73, 80, VI 26, 33, 51, 52, 86, 100, 141, VII 16, 18, 59, 61, VIII 8, 33, 44, 54, IX 3, 32, 57, 107, X 10, 77; Ved arnen, 29, II 5, III 18, 26, 28, 35, 51, 53, 55, IV 6, 35, 44, 52, 66, 86, V 3, 10, 22, 41, 86, VI 10, 13, 92, 127, VII 29, 63, 78, 117, VIII 70, 73, 79, IX 17, 20, 93, X 1, 11, 14, 58, 78, 92; Vega, X 89; Vor tid, V 39, 74, VI 118; Yule, IV 76.*
Personality, and culture, 20; types, 24, 327; changes in, 86-7, 136-9, 184, 211-3, 295, 328. See also Homesickness, Cultural conflict, Identity.
Philblad, Ernest F., Swedish-American, *IX 1.*
Pioneers and pioneering, hardships of, 15, 41, 81, 82, 197, 259-62; baggage and tools, 81-2; pragmatism, 83-4; social relations, 84, 94, 119; family relations, 239; lawlessness, 190, 211-2; saloons, 225-6.
Politics, Scandinavian, 102, 104-5, 160; American, 160-6; Republican party, 162-3, 201; Democratic party, 162; Populists and agrarian radicals, 163-4, 165, 203, 213, 303; Socialism, 200-1; political corruption, 164-5; Scandinavian-American politics, 96, 161-2; citizenship, 87, 159; conservatism, 200-1.
Preservationists, 41, 107, 108, 110, 117, 216-7, 279, 304, 306; defined, 87; cultural pluralism, 107-8; attitude toward language, 90-1, 275; decline of, 111, 117-8. See also Assimilationists, Americanization, Nationality.
Preus, Pastor, Norwegian-American church leader, 167, 175.
Publishers, Scandinavian-American, commercial houses, 35-6; synodical presses, 35; Augsburg Publishing House, 32, 35; Augustana Book Concern, 35; Lutheran Publishing House, 31; John Anderson Publishing Company, 35; Waldem. Kriedt 37; B. Anundsen, 30.
Pure Gold, novel by O. E. Rølvaag, 189.

Railroads, U. S., 74, 257.
Red River Valley (Minnesota), 40, 52, 83, 175, 201, 317.
Religion, Scandinavian-American, dominance in cultural life, 170, 279; Lutheranism, 30, 41, 42, 44, 95-6, 106; piety and pietism, 100, 110, 131, 147, 178, 227, 229, 233-4, 280; Lutheran church organization, 167, 170-3; synods, 30-2, 35, 172, 175, 176-7, 179; controversy in, 30, 96, 102, 108, 148, 169, 173-81, 219, 227-8, 230; language conflict in, 147-8, 273-4, 311, 313; attitudes toward ministers, 125, 130-3, 219-20; Methodists, 30, 146, 158, 168, 182, 229; Baptists, 30, 182; church periodicals, 30-2; religious education, 146-8, 301-2; ministers' training, 129, 140, 148; failure in leadership, 218-9, 279-80; ministers' attitudes toward civil marriage, 238, drink, 227-8, literature, 280, English language, 116, 294, 301, public schools, 145, secret societies, 235.
Riis, Jacob, Danish-American journalist, 46, 115.
Rock Island (Illinois), 27, 35, 46; place of publication 33, 265.
Roedder, Karsten, Norwegian-American journalist, 19n.
Rølvaag, Ella V., *IX 86, 91.*
Rygg, A. N., American scholar, *II 4.*

Saaledes blev jeg hjemløs, novel by Enok Mortensen, 114-5.
Saint Olaf College (Northfield, Minnesota), 27, 39, 46, 150.
Saloons, see Temperance movement, Pioneers.
Sandburg, Carl, American poet, 47, 50.
Scandinavia, definition of, 16-17, *I 4;* geography, 78, 262-3; national character, 97-103. See also Scandinavian culture and institutions.
Scandinavian-American culture, described, 104-6, 152-3, 279; ethnic communities, 103-4, 258; cultural societies, 33, 105, 151-3, 154, 232; customs and folkways,

ERRATA

P. 34: The name of *Busletts* magazine should be spelled without an apostrophe.

P. 49: The publication date of Skulda Banér's *Latchstring Out* is misprinted as 1954; it should be 1944.

P. 49: The first volume of Lillian Budd's trilogy, *April Snow,* is laid entirely in Sweden and therefore deals with Swedes, not Swedish-Americans.

P. 50: The name of Albert Edward Johansson has only one *n*.

P. 88: The third line of the poem cited should read, 'And when we *lose* that language...'

P. 96: In the last line before the subtitle, Chapter Seven should be Chapter Six.

P. 115: The title of Jacob Riis' autobiography as given here was translated from the Danish. When the book was published in English, the title was changed to *The Making of an American.*

P. 333: The Augustana Historical Society (Rock Island, Illinois) should also be mentioned for its specialized publications in Swedish-American history. There are of course other general histories of Scandinavian immigrant life than those listed here as examples.